A New Star-R
& Other Ex
from Frommer's:

In our continuing effort to publish the savviest, most up-to-date, and most appealing travel guides available, we've added some great new features.

Frommer's guides now include a new **star-rating system.** Every hotel, restaurant, and attraction is rated from 0 to 3 stars to help you set priorities and organize your time.

We've also added **seven brand-new features** that point you to the great deals, in-the-know advice, and unique experiences that separate travelers from tourists. Throughout the guide, look for:

Finds	Special finds—those places only insiders know about
Fun Fact	Fun facts—details that make travelers more informed and their trips more fun
Kids	Best bets for kids—advice for the whole family
Moments	Special moments—those experiences that memories are made of
Overrated	Places or experiences not worth your time or money
Tips	Insider tips—some great ways to save time and money
Value	Great values—where to get the best deals

We've also added a **"What's New"** section in every guide—a timely crash course in what's hot and what's not in every destination we cover.

Here's what the critics say about Frommer's:

"Amazingly easy to use. Very portable, very complete."

—*Booklist*

"Detailed, accurate, and easy-to-read information for all price ranges."
—*Glamour Magazine*

"Hotel information is close to encyclopedic."

—*Des Moines Sunday Register*

"Frommer's Guides have a way of giving you a real feel for a place."
—*Knight Ridder Newspapers*

Frommer's®

San Antonio & Austin

5th Edition

by Edie Jarolim

Wiley Publishing, Inc.

About the Author

Edie Jarolim was a senior editor at Frommer's in New York before she indulged her Southwest fantasies and moved to Tucson, Arizona. She has since written about the Southwest and Mexico for a variety of national publications, ranging from America West Airlines Magazine, Art & Antiques, and Brides to the New York Times Book Review and the Wall Street Journal.

Published by:

Wiley Publishing, Inc.

111 River St.
Hoboken, NJ 07030

ISBN 0-7645-2459-3
ISSN 1080-9104

Editor: Paul Karr
Production Editor: Suzanna R. Thompson
Cartographer: Roberta Stockwell
Photo Editor: Richard Fox
Production by Wiley Indianapolis Composition Services

Front cover photo: The River Walk in San Antonio
Back cover photo: A mural in Market Square, San Antonio

For information on our other products and services or to obtain technical support, please contact our Customer Care Department within the U.S. at 800-762-2974, outside the U.S. at 317-572-3993 or fax 317-572-4002.

Wiley also publishes its books in a variety of electronic formats. Some content that appears in print may not be available in electronic formats.

Manufactured in the United States of America

5   4   3   2

Contents

Appendix A: San Antonio & Austin in Depth 262

Appendix B: For International Visitors 273

Appendix C: Useful Toll-Free Numbers & Websites 286

Index 289

List of Maps

An Invitation to the Reader

In researching this book, we discovered many wonderful places—hotels, restaurants, shops, and more. We're sure you'll find others. Please tell us about them, so we can share the information with your fellow travelers in upcoming editions. If you were disappointed with a recommendation, we'd love to know that, too. Please write to:

Frommer's San Antonio & Austin, 5th Edition
Wiley Publishing, Inc. • 111 River St. • Hoboken, NJ 07030

An Additional Note

Please be advised that travel information is subject to change at any time—and this is especially true of prices. We therefore suggest that you write or call ahead for confirmation when making your travel plans. The authors, editors, and publisher cannot be held responsible for the experiences of readers while traveling. Your safety is important to us, however, so we encourage you to stay alert and be aware of your surroundings. Keep a close eye on cameras, purses, and wallets, all favorite targets of thieves and pickpockets.

New! Frommer's Star Ratings & Icons

Every hotel, restaurant, and attraction listing in this guide has been ranked for quality, value, service, amenities, and special features using a star-rating scale. In country, state, and regional guides, we also rate towns and regions to help you narrow down your choices and budget your time accordingly. Hotels and restaurants are rated on a scale of one (highly recommended) to three stars (exceptional). Attractions, towns, and regions are rated according to the following scale: zero stars (recommended), one star (highly recommended), two stars (very highly recommended), and three stars (must-see).

In addition to the rating system, we also use seven icons to highlight insider information, useful tips, special bargains, hidden gems, memorable experiences, kid-friendly venues, places to avoid, and other useful information:

(Finds   (Fun Fact   (Kids   (Moments   (Overrated   (Tips   (Value

The following abbreviations are used for credit cards:

AE American Express	DISC Discover	V Visa
DC Diners Club	MC MasterCard	

FROMMERS.COM

Now that you have the guidebook to a great trip, visit our website at **www.frommers.com** for travel information on nearly 2,500 destinations. With features updated regularly, we give you instant access to the most current trip-planning information available. At Frommers.com, you'll also find the best prices on airfares, accommodations, and car rentals—and you can even book travel online through our travel booking partners. At Frommers.com, you'll also find the following:

- Online updates to our most popular guidebooks
- Vacation sweepstakes and contest giveaways
- Newsletter highlighting the hottest travel trends
- Online travel message boards with featured travel discussions

What's New in San Antonio & Austin

Several projects in San Antonio and Austin were put on hold as the economy slowed down in 2001 and 2002; high-wired Austin was especially hard hit by the tech bust. But both cities kept shape-shifting nevertheless.

SAN ANTONIO

PLANNING YOUR TRIP If you're a squeezebox fan, you might want to plan your visit to San Antonio to coincide with the **International Accordion Festival** (📞 210/222-ARTS; www.internationalaccordionfestival. org). Inaugurated in October 2001, it was so successful that it became an annual event. See chapter 2 for additional details.

ACCOMMODATIONS The only new hotel to open on the River Walk in several years, the **Hotel Valencia Riverwalk**, 405 North St. Mary's, San Antonio, TX 78205 (📞866/842-0100; www.hotelvalencia.com), wasn't completed in time for it to be reviewed (it debuted Jan 2003), but, based on a hard-hat tour and model room peek (they're techno chic), it looks like a winner. Restoring a historic building and adding all kinds of high-tech accoutrements doesn't come cheap: Lodgings with a river view at this boutique property run $375 and up. And San Antonio's recycling of its historic downtown buildings doesn't always stop at a single go-round. A major revamp of the **Emily Morgan**, 705 E. Houston St. (📞 800/824-6674), a Ramada since the mid-1980s, transformed the dowdy discount dowager into a fashionable gal-about-town with somewhat more expensive tastes.

Opened on the west side in 2002, the **Radisson Resort Hill Country,** 9800 Westover Hills Blvd. (📞 800/333-3333), is a good option for families who want to stay near SeaWorld. Name and generous recreational facilities notwithstanding, it's not really a resort—but when the tab arrives, that's not necessarily a bad thing. Right next door at the **Hyatt Regency Hill Country Resort,** 9800 Hyatt Resort Dr. (📞 800/233-1234), the premiere of the terrific **Windflower** spa gilds the lily of a property that was already top notch. See chapter 4 for more information.

DINING Dishing out regional Mexican cuisine rather than typical Tex-Mex, **Manduca,** 215 Losoya St. (📞 210/475-9099), is a welcome addition to the generally touristy River Walk. After it moved last year from the Brackenridge Park area to the King William historic neighborhood and expanded its menu of salads, sandwiches, and desserts, **Madhatters,** 320 Beauregard St. (📞 210/212-4832), has won favor with locals and with tourists who need sustenance for mansion ogling. Similarly beneficial to visitors was the move made by the excellent northern Italian restaurant **Massimo,** 1896 Nacogdoches Rd. (📞 210/342-8556), from a frontage road near the airport to Alamo

Heights. That doesn't mean you'll be without good dining options in case of a flight delay: A branch of **Rosario's** is now open at Terminal 2. Find out more about all these restaurants in chapter 5.

SIGHTSEEING   Even with hotel construction on hold, downtown San Antonio never stays the same. The **Herzburg Circus Collection,** a long-time favorite attraction, disappeared from view in 2001 when rain damage made the historic building in which it was housed unsafe for visitors. Part of its excellent array of historic circus artifacts resurfaced at the **San Antonio Central Library,** 600 Soledad (© 210/207-2500), which was sturdily (and creatively) constructed in the mid-1990s. Here, they're safely archived and, on occasion, displayed. With the stabilization of its foundation and improvement of its lighting and acoustics in 2002, the **San Fernando Cathedral,** 115 Main Plaza (© 210/ 227-1297), completed the initial part of its three-phase restoration. The most impressive new addition, a 24-foot-high gilded *retablo* (gradine), is slated to be unveiled sometime after Easter 2003. When downtown isn't restoring its old buildings, it's building huge new sports arenas. In October 2002—less than a decade after the debut of the Alamodome—the **SBC Center,** One SBC Center Parkway (© 210/444-5000), opened with a pre-season basketball game between the New York Knicks and the San Antonio Spurs. The high-tech stadium will not only house the Spurs, but, starting with the 2003 season, it will also host the WNBA team formerly known as the Utah Starzz (now known as the **San Antonio Silver Stars**). The San Antonio Rampage hockey team will also take to the (artificial) ice at this arena, and major concerts will be held here.

On the outskirts of town, San Antonio's two major theme parks constantly compete to outdo each other.

In 2001, **SeaWorld San Antonio,** 10500 SeaWorld Dr. (© 210/523-3611), added a three-story water fun house called Splash Attack to its Lost Lagoon section; in 2003, a Sea Star "4D" Theater, featuring a large-screen film viewable with 3D glasses and seats that spout water, will premiere. Scooby-Doo Ghostblasters, an interactive haunted mansion, was the contribution to the thrillfest made in 2002 by **Six Flags Fiesta Texas,** 17000 I-10 West (© 800/473-4378). See chapter 6 for more information on all these attractions.

AUSTIN

PLANNING YOUR TRIP   As though the S×SW music extravaganza in spring weren't enough, another major tune-up has been added to Austin's calendar. In September 2002, the first 2-day **Austin City Limits Music Festival** (© 512/478-4811 or 512/478-7211) was held, featuring Emmylou Harris, Jimmy Vaughan, Shawn Colvin, and others performers in a variety of genres—just like the acts on the long-running public TV show for which the festival is named.

In fall 2002, **Frontier Airlines** (© 800/432-1359) initiated two daily nonstop flights from its home city, Denver, to Austin-Bergstrom International Airport. Direct service from Austin to Seattle and Reno/Lake Tahoe was introduced too. US Airways had also planned to start flying into Austin in fall 2002, but postponed service until the following spring.

ACCOMMODATIONS   The expansion of Austin's convention center to double its previous size, completed in spring 2002, resulted in an accompanying increase in the number of downtown hotel rooms. Although the opening of a high-rise Hilton was delayed until early 2004, a new Hampton Inn opened near the convention center at the end of 2002.

Chain hotels also continue to spring up near the Austin-Bergstrom International Airport, still a relative newcomer to town (1999).

But not all the lodgings that arrived in Austin recently were of the chain variety. The **Austin Folk House,** 506 West 22nd St. (© **866/472-6700**), a bed-and-breakfast near the University of Texas, combines historic character with contemporary amenities. That's true too of Austin's most venerable property, **The Driskill,** 604 Brazos St. (© **800/252-9367**). After a multimillion-dollar remake in time for the new millennium, the hotel further burnished its image by adding a posh new spa and retro-chic cafe. See chapter 12 for more information.

DINING   It's tough to keep track of the culinary comings and goings around town. Recently it was bye-bye Brio Vista, hello **Eddie V's Edgewater Grill,** 9400B Arboretum Blvd. (© **512/342-6242**), a seafood and steak restaurant by Brio Vista's originators: Same team, same location, new decor and concept. Eddie V's has a branch downtown, where other recent arrivals include **La Traviata,** 314 Congress Ave. (© 512/479-8131), a casual trattoria; **Noodle-ism,** 107 W. 5th St. (© 512/275-9988), an Asian-inspired pasta house; **Gumbo's,** 701 Colorado (© 512/480-8053), serving Cajun fare in the historic Brown Building; and **Wink,** 1014 N. Lamar (© 512/482-8868), another entry into the only-use-fresh-local-ingredients arena.

Also relatively new to Austin, **Emilia's,** 600 E. 3rd St. (© **512/469-9722**), lit up the city's dining scene with its dazzling New American cuisine. In 2002 there was proof that the restaurant has a wine list to match: Emilia's was the sole recipient in Austin (and only one of three in Texas) of the *Wine Spectator*'s Best of Award of Excellence. Chapter 13 provides details on all.

SIGHTSEEING   Austin is surprisingly sluggish when it comes to its major art venues—the openings of the new buildings for the Austin Museum of Art–Downtown and the Jack S. Blanton Museum of Art, originally scheduled for completion by now, are still several years away—but it shines when it comes to tour guidance. The "O. Henry Trail" brochure is a recent addition to the excellent collection of free self-guided tours prepared by the Austin Convention and Visitors Bureau. The new **Hit the Road Austin** (© **512/335-3300;** www. hittheroadtours.com) audio tour lets you drive around at your leisure listening to a lively historic narrative and music. You'll be glad that you'll have more than just a disembodied voice to accompany you on the **Austin Ghost Tours** (© **512/695-7297** www.austin ghosttours.com), since there'll be sufficient discussion of disembodiment to keep you happily spooked. See chapter 14 to find out more.

THE HILL COUNTRY

The relatively rural region around San Antonio and Austin changes less readily and steadily than the big cities—except when it comes to **Fredericksburg,** the most popular of the Hill Country towns. A $1.1 million visitors center, opened in early 2003, includes a 46-seat theater that screens a historical video, as well as several computers where travelers can check their e-mail. More Fred-burg buzz: Yet another *gasthaus* reservation service was added to the places that will book you a stay at one of the town's unique B&Bs (more than 300 of them at last count). And the six super-trendy Homestead stores were consolidated into a single three-story yuppie furnishings emporium on the town's main street.

In **San Marcos,** the Aquarena Center continues to move beyond its politically incorrect past (which included Ralph the Swimming Pig) by adding an aquarium and nature walks to its newly eco-conscious exhibits. South of San Marcos in Kyle but under the aegis of the Southwest Texas University's Southwest Writers Collection, a house devoted to the author Katherine Anne Porter was opened to the public (by appointment).

The art museum in downtown **New Braunfels** that formerly housed an extensive collection of Hummels moved to the adjacent village, Gruene, where it was reincarnated as the New Braunfels Museum of Art & Music; it now offers excellent Texas-themed shows and is blissfully Hummel-free.

See chapter 17 for details on these and other Hill Country towns.

1

The Best of San Antonio

Call it the Fiesta City or the Alamo City; each of San Antonio's nicknames reveals a different truth. Visitors come here to kick back and party, but they also come to seek Texas's history—some would say its soul. They come to sit on the banks of a glittering river and sip cactus margaritas, but also to view Franciscan missions that rose along the same river more than 2½ centuries ago.

Multiculturalism isn't just an academic buzzword in San Antonio, the only major Texan city founded before Texas won its independence from Mexico. During its early days, it was populated by diverse groups with distinct goals: Spanish missionaries and militia men, German merchants, Southern plantation owners, Western cattle ranchers, and Eastern architects. All have left their mark, both tangibly on San Antonio's downtown and subtly on the city's culture and cuisine.

With its German, Southern, Western, and, above all, Hispanic influences— the city is nearly 60% Mexican-American—San Antonio's cultural life is rich and complex. At the New Orleans–like Fiesta, for example, San Antonians might break confetti eggs called *cascarones,* listen to oompah bands, and cheer rodeo bull riders. Countless country-and-western ballads twang on about "San Antone"—no doubt because the name rhymes with "alone"—which is also America's capital for Tejano music, a unique blend of Mexican and German sounds. And no self-respecting San Antonio festival would be complete without Mexican tamales and tacos, Texan chili and barbecue, Southern hush puppies and glazed ham, and German beer and bratwurst.

The city's architecture also reflects its multiethnic history. After the Texas revolution, Spanish viga beams began to be replaced by southern Greek revival columns, German *fachwerk* (half-wooden) pitched roofs, and East Coast Victorian gingerbread facades. San Antonio, like the rest of the Southwest, has now returned to its Hispanic architectural roots—even chain hotels in the area have red-clay roofs, Saltillo tile floors, and central patios—but updated versions of other indigenous building styles are also popular. The rustic yet elegant Hill Country look, for example, might use native limestone in structures that combine sprawling Texas ranch features with more intricate German details.

These days, San Antonio is simultaneously moving backwards and forwards. The city is succumbing to the proliferation of highways, faceless housing developments, and homogenous restaurant and lodging chains that so many Southwestern cities seem to equate with progress; in fact, early in the 20th century it almost paved over the river on which the city was founded. But it's also making a concerted effort to preserve its past, and for economic—not sentimental—reasons; cultural tourism sells, after all. Amid San Antonio's sprawl, it's the winding downtown streets that most visitors recall, and that once-endangered river. Few who come here leave without a memory of a moment, quiet or heart-quickening, sunlit or sparkling with tiny tree-draped lights, when the river somehow worked its magic on them.

1 Frommer's Favorite San Antonio Experiences

- **Recapturing Texas's Fight for Independence at the Alamo.** It's hard to imagine the state's prime attraction as a battle site, surrounded as it is now by hotels and shops—that is, until you step inside the Long Barrack, where Texas's most famous fighters prepared to fight General Santa Anna's troops. Here, you just might shut out those modern images (if not the crowds) for a moment. See p. 72.

- **Attending a Mariachi Mass at Mission San José.** It's very moving to watch members of the congregation of this largest of the mission churches raise their voices in spirited musical prayer each Sunday at noon. Come early, as seats are limited and this is a popular thing to do. See p. 80.

- **Strolling Along San Antonio's River Walk.** Whether you opt for the buzz of the busy South Bank portion of the River Walk, or decide to escape to one of its quieter stretches, the green, lush banks of San Antonio's river will match your mood, day or night. See p. 90.

- **Seeing a Show at the Majestic Theatre.** As it happens, the restored Majestic offers top-notch shows of all kinds, but the venue itself is worth the price of admission alone. Book a seat in the front rows, or try the upstairs mezzanine so you can gaze at the star-studded ceiling. See p. 111.

- **Climbing into a Treehouse at the Witte Museum.** You can recapture your youth (or enjoy your kids relishing theirs) at the Witte, where the HEB Treehouse has interactive science exhibits galore. See p. 79.

- **Lazing in the Courtyard at the Marion Koogler McNay Art Museum.** Art, shmart. As interesting as the paintings are, when it comes to transcendent experiences, you can't beat sitting out on the lovely tree-shaded patio of the McNay. See p. 78.

- **Pretending You Live in the King William District.** The opulent mansions homes built here by German merchants in the 19th century are eye-popping. You can't enter most of them (unless you're staying at one of the area's many B&Bs), but the fantasizing is free. See chapter 6.

- **Ascending the Tower of the Americas.** In the daytime, the tower provides a great way to get the lay of the land. At sunset, it's transformed from pragmatic to romantic as you sip a drink and watch the city lights wink on. See chapters 6 and 8.

- **Buying Day of the Dead Souvenirs in Southtown.** The Day of the Dead (actually 2 days, Nov 1 and 2) is commemorated throughout the largely Hispanic Southtown, but you can buy T-shirts with dancing skeletons and folk art tableau typical of the holiday at Tienda Guadalupe year-round. See chapter 7.

- **Checking out the Headgear at Paris Hatters.** Even if you're not in the market for a Stetson, you should at least wander over to this San Antonio institution that has sold hats to everyone from Pope John Paul II and Queen Elizabeth to lesser lights like, well, TV's Jimmy Smits. See how big your head is compared to that of the stars. See p. 107.

- **Grooving to Jazz at The Landing.** Jim Cullum and his band play cool jazz at a cool location—the River Walk. A groove doesn't get much mellower than this. See p. 112.

2 Best San Antonio Hotel Bets

- **Best Historic Hotel:** Who can resist a place that's right across the street from the Alamo and still has the bar where Teddy Roosevelt recruited his Rough Riders? A 19th-century gem, the **Menger,** 204 Alamo Plaza (℗ **800/345-9285** or 210/223-4361), still sparkles. See p. 41.

- **Best for Business Travelers:** The Guest Office rooms at the **Westin Riverwalk Inn,** 420 W. Market St. (℗ **800/WESTIN-1** or 210/224-6500), are equipped with high-speed Internet access—still a relative rarity in San Antonio—along with other convenient-for-work perks. The sleek hotel bar, with its top-notch martinis, is a fine place to schmooze clients. River view rooms are pricey for leisure travelers, but if your company's footing the bill, try to enjoy one. See p. 38.

- **Best for Families:** If you can afford it, the **Hyatt Regency Hill Country Resort,** 9800 Hyatt Resort Dr. (℗ **800/233-1234** or 210/647-1234), just down the road from SeaWorld, is ideal for a family getaway. Kids get to splash in their own shallow pool, go tubing on a little river, and be entertained in a kids' camp—and you get to relax in the resort's spiffy new spa. See p. 52.

- **Best Moderately Priced Hotel:** The **Drury Inn & Suites,** 201 N. St. Mary's St. (℗ **800/DRURY-INN** or 210/212-5200), is a good, economical downtown bet located in a historic building right on the river. Breakfast and afternoon cocktails are included in the room rate, and in-room fridges and microwaves mean you can cut down on food costs in this pricey area even further. See p. 42.

- **Best Budget Lodging:** How do I love the savings at the **Best Western Sunset Suites,** 1103 E. Commerce St. (℗ **866/560-6000** or 210/223-4400)? Let me count the ways: Low room rates, lots of free perks, and a convenient location near downtown, plus very attractive rooms, make staying here a super deal. See p. 43.

- **Best B&B:** The King William area abounds with B&Bs, but the **Ogé House,** 209 Washington St. (℗ **800/242-2770** or 210/223-2353), stands out as much for its professionalism as for its gorgeous mansion and lovely rooms. You don't need to sacrifice service for warmth here. See p. 44.

- **Best Health Club:** Not only does the health club at the **Marriott Rivercenter,** 101 Bowie St. (℗ **800/228-9290** or 210/223-1000), have the best weight machines and cardiovascular equipment of all the city's downtown hotels, but it's on the same floor as the hotel's free washers and dryers. Hop on a treadmill while your duds exercise the spin cycle. See p. 38.

- **Hippest Hotel:** With its super-cool cigar bar, faux porter trunk–era furnishings, and laid-back atmosphere, the **Havana Riverwalk Inn,** 1015 Navarro (℗ **888/224-2008** or 210/222-2008), is as much a scene as a place to bed down. See p. 42.

- **Best Place to Spot Celebrities:** Everyone from Paula Abdul to ZZ Top (hey, they're big in Texas) has stayed at **La Mansión del Río,** 112 College St. (℗ **800/292-7300** or 210/225-2581); discretion, a willingness to cater to special requests, and a location that's just slightly away from the action might explain why. See p. 38.

- **Best for River Views:** La Mansión del Río, the Marriott Rivercenter, and the Westin Riverwalk each boast prime watery views from some of their rooms, but if you stay at the **Hyatt Regency on the River Walk,** 123 Losoya St. (© **800/233-1234** or 210/222-1234), you can book less expensive atrium-view lodgings and still glimpse a bit of the river running through the lobby. See. p. 37.

- **Best New Addition to San Antonio's Lodging Scene:** With

construction on the wane over the past couple of years, the **Radisson Resort Hill Country,** 9800 Westover Hills Blvd. (© **800/333-3333** or 210/509-9800), didn't have much competition in this category. But with a prime vacation location near SeaWorld and excellent recreational facilities, it's a winner in any case. See. p. 52.

3 Best San Antonio Dining Bets

- **Best for a Romantic Dinner:** On a quiet stretch of the River Walk, **Las Canarias,** at the Mansión del Río, 112 College St. (© **210/518-1063**), avoids the noise that plagues most water-view restaurants. You'll enjoy candlelight and superb, discreet service. See p. 56.
- **Best Moveable Feast:** It used to be that you could dine on the river only if you were with a group, but among the restaurants that now offer reservations on communal tables to individuals and couples, **Boudro's,** 421 E. Commerce St./River Walk (© **210/224-8484**), tops the meals-on-river-barge-wheels list. See p. 58.
- **Best American Cuisine:** When I give the nod to **Silo,** 1133 Austin Hwy. (© **210/824-8686**), as tops in American cuisine, I'm not talking meat loaf and mashed potatoes (although versions of both dishes may turn up on the menu). Silo's New American recipes, which rely on fresh seasonal and regional ingredients, will dazzle those willing to expand their culinary horizons. See p. 66.
- **Best Continental Cuisine:** Get out those elastic-waist clothes for **Bistro Time,** 5137 Fredericksburg Rd. (© **210/344-6626**), where

wonderfully rich sauces hearken back to the days before the word "cholesterol" entered the national vocabulary. See p. 69.
- **Best Italian Cuisine:** The risotto, potato gnocchi, and saltimbocca are among the dishes perfected by a chef from Rome that make it worth the trip to **Massimo,** 1896 Nacogdoches Rd. (© **210/342-8556**), in the posh Alamo Heights area. See p. 66.
- **Best Mexican Cuisine:** This is a tough one to call in a city with so many worthy contenders, but **Rosario's,** 910 S. Alamo (© **210/223-1806**), offers great atmosphere along with great food—not to mention some of the most potent margaritas in town. See p. 63.
- **Best Blast from the Past:** **Schilo's,** 424 E. Commerce St. (© **210/223-6692**), not only serves up German deli in portions that date back to pre-cholesterol-conscious days but also retains prices from that era. See p. 61.
- **Best New Restaurant:** With its dazzling Asian-inspired French cuisine, **Frederick's,** 771 Broadway, Suite 20 (© **210/828-9050**), is a reminder of why the whole "fusion" trend took off. See p. 66.

- **Best Place to Encounter Artists:** Terrific food, a nice selection of libations, good prices, and a fun, funky atmosphere draw creative types of all kinds to the **Liberty Bar,** 328 E. Josephine St. (© **210/ 227-1187**). See p. 64.

Site Seeing: San Antonio's Best Websites

www.mysanantonio.com: The website of the city's only mainstream newspaper, the *San Antonio Express-News,* is a one-stop e-shop for the city: In addition to providing the daily news, it also links to local business such as dry cleaners and florists (via its Power Pages) and to movie, nightlife, and restaurant listings and reviews (under Entertainment). One caveat: Many of the searches require zip codes, so be sure to know the one you'll be traveling from when you log on.

www.sanantonio.gov: The City of San Antonio's website offers timely information on such topics as traffic and street closures. Some of its other tourist-friendly sections, such as cultural affairs (www.san antonio.gov/art), which has links to local galleries, are also excellent. But not all the topics are updated regularly. When I last checked the airport information, for example, it was a year and a half out of date.

www.sanantoniovisit.com: You're not going to get honest critiques of restaurants, hotels, and attractions on the San Antonio Convention and Visitors Bureau's website. You are, however, going to get current admission fees and hours, as well links to many restaurants and hotels. The "Special Values" section is especially good if you're looking for discounts on everything from accommodations to theme parks.

http://sanantonio.citysearch.com: I don't always agree with this site's reviews, but it's always good to have a variety of opinions about dining, nightlife, and shopping (even if mine are ultimately right). And there are a few things I can't do—like provide you with an up-to-date weather report or driving directions—that this site can.

www.texasmonthly.com: You won't necessarily find San Antonio stories on the *Texas Monthly* site, but the state's best magazine offers in-depth treatments of lots of interesting topics, so you'll be keyed into a Texas mindset. And the site sometimes highlights hot new San Antonio dining spots.

2

Planning Your Trip to San Antonio

Spontaneity is all well and good once you get to where you're going, but advance planning can make or break a trip. San Antonio is becoming more and more popular; therefore, it's best to book your vacation here well in advance. If you're thinking of coming for April's huge Fiesta bash, for example, try to reserve accommodations at least 6 months ahead of time to avoid disappointment.

1 Visitor Information

Contact the **San Antonio Convention and Visitors Bureau (SACVB)**, P.O. Box 2277, San Antonio, TX 78298 (✆ **800/447-3372**), for a useful pre-trip information packet, including a visitors' guide and map, lodging guide, detailed calendar of events, arts brochure, and "SAVE San Antonio" booklet with discount coupons for a number of hotels and attractions. You can also get pre-trip information, sans discount coupons, online at the SACVB's website, **www.sanantoniovisit.com**.

Phone or fill out an online form on the website of the **Texas Department of Tourism** (✆ **800/8888-TEX;** www.traveltex.com) to receive the *Texas State Travel Guide,* a glossy book chockfull of information about the state, along with a statewide accommodations booklet; you can also request it in CD-ROM form. The **Texas Travel Information Center** has a toll-free number (✆ **800/452-9292**) to call for the latest on road conditions, special events, and general attractions in the areas you're interested in visiting; traveler counselors will even advise you on the quickest or most scenic route to your intended destination. *Texas Monthly* magazine, another good source of information, can be accessed at **www.texasmonthly.com**.

2 Money

Like most tourist-oriented cities, San Antonio has two price structures: one for locals, and another for visitors. You can expect everything from food to hotels to souvenirs to be fairly pricey on the River Walk and at theme parks such as SeaWorld. In general, however, the average San Antonio salary is not terribly high, and the cost of living is about 10% lower than the country's average, so prices tend to be moderate.

Minimal cash is required, since credit cards are accepted nearly universally, and automatic teller machines linked to national networks are strewn around tourist destinations and, increasingly, within hotels. **Cirrus** (✆ **800/424-7787;** www.mastercard.com) and **PLUS** (✆ **800/843-7587;** www.visa.com) are the two most popular networks; call or check online for ATM locations in San Antonio.

What Things Cost in San Antonio	U.S. $	U.K. £
Taxi from the airport to the city center	16.00	10.00
Streetcar ride between any two downtown points	.50	.30
Local telephone call	.50	.30
Long-neck beer	2.00–3.00	1.25–1.90
Double at Westin Riverwalk Inn (very expensive)	365.00	228.10
Double at Drury Inn & Suites San Antonio Riverwalk (moderate)	129.00	80.60
Double at Best Western Sunset Suites (inexpensive)	89.00	55.60
Lunch for one at Rosario's (moderate)	10.00	6.25
Lunch for one at Twin Sisters (inexpensive)	5.50	3.45
Dinner for one, without wine, at Las Canarias (very expensive)	50.00	31.25
Dinner for one, without beer, at La Fonda on Main (moderate)	13.00	8.10
Dinner for one, without beer, at Schilo's (inexpensive)	8.00	5.00
Coca-Cola	1.00–1.50	.60–.95
Cup of espresso	1.50–2.25	.95–1.40
Roll of ASA 100 Kodacolor film, 24 exposures	5.25	3.30
Admission to the Witte Museum	5.95	3.70
Movie ticket	.50–7.75	30p–4.85
Ticket to the San Antonio Symphony	18.00–55.00	11.25–34.40
Ticket to a Spurs game	9.00–69.00	5.60–43.10

The three major traveler's checks agencies are **American Express** (© 800/221-7282), **MasterCard** (© 800/223-9920), and **Visa** (© 800/732-1322). See also Appendix B, "For International Visitors."

3 When to Go

Most tourists visit San Antonio in summer, though it's not the ideal season: The weather is often steamy, and restaurants and attractions tend to be crowded. That said, there are plenty of places to cool off around town, and hotel rates are generally lower (conventioneers come in the fall, winter, and spring) during this time of year. Also consider that some of the most popular outdoor attractions, such as SeaWorld and Six Flags Fiesta Texas, either open only in summer or keep far longer opening hours in summer. Fall and spring are less crowded with tourists, and the weather is much more pleasant. Time of week is also a consideration: San Antonio is the single most popular destination in the state for Texans, many of whom drive in just for the weekend, and you may encounter full hotels or higher rates on weekends. The city's business hotels are busy during the week, so consider booking a B&B or hotel that's not business-oriented if you'll be staying weekdays.

CLIMATE

Complain to San Antonians about their city's heat on a sultry summer day and you're likely to be assured that it's far more humid in say, Houston, or anywhere in East Texas. This may be true, but it won't make you feel any less sweaty. From late May to early September, expect regular high temperatures and high humidity.

Fall and spring are generally prime times to visit; the days are pleasantly warm and, if you come in late March or early April, the wildflowers in the nearby Hill Country will be in glorious bloom. Temperate weather combined with the lively celebrations surrounding Christmas also make November and December good months to visit. January and February can be a bit raw, relatively speaking— though, if you're from up north, you probably won't even notice.

San Antonio's Average Monthly Temperature & Rainfall

	Jan	Feb	Mar	Apr	May	June	July	Aug	Sept	Oct	Nov	Dec
Avg. Temp. (°F)	52	55	61	68	75	82	84	84	80	71	60	53
Avg. Temp. (°C)	11	13	16	20	24	28	29	29	26	21	15	12
Rainfall (in.)	1.66	2.06	1.54	2.54	3.07	2.79	1.69	2.41	3.71	2.84	1.77	1.46

SAN ANTONIO CALENDAR OF EVENTS

Please note that the information contained below is always subject to change. For the most up-to-date information on these events, call the number provided, or check with the Convention and Visitors Bureau (© 800/447-3372; www.SanAntonio Visit.com). You can also find a detailed calendar of downtown events on the website for the Downtown Alliance San Antonio, http://downtownsanantonio.org/calendar.html.

January

River Walk Mud Festival, River Walk. Every year, when the horseshoe bend of the San Antonio River Walk is drained for maintenance purposes, San Antonians cheer themselves up by electing a king and queen to reign over such events as Mud Stunts Day and the Mud Pie Ball. © 210/227-4262; www.thesanantonioriverwalk.com. Mid-January.

February

Stock Show and Rodeo, SBC Center. In early February, San Antonio hosts more than 2 weeks of rodeo events, livestock judging, country-and-western bands, and carnivals. It's been going (and growing) since 1949. © 210/225-5851; www.sarodeo.com. Early February.

San Antonio CineFestival, Guadalupe Cultural Arts Center. The nation's oldest and largest Chicano/Latino film festival screens more than 70 films and videos. © 210/271-3151; www.guadalupecultural arts.org. Mid- to late February.

March

Dyeing O' The River Green and Pub Crawl. Are leprechauns responsible for turning the San Antonio River into the green River Shannon? Irish dance and music fill the Arneson River Theatre from the afternoon on. © 210/227-4262; www.

> *Fun Fact* **The Fiesta City**
>
> San Antonio's nickname refers to its huge April bash, but it also touches on the city's tendency to party at the drop of a sombrero. It's only natural that a place with strong Southern, Western, and Hispanic roots would know how to have a good time: Elaborately costumed festival queens, wild-and-woolly rodeos, and Mexican food and mariachis are rolled out year-round. And where else but San Antonio would something as potentially dull as draining a river turn into a cause for celebration?

thesanantonioriverwalk.com. March 16–17.

April

Starving Artist Show, River Walk and La Villita. Part of the proceeds of the works sold by nearly 900 local artists go to benefit the Little Church of La Villita's program to feed the hungry. ✆ **210/226-3593;** www.lavillita.com. First weekend of the month.

Fiesta San Antonio. What started as a modest marking of Texas's independence in 1891 is now a huge event, with an elaborately costumed royal court presiding over 10 days of revelry: parades, balls, food fests, sporting events, concerts, and art shows all over town. Call ✆ **210/ 227-5191,** or 877/SA-FIESTA within Texas, for details on tickets and events, or log on to **www.fiesta-sa.org**. Starts the third week of the month.

May

Tejano Conjunto Festival, Rosedale Park and Guadalupe Theater. This annual festival, sponsored by the Guadalupe Cultural Arts Center, celebrates the lively and unique blend of Mexican and German music born in south Texas. The best conjunto musicians perform at the largest event of its kind in the world. Call ✆ **210/271-3151** for schedules and ticket information, or check the website, **www.guadalupe culturalarts.org**. Mid-May.

Return of the Chili Queens, Market Square. An annual tribute to chili, said to have originated in San Antonio, with music, dancing, crafts demonstrations, and (of course) chili aplenty. Bring the Tums. ✆ **210/ 207-8600;** jessemo@sanantonio. gov. Memorial Day weekend.

June

Texas Folklife Festival, Institute of Texas Cultures. Ethnic foods, dances, crafts demonstrations, and games celebrate the diversity of Texas's heritage. ✆ **210/558-2300;** www.texancultures.utsa.edu. Four days in June.

Juneteenth, various venues. The anniversary of the announcement of the Emancipation Proclamation in Texas in 1865 is the occasion for a series of African-American celebrations, including an outdoor jazz concert, gospel fest, parade, picnic, and more. Call the San Antonio Convention and Visitors Bureau for details at ✆ **800/447-3372;** www. SanAntonioVisit.com. June 19.

July

Contemporary Art Month, various venues. You can pick up a calendar of the more than 70 events that get the city's creative (and acquisitive) juices flowing throughout July at the Blue Star Arts Complex. ✆ **210/227-6960;** www.blue starartspace.org or www.sanantonio. gov/art/website/calendar.asp.

September

Diez y Seis. Mexican independence from Spain is feted at several different downtown venues, including La Villita, the Arneson River Theatre, and Guadalupe Plaza. Music and dance, a parade, and a *charreada* (rodeo) are part of the fun. ☎ 210/223-3151; www.agatx.org. Weekend nearest Sept. 16.

Jazz'SAlive, Travis Park. Bands from New Orleans and San Antonio come together for a weekend of hot jazz. ☎ 210/207-3000. Third weekend in September.

International Accordion Festival, La Villita. Inaugurated in 2001, this squeezebox fest was such a success it became an annual event. In 2002, close to 20 ensembles played music from around the globe, from Cajun, merengue, zydeco, and conjunto to klezmer, Basque, and Irish music. ☎ 210/222-ARTS; www.internationalaccordionfestival.org. Sept. 20–21 in 2003; call for 2004 dates.

October

Oktoberfest, Beethoven Home. San Antonio's German roots show at this festival with food, dance, oompah bands, and beer. ☎ 210/222-1521. Early October.

November

New World Wine and Food Festival, various venues. Celebrity chefs from around Texas help celebrate San Antonio's culinary roots with everything from tequila tastings and chocolate seminars to cooking classes. It's a taste treat, and all for charity. ☎ 210/930-3232. www.newworldwinefood.org. Early November.

Lighting Ceremony and River Walk Holiday Parade. Trees and bridges along the river are illuminated by some 120,000 lights, and Santa Claus arrives on a boat during this floating river parade. ☎ 210/227-4262; www.thesanantonioriverwalk.com. Friday following Thanksgiving.

December

Fiestas Navideñas, Market Square. The Mexican market hosts piñata parties, a blessing of the animals, and surprise visits from Pancho Claus. ☎ 210/207-8600. Weekends in December.

Rivercenter Christmas Pageant. River barges in the Rivercenter complex are the untraditional setting for the traditional Christmas story. ☎ 210/225-0000; www.shoprivercenter.com. December weekends leading up to the holiday.

Las Posadas, River Walk. Children carrying candles lead the procession along the river, reenacting the search for lodging in a moving multifaith rendition of the Christmas story. ☎ 210/224-6163; www.saconservation.org. Second Sunday in December.

4 Insurance

There are three kinds of travel insurance: trip cancellation, medical, and lost luggage. Trip cancellation insurance is a good idea if you have paid a large portion of your vacation expenses up front.

But the other two types of insurance don't make sense for most travelers. Your existing health insurance should cover you if you get sick while on vacation (although if you belong to an HMO, you should check to see whether you are fully covered when away from home). And your homeowner's insurance should cover stolen luggage if you have off-premises theft. Check your existing policies before you buy any additional coverage. The airlines are responsible for $2,500 on domestic flights if they lose your luggage; if you plan to carry anything more valuable than that, keep it in your carry-on bag.

Some credit cards (American Express and certain gold and platinum Visas and MasterCards, for example) offer automatic flight insurance against death or dismemberment in case of an airplane crash. If you still feel you need more insurance, try one of the companies listed below. But don't pay for more insurance than you need. For example, if you need only trip cancellation insurance, don't purchase coverage for lost or stolen property. Trip cancellation insurance costs approximately 6% to 8% of the total value of your vacation. Reputable issuers of travel insurance include **Access America** (© 800/284-8300; www.accessamerica.com); **Travelex Insurance Services** (© 800/228-9792; www.travelex-insurance.com); **Travel Guard International** (© 800/826-1300; www.travelguard.com); and **Travel Insured International, Inc.** (© 800/243-3174; www.travelinsured. com).

5 Tips for Travelers with Special Needs

FOR TRAVELERS WITH DISABILITIES

Lots of work has been done in recent years to make San Antonio friendlier to those who use wheelchairs. The Riverwalk Trolley Station, for example, was built with a large elevator to transport people down to the water. Contact the **San Antonio Planning Department** (© 210/207-7245, voice and TTY) for additional information (including a map of River Walk access), or click on to the disability access section of the department's website (www.sanantonio. gov/planning/disability_access.asp). Several taxis have also been equipped with lifts and ramps; **Yellow-Checker** (© 210/222-2222) has most of them. And two downtown trolleys and about 85% of the public buses are now accessible. For **VIA Trans Disabled Accessibility Information,** phone © 210/362-2140 (voice) or 210/362-2217 (TTY) or log on to www. viainfo.net/accessible_services. In addition, the Weekender section of the *San Antonio Express-News* includes accessibility symbols for restaurants, theaters, galleries, and other venues.

Access-Able Travel Source (www. access-able.com) is a comprehensive database of travel agents who specialize in travel for disabled individuals; it's also a clearinghouse for information about accessible destinations around the world, including Texas. Another excellent resource for travelers with any type of disability is **Mobility International USA** (© 541/343-1284, voice and TDD; www. miusa.org), a nonprofit organization involved in promoting travel awareness for people who have difficulty getting around. The organization publishes *A World of Options,* a 658-page book of resources for travelers with disabilities, covering everything from biking trips to scuba outfitters. Annual membership is $35.

FOR GAY & LESBIAN TRAVELERS

San Antonio has a fairly large, but not exceedingly visible, gay and lesbian population. The website of the **Gay and Lesbian Community Center of San Antonio,** 611 E. Myrtle St. (© 210/223-6106; www.glccsa.org), includes a calendar of events—many of which are held at **The Esperanza Peace & Justice Center,** 922 San Pedro (© 210/228-0201; www. esperanzacenter.org), which often screens films or has lectures on topics of interest to gays, lesbians, and transgenders. If you stay at the **Painted**

Lady Inn, a lesbian-owned bed-and-breakfast at 620 Broadway (✆ 210/220-1092; www.thepaintedladyinn.com), you can also find out all you want to know about the local scene. See also chapter 8 for information about gay bars.

The **International Gay & Lesbian Travel Association (IGLTA)** (✆ 800/448-8550 or 954/776-2626; fax 954/776-3303; www.iglta.org) links travelers up with gay-friendly hoteliers, tour operators, and airline and cruise-line representatives. It offers monthly newsletters, marketing mailings, and a membership directory that's updated once a year. Membership is $200 yearly, plus a $100 administration fee for new members.

FOR SENIORS

If you're like many people these days, getting older doesn't necessarily mean slowing down. And, if you're savvy, you can even make those gray hairs pay off. For example, most major domestic airlines offer discount programs for senior travelers; be sure to ask whenever you book a flight. In most cities, including San Antonio and Austin, people over the age of 60 (or 62 or 65) qualify for reduced admission to theaters, museums, and other attractions, as well as discounted fares on public transportation (see the "One-Day Ticket, Yeah" sidebar in chapter 3).

Not yet 60? You can still reap the benefits of the maturity that your birth certificate indicates you've achieved. By joining the **AARP,** 601 E St. NW, Washington, DC 20049 (✆ 202/434-2277), those over age 50 can get good discounts on many hotels, rental cars, and sights; at extra cost, the Amoco Motoring Plan offers trip-routing information and emergency road service.

Always remember to ask about any senior discounts in advance—for example, when you're booking a room or renting a car, not when you're checking out or returning the vehicle.

The nonprofit **Elderhostel,** 75 Federal St., 3rd Floor, Boston, MA 02110 (✆ 617/426-7788; www.elderhostel.org), has a great variety of inexpensive and interesting study programs, including room and board, for travelers ages 55 and older; find the complete catalog online or mail away for one. San Antonio–based courses may range from a general introduction to Texas history to more specialized subjects, such as the architecture of the Spanish missions.

FOR FAMILIES

The family vacation is a rite of passage for many households. As any veteran family vacationer will assure you, a family trip can be among the most pleasurable and rewarding times of your life; it can also quickly devolve into a farce worthy of a *National Lampoon* movie. Good advance travel planning is essential.

The San Antonio edition of the free monthly *Our Kids* magazine includes a calendar that lists daily local activities oriented toward children. You can read it online at www.parenthoodweb.com; order it in advance from 8400 Blanco, Suite 201, San Antonio, TX 78216 (✆ 210/349-6667); or find it in San Antonio at HEB supermarkets, Wal-Mart stores, Hollywood Video, and most major bookstores. Call to find out other additional locations where it's available.

The **Family Travel Times** newsletter, *Travel with Your Children,* 40 Fifth Ave., New York, NY 10011 (✆ 888/822-4388 or 212/477-5524; www.familytraveltimes.com), published six times a year, offers good general information, as well as destination-specific articles. Subscriptions cost $39; get one online, by phone, or by snail mail.

Plugged in? **Family Travel Network** (www.familytravelnetwork.com) offers travel tips and reviews of family-friendly destinations, vacation deals, and thoughtful features such as "What to Do When Your Kids Are Afraid to Travel" and "Kid-Style Camping." **Travel Internationally with Your Children** (www.travelwithyourkids.com) is a comprehensive site offering sound advice for traveling with children. **The Busy Person's Guide to Travel with Children** (http://wz.com/travel/TravelingWithChildren.html) features a "45-second newsletter" where experts weigh in on the best websites and resources for tips for traveling with children.

FOR STUDENTS

You don't have to be a student—or even a youth—to join Hostelling International–American Youth Hostels, 733 15th St. NW, Suite 840, Washington, DC 20005 (✆ **202/783-6161;** www.iyhf.org), which gives its members discounts at its dorm-style hostels around the world, and also offers rail and bus travel discounts in many places. **STA Travel** (✆ **800/781-4040;** www.statravel.com) is another travel agency catering especially to young travelers, although their bargain-basement prices are available to people of all ages. In Canada, **Travel CUTS** (✆ **800/667-2887** or 416/614-2887; www.travelcuts.com), offers similar services.

Although San Antonio has 12 2- and 4-year institutions of higher education, it's not really a college town, and there's no general gathering place for college-agers (though they tend to gravitate toward the entertainment strip on N. St. Mary's St. during weekends). The local branch of the state system, the **University of Texas at San Antonio,** has two campuses: one north of town at 6900 N. Loop 1604 (✆ **210/458-4011**), and a newer one on the western side of downtown, at 501 W. Durango (✆ **210/458-2700**). The city's other major universities, **Trinity,** 715 Stadium Dr. (✆ **210/999-7011**); **St. Mary's,** 1 Camino Santa Maria (✆ **210/436-3011**); and **University of the Incarnate Word,** 4301 Broadway (✆ **210/829-6000**), are all private. The best source of local information for student visitors is probably **Hostelling International–San Antonio** (see chapter 4).

6 Getting There

BY PLANE
THE MAJOR AIRLINES

The major domestic carriers serving San Antonio are **America West** (✆ 800/235-9292; www.americawest.com), **American** (✆ 800/433-7300; www.aa.com), **Continental** (✆ 800/525-0280; www.continental.com), **Delta** (✆ 800/221-1212; www.delta.com), **Midwest Express** (✆ 800/452-2022; www.midwestexpress.com), **Northwest** (✆ 800/225-2525; www.nwa.com), **Southwest** (✆ 800/435-9792; www.iflyswa.com), and **United** (✆ 800/241-6522; www.united.com). **Aerolitoral** (✆ 800/237-6639; www.aerolitoral.com), **Aeromar** (✆ 888/627-0207; www.aeromarairlines.com),

Continental and **Mexicana** (✆ 800/531-7921; www.mexicana.com) offer service to and from Mexico.

For the most current information on who jets into town, call 210/207-3450. Because San Antonio isn't a hub, service to the city has been circuitous in the past, but airlines servicing San Antonio currently provide nonstops to such major U.S. cities as Austin, Atlanta, Baltimore, Chicago, Cincinnati, Dallas-Fort Worth, Denver, El Paso, Houston, Kansas City, Las Vegas, Los Angeles, Memphis, Minneapolis/St. Paul, Nashville, Newark, Orlando, Phoenix, Tampa, Salt Lake City, and St. Louis.

Air Travel Security Measures

In the wake of the terrorist attacks of September 11, 2001, the airline industry implemented sweeping security measures in airports. Although regulations vary from airline to airline, you can expedite the check-in process and alleviate airport stress by taking the following steps:

- **Arrive early.** Times vary from airport to airport, depending on their size. Figure on arriving for check-in anywhere from a minimum of an hour in advance to at least 2 hours before your scheduled flight.
- **Don't count on curbside check-in.** Some airlines and airports have stopped curbside check-in altogether, whereas others offer it on a limited basis. For up-to-date information on specific regulations and implementations, check with your airline.
- **Be sure to carry documentation.** A government-issued photo ID (federal, state, or local) is now required. Have it easily accessible to show at various checkpoints. With an E-ticket, you may also be required to have with you printed confirmation of purchase, and perhaps even the credit card with which you bought your ticket. Again, this varies from airline to airline, so call ahead to make sure you have the proper documentation.
- **Know what you can carry on-and what you can't.** Travelers in the United States are now limited to one carry-on bag, plus one personal bag (such as a purse or a briefcase). The **Transportation Security Administration** has also issued a list of banned carry-on items; for more information, check the TSA's website at www.tsa.gov. Your airline may have additional restrictions on carry-on items, so call ahead to avoid problems.
- **Prepare to be searched.** Expect spot-checks. Electronic items, such as a laptop or cell phone, are likely to be subject to additional screening. Be prepared to shift your jewelry, loose change, and any other metallic items on your person to bins before you go through security.
- **It's no joke.** If anyone asks you security-related questions, don't be flip. The agents will not hesitate to call security.

FLYING FOR LESS: TIPS FOR GETTING THE BEST AIRFARE

Airfares are capitalism at its purest. Passengers within the same cabin on an airplane rarely pay the same fare. Rather, they pay what the market will bear.

Business travelers who need the flexibility to buy their tickets at the last minute and change their itinerary at a moment's notice, and whose priority it is to get home before the weekend, pay the premium rate, known as the full fare (at least their companies do). Passengers who can book their ticket long in advance, who don't mind staying over Saturday night, or who are willing to travel on a Tuesday, Wednesday, or Thursday pay the least, usually a fraction of the full fare. On most flights, even the shortest hops, the full fare is close to $1,000 or more, but a 7-day or 14-day advance purchase ticket is closer to $200 to $300. Obviously, it pays to plan ahead.

The airlines also periodically hold sales, in which they lower the prices on their most popular routes. These fares have advance purchase requirements and date-of-travel restrictions, but you can't beat the prices. Keep your eyes open for these sales, which tend to take place in seasons of low travel volume, as you're planning your vacation. You'll almost never see a sale around the peak summer vacation months of July and August, or around Thanksgiving or Christmas, when people have to fly regardless of the fare they have to pay.

Here are some other ways to save:

- **Consolidators,** also known as bucket shops, are a good place to check for the lowest fares. Their prices are much better than the fares you could get yourself, and are often even lower than what your travel agent can get you. You see their ads in the small boxes at the bottom of the page in your Sunday travel section. Some of the most reliable consolidators include **Cheap Tickets** (© **800/ 377-1000;** www.cheaptickets. com), which also offers discounts on car rentals and hotel rooms; **Travac Tours & Charters** (© **877/ 872-8221;** www.thetravelsite. com), with useful links to lots of different travel websites; and Fly-Cheap (© **800/FLY-CHEAP;** www.flycheap.com), which requires you to provide a lot of information about yourself before you can find out very much about them.

- Another way to find the cheapest fare is to **scour the Internet.** That's what computers do best—search through millions of pieces of data and return information in ranking order. The number of virtual travel agents on the Internet has increased exponentially in recent years. See "Planning Your Trip Online," below, for more information.

- Great last-minute deals are also available directly from the airlines themselves through a free e-mail service called **E-savers.** Each week, the airline sends you a list of discounted flights, usually leaving the upcoming Friday or Saturday, and returning the following Monday or Tuesday. You can sign up for all the major airlines at once by logging on to **Smarter Living** (www.smarterliving.com), or go to each individual airline's website. These sites offer schedules, flight booking, and information on late-breaking bargains.

BY CAR

As has been said of Rome, all roads lead to San Antonio. The city is fed by four interstates (I-35, I-10, I-37, and I-410), five U.S. highways (U.S. 281, U.S. 90, U.S. 87, U.S. 181, and U.S. 81), and five state highways (Hwy. 16, Hwy. 13, Hwy. 211, Hwy. 151, and Hwy. 1604). In San Antonio, I-410 and Hwy. 1604, which circle the city, are referred to as Loop 410 and Loop 1604. All freeways lead into the central business district; U.S. 281 and Loop 410 are closest to the airport.

San Antonio is 975 miles from Atlanta, 1,979 miles from Boston, 1,187 miles from Chicago, 1,342 miles from Los Angeles, 1,360 miles from Miami, 527 miles from New Orleans, 1,781 miles from New York, 1,724 miles from San Francisco, and 2,149 miles from Seattle. The distance to Dallas is 282 miles, to Houston 199 miles, and to Austin 80 miles.

BY TRAIN

Amtrak provides service three times a week, going east to Orlando (via Houston, Lafayette, and New Orleans), and west to Los Angeles (via El Paso and Tucson). Trains leave from the depot at 350 Hoefden (© **210/ 223-3226**). There is also daily service between San Antonio and Chicago via Austin, Fort Worth, Dallas, Little Rock, and St. Louis. Call © **800/ USA-RAIL** or log on to www.amtrak. com for current fares, schedules, and reservations.

BY BUS

San Antonio's **Greyhound** station, 500 N. St. Mary's St. (© **210/270-5824**), is located downtown about 2 blocks from the River Walk. This bustling station, which is open 24 hours, is within walking distance of a number of hotels, and many public streetcar and bus lines run nearby. Look for Greyhound's advance specials, companion specials (if you book a round-trip at least 3 days in advance, a companion rides free), and other promotional discounts. For all current price and schedule information, call © **800/ 229-9424** (© 800/345-3109 TTY; 800/752-4841 for assistance for people with disabilities), or log on to www.greyhound.com.

7 Planning Your Trip Online

Researching and booking your trip online can save time and money. Then again, it may not. It is simply not true that you always get the best deal online. Most booking engines do not include schedules and prices for budget airlines, and from time to time you'll get a better last-minute price by calling the airline directly, so it's best to call the airline to see if you can do better before booking online.

On the plus side, Internet users today can tap into the same travel-planning databases that were once accessible only to travel agents—and do it at the same speed. Sites such as **Frommers.com, Travelocity.com, Expedia.com,** and **Orbitz.com** allow consumers to comparison shop for airfares, access special bargains, book flights, and reserve hotel rooms and rental cars.

But don't fire your travel agent just yet. Although online booking sites offer tips and hard data to help you bargain shop, they cannot endow you with the hard-earned experience that makes a seasoned, reliable travel agent an invaluable resource, even in the Internet age. And for consumers with a complex itinerary, a trusty travel agent is still the best way to arrange the most direct flights to and from the best airports.

Still, there's no denying the Internet's emergence as a powerful tool in researching and plotting travel time. The benefits of researching your trip online can be well worth the effort.

Last-minute specials, such as weekend deals or Internet-only fares, are offered by airlines to fill empty seats. Most of these are announced on Tuesday or Wednesday and must be purchased online. They are only valid for travel that weekend, but some can be booked weeks or months in advance. Sign up for weekly e-mail alerts at airline websites or check mega-sites that compile comprehensive lists of last-minute specials, such as **Smarter Living** (www.smarter living.com) or **WebFlyer** (www.web flyer.com).

Some sites, such as Expedia.com, will send you **e-mail notification** when a cheap fare becomes available to your favorite destination. Some will also tell you when fares to a particular destination are lowest.

TRAVEL PLANNING & BOOKING SITES

Keep in mind that because several airlines are no longer willing to pay commissions on tickets sold by online travel agencies, these agencies may either add a $10 surcharge to your bill if you book on that carrier—or neglect to offer those carriers' schedules.

The list of sites below is selective, not comprehensive. Some sites will have evolved or disappeared by the time you read this.

- **Travelocity** (www.travelocity.com or http://frommers.travelocity.com) and **Expedia** (www.expedia.com) are among the most popular sites,

Frommers.com: The Complete Travel Resource

For an excellent travel-planning resource, we highly recommend **Frommers.com** (www.frommers.com). We're a little biased, of course, but we guarantee that you'll find the travel tips, reviews, monthly vacation giveaways, and online-booking capabilities thoroughly indispensable. Among the special features are our popular **Message Boards,** where Frommer's readers post queries and share advice (sometimes even our authors show up to answer questions); **Frommers.com Newsletter,** for the latest travel bargains and inside travel secrets; and Frommer's **Destinations Section,** where you'll get expert travel tips, hotel and dining recommendations, and advice on the sights to see for more than 2,500 destinations around the globe. When your research is done, the **Online Reservation System** (www.frommers.com/booktravelnow) takes you to Frommer's favorite sites for booking your vacation at affordable prices.

each offering an excellent range of options. Travelers search by destination, dates and cost.

- **Orbitz** (www.orbitz.com) is a popular site launched by United, Delta, Northwest, American, and Continental Airlines. With this site, you're granted access to the largest databank of low rates, airline tickets, rental cars, hotels, vacation packages, and other travel products. You get, among other offerings, available fares from more than 450 airlines.
- **Qixo** (www.qixo.com) is another powerful search engine that allows you to search for flights and accommodations from some 20 airline and travel-planning sites (such as Travelocity) at once. Qixo sorts results by price.
- **Priceline** (www.priceline.com) lets you "name your price" for airline tickets, hotel rooms, and rental cars. For airline tickets, you can't say what time you want to fly—you have to accept any flight between 6am and 10pm on the dates you've selected, and you may have to make one or more stopovers. Tickets are nonrefundable, and no frequent-flier miles are awarded.

SMART E-SHOPPING

The savvy traveler is armed with insider information. Here are a few tips to help you navigate the Internet successfully and safely.

- **Know when sales start.** Last-minute deals may vanish in minutes. If you have a favorite booking site or airline, find out when last-minute deals are released to the public. (For example, Southwest's specials are posted every Tues at 12:01am Central time.)
- **Shop around.** If you're looking for bargains, compare prices on different sites and airlines—and against a travel agent's best fare. Try a range of times and alternative airports before you make a purchase.
- **Stay secure.** Book only through secure sites (some airline sites are not secure). Look for a key icon (Netscape) or a padlock (Internet Explorer) at the bottom of your web browser before you enter credit card information or other personal data.
- **Avoid online auctions.** Sites that auction airline tickets and frequent-flier miles are the

number-one perpetrators of Internet fraud, according to the National Consumers League.
• **Maintain a paper trail.** If you book an E-ticket, print out a confirmation, or write down your confirmation number, and keep it safe and accessible—or your trip could be a virtual one!

8 Recommended Reading

Before Frederick Law Olmsted became a landscape architect—New York's Central Park is among his famous creations—he was a successful journalist; his 1853 *A Journey Through Texas* includes a delightful section on his impressions of early San Antonio. William Sidney Porter, better known as O. Henry, had a newspaper office in San Antonio for a while; two collections of his short stories, *Texas Stories* and *Time to Write,* include a number of pieces set in the city, among them "A Fog in Santone," "The Higher Abdication," "Hygeia at the Solito," "Seats of the Haughty," and "The Missing Chord."

O. Henry wasn't very successful at selling his newspaper *Rolling Stone* (no, not *that* one) in San Antonio during the 1890s, but there's a lively literary scene in town today. Resident writers include Sandra Cisneros, whose powerful, critically acclaimed short stories in *Women Hollering Creek* are often set in the city; novelist Sarah Bird, whose humorous *The Mommy Club* pokes fun at the yuppies of the King William area; and mystery writer Jay Brandon, whose excellent *Loose Among the Lambs* kept San Antonians busy trying to guess the identities of the local figures they (erroneously) thought had been fictionalized therein. Stephen Harrigan's *The Gates of the Alamo* is a gripping, fictionalized version of Texas's most famous battle. For a hard-boiled detective take on the city, check out *Tequila Red* and other novels by Rick Riordan set in an appropriately seamy San Antonio.

3

Getting to Know San Antonio

For visitors, San Antonio is really two cities. Downtown, site of the original Spanish settlements, is the compact, eminently strollable tourist hub. The River Walk and its waterside development have revitalized a once-decaying urban center that now buzzes with hotels, restaurants, and shops. And thanks in large part to the San Antonio Conservation Society, many of downtown's beautiful old buildings are still intact; some house popular tourist attractions and hotels, while others are occupied by the large businesses that are increasingly trickling back to where it all began. Public transportation is cheap and plentiful downtown, and as a result a car tends to be more of a hindrance than a help.

The other San Antonio is spread out, mostly low-rise, and connected by more than its fair share of freeways.

The city's most recent growth has been toward the northwest, where you'll find the sprawling South Texas Medical Center complex and, farther out, the ritzy Dominion Country Club and housing development, the Six Flags Fiesta Texas theme park, and the Westin La Cantera Resort. The old southeast section, home to four of the five historic missions, remains largely Hispanic, while much of the southwest is taken up by Kelly and Lackland Air Force Bases. Whether you fly or drive in, you're likely to find yourself in the northeastern reaches of the city at some point: Along with the airport, this section hosts the Brackenridge Park attractions and some of the best restaurants and shops in town. You'll probably want your own wheels if you're staying in this second San Antonio.

1 Orientation

ARRIVING

BY PLANE The two-terminal **San Antonio International Airport** (© **210/207-3411;** www.sanantonio.gov/airport), about 13 miles north of downtown, is compact, clean, well marked—even cheerful. Among its various amenities are a postal center, ATM, foreign-currency exchange, game room, and well-stocked gift shops. Advantage, Alamo, Avis, Budget, Dollar, Enterprise, Hertz, and National all have desks at both of the airport terminals.

Loop 410 and U.S. 281 south intersect just outside the airport. If you're renting a car here (see "By Car" in "Getting Around," below), it should take about 15 to 20 minutes to drive downtown via U.S. 281 south.

Impressions
We were already almost out of America and yet definitely in it and in the middle of where it's maddest. Hotrods blew by. San Antonio, ah-haa!
—Jack Kerouac, *On the Road* (1955)

Most of the hotels within a radius of a mile or two offer **free shuttle service** to and from the airport (be sure to check when you make your reservation). If you're staying downtown, you'll most likely have to pay your own way.

VIA Metropolitan Transit's **bus no. 2** is the cheapest (80¢) way to get downtown but also the slowest, stopping first at the North Star shopping center. Unless you've come without luggage and want to stop off at the mall to buy a few things, the trip should take from 40 to 45 minutes. You need exact change.

SATRANS (© 800/868-7707 or 210/281-9900, www.saairportshuttle. com), with a booth outside each of the terminals, offers shared van service from the airport to the downtown hotels for $9 per person one-way, $16 round-trip. Check the website for prices to other destinations. Vans run from about 6am until 1am; phone 24 hours in advance for van pickup from your hotel.

There's a **taxi** queue in front of each terminal. The base charge on a taxi is $1.60; add $1.50 for each mile. It should cost you about $14 to $16 to get downtown, including the 50¢ airport departure fee; from 9pm to 5am the base charge is $2.60, plus the usual $1.50 per additional mile.

BY TRAIN   San Antonio's train station is located in St. Paul's Square, on the east side of downtown near the Alamodome and adjacent to the Sunset Station entertainment complex. Unfortunately, both eastbound and westbound long-distance trains come into San Antonio at ungodly hours (after 3am and 4am, respectively), making this a difficult option; you're not going to be able to jump straight into your vacation, but at least you can easily get a cab here. Drink and snack machines are available inside the station, and there's an ATM at the Alamodome—just *don't* try walking to the dome before daylight, as it's located in a bad area. Lockers are not available (for security reasons), but Amtrak will hold passengers' bags in a secure location for $1.50 per bag. Information about the city is available at the main counter.

VISITOR INFORMATION

The main office of the **City of San Antonio Visitor Information Center** is across the street from the Alamo, at 317 Alamo Plaza (© 210/207-6748). Hours are daily 8:30am to 6pm, except Thanksgiving, Christmas, and New Year's, when the center is closed.

Publications such as the free *Fiesta,* a glossy magazine with interesting articles about the city, and *Rio,* a tabloid focusing on the River Walk, are available at the Visitor Information Center, as well as at most downtown hotels and many shops and tourist sights. Both of these advertising-heavy publications list sights, restaurants, shops, cultural events, and some nightlife, though there's an obvious bias toward advertisers. Also free—but more objective—is San Antonio's alternative paper, the *Current.* Though skimpy, it is a good source for nightlife listings; don't depend on it for movie schedules, however. Check out the *Current's Visitors Guide to the Alamo City,* published four times a year and available at most River Walk hotels, restaurants, and bars, for an offbeat take on the usual tourist attractions and other suggestions for unusual things to do around town.

The *San Antonio Express-News* is the local newspaper. It's got a good arts/entertainment section called "The Weekender," which comes out on Friday and is available for free around town.

Arguably the best state-oriented magazine in the country, *Texas Monthly* contains excellent short reviews of restaurants in San Antonio, among other cities; its incisive articles about local politics, people, and events are a great way to get acquainted with Lone Star territory in general. You can buy a copy at almost any city bookstore, grocery, or newsstand.

CITY LAYOUT

Although it lies at the southern edge of the Texas Hill Country, San Antonio itself is basically flat. As I noted earlier, the city divides into two distinct districts: a compact central downtown surrounded by a Western-style, freeway-laced sprawl. Neither section is laid out in a neat grid system; many of downtown's streets trace the meandering course of the San Antonio River, while a number of the thoroughfares in the rest of town follow old conquistador routes or 19th-century wagon trails.

MAIN ARTERIES & STREETS   Welcome to loop land. Most of the major roads in Texas meet in San Antonio, where they form a rough wheel-and-spoke pattern: I-410 traces a 53-mile circumference around the city, and Hwy. 1604 forms an even larger circle around them both. I-35, I-10, I-37, U.S. 281, U.S. 90, and U.S. 87, along with many smaller thoroughfares, run diagonally, but not always separately, across these two loops to form its main spokes. For example, U.S. 90, U.S. 87, and I-10 converge for a while in an east–west direction just south of downtown, while U.S. 281, I-35, and I-37 run together on a north–south route to the east; I-10, I-35, and U.S. 87 bond for a bit going north–south to the west of downtown. As a result, you may hear locals referring to something as being "in the loop." That doesn't mean it's privy to insider information; rather, it lies within the circumference of I-410. True, this covers a pretty large area, but with the spreading of the city north and west, it's come to mean central.

Among the most major of the minor spokes are Broadway, McCullough, San Pedro, and Blanco, all of which lead north from the city center into the most popular shopping and restaurant areas of town. Fredericksburg goes out to the Medical Center from just northwest of downtown.

Downtown is bounded by I-37 to the east, I-35 to the north and west, and U.S. 90 (which merges with I-10) to the south. Within this area, Durango, Commerce, Market, and Houston are the important east–west thoroughfares. Alamo on the east side and Santa Rosa (which turns into South Laredo) on the west side are the major north–south streets. *Note:* A lot of the north–south streets change names midstream (or should I say mid-macadam). That's another reason, besides the confusing one-way streets, to consult a map carefully before attempting to steer your way around downtown.

FINDING AN ADDRESS   Few locals are aware that there's any method to the madness of finding downtown addresses, but in fact directions are actually based on the layout of the first Spanish settlements—back when the San Fernando cathedral was at the center of town. Market is the north–south street divider, and Flores separates east from west. Thus, South St. Mary's becomes North St. Mary's when it crosses Market, with addresses starting from zero at Market going in both directions. North of downtown, San Pedro is the east–west dividing line, although not every street sign reflects this fact.

There are few clear-cut rules like this in loop land, but on its northernmost stretch, Loop 410 divides into east and west at Broadway; at Bandera Road, it splits into Loop 410 north and south. Keep going far enough south, and I-35 marks yet another boundary between east and west. Knowing this will help you a little in locating an address, and explains why, when you go in a circle around town—you probably won't do this on purpose, unless you're trying to put a baby

San Antonio at a Glance

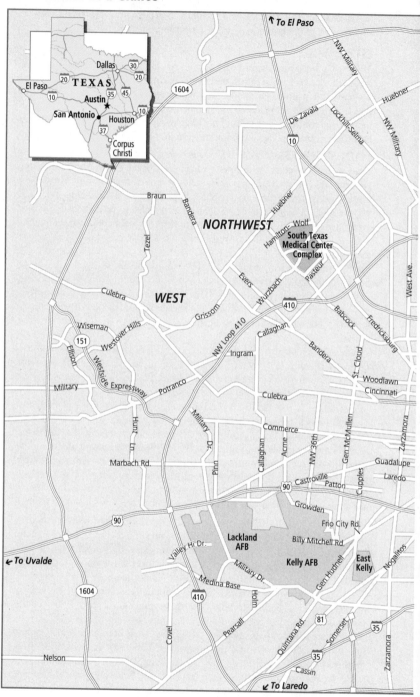

To El Paso

Dallas
El Paso
TEXAS
Austin
San Antonio
Houston
Corpus
Christi

1604

NW Military
Huebner
NW Military
De Zavala
Lockhill-Selma
10

Braun
Bandera
Huebner
NORTHWEST
Wolf
Hamilton
South Texas
Medical Center
Complex
Pasteur
West Ave.

Tezel
Culebra
WEST
Evers
Wurzbach
410
Babcock
Fredricksburg

Wiseman
Westover Hills
Grissom
NW Loop 410
Callaghan
Bandera
St. Cloud
Woodlawn
151
Ingram
Cincinnati
Ellison
Westside Expressway
Potranco
Culebra
Military
Commerce
Callaghan
Acme
NW 36th
Gen McMullen
Zarzamora
Hunt Ln
Military Dr.
Guadalupe
Marbach Rd.
Pinn
Castroville
Laredo
90
Patton
Cupples
Growden
Frio City Rd.
90
Valley Hi Dr.
Lackland
AFB
Billy Mitchell Rd.
East
Kelly
To Uvalde
Military Dr.
Kelly AFB
Gen Hudnell
Nogalitos
1604
Medina Base
Holm
410
Covel
Pearsall
Quintana Rd.
81
Somerset
35
Zarzamora
Nelson
Cassin
35

To Laredo

26

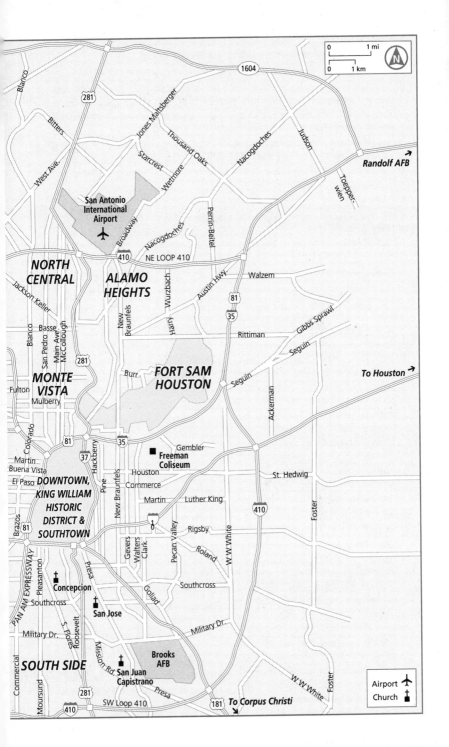

to sleep (as one friend of mine successfully did)—you'll notice that the directions marked on overhead signs have suddenly completely shifted.

STREET MAPS   The Visitor Information Center (see "Visitor Information," above) and most hotels distribute the free street maps published by the **San Antonio Convention and Visitors Bureau (SACVB).** They mark the main attractions in town and are useful enough as a general reference, especially if you're on foot; they even indicate which downtown streets are one-way—a bonus for drivers. But if you're going to do much navigating around town, you'll need something better. Both **Rand McNally** and **Gousha**'s maps of San Antonio are reliable; you'll find one or the other at most gas stations, convenience stores, drugstores, bookstores, and newsstands.

THE NEIGHBORHOODS IN BRIEF

The older areas described here, from downtown through Alamo Heights, are all "in the loop" (410). The Medical Center area in the Northwest lies just outside it, but the rest of the Northwest, as well as North Central and the West, are expanding beyond even Loop 1604.

Downtown   Site of San Antonio's three oldest Spanish settlements, this area includes the Alamo and other historic sites, along with the River Walk, the Alamodome, the convention center, the Rivercenter Mall, and many high-rise hotels, restaurants, and shops. It's also the center of commerce and government; many banks and offices, as well as most city buildings, are located here. Once seedy and largely deserted at night, it has rebounded with a vengeance—a proliferation of bars and clubs catering to younger crowds even resulted in a city ordinance restraining the volume of outdoor noise.

King William   The city's first suburb, this historic district directly south of downtown was settled in the mid- to late 1800s by wealthy German merchants who built some of the most beautiful mansions in town. It began to be yuppified in the 1970s, and, at this point, you'd never guess it had ever been allowed to deteriorate. Only two of the area's many impeccably restored homes are generally open to the public, but a number have been turned into bed-and-breakfasts.

Southtown   Alamo Street marks the border between King William and Southtown, an adjoining commercial district. Long a depressed area, it's slowly becoming trendy thanks to a Main Street refurbishing project and the opening of the Blue Star arts complex. You'll find a nice mix of Hispanic neighborhood shops and funky coffeehouses and galleries here.

South Side   The old, largely Hispanic southeast section of town that begins where Southtown ends (there's no agreed-upon boundary, but I'd say it lies a few blocks beyond the Blue Star arts complex) is home to four of the city's five historic missions. Thus far, it hasn't been experiencing the same gentrification and redevelopment as much of the rest of the city—but that could change when the hike-and-bike trail along a stretch of the San Antonio River here is completed.

Monte Vista Area   Immediately northwest of downtown, Monte Vista was established soon after King William by a conglomeration of wealthy cattlemen, politicos, and generals who moved "on to the hill" at the turn of the century. A number of the area's large houses have been split into apartments for students of nearby Trinity University and San Antonio Community College, but many lovely old homes have been restored in the past 30 years. It hasn't reached King William status yet, but this is already a highly desirable (read: pricey) place to live. Monte Vista is close to the once thriving, but now less lively, restaurant and entertainment district along North St. Mary's Street between Josephine and Magnolia known locally as **The Strip.**

Fort Sam Houston Built in 1876 to the northeast of downtown, Fort Sam Houston boasts a number of stunning officers' homes. Much of the working-class neighborhood surrounding Fort Sam is now run-down, but renewed interest in restoring San Antonio's older areas is beginning to have some impact here, too.

Alamo Heights Area In the 1890s, when construction in the area began, Alamo Heights was at the far northern reaches of San Antonio. It has slowly evolved into one of the city's most exclusive neighborhoods, and is now home to wealthy families, expensive shops, and trendy restaurants. **Terrell Hills** to the east, **Olmos Park** to the west, and **Lincoln Heights** to the north are all offshoots of this moneyed area; the latter is home to the Quarry, once just that, but now a ritzy golf course and huge shopping mall. Shops and restaurants are concentrated along two main drags: Broadway and, to a lesser degree, New Braunfels. Most of these neighborhoods share a single ZIP code ending in the numbers "09"—thus the local term "09ers," referring to the area's affluent residents. The Witte Museum, San Antonio Botanical Gardens, and Brackenridge Park are all in this part of town.

Northwest The mostly character-less neighborhood surrounding the South Texas Medical Center (always just referred to as **Medical Center**), which hosts the majority of San Antonio's hospitals and health care facilities, is one of the city's more recently established areas. Many of the homes occupied by the young professionals who have been moving here are condominiums and apartments, and much of the shopping and dining is in strip malls (the trendy, still-expanding Heubner Oaks retail center is an exception). The farther north you go, the nicer the housing complexes get. The high-end Westin La Cantera resort, the exclusive La Cantera and Dominion residential enclave, and several tony new golf courses mark the direction that development is taking in the far northwest part of town, just beyond Six Flags Fiesta Texas and near the public Friedrich Park. It's becoming one of San Antonio's prime growth areas.

North Central San Antonio is inching towards Bulverde and other Hill Country towns via this major corridor of development clustered from Loop 410 north to Loop 1604, east of I-10 and west of I-35, and bisected by U.S. 281. The **airport** and many developed industrial strips line U.S. 281 in the southern section, but the farther north you go, the more you see the natural beauty of this area, hilly and dotted with small canyons. Recent city codes have motivated developers to retain trees and native plants in their residential communities.

West Although SeaWorld has been out here since the late 1980s, and the Hyatt Regency Hill Country Resort settled here in the early 1990s, other development was comparatively slow in coming. Now the West is booming with new mid-price housing developments, strip malls, schools, and businesses. Road building hasn't kept pace with growth, however, so traffic can be a bear.

2 Getting Around

BY PUBLIC TRANSPORTATION

BY BUS   San Antonio's public transportation system is visitor friendly; although prices have gone up in recent years, they're still very reasonable. The 104 **VIA Metropolitan Transit Service** bus routes cost 80¢ for regular lines, with an additional 15¢ charge for transfers, and $1.60 for express buses (15¢ for transfers). You'll need exact change. Call © **210/362-2020** for transit information, check the website at **www.viainfo.net**, or stop in at VIA's downtown center, 260 E. Houston St; it's open Monday to Friday 7am to 6pm, Saturday 9am to 2pm. *Tip:* During large festivals such as Fiesta and the Texas Folklife Festival, VIA offers many park-and-ride lots that allow you to leave your car and bus it downtown.

BY STREETCAR   In addition to its bus lines, VIA offers four convenient downtown streetcar routes that cover all the most popular tourist stops. Designed to look like the turn-of-the-century trolleys used in San Antonio until 1933, the streetcars cost 50¢ (exact change required, drivers carry none). The trolleys, which have signs color-coded by route, display their destinations.

BY CAR

If you can avoid driving downtown, by all means do so. The pattern of one-way streets is confusing and parking is extremely limited. It's not that the streets in downtown San Antonio are narrower or more crowded than those in most old city centers; it's just that there's no need to bother when public transportation is so convenient. There's also the matter of the 3-second traffic light (I'm not making this up; I timed them) many downtown streets have. The continuous stop-and-go can get old pretty fast.

As for highway driving, pay attention. Because of the many convergences of major freeways in the area—described in the "Main Arteries & Streets" section, above—you could suddenly find yourself in an express lane headed somewhere you really don't want to go. Don't let your mind wander; watch signs carefully, and be prepared to make lots of quick lane changes.

Rush hour lasts from about 7:45 to 9am and 4:30 to 6pm Monday through Friday. The crush may not be bad compared with that of Houston or Dallas, but it's getting worse all the time. Because of San Antonio's rapid growth, you can also expect to find major highway construction or repairs going on somewhere in the city at any given time. Areas that will be particularly hard hit in the next few years are the Loop 410/I-10 and Loop 410/U.S. 281 links, where four-level interchanges, with ramps directly connecting the respective freeways with one another, are in the works. Construction is not scheduled to be completed until 2005 or 2006. For the gory details, log on to the Texas Department of Transportation's website at **www.dot.state.tx.us**.

RENTALS   **Advantage** (© 800/777-5500; www.arac.com), **Alamo** (© 800/327-9633; www.goalamo.com), **Avis** (© 800/831-2847; www.avis.com), **Budget** (© 800/527-0700; www.budget.com), **Dollar** (© 800/800-4000; www.dollar.com), **Enterprise** (© 800/736-8222; www.pickenterprise.com), **Hertz** (© 800/654-3131; www.hertz.com), **National** (© 800/227-7368; www.nationalcar.com), and **Thrifty** (© 800/367-2277; www.thrifty.com) all have desks at both of the airport terminals. **Hertz** is also represented downtown at the Marriott Rivercenter at Bowie and Commerce (© **210/225-3676**).

One-Day Ticket, Yeah!

A $2 day-tripper pass, good for an entire day of travel on all VIA transportation except express buses, can be purchased at VIA's downtown Information Center (see the "By Bus" section, above). Seniors (62 and over) can also get a discount card there and at several other locations (if downtown isn't convenient, phone the downtown office or check the website to locate the office closest to you). You have to go in person, with proof of age and a Social Security card; the picture ID that you receive on the spot will entitle you to ride for 20¢ Monday to Friday from 9am to 3pm and all day Saturday and Sunday, and for 40¢ before 9am and after 3pm, with a 7¢ transfer fee at all times.

Almost all the major car-rental companies have their own discount programs. Your rate will often depend on the organizations to which you belong, the dates of travel, and the length of your stay. Some companies give discounts to AAA members, for example, and some have special deals in conjunction with various airlines or telephone companies. Off-season rates are likely to be lower, and prices are sometimes reduced on weekends (or midweek). Call as far in advance as possible to book a car, and always ask about specials.

On top of the standard rental prices, other optional charges apply to most car rentals. The Collision Damage Waiver (CDW), which requires you to pay for damage to the car in a collision, is illegal in some states but not Texas. It is, however, covered by many credit card companies. Check with yours before you go so you can avoid paying this hefty fee (as much as $15 a day).

The car-rental companies also offer additional liability insurance (if you harm others in an accident), personal accident insurance (if you harm yourself or your passengers), and personal effects insurance (if your luggage is stolen from your car). If you have insurance on your car at home, you are probably covered for most of these unlikelihoods. If your own insurance doesn't cover rentals, or if you don't have auto insurance, you should consider the additional coverage (keeping in mind that the car-rental companies are liable for certain base amounts).

There are Internet resources that can make comparison shopping easier. All the major booking sites—**Travelocity** (www.travelocity.com), **Expedia** (www.expedia.com), and **Cheap Tickets** (www.cheaptickets.com), for example—have search engines that can dig up discounted car-rental rates. Just enter the size car you want, the rental and return dates, and the city where you want to rent, and the server returns a price. It will even make your reservation for you.

And in case you were wondering, yes—the Alamo car-rental company got its start right here in San Antonio.

PARKING   Parking meters are not plentiful in the heart of downtown, but you can find some on the streets near the River Walk and on Broadway. The cost is $1 per hour (which is also the time limit) in San Fernando Plaza and near the courthouse, 75¢ in other locations. There are some very inexpensive (2 hr. for $1) meters at the outskirts of town; the trick is to find one. If you don't observe the laws, you'll be quickly ticketed. Note that, although very few signs inform

---

(Tips) Free Parking

If you're staying for only a short time, consider leaving your car in the Rivercenter Mall garage and getting your ticket validated at one of the shops; you don't have to buy anything, and you'll have 2 hours of free parking. This is only a good idea, however, if you have an iron will or are allergic to shopping; otherwise, you could end up spending a lot more than at a parking garage.

---

you of this fact, parking at meters is free after 6pm Monday through Saturday and free all day Sunday except during special events.

Except during Fiesta or other major events, you shouldn't have a problem finding a parking lot or garage for your car; rates run from $5 to $7 per day—the closer you get to the Alamo and the River Walk, the more expensive they become. Prices tend to go up during special events and summer weekends; a parking lot that ordinarily charges $5 a day is likely to charge $7 or more.

DRIVING RULES   Right turns on red are permitted after a full stop. Left turns on red are also allowed, but only if you're going from a one-way street onto another one-way street. Seat belts and child restraint seats are mandatory.

BY RIVER TAXI

Yanaguana Cruises (see "Organized Tours," in chapter 6) runs the **Rio Trans River Shuttle** (© **210/244-5700** or www.sarivercruise.com), with ten ticket locations on the River Walk: the Four Points Sheraton, Joe's Crabshack, the Marriott Riverwalk, the Convention Center, the Fig Tree Restaurant, the Tower Life Building, Hawthorne Suites, IBC Bank, the Mexican Manhattan, and the Adam's Mark Hotel. Shuttle stops on the River Walk are marked by Rio Trans signs, but you have to get your ticket before you board. At $3.50 one-way, $10 for an all-day pass, or $25 for a 3-day pass, it's more expensive than ground transport, but it's a treat.

BY TAXI

Cabs are available outside the airport, near the Greyhound and Amtrak terminals (only when a train is due, however), and at most major downtown hotels, but they're next to impossible to hail on the street; most of the time, you'll need to phone for one in advance. The best of the taxi companies in town (and also the biggest, since it represents the recent consolidation of two of the majors) is **Yellow-Checker Cab** (© **210/222-2222**), which has an excellent record of turning up when promised. See "By Plane" in the "Arriving" section above for rates. Most cabbies impose a minimum of $8 for trips from the airport, $3 for rides downtown.

ON FOOT

Downtown San Antonio is a treat for walkers, who can perambulate from one tourist attraction to another or stroll along a beautifully landscaped river. Traffic lights even have buttons to push to make sure the lights stay green long enough for pedestrians to cross without putting their lives in peril. Jaywalking is a ticketable offense, but it's rarely enforced.

FAST FACTS: San Antonio

Airport See "Arriving," earlier in this chapter.

Area Code The telephone area code in San Antonio is **210.**

Business Hours Banks are open Monday to Friday 9am to 4pm, Saturday 9am to 1pm. Drive-up windows are open 7am to 6pm Monday to Friday, and 9am to noon on Saturday. Office hours are generally weekdays from 9am to 5pm. Shops tend to be open from 9 or 10am until 5:30 or 6pm Monday to Saturday, with shorter hours on Sunday. Most malls are open Monday to Saturday from 10am to 9pm, Sunday from noon to 6pm. The majority of bars and clubs boot their last customers out at 2am.

Camera Repair Havel Camera Service, 1102 Basse Rd. (© **210/735-7412**), a reputable camera repair shop, is about 15 minutes north of downtown.

Car Rentals See "Getting Around," earlier in this chapter.

Climate See "When to Go," in chapter 2.

Dentist To find a dentist near you in town, contact the San Antonio District Dental Society, 3355 Cherry Ridge, Ste. 214 (© **210/732-1264**).

Doctor For a referral, contact the Bexar County Medical Society at 202 W. French Pl. © **210/301-4368**).

Driving Rules See "Getting Around," earlier in this chapter.

Drugstores Most branches of Eckerd and Walgreens, the major chain pharmacies in San Antonio, are open late Monday through Saturday. There's an Eckerd downtown at 211 Losoya/River Walk (© **210/224-9293**). Call © **800/925-4733** to find the Walgreens nearest you; punch in the area code and the first three digits of the number you're phoning from and you'll be directed to the closest branch (or, if you choose, the closest one that has 24-hr. service).

Embassies/Consulates See "Fast Facts: For the International Traveler," in Appendix B.

Emergencies For police, fire, or medical emergencies, dial © **911.** The Sheriff's Department number is © **210/270-6000,** and the Texas Department of Public Safety, including the Texas Highway Patrol, can be reached at © **210/533-9171.**

Eyeglass Repair North of the airport, Texas State Optical (TSO), 16111 San Pedro (© **210/545-5755**), is a trusted name for glasses. Also near the airport, Eye Mart, Hwy. 281 and Bitters (© **210/496-6549**), offers quick and friendly service. You'll also find many branches of LensCrafters in town.

Hospitals The main downtown hospital is Baptist Medical Center, 111 Dallas St. (© **210/297-7000**). Christus Santa Rosa Health Care Corp., 333 N. Santa Rosa St. (© **210/704-2011**), is also downtown. Contact the San Antonio Medical Foundation (© **210/614-3724**) for information about other medical facilities in the city.

Hot Lines Contact the National Youth Crisis Hot Line at © **800/448-4663;** Rape Crisis Hot Line at © **210/349-7273;** Child Abuse Hot Line at (© **800/252-5400**); Mental Illness Crisis Hot Line at (© **210/227-4357**); Bexar County Adult Abuse Hot Line at (© **800/252-5400**); and Poison Control Center at (© **800/764-7661**).

Information See "Visitor Information," earlier in this chapter.

Internet You can check your e-mail at the various Kinko's around town; check the Yellow Pages for the location nearest you.

Libraries In 1995, San Antonio opened its magnificent new main library at 600 Soledad Plaza (℃ 210/207-2500); see "More Attractions," in chapter 6, for details.

Liquor Laws The legal drinking age in Texas is 21. Under-age drinkers can legally imbibe as long as they stay within sight of their legal-age parents or spouses, but they need to be prepared to show proof of the relationship. Open containers are prohibited in public and in vehicles. Liquor laws are strictly enforced; if you're concerned, check www.tabc.state.tx.us for the entire Texas alcoholic beverage code.

Lost Property For lost property at the bus station call ℃ 210/270-5824; at the airport, ℃ 210/207-3526 (after 4:30pm, call ℃ 210/207-3526). In addition, each airline operates its own Lost and Found service.

Luggage Storage/Lockers There are lockers at the Greyhound Bus Station and luggage storage at the Amtrak station. But there's nowhere to stow your stuff at the airport.

Maps See "City Layout," earlier in this chapter.

Newspapers/Magazines The *San Antonio Express-News* is the only mainstream source of news in town. See "Visitor Information," above, for magazine recommendations.

Police Call ℃ 911 in an emergency. The Sheriff's Department can be reached at ℃ 210/270-6000; call the Texas Highway Patrol at ℃ 210/533-9171.

Post Office The main post office is at the far northeast part of town at 10410 Perrin-Beitel, but the most convenient location is downtown at 615 E. Houston St., just across from the Alamo. For all postal service, including the location of the post office nearest to your hotel (be sure you know the ZIP code), call ℃ 800/275-8777.

Radio You should be able to find something to suit your radio tastes in San Antonio. KJ97 at 97.3 FM plays country music; KISS at 99.5 FM plays rock music; KONO at 101.1 FM plays oldies; KSMG at 105.3 FM plays easy listening; and KCJZ at 106.7 FM plays rhythm and blues. KSYM at 90.1 FM is the only college alternative station in south Texas. For Tejano music, tune in to KXTN at 107.5 FM. You'll find National Public Radio on KSTX at 89.1 FM, and classical music on sister station KPAC at 88.3 FM. WOAI 1200 on the AM dial is a news/talk radio station.

Restrooms You can use the restrooms downtown at the Rivercenter Mall or duck into any of the free tourist attractions. (Yes, you can go to the bathroom at the Alamo—gratis.) Most restaurants don't mind quick visits, either.

Safety The crime rate in San Antonio has gone down in recent years, and there are frequent police patrols downtown at night; as a result, muggings, pickpocketings, and purse snatchings in the area are rare. Still, use common sense as you would anywhere else: Walk only in well-lit, well-populated streets. Also, it's generally not a good idea to stroll south of Durango Avenue after dark.

Taxes The sales tax here is 7.875%, and the city surcharge on hotel rooms increases to a whopping 16.75%.

Taxis See "Getting Around," earlier in this chapter.

Television The local television affiliates are WOAI on Channel 4 (NBC), KENS on Channel 5 (CBS); KSAT on Channel 12 (ABC); KLRN on Channel 9, (PBS); FOX on Channel 11 (Fox) and KRRT on Channel 7 (WB).

Time Zone San Antonio is on Central Standard Time, one hour behind New York and two hours ahead of Los Angeles. Texas observes daylight saving time.

Transit Information Call ⓒ **210/362-2020.**

Weather Call ⓒ **210/226-3232** or log on to the Weather Channel's website at www.weather.com for forecasts.

4

Where to Stay in San Antonio

You don't have to leave your lodgings to sightsee in San Antonio: This city has the highest concentration of historic hotels in Texas. Even low-end hotel chains are reclaiming old buildings—many examples are covered in this chapter—so don't judge a place by its affiliation. Most of these, as well as other more recently built luxury accommodations, are in the downtown area, which is where you'll likely want to be whether you're here on pleasure or business. Prices in this prime location tend to be high, especially for hotels on the river, but you'll still generally get your money's worth. And if you're willing to forgo your own wheels for a bit—c'mon, you can do it—you'll economize by eliminating car rental and parking fees. Most of the city's tourist attractions are within walking distance or are easily accessible by public transportation anyway, and many restaurants favored by locals are within an inexpensive cab ride from downtown.

In recent years, a number of the old mansions in the King William and Monte Vista historic districts—both close to downtown—have been converted into bed-and-breakfasts; several of them are reviewed in this chapter. For information about additional bed-and-breakfasts in these areas and in other neighborhoods around the city, check out www.sanantoniobb.org, the website of the **San Antonio Bed & Breakfast Association.** Several of San Antonio's inns are also bookable via **Historic Accommodations of Texas,** 3353 Park Lane, Chappell Hill, TX 77426 (© **800/HAT-0368;** www.hat.org).

San Antonio also has two top-notch destination resorts on the outskirts of town, the Hyatt Regency Hill Country Resort and the Westin La Cantera Resort. They're great places to hole up and relax and maybe play some golf, with sightseeing as a secondary potential goal.

Expect most downtown hotels to fall into the Very Expensive or Expensive range, especially if they sit right on the river. With a few notable exceptions, detailed below, only chain hotels on the outskirts of downtown tend to be Moderate or Inexpensive. Pricewise, you'll do better if you stay in a B&B in a historic area near downtown (the Monte Vista neighborhood gives especially good value); you won't have to give up many amenities. Although they're not formally called concierges, B&B owners and innkeepers also do far more to guide their guests around town than employees given that title in many large city hotels. You can also expect B&Bs to be able to provide fax and other business services.

With a few other exceptions, detailed here, the vast majority of the other lodgings around town are low-priced chains; the most convenient are clustered in the northwest near the Medical Center and in the north central area, around the airport. For a full alphabetical listing of the accommodations in the city, mapped by area and including rate ranges as well as basic amenities, phone the **San Antonio Convention and Visitors Bureau** (© **800/447-3372**) and request a lodging guide. The "Accommodations" section of www.SanAntonioVisit.com is a good resource too.

Deal Well, Sleep Well

Don't eliminate a choice because of its price category alone; the prices listed here are the hotel's "rack rates"—the room rate charged without any discount—and you can almost always do better. The San Antonio Convention and Visitors Bureau's annual SAVE (San Antonio Vacation Experience) promotion features discounts on hotel rooms (more than 50 properties participate) as well as on dining and entertainment. Some bed-and-breakfasts and hotels offer better rates to those who book for at least 4 days, although a week is usually the minimum. Even though most leisure travelers visit in summer, rooms tend to be less expensive then; in general, rates are highest from November through April, when conventions converge on the town. Rates also are at their highest when the city's many festivals cause a run on rooms.

But even during peak times, hotel rates vary widely: Some hotels in San Antonio host business clients during the week, whereas others cater to tourists who come on the weekend, so you never know when a property is not fully booked and willing to give you a good deal. In addition, ask about any discounts you can think of—corporate, senior citizen, military, Internet, AAA, entertainment/hotel coupon books, your Uncle Morty's high school friendship with the manager—and about packages such as family, romance, or deals that include meals or sightseeing tours. Bottom line: *Always ask for the lowest-priced room with the most perks available.* Reservation agents are eager to sell rooms, so you shouldn't have a problem getting a good deal.

Wherever you decide to stay, try to book as far in advance as possible—especially if the property is located downtown. And don't even think about coming to town during Fiesta (the 3rd week in Apr) if you haven't reserved a room 6 months in advance.

In the following reviews, price categories are based on rates for a double room in peak season. Don't forget to factor in the 16.75% room tax; price ranges below don't include it.

1 Downtown
VERY EXPENSIVE
Hyatt Regency on the River Walk ★★   There's something stimulating about all that glass and steel rising from this hotel's lobby, where the Hyatt's signature cage elevators ascend and descend the skylit atrium. Maybe it's airiness that determines the difference between a hotel that's bustling and one that just feels overcrowded; this one's definitely bustling, both with business travelers and families who enjoy its convenience to all the downtown attractions. You couldn't be closer to the river's hopping South Bank section, and having a bit of said river running through the lobby adds to the dramatic effect. Guest rooms, done in light woods with Southwestern accents and live plants, are very attractive. And you've got easy access to the New Orleans–oriented bar The Landing, longtime home to the Dixieland jazz of Jim Cullum and his band (see p. 112).

123 Losoya St. (at College St.), San Antonio, TX 78205. ℂ **800/233-1234** or 210/222-1234. Fax 210/227-4925. www.sanantonioregency.hyatt.com. 632 units. $239–$319 double; $328–$768 suite. AE, DC, DISC, MC, V. Self-parking $10; valet parking $14. **Amenities:** Restaurant; 2 bars; outdoor pool; health club; concierge; business center; shopping arcade; limited room service; dry cleaning; club-level rooms. *In room:* A/C, TV w/pay movies, minibar, coffeemaker, hair dryer, iron.

La Mansión del Río 🏨🏨   This lushly landscaped Spanish hacienda–style hotel—converted from a 19th-century seminary in 1968—not only oozes character, but it's also convenient: It sits right on the Paseo del Río, just a block from the Majestic Theater. Moorish arches, Mexican tile, a central patio, wrought-iron balconies, and antique pieces in every nook and cranny combine to create a low-glitz, high-tone Mediterranean atmosphere. The layout is a bit mazelike—the directionally challenged, like me, may find themselves wandering in circles—but staff discretion and a willingness to cater to special requests makes this hotel the pick for many of San Antonio's high-profile visitors (their entourages no doubt steer them in the right direction).

Guest rooms recently underwent a massive revamp and are now better than ever, with rich green, gold and burgundy draperies and bedspreads complementing the rough-hewn beamed ceilings, and brick walls. The more expensive quarters boast balconies overlooking the River Walk, but the interior courtyard views are fine, too. The hotel's dining room, Las Canarias, serves up a terrific river view with its excellent American regional cuisine (see p. 56 for the full review).

112 College St. (between St Mary's and Navarro), San Antonio, TX 78205. ℂ **800/292-7300** or 210/518-1000. Fax 210/226-0389. www.lamansion.com. 337 units. $249–$329 double; $575–$1,949 suite. AE, DC, DISC, MC V. Valet parking $15. Domesticated pets sometimes accepted. **Amenities:** Restaurant; outdoor pool; health club concierge; business center; 24-hr. room service; dry cleaning; babysitting. *In room:* A/C, TV w/pay movies, dataport, minibar, coffeemaker, hair dryer, iron.

Marriott Rivercenter 🏨   Serious retail hounds will find heaven in this glitzy conventioneer high-rise; they can shop more than 100 Rivercenter emporiums until they're ready to drop, and then collapse back into their hotel rooms without ever leaving the mall. Sightseers will be happy here, too; a cruise along the River Walk departs from the mall's downstairs "dock," and the Alamo and HemisFair Park are just a few blocks away.

Convenience is definitely the goal here—free washers and dryers on the same floor as the health club let you bicycle while your clothes cycle. Guest rooms have an earth-toned, simple elegance; many afford spectacular River Walk or city views. If you find all this convenience—and the bustle that goes along with it—a bit overwhelming, an option is to stay at the smaller Marriott Riverwalk across the street. This slightly older and slightly less expensive sister hotel has equally comfortable Southwest-style rooms, and its guests have access to all the facilities of the Rivercenter.

101 Bowie St. (at Commerce St.), San Antonio, TX 78205. ℂ **800/228-9290** or 210/223-1000. Fax 210/223-4092. www.marriotthotels.com. 1,001 units. $279 double; suites from $450. AE, DC, DISC, MC, V. Self-parking $12; valet parking $17. Pets under 20 lb. permitted; $25 deposit required. **Amenities:** 2 restaurants; indoor pool; outdoor pool; health club; sauna; Jacuzzi; concierge; car-rental desk; business center; 24-hr. room service; babysitting; dry cleaning; club-level rooms. *In room:* A/C, TV w/pay movies, dataport, coffeemaker, hair dryer, iron.

Westin Riverwalk Inn 🏨🏨 *(Kids)*   The recycling of downtown historic buildings into hotels is an admirable trend, but there's also something to be said for new construction—at least when it's done right. Opened in late 1999, this ultra-luxe property was designed to blend in architecturally with the older structures

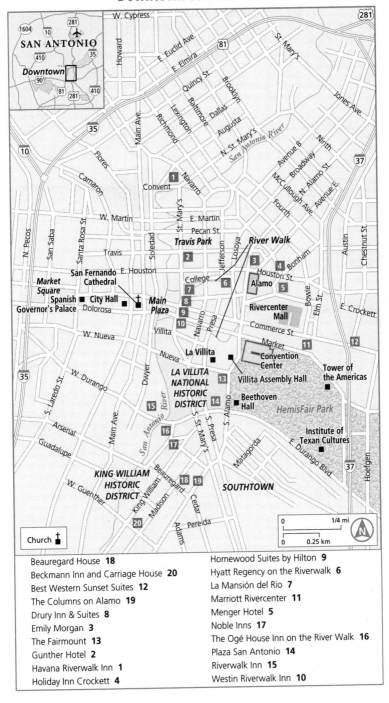

Downtown San Antonio Accommodations

Beauregard House **18**
Beckmann Inn and Carriage House **20**
Best Western Sunset Suites **12**
The Columns on Alamo **19**
Drury Inn & Suites **8**
Emily Morgan **3**
The Fairmount **13**
Gunther Hotel **2**
Havana Riverwalk Inn **1**
Holiday Inn Crockett **4**

Homewood Suites by Hilton **9**
Hyatt Regency on the Riverwalk **6**
La Mansión del Rio **7**
Marriott Rivercenter **11**
Menger Hotel **5**
Noble Inns **17**
The Ogé House Inn on the River Walk **16**
Plaza San Antonio **14**
Riverwalk Inn **15**
Westin Riverwalk Inn **10**

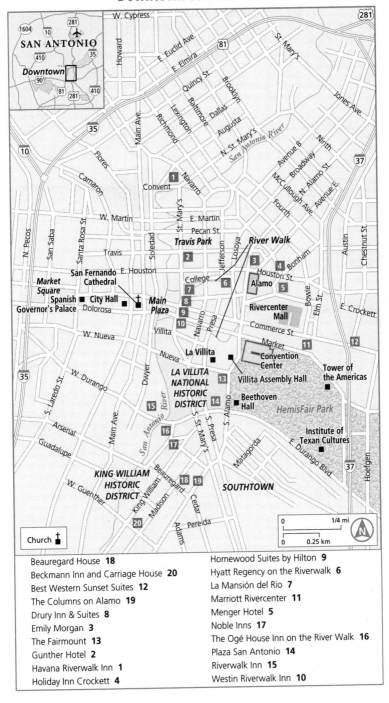

that flank it on this (relatively) quiet section of the river bend, but its clean, elegant lines are attuned to 21st-century sensibilities.

From the lobby to the rooms, earth tones balance with Spanish colonial accents to create an atmosphere that's soothing without being bland. Built-from-scratch also means incorporating the latest amenities, including Westin's signature "Heavenly Beds"—layers and layers of bedding, a guest's dream but a housekeeper's nightmare—and hypoallergenic pillows. The Guest Office units also feature ergonomically designed chairs, halogen lamps, fax/printer/copiers, and all the paper clips and Post-Its you might need. Get one with a river-view balcony, though, and you probably won't want to spend much time at the desk. This Westin has also nicely incorporated several kid-friendly features (see "Family-Friendly Lodgings" on p. 46).

420 W. Market St. (at Navarro), San Antonio, TX 78205. ℭ 800/WESTIN-1 or 210/224-6500. Fax 210/444-6000. www.westin.com./riverwalk. 473 units. $365–$395 double; $395–$425 suite. AE, DC, DISC, MC, V. Self-parking $12; valet parking $22. **Amenities:** Restaurant; outdoor pool; sauna; health club; concierge; business center; 24-hr. room service; dry cleaning. *In room:* A/C, TV w/pay movies, dataport, minibar, coffeemaker, hair dryer, iron, safe.

EXPENSIVE

Emily Morgan ★★ (Value) Emily, we hardly knew you. This hotel—named for the mulatto slave mistress of Mexican general Santa Anna, and reputed to have spied on him for the Texas independence fighters—was long a moderately priced Ramada in a historic building. The location, a musket shot from the Alamo and the River Walk, is as good as ever, and the facade of this 1926 Gothic Revival–style medical arts center (check out the gargoyles, said to have been placed there to help the doctors ward off diseases) was undisturbed, but the dowdy public areas and guest rooms were seriously glamorized in 2002. Now the rooms have a light, contemporary feel, designed to appeal to a young and affluent crowd who go for the pared-down "I don't have time for fuss" look popularized by the W hotel chain. Any industrial chic coldness is offset by lots of dark, burnished wood and such touches as a lit votive candle at turndown. Of course, you aren't going to get 250-count sheets, Aveda bath products, CD players, 27-inch TVs, and (in 115 of the rooms) jetted tubs at Ramada prices; still, this place remains considerably less expensive than many comparable hotels on the river, and its combination of hipness, luxury, and history is hard to beat.

705 E. Houston St. (at Ave. E), San Antonio, TX 78205. ℭ 800/824-6674 or 210/225-8486. Fax 210/225-7227. www.emilymorganhotel.com. 177 units. $189–$229 double; $259–$289 suite. Corporate, promotional rates available. AE, DC, DISC, MC, V. Valet parking $16. **Amenities:** Restaurant; outdoor pool; Jacuzzi; health club; sauna; 24-hr. room service; dry cleaning; concierge. *In room:* AC TV w/pay movies, dataport, coffeemaker, hair dryer, iron.

The Fairmount, A Wyndham Historic Hotel ★ This lovely boutique hotel, built in an ornate Italianate-Victorian style in 1906, is across the street from HemisFair Park, adjacent to La Villita, and within walking distance of the King William historic district—but it wasn't always. In 1985, it was hoisted 6 blocks across town, earning it a place in the *Guinness Book of World Records* as the heaviest building ever moved. Excavations of the site on which it now sits uncovered artifacts from the battle at the Alamo, some of which are showcased in the building's lobby.

The Fairmount once lodged railway travelers, but today's clientele is more likely to jet in; the hotel is sought out by celebs looking for low-key but luxurious digs. The suites are naturally the largest rooms—some have hardwood floors, wet bars, skylights, Jacuzzi tubs, or combinations thereof—but even the double rooms are outstanding. All are individually decorated in muted Southwestern tones, with rich wood furniture (some in craftsman style), plants, and original artwork, and all have balconies overlooking the city or a small central courtyard. Just downstairs, you can enjoy the soft strains of a jazz piano at Polo's lounge (see chapter 8), where deals are closed over single-malt scotches and romantic liaisons are celebrated with champagne.

401 S. Alamo St. (between Nuevo and Durango), San Antonio, TX 78205. ✆ 800/WYNDHAM or 210/224-8800. Fax 210/475-0082. www.wyndham.com. 37 units. $209–$294 double; $244–$559 suite. AE, DC, MC, V. Valet parking $17. **Amenities:** Restaurant; 24-hr. room service; babysitting. *In room:* A/C, TV/VCR w/pay movies, dataport, coffeemaker, hair dryer, iron.

Holiday Inn Crockett Hotel *(Value)*

This hotel comes by its name honestly, unlike many of the places that bank on Davy Crockett's moniker: The famed Alamo hero definitely walked the land on which the hotel rose in 1909, as it—the land, that is—served as the Alamo's battleground. The property is a bit of a hybrid, consisting of the original historical landmark building (expanded in 1927) and several low-slung, motel-style units that surround what may be downtown's nicest swimming pool and a tropical landscaped courtyard. Rooms in both sections of the hotel are consistently attractive, with lots of vibrant Southwest colors and allusions to Texas history (regional artwork, pine beds with Lone Star headboards, and the like). And the rates—discounted for every imaginable reason—are quite good for this prime location between the Alamo and the Rivercenter Mall—and right near several River Walk entrances.

320 Bonham St. (at Houston St.), San Antonio, TX 78205. ✆ 800/292-1050 or 210/225-6500. Fax 210/225-6251. www.crocketthotel.com. 204 units. Rooms $199; suites from $275. Various discounts (including Internet booking) and specials. Pets accepted; $100 deposit required. Valet parking $17. **Amenities:** Restaurant; lounge; unheated outdoor pool and hot tub; limited room service; coin-op laundry; same day dry cleaning. *In room:* A/C, TV w/pay movies, dataport, coffeemaker, iron, hair dryer.

Menger Hotel *

In the late 19th century, no one who was anyone would consider staying anywhere but the Menger, which opened its doors in 1859 and has never closed them. Ulysses S. Grant, Sarah Bernhardt, and Oscar Wilde were among those who walked—or, rumor has it, in the case of Robert E. Lee, rode a horse—through the halls, ballrooms, and gardens. Successfully combining the original, restored building with myriad additions, the Menger now takes up an entire city block. The hotel's location is terrific—smack between the Alamo and the Rivercenter Mall, a block from the River Walk, with the tourist information office on the ground floor. And its public areas, particularly the Victorian Lobby, are gorgeous. The Menger Bar (see chapter 8) is one of San Antonio's great historic taverns, and while nearly every historic hotel in town promotes a ghost, this one claims to have no less than 32. The Menger also has a small spa, a real rarity among San Antonio hotels.

The rooms, however, are somewhat tired, and no longer the bargain they've been in the past. Decor ranges from ornate 19th-century to modern. If you want one of the antiques-filled Victorian rooms, be sure to request it when you book.

204 Alamo Plaza (at Houston St.), San Antonio, TX 78205. ✆ 800/345-9285 or 210/223-4361. Fax 210/228-0022. www.historicmenger.com. 316 units. $195–$215 double; $250–$495 suite. AE, DC, DISC, MC, V. Self-parking $13; valet parking $17. **Amenities:** Restaurant; bar; outdoor pool; Jacuzzi; health club; spa; shopping arcade; limited room service; dry cleaning. *In room:* A/C, TV w/pay movies, dataport, minibar (in suites), fridge rental ($25), hair dryer, iron, safe.

Plaza San Antonio, A Marriott Hotel **

Pheasants stroll the beautifully landscaped grounds of this gracious hotel, located across from HemisFair Park, close to La Villita, and just north of the King William district. Four 19th-century buildings that were saved from HemisFair's bulldozer in 1968 were later incorporated into the Plaza complex. Three are used for intimate conference centers—the initialing ceremony for the North American Free Trade Agreement was held in one of them—and the fourth houses a health club and spa.

This is a place to come and feel pampered, with extras like complimentary shoeshines and evening turndowns with bottled water and filled ice buckets, as well as top-notch, friendly service. Elegant rooms, decorated in muted colors and floral patterns, with antique-style furnishings, looked a tad tired in late 2002, but this is one of the few hotels in town that has lit tennis courts—not to mention a croquet lawn. The Anaqua Grill has had revolving chefs for many years, but when its innovative Southwestern cuisine is good, it's very, very good.

555 S. Alamo St. (at Durango), San Antonio, TX 78205. © 800/727-3239 or 210/229-1000. Fax 210/223-6650. www.plazasa.com. 252 units. $169–$274 double; suites from $420. AE, DC, DISC, MC, V. Self-parking $9; Valet parking $15. Pets up to 20 lbs accepted. **Amenities:** Restaurant; bar; outdoor pool; health club; spa; tennis courts; Jacuzzi; bikes (free); concierge; business center; limited room service; massage; babysitting; dry cleaning. *In room:* A/C, TV w/pay movies, dataport, coffeemaker, hair dryer, iron.

MODERATE

Drury Inn & Suites San Antonio Riverwalk (Value)   One of San Antonio's more recent River Walk conversions, the one-time Petroleum Commerce Building is now a comfortable modern lodging. The polished marble floors and chandeliers in the lobby and the high ceilings and ornate window treatments in the guest rooms hearken back to a grander era, also evoked in business-traveler perks such as free hot breakfasts, free evening cocktails and snacks, and free local phone calls. Guests also appreciate the on-premises Texas Land & Cattle Co. steakhouse (see p. 60), located on the River Walk level—it's a nice, reasonably priced place to schmooze clients—as well as the 24-hour business center. Anyone who wants to economize on meals will also like the fact that many of these attractive Southwest-style rooms are equipped with refrigerators and microwaves.

201 N. St. Mary's St. (at Commerce St.), San Antonio TX 78205. © 800/DRURY-INN or 210/212-5200. Fax 210/352-9939. www.druryinn.com. 150 units. $129–$154 double; $159–$185 suite. AE, DC, DISC, MC, V. Self-parking $8. Small pets accepted. **Amenities:** Restaurant; outdoor pool; Jacuzzi; dry cleaning. *In room:* TV, dataport, fridge (in king rooms and suites), coffeemaker, hair dryer, iron.

Havana Riverwalk Inn ✪   This has got to be *the* hippest place to stay on the river. Decked out to suggest travelers' lodgings circa the 1920s, this intimate inn—built in 1914 in Mediterranean Revival style—oozes character. All of the rooms are delightfully different, with a safari hat covering a temperature control gauge here, an old photograph perched over a toilet paper roll there, gauzy curtains draped on a canopy bed, wooden louvers on the windows, brick walls, and so on. Touches like fresh flowers and bottled water add to the charm, and modern amenities such as irons have not been ignored. Not all rooms have closets, however, so be prepared to have your clothes (ironed or not) hanging in public view if you plan to invite anyone to your room. Singles will absolutely want to hit the hotel's super-hot cigar bar, Club Cohiba.

1015 Navarro (between St. Mary's and Augusta sts.), San Antonio, TX 78205. © 888/224-2008 or 210/222-2008. Fax 210/222-2717. www.havanariverwalkinn.com. 27 units. $109–$209 double; $249–$599 suite. AE, DC, DISC, MC, V. Self-parking $10. Children ages 15 and over only accepted. **Amenities:** Restaurant; bar; concierge; secretarial services; limited room service; dry cleaning. *In room:* A/C, TV w/pay movies, dataport, iron, hair dryer.

Homewood Suites by Hilton ⚡ *Kids*   Opened in the mid-1990s in the former San Antonio Drug Company building (built in 1919), this all-suites hotel is a good downtown deal. Located on a quiet stretch of the river, it's convenient to west-side attractions such as Market Square and located only a few more blocks away from the Alamo. In-room amenities such as microwave ovens, refrigerators with ice makers, and dishwashers appeal to business travelers and families alike; the dining area can double as a work space, and there's a sleeper sofa in each suite as well as two TVs with VCRs—that means fewer squabbles over TV shows and movies. The decor is a cut above that of most chains, with Lone Star–design headboards, wood desks and bureaus, and attractive Southwestern bedspreads and drapes. Two suites have river views.

432 Market St. (at St. Mary's St.), San Antonio, TX 78205. ℂ **800/CALL-HOME** or 210/222-1515. Fax 210/222-1575. www.homewood-riverwalk.com. 146 units. $139–$249 suite. Rates include continental breakfast, afternoon drinks, and snacks. AE, DC, DISC, MC, V. Valet parking $16. **Amenities:** Outdoor pool; Jacuzzi; business center; dry cleaning; concierge. *In room:* A/C, TV/VCR w/pay movies, dataport, kitchenette, coffeemaker, hair dryer.

Riverwalk Inn *Finds*   If you've ever had a hankering to stay in an old log cabin but don't really care to go rustic, consider this unusual bed-and-breakfast. Native Texans Jan and Tracy Hammer had eight 1840s Tennessee cabins taken apart log by log and put back together again near the banks of the San Antonio River, a few blocks south of HemisFair Park and north of the King William area.

Except for a few anachronistic (but welcome) details such as indoor plumbing, refrigerators, and phones with voice mail, everything else in the cabins is authentic. Each room has a fireplace, quilt, braided rug, and fascinating primitive antiques; most also possess balconies or porches fronting the river. Freshly made desserts are served in the parlor each evening. The wooden-plank breakfast table can get a bit crowded on weekend mornings, but that's in keeping with the inn's pioneer spirit. (Note that a maximum of two guests are permitted in each room, which means it's not for families.)

329 Old Guilbeau (off Durango, near Dwyer St.), San Antonio, TX 78204. ℂ **800/254-4440** or 210/212-8300. Fax 210/229-9422. www.riverwalkinn.com. 11 units. $130–$145 non–river view double; $145–$170 river view. Rates include continental breakfast. 2-night minimum required for Fri–Sun stays, 3-night stay required for some holiday weekends. AE, DISC, MC, V. Free off-street parking. *In room:* A/C, TV, fridge, coffeemaker.

INEXPENSIVE

Best Western Sunset Suites ⚡⚡ *Value Kids*   Don't be put off by the bland name or the fact that this all-suites hotel is located on the wrong side of the tracks, er, highway. In a converted turn-of-the-century building you'll find some of the nicest rooms in downtown San Antonio—large, with custom-made Arts and Crafts–style furnishings, including comfy, clean-lined lounge chairs and faux Tiffany lamps. They're also some of the best-equipped rooms around: All offer sleeper sofas, microwaves, minifridges, and 27-inch TVs. And talk about deals: You get a free hot buffet breakfast, free afternoon cocktails, and free local calls. If you don't want to move your car from its free parking spot or take a 10-minute walk to the heart of downtown, you can take advantage of the free trolley passes that'll get you there. With all the money you've saved on perks and on the room, you just might be able to afford dinner at Ruth's Chris Steakhouse, just a few blocks away in the Sunset Station complex.

1103 E. Commerce St. (at Hwy 281), San Antonio, TX 78205. ℂ **866/560-6000** or 210/223-4400. Fax 210/223-4402. www.bestwesternsunsetsuites.com. 64 units. $89–$119 double. Rates include breakfast and trolley pass. Free parking. **Amenities:** Health club; business center. *In room:* A/C, TV w/pay movies, dataport, kitchenette, coffeemaker, iron, hair dryer.

2 King William Historic District

EXPENSIVE

Noble Inns ⭐ It's hard to imagine that Donald and Liesl Noble, both descended from King William founding families, grew up in the neighborhood when it was run-down; the area has undergone an amazing metamorphosis in the short span of the young couple's life. Indeed, their gracious lodgings—the 1894 Jackson House, a traditional-style B&B and, a few blocks away, the 1896 Aaron Pancoast Carriage House, offering three suites with full kitchens—are a tribute to just how far it has come. The decor in both houses hearkens back to the period in which they were built, and manages to do so without being overly fussy. Rooms, individually decorated with fine antiques, are ideal for both business and leisure travelers. All have gas fireplaces; three in the Jackson House feature two-person Jacuzzi tubs. Other luxurious touches include Godiva chocolate at turndown, and fresh flowers. A silver-gray classic Rolls Royce is available for airport transportation or downtown drop-off.

102 Turner St. (off King William St.), San Antonio, TX 78204. ℭ **800/221-4045** or 210/225-4045. Fax 210/227-0877. www.nobleinns.com. 9 units. $130–170 double; $140–$195 suite. Rates at Jackhouse include full breakfast, rates at Carriage House include continental breakfast. Corporate, weekday discounts available. AE, DISC, MC, V. Free off-street parking. **Amenities:** Outdoor pool; Jacuzzi. *In room:* A/C, dataport, kitchen (carriage house suites only).

Ogé House Inn on the River Walk ⭐⭐ One of the most glorious of the mansions that grace the King William district, this 1867 Greek revival–style property is more of a boutique inn than a bed-and-breakfast. You'll still get the personalized attention you would expect from a host home, but it's combined here with the luxury of a sophisticated small hotel. All rooms are impeccably decorated in high Victorian style, yet feature modern conveniences such as small refrigerators; many rooms also have fireplaces and views of the manicured, pecan-shaded grounds, and one looks out on the river from its own wrought-iron balcony. The units downstairs aren't as light as those on the upper two floors, but they're less expensive and offer private entrances.

A bountiful gourmet breakfast is served on individual white-clothed tables set with the finest crystal and china. Travelers can also bury themselves in daily newspapers laid out on the bureau just beyond the dining room.

209 Washington St. (at Turner St.), San Antonio, TX 78204. ℭ **800/242-2770** or 210/223-2353. Fax 210/226-5812. www.ogeinn.com. 10 units. $155 double; $185–$225 suite. Rates include breakfast. Corporate rates available for single business travelers. 2-night minimum stay on weekends; 3 nights during holidays and special events. AE, DC, DISC, MC, V. Free off-street parking. *In room:* A/C, TV, dataport, iron, fridge, hair dryer.

MODERATE

Beauregard House ⭐ *Finds* You can tell that an artist runs this appealing B&B as soon as you walk through the door. Although it's not immediately obvious that owner Lisa Fittipaldi painted most of the vibrant pictures that hang on the walls (and she did it after she lost 90% of her vision), it's clear that someone with a creative flair did the decorating. As you tour the 1908 house, you become aware that Fittipaldi is also something of a historian: She gathered clean-lined antiques contemporary with the period of the rooms, which she then named for authors (Faulkner, Hemingway) who were writing during the era. Although there's a hint of it in the home-baked biscotti you'll find in your room, you'll have to wait until you enjoy your first gourmet breakfast here—served on Royal

Doulton china, dahling—to taste the cooking of Lisa's husband Al, a trained chef who once ran a successful restaurant on Long Island. His 40 morning recipes incorporate organic ingredients whenever possible.

Accommodations here are gorgeous without being fussy—the London Hideaway, which occupies the entire third floor and has a DVD player and library, is especially guy-friendly—and come with extras (such as sewing kits) usually only found in the larger hotels. Two rooms even offer private exits.

215 Beauregard St. (at Madison St.), San Antonio, TX 78204. © **888/667-0555** or 210/222-1198. www.beauregardhouse.com. 6 units. $109–$114 double; $129–$139 suite. Rates include breakfast. Extended stay plans available. 2-night minimum stay required on weekends; 3–4 night stay required during holidays and special events. AE, DISC, MC, V. Free off-street parking. **Amenities:** Bike rentals. *In room:* A/C, TV, TV/VCR (some), dataport (some), fridge, coffeemaker, hair dryer.

Beckmann Inn and Carriage House

Sitting on the lovely wraparound porch of this 1886 Queen Anne home, surrounded by quiet, tree-lined streets on an uncommercialized stretch of the San Antonio River, you can easily imagine yourself in a kinder, gentler era. In fact, you can still see the flour mill on whose property the Beckmann Inn was originally built. Nor will the illusion of time travel be dispelled when you step through the rare Texas red-pine door into the high-ceilinged parlor.

Innkeepers Betty Jo and Don Schwartz filled the house with antique pieces that do justice to the setting, such as the ornately carved Victorian beds in each of the guest rooms. Two of the rooms have private entrances, as does the separate Carriage House, decorated in a somewhat lighter fashion. A full breakfast—perhaps stuffed cinnamon French toast with light cream cheese and pecans—is served in the formal dining room, but you can also enjoy your coffee on a flower-filled sun porch.

222 E. Guenther St. (at Madison St.), San Antonio, TX 78204. © **800/945-1449** or 210/229-1449. Fax 210/229-1061. www.beckmanninn.com. 5 units. $110–$150. Rates include breakfast. AE, DC, DISC, MC, V. Free off-street parking. *In room:* A/C, TV, dataport, fridge, hair dryer.

The Columns on Alamo

Guests at this B&B can stay in the 1892 Greek revival mansion from which the inn derives its name; an adjacent guesthouse, built 9 years later; or a separate limestone cottage that's new, yet built in a rustic, early-1880s style. The mansion, where the innkeepers live, is the most opulent and offers unusual walk-through windows leading to a veranda, while the guesthouse—which houses most of the lodgings—affords more privacy if you're uncomfortable with the idea of staying in someone else's home. Those who really want to hole up should book the Honeymoon and Anniversary cottage, attached to the guesthouse, or the separate Rock House cottage in the back; it's large enough for four.

All the rooms are light, airy, and very pretty, although this is not the place for those allergic to pastels and frills; pink dominates many of the accommodations, and even the darker-toned Imari Room has lace curtains. (The Rock House, done in more casual country style, is the exception.) Several of the units boast two-person Jacuzzis and gas-log fireplaces. Hosts Ellenor and Arthur Link are extremely helpful, and their breakfasts are all you could ask for in morning indulgence.

1037 S. Alamo (at Sheridan, 5 blocks south of Durango), San Antonio, TX 78210. © **800/233-3364** or 210/271-3245. www.columnssanantonio.com. 13 units. $92–$162 double; $162–$255 cottage. Rates include breakfast. Extended stay discounts. AE, DC, DISC, MC, V. Free off-street parking. *In room:* A/C, TV, dataport, fridge, hair dryer, iron.

Kids Family-Friendly Lodgings

Hyatt Regency Hill Country Resort (p. 52) In addition to its many great play areas (including a beach with a shallow swimming area), and its proximity to SeaWorld, this hotel offers Camp Hyatt—a program of excursions, sports, and social activities for children 3 to 12. The program fills up fast during school breaks and other holidays, when reservations are mandatory.

Homewood Suites (p. 43) This reasonably priced all-suites hotel near the River Walk, with in-room kitchen facilities and two TVs per suite (each with its own VCR)—not to mention a guest laundry—is extremely convenient for families.

O'Casey's Bed & Breakfast (p. 47) Usually B&Bs and family vacations are a contradiction in terms, but O'Casey's is happy to host well-behaved kids. *Best bet:* Stay in the separate guesthouse with the fold-out bed, then join the main-house guests for breakfast in the morning.

Terrell Castle (p. 48) Those with relatives stationed at nearby Fort Sam Houston who'd rather stay at a B&B than a chain hotel will enjoy this unique lodging. It's very welcoming to children.

Westin La Cantera (p. 49) It's close to Six Flags Fiesta Texas, it's got two pools just for children, and it offers the Enchanted Rock Kids Club—an activities program for ages 4 through 12—from May through September.

Westin Riverwalk Inn (p. 38) Though not as family-friendly as the Westin La Cantera, this Westin on the River Walk still offers such amenities as free in-room movies, a kids' treat pack upon check-in, and bedtime stories told over the phone.

3 Monte Vista Historic District

MODERATE

The Inn at Craig Place ✦ This 1891 mansion-turned-B&B appeals to history, art, and architecture buffs alike. It was built by one of Texas's preeminent architects, Alfred Giles, for H.H. Hildebrand, one of San Antonio's movers and shakers; the living room boasts a mural by Julian Onderbronk, an influential Texas landscape artist.

But that's all academic. More to the point, this place is gorgeous, with forests of gleaming wood and clean Arts-and-Crafts lines, as well as cushy couches and a wraparound porch. Rooms are at once luxurious—all have working fireplaces, hardwood floors, and come with robes, slippers, feather pillows, and down comforters—and equipped for modern needs. Just to gild the lily, one of the innkeepers, Tamra Black, worked as a professional chef, so you can expect the three-course breakfasts here to be outstanding.

117 W. Craig Place (off N. Main Ave.), San Antonio TX 78212. ℃ **877/427-2447** or 210/736-1017. Fax 210/737-1562. www.craigplace.com. 4 units. $115–$200. Corporate rates available. Rates include breakfast. AE, DC, MC, V. On-street parking. *In room:* A/C, TV, dataport, iron.

INEXPENSIVE

Bonner Garden ⭐ *Value*   Those who like the intimacy of the bed-and-breakfast experience but aren't keen on Victorian froufrou should consider the Bonner Garden, located in the Monte Vista Historic District, about a mile north of downtown. Built in 1910 for Louisiana artist Mary Bonner, this large, Italianate villa has a beautiful, classical simplicity and lots of gorgeous antiques—not to mention a 45-foot sunken swimming pool.

The Portico Room, in which guests can gaze up at a painted blue sky with billowing clouds, offers a private poolside entrance. You don't have to be honeymooners to enjoy the large Jacuzzi tub in the Bridal Suite, perhaps the prettiest room, with its Battenburg lace drapes and blue porcelain fireplace. Most of the rooms feature European-style decor, but Mary Bonner's former studio, separate from the main house, is done in tasteful Santa Fe style. Generous breakfasts are enjoyed around a long, gleaming wood table that once hosted diplomats in Denmark's British Embassy. A rooftop deck with a wet bar affords a sparkling nighttime view of downtown. If you prefer your views to be virtual, take advantage of a desktop computer with DSL access in the living room.

145 E. Agarita (at McCullough), San Antonio, TX 78212. ℭ **800/396-4222** or 210/733-4222. Fax 210/733-6129. www.bonnergarden.com. 6 units. $85–$105 double; $115–$125 suite. Rates include full breakfast. Extended stay (minimum 3 nights) and corporate rates available. AE, DISC, MC, V. Free off-street parking. **Amenities:** Outdoor pool; Jacuzzi; bikes (free). *In room:* A/C, TV/VCR, dataport (some), iron.

O'Casey's Bed & Breakfast *Kids* *Value*   If there's a twinkle in John Casey's eye when he puts on a brogue, it's because he was born on U.S. soil, not the auld sod. But his and his wife Linda Fay's down-home friendliness is no blarney. This Irish-themed B&B is one of the few around that welcomes families, and it's well equipped to handle them. One suite in the main house has a sitting area with a futon large enough for a couple of youngsters; another has a trundle bed for two kids in a separate bedroom. Studio apartments in the carriage house both offer full kitchens.

Which is not to suggest that accommodations are utilitarian—far from it. Rooms in the main house, a gracious structure built in 1904, feature hardwood floors and fine antiques; many bathrooms also sport claw-foot tubs. There's a wraparound balcony upstairs, too. For a treat, ask Linda (a professional pianist) and John (a choir director and singer) to perform a few numbers for you. Just don't ask *too* often; they work hard to run their B&B smoothly and well.

225 W. Craig Place (between San Pedro Ave. and Main St.), San Antonio, TX 78212. ℭ **800/738-1378** or 210/738-1378. www.ocaseybnb.com. 7 units. $79–$99 double; $89–$109 suite. Rates include breakfast. Weekday and extended stay discounts. AE, DISC, MC, V. Street parking. Pets allowed in apartments only; $10 per night. *In room:* A/C, TV, kitchen (some), no phone.

Ruckman Haus ⭐ *Finds*   If you're one of those folks who don't find B&B owners' pets to be substitutes for your personal pooch or feline, good news: This is one of the pet-friendliest B&Bs you could hope to encounter. Your cat or dog can sleep in your room or—in the case of Fido—frisk in a large kennel in the leafy backyard. That's not to suggest that the petless will encounter a menagerie—you're unlikely to see or hear any nonhumans most of the time—or that you won't be petted yourselves. The accommodations in this pretty turn-of-the-century stucco home, just a block from San Pedro Springs Park, are comfy but elegant, with lots of nice antiques and plenty of light. Two offer showers with three body jets—almost as good as an in-room massage (which is also available). One unit, the Highlands, is large enough to sleep four (people, that is), should you decide to bring the kids along with the animals. Breakfasts are generous and, if you haven't already encountered them in the morning, you can bond with fellow guests over afternoon drinks on either the covered deck or the fern-shaded side patio.

629 W. French St. (at Breeden, 1 block west of San Pedro Ave.), San Antonio, TX 78212. © **866/736-1468** or 210/736-1468. Fax 210/736-1468. www.ruckmanhaus.com. 5 units. $85–$100 double; $120 suites. Rates include breakfast. Corporate rates for single travelers, summer specials. AE, DISC, MC, V. Free off-street parking. Pets accepted. *In room:* A/C, TV, dataport, fridge (in all but 1 unit), coffeemaker.

4 Fort Sam Houston Area

MODERATE

Terrell Castle *(Kids)*   Unless a trip to Scotland is in the cards, this could be your best chance to spend a night in a castle. Built in 1894 by English-born architect Alfred Giles, this massive limestone structure was commissioned by Edwin Terrell, a statesman who fell in love with the European grand style while serving as U.S. ambassador to Belgium. Turned into a bed-and-breakfast in 1986, it's an anomaly in the working-class area near the Fort Sam Houston quadrangle. Guest rooms don't feature as many antiques as you'll see in the public areas, but they're comfortable and clean; several offer fireplaces. A variety of suites, as well as free lodging for children under 6 and the free use of a crib, make this B&B uncharacteristically family-friendly. Breakfasts, served in the formal dining room, are copious and elaborate.

950 E. Grayson St., San Antonio, TX 78208. © **800/481-9732** or 210/271-9145. Fax 210/527-1455. www.terrellcastle.com. 8 units. $105–$120 double; $140 suites. Rates include full breakfast. Corporate, government, military rates available. AE, DISC, MC, V. Free off-street parking. Take Exit 159A off I-35, turn right to gate at Fort Sam Houston; take left on Grayson St., go approximately 4½ blocks. *In room:* A/C, TV, no phone.

INEXPENSIVE

Bullis House Inn *(Value)*   This graceful neoclassical mansion, just down the street from the Fort Sam Houston quadrangle and easily accessible from the airport and downtown by car, is an excellent bed-and-breakfast bargain, especially for those who don't mind sharing bathrooms. Beautifully restored in the 1980s, it was built from 1906 to 1909 for General John Lapham Bullis, a frontier Indian fighter who played a key role in capturing Geronimo (some claim the Apache chief's spirit still roams the mansion). More concerned with creature comforts when he retired, the general had oak paneling, parquet floors, crystal chandeliers, and marble fireplaces installed in his home, which is now often used for wedding receptions. Guest rooms all have 14-foot ceilings and are furnished with some period antiques along with good reproductions; three of them feature fireplaces, and one offers a private bathroom. The family room, which sleeps up to six, also has a refrigerator. Movie nights and VCR and video rentals are among the other perks.

621 Pierce St. (at Grayson, directly across from Fort Sam Houston), San Antonio, TX 78208. © **210/223-9426**. Fax 210/299-1479. 5 units. $59–$79 double with shared bathroom; $89 double with private bathroom. Weekly rates available. Rates include continental breakfast. AE, MC, V. Free off-street parking. **Amenities:** Outdoor pool. *In room:* A/C, no phone.

Hostelling International—San Antonio   Right next door to the Bullis House Inn (see above), this youth hostel has a reading room, small kitchen, dining area, lockers, and picnic tables, in addition to male and female dorms. Hostelers are welcome at the Bullis House Inn on film nights, and the two lodgings share a pool. A continental breakfast, served at the inn, is available for an additional $4.50.

621 Pierce St. (at Grayson, directly across from Fort Sam Houston), San Antonio, TX 78208. © 210/223-9426. Fax 210/299-1479. HISanAnton@aol.com. 38 beds. $15–$20 per person. AE, MC, V. **Amenities:** Outdoor pool. *In room:* No phone.

5 Northwest

VERY EXPENSIVE

Westin La Cantera ★★★ *Kids* Locals like to joke that the 1999 opening of this posh northwest property doubled the number of resorts in San Antonio. No doubt about it: This lovely retreat is giving the Hyatt Regency Hill Country Resort (see under "West," below) a run for the high-end-visitor money. They're similar in many ways, with knockout facilities, sprawling, gorgeous grounds, and loads of Texas character. Both are family-friendly, with theme parks in their backyards (here it's Six Flags Fiesta Texas) and excellent children's programs. But the Westin has the edge when it comes to golf, boasting two championship courses (in addition to the much-praised La Cantera, there's a newer Arnold Palmer–designed course) plus a professional golf school. It's a tad more romantic, too, with dramatic rocky outcroppings and drop-dead gorgeous views from its perch on one of the highest points in San Antonio.

The resort is elaborately designed around state historical motifs. The Texas colonial architecture is impressive, and the tales and legends detailed in plaques in the various rooms are interesting, but you'll probably be too busy having fun to pay them much mind. Likewise, the casual elegant rooms—beautifully decorated in muted earth tones and subtle florals and equipped with all the business amenities conference attendees need—are likely to be abandoned for the resort's myriad recreational areas, or at least for the balconies that many of the guest quarters offer. Remnants of the limestone quarry on which the resort was built were incorporated into the five swimming pools interconnected with bridges and channels and a dramatic waterfall. And the indigenous plant life and animal life—deer, rabbits, and wild turkeys come out at dusk—should have you oohing and cooing. So will the Southwest cuisine—speaking of game—and the sundown vistas of Francesca's at Sunset (see p. 68).

16641 La Cantera Parkway, San Antonio, TX 78256. © 800/WESTIN-1 or 210/558-6500. Fax 210/641-0721. www.westin.com/lacantera. 508 units. $200–$500 double; $380–$1,800 suite; $350–$1,200 casita. AE, DC, DISC, MC, V. Free self-parking; valet parking $10. Take the La Cantera Parkway exit off I-10 and turn left. Resort entrance is ¾ mile ahead, on the right. **Amenities:** 3 restaurants; 2 bars; outdoor pool; 2 golf courses; tennis courts; health club; spa; Jacuzzi; children's center; video arcade; concierge; car-rental desk; business center; 24-hr. room service; massage; dry cleaning. *In room:* A/C, TV w/pay movies, dataport, minibar, coffeemaker, hair dryer, iron, safe.

EXPENSIVE

Omni San Antonio ★ *Kids* This polished granite high-rise off I-10 west is convenient to SeaWorld, Six Flags Fiesta Texas, the airport, and the Hill Country, and the shops and restaurants of the 66-acre Colonnade complex are within easy walking distance. The lobby is soaring and luxurious, and guest rooms, updated in 2001, are well appointed in a traditional European style. The proximity to the theme parks as well as in-room Nintendo and various other Omni Kids features makes this hotel as appealing to families as it is to business travelers, who appreciate its exercise facilities, better than most in San Antonio and definitely the best in this part of town, dominated by inexpensive chains. Although the hotel sees a lot of tourist and Medical Center traffic, service here is always prompt and courteous.

Greater San Antonio Accommodations & Dining

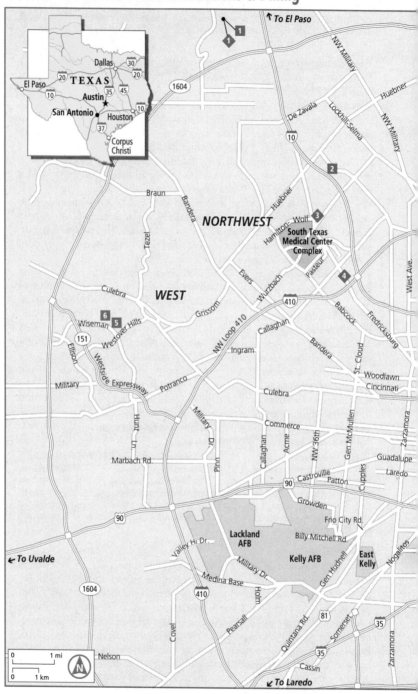

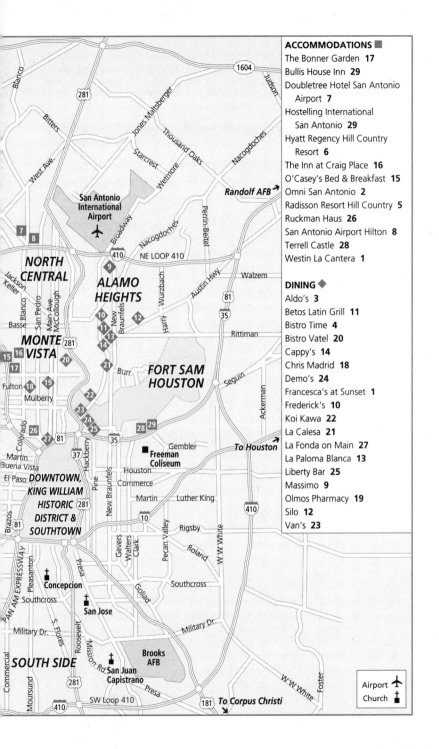

ACCOMMODATIONS ■
The Bonner Garden **17**
Bullis House Inn **29**
Doubletree Hotel San Antonio Airport **7**
Hostelling International San Antonio **29**
Hyatt Regency Hill Country Resort **6**
The Inn at Craig Place **16**
O'Casey's Bed & Breakfast **15**
Omni San Antonio **2**
Radisson Resort Hill Country **5**
Ruckman Haus **26**
San Antonio Airport Hilton **8**
Terrell Castle **28**
Westin La Cantera **1**

DINING ◆
Aldo's **3**
Betos Latin Grill **11**
Bistro Time **4**
Bistro Vatel **20**
Cappy's **14**
Chris Madrid **18**
Demo's **24**
Francesca's at Sunset **1**
Frederick's **10**
Koi Kawa **22**
La Calesa **21**
La Fonda on Main **27**
La Paloma Blanca **13**
Liberty Bar **25**
Massimo **9**
Olmos Pharmacy **19**
Silo **12**
Van's **23**

Airport ✈
Church ■

9821 Colonnade Blvd. (at Wurzbach), San Antonio, TX 78230. ℂ 800/843-6664 or 210/691-8888. Fax 210/691-1128. www.omnihotels.com. 326 units. $169 double; $300–$600 suite. Packages available. AE, DC, DISC, MC, V. Free self-parking; valet parking $7. Pets 25 lb. or under permitted; $50 deposit required. **Amenities:** Restaurant; bar; indoor pool; outdoor pool; health club; Jacuzzi; sauna; game room; concierge; courtesy car; business center; limited room service; babysitting; dry cleaning; club-level rooms. *In room:* TV w/pay movies, dataport, minibar, coffeemaker, hair dryer, iron.

6 West

VERY EXPENSIVE

Hyatt Regency Hill Country Resort ★★★ *Kids*   If I were feeling flush and didn't want to spend a lot of time downtown, this would be my favorite place to settle in for a week. The setting, on 200 acres of former ranchland on the far west side of San Antonio, is idyllic. The resort's low-slung native limestone buildings, inspired by the architecture of the nearby Hill Country, showcase the best of Texas design. The on-site activities, ranging from golf to tubing on the 950-foot long Ramblin' River, are endless. And the rooms are done in an appealing updated country style—carved maple beds topped with quilt-style covers, stenciled wall borders, clean unfussy lines—most featuring French doors that open out onto wood-trimmed porches. Not one to rest on its laurels, the resort even added a fantastic new spa in 2002, definitely the best pampering palace in this part of Texas. It's a low-key and relaxing place.

The resort is also extremely family-friendly: SeaWorld sits at your doorstep, there are free laundry facilities and a country store for supplies, and every room has a refrigerator (not stocked with goodies, alas). When you're tired of all that family bonding, the Hyatt Kids Club will keep the youngsters happily occupied while you spend some quality time relaxing on Ramblin' River.

9800 Hyatt Resort Dr. (off Hwy. 151, between Westover Hills Blvd. and Potranco Rd.), San Antonio, TX 78251. ℂ 800/233-1234 or 210/647-1234. Fax 210/681-9681. http://hillcountry.hyatt.com. 500 units. $275–$380 double; $450–$1,550 suite. Rates lower late Nov to early Mar; packages available. AE, DC, DISC, MC, V. Free self-parking; Valet parking $8. **Amenities:** 4 restaurants; 2 bars; outdoor pool; golf course; 3 tennis courts; health club; spa; Jacuzzi; bike rentals; children's programs; game room; concierge; car-rental desk; business center; limited room service; laundry service; dry cleaning; club-level rooms. *In room:* A/C, TV w/pay movies, dataport, fridge, hair dryer, iron.

EXPENSIVE

Radisson Resort Hill Country ★ *Kids*   The name of this new (opened 2002) property is a bit misleading: A spa and proximity to a golf course do not a resort make. And the Radisson is a pretty blatant knockoff of its ritzier next-door neighbor, the Hyatt Regency Hill Country Resort (see above), down to the Ralph Lauren-does-Texas lobby and the on-site ATM and upscale convenience store. But that doesn't mean it isn't a nice place to stay. It's got plenty of family appeal, including a nice pool complex. And SeaWorld is just down the road. Vacationers and conventioneers alike will enjoy the generous menu of spa treatments and products, as well as guest privileges at two good golf courses. Rooms are attractive in a dark, masculine way. Suites offer jetted tubs and rainforest shower heads, and all accommodations feature cushy "seven-layer beds" as well as an atypical of San Antonio perk: inexpensive ($9.95 per day) unlimited Internet access via your television allows you to compulsively check email 24/7 (not that I would do that).

9800 Westover Hills Blvd. (off Hwy 151), San Antonio TX 78251. ℂ 800/333-3333 or 210/509-9800. Fax 210/509-9814. www.radisson.com/sanantoniotx-resort. 227 units. $209–$229 double; $289–$429 suite. AE, DC, DISC, MC, V. Free parking. **Amenities:** 2 restaurants; bar; outdoor pools; health club; spa; Jacuzzi; business center; limited room service; dry cleaning. *In room:* A/C TV w/pay movies, dataport, fridge, coffeemaker, hair dryer, iron.

La Paloma Blanca ✿ (Alamo
 Heights Area, $, p. 67)
Mi Tierra (Downtown, $, p. 61)
Rosario's ✿ (Southtown, $$, p. 63)

IN AMERICAN
tos Latin Grill (Alamo Heights
 Area, $, p. 68)

AMERICAN
 on the Banks ✿ (Downtown,
 $$, p. 56)
 ro's ✿✿ (Downtown, $$$,
 8)
 narias ✿ (Downtown, $$$$,
)
 Bar ✿ (Monte Vista Area,
 64)
 ✿ (Alamo Heights Area,
 66)

MEXICAN
 ✿ (Alamo Heights Area,
 Main ✿ (Monte
 $$, p. 64)

La Paloma Blanca ✿ (Alamo
 Height Area, $$, p. 67)
Manduca ✿ (Downtown, $$$,
 p. 59)
Rosario's ✿ (Southtown, $$, p. 63)

SOUTHWESTERN
Francesca's at Sunset ✿ (North-
 west, $$$$, p. 68)
Zuni Grill ✿ (Downtown, $$$,
 p. 59)

STEAKS
Little Rhein Steakhouse (Downtown, $$$$, p. 58)
Texas Land & Cattle Co. (Down-
 town, $$, p. 60)

VEGETARIAN
Twin Sisters (Downtown, $, p. 61)

VIETNAMESE
Van's (Alamo Heights Area, $$,
 p. 68)

VE

s ✿ NEW AMERICAN With its new millennium move
ne of San Antonio's earliest culinary innovators got a venue
legant, bold, and contemporary. Clean lines, high ceilings,
 and lots of seraglio (sexy white draperies)—plus a balcony
ews—set the scene for chef/owner Bruce Auden's consis-
e. The game packet starters, for example, cross a few con-
s and Asia in spring-style rolls filled with minced venison,
asant accompanied by two spicy dipping sauces. The T-
ashers" and beer-battered onion rings raises comfort-
eights, and the variations on a theme in the Paseo de
 you happily into sugar shock, international style.
he bad news is that Auden seems to be spending less
 food is not nearly as dazzling as it was when the set-
, it's way above average, and if you're willing to eat
n sample a three-course meal for a bargain $29 per

/River Walk. ✆ **210/225-0722.** Reservations recommended. Main
 Mon–Thurs 5:30–10pm; Fri–Sat 5:30–11pm; Sun 11am–2:30pm

CAN The fine dining room at La Mansión del
 or it: the setting and the food. You have a choice
 tifully presented cuisine on a lovely riverside

---

7 North Central (Near the Airport)

EXPENSIVE

San Antonio Airport Hilton ✿ You'll go straight from the airport to the heart of Texas if you stay at this friendly hotel, where the cheerful lobby has a bull-rider mural and the guest quarters feature Lone Star–pattern chairs and cowboy lamps. The decor may be fun, but the rooms, loaded with up-to-date amenities, also get down to business. Jocks will like Tex's sports bar (see chapter 8), with Texas sports memorabilia and enough TVs to let patrons tune in to their favorite home games. One caveat: Despite the 24-hour security guards, this Hilton is locally notorious for its parking lot break-ins. Don't leave any valuables in your car if you stay here.

611 NW Loop 410 (San Pedro exit), San Antonio, TX 78216. ✆ **800/HILTONS** or 210/340-6060. Fax 210/377-4674. www.hilton.com. 386 units. $165–$175 double; $425–$550 suite. Romance, weekend packages available. AE, DC, DISC, MC, V. Free covered parking. Pets up to 20 lb. accepted. **Amenities:** Restaurant; bar; outdoor pool; sauna; Jacuzzi; video arcade; courtesy car; business center; limited room service; dry cleaning; club-level rooms. *In room:* TV w/pay movies, dataport, coffeemaker, hair dryer, iron.

MODERATE

Doubletree Hotel San Antonio Airport ✿ For an airport hotel, the Doubletree is surprisingly serene. The same developer who converted a downtown seminary into the posh La Mansión del Río hotel (see above) was responsible for this hotel's design. Moorish arches, potted plants, stone fountains, and colorful Mexican tile create a Mediterranean mood in the public areas; intricate wrought-iron elevators descend from the guest floors to the lushly landscaped pool patio, eliminating the need to tromp through the lobby in a swimsuit. Guest rooms are equally appealing, with brick walls painted in peach or beige, wood-beamed ceilings, draped French doors, and colorful contemporary art. This hotel draws a large business clientele, much of it from Mexico.

37 NE Loop 410 (McCullough exit), San Antonio, TX 78216. ✆ **800/535-1980** or 210/366-2424. Fax 210/341-0410. www.sanantonio.doubletreehotels.com. 291 units. $130–$170 double; $230–$300 suite. Packages available. AE, DC, DISC, MC, V. Free self-parking. **Amenities:** Restaurant; 2 bars; outdoor pool; health club; Jacuzzi; sauna; concierge; courtesy car; business center; limited room service; dry cleaning; club-level rooms. *In room:* A/C, TV w/pay movies, dataport, coffeemaker, hair dryer, iron.

5

Where to Dine in San Antonio

It's easy to eat well in San Antonio, especially if you enjoy Mexican food—or are willing to give it a try. But that's hardly all there is to eat in town. New American cuisine, emphasizing fresh regional ingredients and spices combined in exciting ways, is served in some of the most chic dining rooms in town, as well as in some unlikely dives. Then there's high-class French, chicken-fried steak, burgers, barbecue . . . in short, something to satisfy every taste and wallet. The national chains are represented here, naturally—everything from McDonald's to Morton's of Chicago—but I've concentrated on eateries that are unique to San Antonio, or at least to Texas.

The downtown dining scene, especially that on the River Walk, continues to expand. But although dining on the river is a unique, not-to-be-missed experience, many of the restaurants that overlook the water are overpriced and overcrowded. Downtown eateries that aren't on the water tend to be pricey, too. And parking is either tough to find or expensive (on busy weekend nights, when garage space may sell out, it can be both). In short,

even if you're willing to pass up a river view, downtown is not the best place for economical or serene fine dining.

There are some good restaurants in Southtown, the aptly named area just below downtown, but most prime places to chow down are scattered throughout the north. By far the most fertile ground for outstanding San Antonio dining is on and around Broadway, starting a few blocks south of Hildebrand, extending north to Loop 410, and comprising much of the posh area known as Alamo Heights. Brackenridge Park, the zoo, the botanical gardens, and the Witte and McNay museums are all located in this part of town, so you can combine the sightseeing with some serious eating. Although I've pretty much stuck to areas that out-of-towners are likely to visit, I've also included a few restaurants worth driving out of your way to find. (To locate restaurants outside of Downtown, see the map on p. 50.)

A number of popular places don't take reservations; if you arrive around 8pm when everyone else does, you can expect to wait up to an hour for a table. Book a table wherever you can.

RESTAURANT CATEGORIES

Rather than trying to make sharp distinctions between Regional American, New Texan, and American Fusion cuisine, as some chefs try to do, I defined any menu likely to include things like mashed potatoes, feta cheese, pesto, and chorizo (not necessarily all in the same dish) as **New American. Southwestern,** on the other hand, is a contemporary cooking style that tends to confine itself to ingredients from the American Southwest (blue corn and jicama, say). I have merged Tex-Mex and northern Mexican cuisine, which are inextricably intertwined, into a single **Mexican** category. **Regional Mexican** cooking encompasses cuisine from other parts of Mexico.

> **Tips The Early Bird**
>
> If you're budget conscious, consider eating early, when so
> have early-bird specials, or hitting the expensive resta
> some of the most upscale eateries in town have good l

The price categories into which the restaurants ha rough approximations, based on the average costs of th ordering carefully or splurging, you can eat more or l place you choose.

1 Restaurants by Cuisine

AMERICAN
Cappy's ★ (Alamo Heights Area, $$$, p. 65)
Chris Madrid (Monte Vista Area, $, p. 64)
Guenther House ★ (Southtown, $, p. 63)
Little Rhein Steak House (Downtown, $$$$, p. 58)
Olmos Pharmacy (Alamo Heigh Area, $, p. 68)
Texas Land & Cattle Co. (De town, $$, p. 60)

ASIAN FUSION
Frederick's ★★ (Alamo F Area, $$$, p. 66)

CHINESE
Van's (Alamo Height p. 68)

CONTINENTAL
Bistro Time ★★ p. 69)

DELI
Madhatters
Pecan Str town,
Schilo's
Twin

ECLE
M

FRE
P

NEW
Biga
$$
Boud
P.
Las Ca
P. 50
Liberty
$$, p.
Silo ★★
$$$, p

REGIONA
La Calesa ★
$$, P. 67
La Fonda on
Vista Area

2 Downtow
VERY EXPENS
Biga on the Ban
to the River Walk, to match its menu: gleaming wood floors with dramatic river v tently interesting cuisi tinents, combining Tex buffalo, ostrich, and ph bone steak with garlic " cum-bar cuisine to new Chocolate dessert will se That's the good news. time in the kitchen, and th ting was more low key. Still early (5:30–6:30pm), you c person.
International Center, 203 S. St. Mary's S courses $17–$35. AE, DC, DISC, MC, V (brunch) and 5:30–10pm.

Las Canarias ★ NEW AMER Río has a couple of things going of dining on inventive and bea

Key to Abbreviations: $$$$ = ve

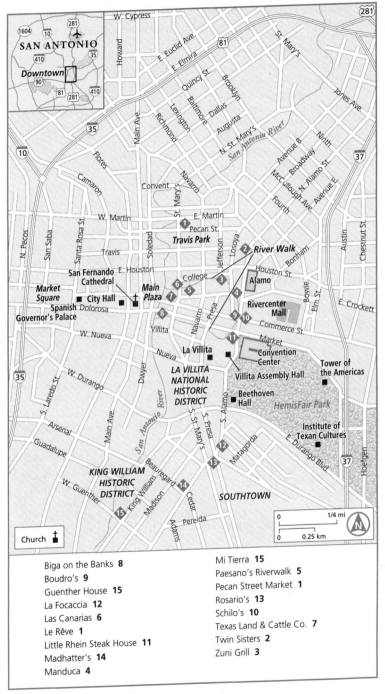

Downtown San Antonio Dining

Biga on the Banks **8**
Boudro's **9**
Guenther House **15**
La Focaccia **12**
Las Canarias **6**
Le Rêve **1**
Little Rhein Steak House **11**
Madhatter's **14**
Manduca **4**

Mi Tierra **15**
Paesano's Riverwalk **5**
Pecan Street Market **1**
Rosario's **13**
Schilo's **10**
Texas Land & Cattle Co. **7**
Twin Sisters **2**
Zuni Grill **3**

veranda; a palm-decked, Mexican-tiled patio; or inside in one of several cozy, antiques-filled interior rooms where you can listen to the soft music of a grand piano or a classical guitar.

Menus change seasonally, but such dishes as seared yellowfin tuna with saffron grits and grilled venison loin with roasted corn flan demonstrate the chef's ability to balance unusual textures and flavors. Appetizers are equally exciting, but you'll want to share to leave room for dazzling desserts like the phyllo-crusted banana cream pie with chocolate pecan ice cream on the side. *One caveat:* All types of (legal) smoking are permitted in the outdoor areas; if someone is stoking a stogie at the next table, your al fresco dining experience can be ruined.

La Mansión del Río, 112 College St./River Walk. ✆ **210/518-1063.** Reservations recommended. Main courses $19–$36; 6-course tasting menu $50 ($65 paired with wine); champagne brunch $30. AE, DC, DISC, MC, V. Sun–Thurs 6:30am–10:30pm; Fri–Sat 6:30am–11pm; Sun brunch 10:30am–2:30pm.

Le Rêve ★★ FRENCH   Chef/owner Andrew Weissman, a local boy who studied in France and did a stint at New York's famed Le Cirque, is very serious about his food—and it shows (and tastes). Presentations are gorgeous, and everything's made from scratch with the freshest of ingredients, so such dishes as the caramelized onion tart appetizer, duck breast with foie gras and calvados apples, or the light but rich sour cream cheesecake are sensual delights.

But Weissman expects patrons to take food as seriously as he does. The staff has been known to give tables away when diners don't show up in time for their reservations, or berate patrons who ordered their meat prepared well done. This is also the only place in town that requires men to wear jackets. I don't think the food justifies the attitude (yo! this is San Antonio, not Paris); it's excellent, not transcendent. Still, this tiny, chic dining room with a peek-a-boo view of the river is one of the prime see-and-be-seen spots in town. If you want to experience Weissman's cooking in the Alamo City (as opposed to Houston, where the chef is planning to move by 2004), now's your chance.

152 E. Pecan St. at St. Mary's. ✆ **210/212-2221.** Reservations required. Jacket required for men. 3 courses $65, 4 courses $75, 5 courses $85. AE, DC, DISC, MC, V. Tues–Sat 5:30–11pm (last reservation taken for 8:30pm seating).

Little Rhein Steak House AMERICAN/STEAKS   Built in 1847 in what was then the Rhein district, the oldest two-story structure in San Antonio has hosted an elegant steakhouse abutting the river and La Villita since 1967. Antique memorabilia decks the indoor main dining room, and a miniature train surrounded by historic replicas runs overhead. Leafy branches overhanging the River Walk patio—elevated slightly and railed off for privacy—are draped in little sparkling lights.

The setting is pretty as ever, and the choice USDA Prime steaks from the restaurant's own meat plant are tasty, but recent competition from chains such as The Palm and Morton's nearby have resulted in a price hike. Now everything here is a la carte: You'll shell out $4.75 for a baked potato, another $6.95 for creamed spinach (you do still get a loaf of fresh wheat bread, gratis). The restaurant can also get quite noisy. That said, this is still one of the few family-owned steakhouses around, and it offers a unique River Walk dining experience.

231 S. Alamo at Market. ✆ **210/225-2111.** Reservations recommended. Main courses $20–$35. AE, DC, DISC, MC, V. Daily 5–10pm.

EXPENSIVE

Boudro's ★★ NEW AMERICAN   Locals tend to look down their noses at River Walk restaurants—that is, with the long-running exception of Boudro's.

And with good reason. The kitchen uses fresh local ingredients—Gulf Coast seafood, Texas beef, Hill Country produce—and the preparations and presentations do them justice. The setting is also out of the ordinary: a turn-of-the-century limestone building with hardwood floors and a handmade mesquite bar.

You might start with the guacamole, prepared tableside and served with tostadas, or the pan-fried Texas crab cakes. The prime rib, blackened on a pecan-wood grill, is deservedly popular, as are the lamb chops with peach chutney and garlic mashed potatoes. The food may be innovative, but portions are hearty nevertheless. Lighter alternatives include the coconut shrimp with orange horse-radish and the grilled yellowfin tuna. For dessert, the whisky-soaked bread pudding is fine, and the lime chess pie with a butter pastry crust . . . divine. Service is very good, especially considering the volume of business and the time the servers spend mixing up guacamole.

421 E. Commerce St./River Walk. ℂ 210/224-8484. Reservations strongly recommended. Main courses $15–$32. AE, DC, DISC, MC, V. Sun–Thurs 11am–11pm; Fri–Sat 11am–midnight.

Manduca ⭐ REGIONAL MEXICAN   It's not easy to find genuine Mexican food—as opposed to Tex-Mex—everywhere in San Antonio, so it's especially surprising to find a well executed, wide-ranging south-of- the-border menu on the tourist-driven River Walk. Thank Jorge Cosio, a young chef from Mexico City, who's betting that gringos will like his adventurous fare if they just give it a chance. I hope he's right. I was certainly pleased with my samplings of the *sopa azteca*, a variation on the traditional soup that uses black beans instead of clear broth; the Veracruz-style fish, as tasty as any I've had in Mexico; and the Friday regional special, *puntas rancheras*, tender beef tips grilled in a tangy tomato-based sauce. "Manduca" means "to have a large feast," and come prepared to do just that.

215 Losoya St./River Walk. ℂ 210/475-9099. Reservations recommended on weekends. Main courses $13–$25. AE, DISC, DC, MC, V. Sun–Thurs 11am–10pm; Fri–Sat 11am–11pm.

Paesano's Riverwalk ⭐ ITALIAN   This River Walk incarnation of a long-time San Antonio favorite relinquished its old Chianti bottle–kitsch decor for a soaring ceiling, lots of inscrutable contemporary art, and a more up-to-date menu. But the one thing the restaurant couldn't give up, at the risk of a local insurrection, was the signature shrimp Paesano's. The crispy crustaceans are as good as their devotees claim, as are the reasonably priced pizzas, including the one topped with grilled chicken, artichokes, basil pesto, and feta cheese. Other good values: Hearty southern Italian staples such as lasagna with meat sauce. Standouts among the pricier entrees include the grilled pork chops with potato gnocchi, and pan-seared trout with almonds on linguini. There's another, newer—and somewhat quieter—Paesano's, across from the Quarry Golf Club at 555 Basse Rd., Suite 100 (ℂ **210/828-5191**).

111 W. Crockett, Suite 101/River Walk. ℂ 210/227-4102. Reservations accepted for 10 or more only. Pizzas $13; pastas $8.95–$19; main courses $20–$29. AE, DISC, MC, V. Daily 11am–11pm.

Zuni Grill ⭐ SOUTHWESTERN   With its chile strings, stylized steers, and chic Southwestern menu, this popular River Walk cafe is a little bit of Santa-Fe-on-the-San-Antonio. If you've never had a prickly pear margarita, this is the place to try one: Puréed cactus fruit, marinated overnight in tequila and cactus-juice schnapps, turns the potent, delicious drink a shade ranging from pink to startling purple, depending on the ripeness of the fruit.

This is a good place to come from morning 'til dark. Kick-start your day with a breakfast taco, or take a mid-afternoon break with a grilled salmon sandwich

San Antonio's Moveable Feasts

Not satisfied to dine with an immobile river view? Several River Walk restaurants recommended in this chapter—Paesano's, Boudro's, Zuni Grill, Manduca, and the Texas Cattle Company—offer communal river barge dinners, which let you book a place (or two or three or four) on one of the restaurant's regular river runs. It's a terrific sightseeing-while-snacking experience, but not especially romantic, as you'll be sitting with a bunch of strangers around a long table. Other caveats: The boats don't have kitchens, so the menu is more limited than it would be if you were dining in the restaurant itself (you get only a few appetizers, entrees, and desserts to select from). And if you don't like the way something is cooked, you can't send it back.

Prices and schedules vary; call the restaurants, all listed in the Downtown section, for details. Not enough choices? Check with Yanaguana Cruises (© **800/417-4139** or 210/244-5700; www.sarivercruise.com), which operates the barges, for information on other eateries that'll let you sit in on their splashy foodfests.

with black bean and corn relish. At night, vegetarians will appreciate the gardener and gatherer platter (grilled vegetables accompanied by roasted garlic mashed potatoes and wilted spinach). For something more substantial, try the honey-coriander pork loin with adobo sauce or seared ahi with polenta. You might want to finish with another culinary dazzler: a pecan crème brûlée that tastes every bit as good as it sounds.

223 Losoya St./River Walk. © **210/227-0864.** Reservations accepted only for parties of 6 or more. Main courses $14–$25. AE, DC, DISC, MC, V. Daily 8am–10pm.

MODERATE
See also La Paloma Blanca on p. 67.

La Margarita *(Overrated* MEXICAN It's overrun by tourists, the food is just okay, and the namesake drinks aren't very strong, but if you want to refuel after Market Square shopping, La Margarita is convenient. And you won't go away hungry. This lively restaurant is known for its fajitas and for its *parilla* platters: huge mounds of charbroiled sausage, chicken, and beef accompanied by *queso flameado* (melted cheese), fried potatoes, beans, guacamole, pico de gallo, and hot flour tortillas. Don't want to consume an entire week's calorie allotment in a single meal? Sit outdoors with some nachos and a margarita; the people-watching is great.

120 Produce Row (Market Sq.). © **210/227-7140.** Reservations accepted for large groups. Main courses $7.25–$16. AE, DC, DISC, MC, V. Sun–Thurs 11am–10pm; Fri–Sat 11am–midnight.

Texas Land & Cattle Co. *(Value* AMERICAN/STEAKS If you're hankering for a big meat fix, slip into some jeans and mosey on down to this dining room that shouts "Texas" from its branding irons to its wagon-wheel chandeliers to its huge, mesquite-grilled steaks. Located on a quiet stretch of the river, this is a kicked-back downtown bargain—not as fancy as the likes of Morton's or Ruth's Chris, but not nearly as pricey, either. Nor will you find Mexican charro-style steaks served with pico de gallo and two cheese enchiladas with chili con carne at those haute steak chains, or great baby-back ribs, or sides such as Caesar salads and tortilla soup included with the meal, or desserts like the outrageous brownie/ice cream sundae.

201 N. St. Mary's St. © 210/222-2263. Main courses $11–$22. AE, DC, DISC, MC, V. Sun–Thurs 11am–10pm; Fri–Sat 11am–11pm.

INEXPENSIVE

Mi Tierra MEXICAN Almost anyone who's ever been within striking distance of San Antonio has heard of this Market Square restaurant, open since 1946. Much expanded and gussied up since then, it still draws a faithful clientele of Latino families and businesspeople—along with busloads of tourists. Perhaps its prime asset is its round-the-clock schedule: If you're looking for chorizo and eggs or an 8-ounce charbroiled rib eye at 2am, this is the place to come. Not that hungry? Mi Tierra has a *panadería* (bakery), and you can get all kinds of good *pan dulces* to go along with a cup of coffee or Mexican hot chocolate.

218 Produce Row (Market Sq.). © 210/225-1262. Reservations accepted for large groups only. Main courses $7.25–$17. AE, MC, V. Open 24 hr.

Pecan Street Market ✦ DELI Choosing a sandwich can be difficult at this downtown deli and gourmet mini-market on the ground floor of the historic Exchange Building. Picking the condiment alone is a challenge—will it be chipotle mayonnaise, cranberry Dijon, or sun-dried tomato spread? Area businesses, long stuck with the same old choices, embraced this little industrial chic spot and its fresh soups, salads, specialty sandwiches (think focaccia with veggies and smoked gouda cheese), and tempting desserts. Heart-healthy items—sorry, no desserts among 'em—are noted. If you want to hole up in your hotel room during lunch and don't like the room service, you can also order in from here. Too bad it's closed weekends.

152 E. Pecan St., no. 102 (across from the Greyhound Station). © 210/227-3226. Sandwiches $4.25–$6. AE, DC, DISC, MC, V. Mon–Fri 10am–2:30pm.

Schilo's *Value* *Kids* GERMAN/DELI You can't leave town without stopping in at this San Antonio institution, if only for a hearty bowl of split-pea soup or a piece of the signature cherry cheesecake. The large, open room with its worn wooden booths is a door into the city's German past. The waitresses—definitely not "servers"—wear dirndl-type outfits, and live German bands play on Saturday from 5 to 8pm. It's a great refueling station near Alamo Plaza for the entire family, with a large kid-friendly selection and retro low prices. For around $5, a good, greasy Reuben or a kielbasa plate should keep you going the rest of the day.

424 E. Commerce St. © 210/223-6692. Reservations for large groups for breakfast and dinner only. Sandwiches $2.90–$4.75; hot or cold plates $4.75–$5.45; main dishes (served after 5pm) $6.85–$8.95. AE, DC, DISC, MC, V. Mon–Sat 7am–8:30pm.

Twin Sisters *Finds* HEALTH FOOD/DELI If you want to avoid overpriced sandwiches and junk food while sightseeing, join the downtown working crowd at this bakery and health-food cafe just a few blocks from the Alamo. Eggless and meatless doesn't mean tasteless here—you can get great Greek salads, spicy tofu scrambles, and salsa-topped veggie burgers—but carnivores can also indulge in the likes of ham, pastrami, and salami sandwiches on the excellent bread made on the premises.

It's Always Chili in San Antonio

It ranks up there with apple pie in the American culinary pantheon, but nobody's mom invented chili. The iconic stew of meat, chiles, onions, and a variety of spices was likely conceived around the 1840s by Texas cowboys who needed to make tough meat palatable—while also covering up its taste as it began to go bad. The name is a Texas corruption of the Spanish "chile" ("*chee*-leh"), after the peppers—which are not really peppers at all, but that's another story—most conventionally used in the stew.

The appellation chili *con carne* is really redundant in Texas, where chili without meat isn't considered chili at all; indeed, most Texans think that adding beans is only for wusses. Beef is the most common base, but everything from armadillo to venison is acceptable.

No one really knows exactly where chili originated, but San Antonio is the prime candidate for the distinction: In the mid–19th century, accounts were widespread of the town's "chili queens," women who ladled steaming bowls of the concoction in open-air markets and street corners. It wasn't until the 1940s that they stopped dishing out chili in front of the Alamo.

William Gebhardt helped strengthen San Antonio's claim to chili fame when he began producing chili powder in the city in 1896. His Original Mexican Dinner package, which came out around 20 years later, included a can each of chili con carne, beans, and tamales, among other things; it fed five for $1. This precursor of the TV dinner proved so popular that it earned San Antonio the nickname "Tamaleville."

Oddly enough, chili isn't generally found on San Antonio restaurant menus. But modern-day chili queens come out in force for special events at Market Square, as well as for Nights in Old San Antonio, one of the most popular bashes of the city's huge Fiesta celebration. And there's not a weekend that goes by without a chili cook-off somewhere in the city.

Tip: This popular place fills up by 11:30am but empties after 12:45pm, so gauge your visit accordingly. A branch in Alamo Heights, 6322 N. New Braunfels (*© **210/822-2265***), has longer hours (Mon–Sat 7am–9pm, Sun 9am–2pm).

124 Broadway at Travis. *© **210/354-1559.*** Reservations not accepted. $1.80–$6 breakfast; $3.80–$8.80 lunch. MC, V. Mon–Fri 8am–3pm.

3 Southtown

MODERATE

La Focaccia *(Finds* ITALIAN   In spite of its trendy name and its funky former gas-station setting, this restaurant is about as traditional as they come. Owner/chef Luigi Ciccarelli was born and raised in Rome; his recipes were handed down from his grandfather, who used to be a chef for Italian royals (the Savoys). Lunch is casual, with lots of calzones, sandwiches, and subs as well as pizzas on offer. For dinner, you've got well-prepared versions of lasagna or spaghetti and meatballs; the seafood dishes are especially good. The salad bar, which includes such unusual dishes as marinated grilled eggplant and mushrooms, is well worth the $3.75 investment (if you get it without an entree). Portions are large, so try to resist scarfing down the basket of focaccia, made in the wood-burning pizza oven.

800 S. Alamo. © 210/223-5353. Reservations required for 5 or more only. Pizzas $6.95–$8.95; pastas $7.75–$16; main courses $11–$20 (lobster higher). AE, DC, DISC, MC, V. Mon–Thurs 11am–2:30pm and 5–10pm; Fri 11am–2:30pm and 5–11pm; Sat noon–11pm; Sun noon–10pm.

Rosario's ✦ MEXICAN/REGIONAL MEXICAN   When it relocated to a new, much larger space a few years ago, this long-time Southtown favorite lost some of its coziness, but it also became hipper and more colorful than ever: Think witty Frida Kahlo and Botero knock-offs and abundant neon—and knockout margaritas. This is the place to sample tasty versions of such adventurous regional dishes as *camote y pollo adobado*—sweet potato and chicken casserole in a sweet and spicy ancho chile sauce—or *nopalito* (cactus pad) tacos, as well as Tex-Mex standards, all prepared with fresh ingredients. You might start with the shrimp nachos with all the fixin's or the more restrained seafood ceviche (scallop, shrimp, and fish marinated in lime juice), and then go on to the delicious chile relleno, with raisins and potatoes added to the chopped beef stuffing. The noise level can make conversation difficult.

A branch of Rosario's opened at the airport (Terminal 2, near Gate 34) in 2002. The menu here is limited, but there's still a full bar and cool waitstaff.

910 S. Alamo. © 210/223-1806. Reservations not accepted. Main courses $7.25–$13. AE, DC, DISC, MC, V. Mon 11am–3pm; Tues–Thurs 11am–10pm; Fri and Sat 11am–11pm (bar until 2am on Fri).

INEXPENSIVE

Guenther House ✦ *Value* AMERICAN   If you're not staying in a King William B&B, this is your chance to chow down in one of the neighborhood's historic homes. And it's a winner. Hearty breakfasts and light lunches are served both indoors—in a pretty art nouveau–style dining room added on to the Guenther family residence (built in 1860)—and outdoors on a trellised patio. The biscuits and gravy are a morning specialty, and the chicken salad (made with black olives) at lunch is excellent, but you can't go wrong with any of the wonderful baked goods made on the premises, either. Adjoining the restaurant are a small museum, a Victorian parlor, and a mill store featuring baking-related items, including mixes for lots of the Guenther House goodies. The house fronts a lovely stretch of the San Antonio River.

205 E. Guenther St. © 210/227-1061. Reservations not accepted. Breakfast $3.25–$6.25; lunch $4.75–$6.95. AE, DC, DISC, MC, V. Daily 7am–3pm (the house and mill store are open Mon–Sat 8am–4pm; Sun 8am–3pm).

Madhatters *Finds* *Kids* DELI/ECLECTIC   Recently transplanted to Southtown from the Brackenridge Park area, this colorful, sprawling storefront attracts everyone from nouveau hippies to buttoned-down refugees from the convention center 5 minutes away. They come for Age-of-Aquarius-meets-south-of-the-border food: granola bowls and breakfast burritos in the morning, veggie sandwiches and pork tamales in the evening. After work (or protests), there are cold cases full of reasonably priced wines and beers. Anglophiles won't be disappointed, either: Among the various tea parties offered, there's one for kids that includes peanut butter-and-jelly sandwiches (crusts cut off, naturally). Don't worry about the NO CELL PHONES sign: Everyone in the bustling front room seems to ignore it, while those seeking quietude head for a cozy enclave in back.

320 Beauregard St. ② **210/212-4832.** Reservations not accepted. Breakfasts $3.30–$11, sandwiches and salad plates $5.95–$7.95. AE, MC, V. Mon 7am–6pm; Tues–Thurs 7am–10pm; Sat 9am–11pm; Sun 9am–6pm.

4 Monte Vista Area
MODERATE

La Fonda on Main ✦ *Value* *Kids* MEXICAN/REGIONAL MEXICAN   One of San Antonio's oldest continually operating restaurants, established in 1932, has revamped both its premises and menu, thanks to Cappy Lawton of Cappy's fame (see p. 65), who acquired it in the late 1990s. The lovely red-tile-roof residence has been spiffed up, rendering the dining rooms cheerful and bright—almost as inviting as the garden-fringed outdoor patio. And the tinkering continues. Although the revamped menu was initially classic Tex-Mex, featuring giant combination plates such as the La Fonda Special (one cheese enchilada, one beef or chicken taco with rice and refried beans), more recently a "Cuisines of Mexico" section was added, including such traditional dishes as *mojo de ajo* (Gulf shrimp with garlic butter served with squash). Many celebrities dined here in the old days—including Franklin Roosevelt, John Wayne, and Yul Brenner, among others—and the fresh, tasty, generous specialties dished up here daily still attract power lunchers and local families alike.

2415 N. Main. ② **210/733-0621.** Reservations recommended for 6 or more. Main courses $6.95–$12. AE, DC, MC, V. Mon–Thurs 11am–3pm and 5–9:30pm; Fri–Sat 11am–3pm and 5–10:30pm; Sun brunch 11am–3pm.

Liberty Bar ✦ *Finds* NEW AMERICAN   You'd be hard-pressed to guess that this ramshackle former brothel (which opened in 1890, in case you were wondering) near the Hwy. 281 underpass hosts one of the hippest haunts in San Antonio. But, as every foodie in town can tell you, it's bright and inviting inside, and you'll find everything from comfort food (pot roast, say, or a ham-and-Swiss sandwich) to regional Mexican cuisine (the *chiles rellenos en nogada* are super). The toasted English bread with roast garlic spread or eggplant purée goes great with many of the fine—and generally affordable—wines available by the glass; there's a good beer selection, too. And don't worry—even if you've had a few too many, you're not imagining it: The house really *is* leaning.

328 E. Josephine St. ② **210/227-1187.** Reservations recommended. Main courses $6.95–$19. AE, MC, V. Sun–Thurs 11:30am–10:30pm; Fri–Sat 11:30am–midnight; Sun brunch 10:30–2pm (bar until midnight Sun–Thurs; 2am Fri–Sat).

INEXPENSIVE

Chris Madrid *Kids* AMERICAN/BURGERS   It's hard to drop much money at this funky gas station turned burger joint, but you might lose your shirt—over the years, folks have taken to signing their tees and hanging them on the walls. An even more popular tradition is trying to eat the macho burger, as huge as its name and topped with cheese and jalapeños. The menu is pretty much limited to burgers, nachos, fries, and various combinations thereof, but the casual atmosphere and down-home cooking keep the large outdoor patio filled.

1900 Blanco. ② **210/735-3552.** Reservations not accepted. Main courses $3.50–$6. AE, DC, DISC, MC, V. Mon–Sat 11am–10pm.

Demo's *Value* GREEK   Demo's is a little bit of Greece in San Antonio, across from a Greek Orthodox church. Either on the airy patio or in a two-tiered dining room with lots of murals of Greek island scenes, you can enjoy gyros, Greek burgers, dolmas, spanakopita, and other Mediterranean specialties; if you go for

(Kids) Family-Friendly Restaurants

Betos (p. 68), **La Calesa** (p. 67), and **La Fonda** (p. 64) All three are great places to introduce your kids to Mexican food. The latter two offer inexpensive children's plates, and Betos has plenty of child-friendly choices—not to mention a sandbox.

Madhatters (p. 63) Even if your kids aren't up for an entire children's tea, they'll be happy to find their faves on the menu, from PB&J to plain turkey or cheese sandwiches. The chocolate chip cookies and brownies won't be sneezed at, either.

Olmos Pharmacy (p. 68) Kids entertain themselves by swiveling in the seats at this classic soda fountain, where the food is as reasonable as it comes. They won't even mind too much when you go on and on about how this is ice cream the way it's *supposed* to be.

Schilo's (p. 61) A high noise level, a convenient location near the River Walk (but with prices far lower than anything you'll find there), and a wide selection of familiar food make this German deli a good choice.

Dieter's Special—a Greek salad with your choice of gyros or souvlaki (beef or chicken)—you might be able to justify the baklava. In addition to this location, there's the original at 7115 Blanco Rd. (© 210/342-2772) near Loop 10 across from what used to be Central Park Mall. A belly dancer gyrates at the Blanco Road location on Monday nights, and at the N. St. Mary's Street location on Wednesdays.

2501 N. St. Mary's St. © 210/732-7777. Reservations accepted for parties of 10 or more only. Main courses $5–$9. AE, DC, DISC, MC, V. Mon–Thurs 11am–9pm; Fri–Sat 11am–10pm.

5 Alamo Heights Area

EXPENSIVE

Bistro Vatel ★★ (Value) FRENCH Talk about a pressure cooker: In 1671, the great French chef Vatel killed himself out of shame because the fish for a banquet he was preparing for Louis XIV wasn't delivered on time. Fortunately, his descendant, Damian Watel, has less stress to contend with in San Antonio, where diners are very appreciative of the chef's efforts to bring them classic French cooking at comparatively reasonable prices.

The restaurant's strip mall location isn't exactly inspiring, and the dining room has a low, acoustic-tile ceiling, but copper pots, wine racks, and white tablecloths help create a charming, intimate atmosphere. You can't go wrong with the rich escalope of veal with foie gras, and fans of sweetbreads will be pleased to find them here beautifully prepared in truffle creme fraiche sauce. Your best bet is the bargain prix-fixe dinner, where you can choose one each from a trio of appetizers, entrees, and desserts of the day.

218 E. Olmos Ave. at McCullough. © 210/828-3141. Reservations recommended on the weekends. Main courses $15–$22; prix-fixe $27 dinner. AE, MC, V. Tues–Fri 11:30am–1:30pm; Tues–Sat 5:30–9:30pm.

Cappy's ★ AMERICAN One of the earliest businesses to open in the now-burgeoning Alamo Heights neighborhood, Cappy's is set in an unusual broken-brick structure dating back to the late 1930s. But there's nothing outdated about this cheerful, light-filled place—high, wood-beam ceilings, hanging plants, colorful work by local artists—or its romantic, tree-shaded outdoor patio.

The enticing smell of a wood-burning grill (no, not mesquite, but the somewhat milder live oak) gives a hint of some of the house specialties: the prime rib eye or slow-roasted Italian chicken with risotto. Lighter fare includes snapper with shrimp and artichoke hearts over pasta. A chef's prix fixe lets you choose an appetizer, salad, and entree. See chapter 8 for **Cappycino** 🐟, an offshoot of Cappy's down the block with a great by-the-glass wine list and a more casual Southwest menu. It's my San Antonio niece's favorite dinner spot; her new baby is even welcome there.

5011 Broadway (behind Twig Book Store). ℂ **210/828-9669.** Main courses $15–$25; prix-fixe $35. AE, DC, MC, V. Daily 11am–3pm and 5:30–10pm.

Frederick's 🐟🐟 *Finds* FRENCH/ASIAN FUSION Among the recently opened restaurants in San Antonio that I have tried, this one—in the back of a Broadway strip mall—is my hands-down favorite. The setting is nothing special, although the low-ceiling, darkish room has been prettified by white draperies and sunny antiqued walls. But once the food started arriving at the table, I wouldn't have noticed if I'd been dining inside a concrete bunker.

For starters, I had tempura-battered sushi, strange in the abstract but actually wonderful; oh-so-crispy spring rolls of shrimp, pork, and mushrooms; and a delicate crab salad with avocado. Those were followed by an entree of sea bass with bok choy and shiitake over a sesame galette. (yes, the restaurant's specialty is seafood). Call the cuisine Indochine—it's a mix of French and Vietnamese—or call it French fusion, as the menu does. I call it delicious.

771 Broadway, Suite 20 (in the back of Dijon Plaza). ℂ **210/828-9050.** Reservations recommended on weekends. Main courses: $17–$29. AE, MC, V. Mon–Thurs 11:30am–2pm and 5:30–10pm; Fri 11:30am–2pm and 5:30–11pm; Sat 5:30–11pm.

Massimo 🐟🐟 ITALIAN There's lots of good Americanized Italian fare in San Antonio, but for authentic *cucina italiana,* prepared by a chef from Rome (by way of New York), this is the place. The kitchen is particularly strong in pastas and risotto, all made fresh on the premises; the potato gnocchi are a special treat. Massimo's move in 2002 from a frontage road near the airport to a shopping complex in Alamo Heights (hey, the neighborhood is right anyway, and it's hard to avoid strip centers in the west) made it far easier to enjoy his food. The Tuscan yellow dining rooms are airy, even if some of the tables are a bit too close together, and the romantic Red Room Bar has become a popular place to listen to live music on the weekends.

Tip: If you want to economize, share a generous salad (such as the primavera with artichokes, asparagus, and hearts of palm) followed by pasta. Of course, then you'd miss such excellent *secondi* as duck breast in a delicate balsamic sauce or the saltimbocca, a Roman specialty.

1896 Nacogdoches Rd. ℂ **210/342-8556.** Reservations recommended on weekends. Pastas $13–$18; main courses $18–$26. AE, DC, DISC, MC, V. Mon–Fri 11am–2:30pm and 5:30–10:30pm; Sat 5:30–10:30pm (Bar Mon–Sat 5pm–2am).

Silo 🐟🐟🐟 NEW AMERICAN Silo is consistently top-listed by San Antonio foodies, and deservedly so. More than the other chic restaurants in town, it has concentrated more on food than on attitude, consistently presenting a small but well-balanced menu using fresh ingredients in fresh combinations. Starters such as the seared sea scallop on a roasted garlic potato blini or a salad of endive, apples, spicy pecans, and blue cheese get the mix of textures and tastes just right, as do entrées like seared yellowfin tuna with a blue crab spring roll or pork tenderloin on a bacon, corn, and potato hash. Desserts, which change nightly, are divine too. Although the chic, industrial-design perch (the "Elevated Cuisine" alluded to in the restaurant's logo) makes for a somewhat cold setting, service is warm and super-efficient to boot. Nonsmokers take note: Silo's has one of the few bars in San Antonio where puffing isn't permitted.

1133 Austin Hwy. ℭ 210/824-8686. Reservations not accepted except for large private parties. Main courses $16–$24. AE, DC, DISC, MC, V. Sun–Thurs 5:30–9:30pm; Fri–Sat 5:30–10:30pm.

MODERATE

Koi Kawa ⭐ JAPANESE   Sushi rules at Koi Kawa, which has won die-hard fans because of its high-quality ingredients, such as real crabmeat and hothouse-grown cucumbers. But if you're not in a raw fish mood (today or ever), you've got plenty of other options. The crispy vegetable, seafood, and shrimp tempuras get a lot of attention, as do the various *udon* (wheat noodle) and *soba* (cold buck-wheat noodle) soups, meals in themselves. In the back of the Boardwalk complex, with a view of the tree-shaded banks of the San Antonio River (admittedly, a generally stagnant section), Koi Kawa is a bit hard to locate, but by all means persevere if you're a Japanese food fan.

A newer, smaller version in the Quarry shopping complex, 255 E. Basse Rd. (ℭ **210/930-6042**), dazzles with a sushi conveyor belt, but most locals remain loyal to the less gimmicky original.

4051 Broadway (in back corner of Boardwalk Complex, close to Witte Museum). ℭ 210/805-8111. Reservations recommended on weekends. Main courses $10–$22. AE, DISC, DC, MC, V. Mon–Fri 11:30am–2pm and 5:30–10pm; Sat 5:30–10pm.

La Calesa ⭐ *(Kids)* REGIONAL MEXICAN   Tucked away in a small house just off Broadway—look for Earl Abel's large sign across the street—this family-run restaurant features several dishes from the southern Yucatán region, as well as the more familiar ones from northern Mexico. The difference is mainly in the sauces, and they're done to perfection here. The mole, for example, strikes a fine balance between its rich chocolate base and its spices, and the achiote marinade lends a piquancy to the *conchinita pibil,* a classic Yucatan pork dish. Rice and black beans (more flavorful than the usual pintos) accompany many of the meals. You can eat indoors in one of three cozy dining rooms, decorated with Mexican art prints and tile work, or outside on the small flower-decked wooden porch.

2103 E. Hildebrand (just off Broadway). ℭ 210/822-4475. Reservations required for 6 or more. Main courses $5.95–$16. AE, DC, DISC, MC, V. Mon–Thurs 11am–9:30pm; Fri 11am–10:30pm; Sat 11:30am–10:30pm; Sun 11:30am–8pm.

La Paloma Blanca ⭐ MEXICAN/REGIONAL MEXICAN   Don't be deceived by this restaurant's tiny blue mosaic tiled entryway. Downstairs, a series of spacious high-ceiling rooms are divided by graceful archways; large as the rooms are, all their tables are likely to be filled, especially at midday when neighborhood office workers pile in for their favorites: enchiladas *verdes* in a tangy green tomatillo sauce, or the vegetable chile relleno, a light, delicious version of this popular dish. You're also likely to find chef/owner Blanca Aldaco working the room, greeting regulars and explaining some of the less familiar fare inspired by her birthplace, Guadalajara. Her second restaurant, **Aldaco's,** 100 Hoefgen St. in Sunset Station (ℭ **210/222-0561**), is more determinedly Tex-Mex but both eateries feature the chef's justifiably renowned traditional *tres leches* (three-milk) cake.

5148 Broadway. ⓒ 210/822-6151. Reservations recommended for dinner. Main courses $6.95–$15. AE, MC, V. Sun–Wed 11am–9pm; Thurs–Fri 11am–10pm; Sat 8am–10pm.

Van's CHINESE/JAPANESE/VIETNAMESE   Talk about pan-Asian. The sign outside announces that Van's is a "Chinese Seafood Restaurant and Sushi Bar," but you'll also find Vietnamese dishes on the huge menu. The dining room is low-key but appealing, with crisp green and white cloth table coverings. If you like seafood, go for the shrimp in a creamy curry sauce or the fresh crab with black-bean sauce. Alternatively, consider one of the meal-size soups—beef brisket with rice noodles, say, or a vegetable clay pot preparation—or tasty versions of such Szechuan standards as spicy kung pao chicken with carrots and peanuts. Bonus: Van's has a surprisingly large wine list; scour the shelves and cold cases for a bottle.

3214 Broadway. ⓒ 210/828-8449. Reservations for large parties only. Main courses $8.95–$20. AE, DC, DISC, MC, V. Daily 11am–10pm.

INEXPENSIVE

Olmos Pharmacy (Finds) (Kids) AMERICAN   When was the last time you drank a rich chocolate malt served in a large metal container—with a glass of whipped cream on the side? Grab a stool at Olmos's Formica counter and reclaim your childhood. Olmos Pharmacy, opened in 1938, also scoops up old-fashioned ice-cream sodas, Coke or root beer floats, sundaes, banana splits . . . if it's cold, sweet, and nostalgia-inducing, they've got it. This is also the place to come for filling American and Mexican breakfasts, a vast array of tacos, and classic burgers and sandwiches, all at seriously retro prices.

3902 McCullough. ⓒ 210/822-3361. Main courses $1.50–$5.50. AE, MC, V. Mon–Fri 7am–5:30pm (fountain until 6pm); Sat 8am–5pm (fountain until 5:30pm).

Betos Latin Grill (Value) (Kids) LATIN AMERICAN/MEXICAN   The colorful, tropical shack–style Betos is a hot, hot, hot Alamo Heights spot to listen to live Latin music and drink sangria while munching *tacos al pastor*—slow-roasted pork basted with an spicy *adobado* pineapple sauce. But it's also a great place to bring kids, who can be as messy as they like on the picnic tables on the covered back deck. You'll find all the usual Tex-Mex suspects such as nachos, quesadillas, and fajitas, along with Mexican regional specialties and South American-influenced dishes. The Sunday all-you-can-eat breakfast bar ($6.95) is especially popular, featuring *chilaquiles, posole,* soups, fruit, and desserts.

7325 Broadway. ⓒ 210/930-9393. Reservations not accepted. Empanadas, tacos and sandwiches $2.40–$6.95, combination plates $7.95–$14. AE, DISC, MC, V. Mon–11am–9pm; Thurs–Sat 11am–10pm; Sun 10am–2pm.

6 Northwest

VERY EXPENSIVE

Francesca's at Sunset ⭐ SOUTHWESTERN   A menu created by chef Mark Miller of Coyote Café fame, an excellent wine list (150 bottles, including 30 by the glass), fine service, and idyllic Hill Country views from an ultra-romantic terrace—what's not to like about Francesca's at Sunset? Starters such as the wild mushroom tamale or quail on a smoked cheddar potato cake are unqualified sensations. The wild boar chops with fig mole also wins raves from diners, and I am very happy with the sea bass with smoked mussel hash. However, both the ancho honey–glazed chicken and the pepper mustard–rubbed rib eye might be a bit too hot to handle even by the chile-tolerant, so inquire about the heat level when ordering. Of course, you can always placate your palate with excellent house-made sorbets or a Jack Daniels pecan tart. Menus change seasonally.

Westin La Cantera, 16641 La Cantera Parkway. © **210/558-6500.** Reservations strongly recommended. Main courses $25–$36. AE, DC, DISC, MC, V. Tues–Thurs 6–10pm; Fri–Sat 6–11pm.

EXPENSIVE

Aldo's ITALIAN A northwest San Antonio favorite, Aldo's offers good, old-fashioned Italian food in a pretty, old-fashioned setting. You can enjoy your meal outside, on a tree-shaded patio, or inside a 100-year-old former ranch house in one of a series of Victorian-style dining rooms. The scampi Valentino—sautéed shrimp with a basil cream sauce—is a nice starter, as are the lighter steamed mussels in marinara sauce, available seasonally. A house specialty, sautéed snapper di Aldo, comes topped with fresh lump crabmeat, artichoke hearts, mushrooms, and tomatoes in a white-wine sauce.

8539 Fredericksburg Rd. © **210/696-2536.** Reservations recommended, especially on weekends. Pastas $12–$21, main courses $15–$29. AE, DC, DISC, MC, V. Mon–Thurs 11am–10pm; Fri 11am–11pm; Sat 5–11pm; Sun 5–10pm.

Bistro Time ★★ (Finds CONTINENTAL Hidden within a nondescript mall, which is itself buried in a nondescript northwest neighborhood, is one gem of a restaurant. This elegant place, with a central fountain and candlelit tables, features a series of weekly alternating menus highlighting French, Asian, American, and northern European dishes. Whichever part of the globe you visit, expect to be satisfied; when in doubt, you can't go wrong with the signature rack of lamb with blackberry peppercorn sauce. And, although I don't generally like buffets, the one served here (Tues–Fri 11:15–11:45pm) is a gourmet treat as well as a bargain (it's just $12). This is not a place to watch your weight, however: Portions are huge, and rich sauces are a specialty. Desserts are particularly hard to resist; if you're lucky, a supremely chocolaty Sacher torte might be in your stars.

Tip: The pre-6pm early-bird specials include soup, salad, and dessert with an entree for no additional charge.

5137 Fredericksburg Rd. at Callaghan. © **210/344-6626.** Reservations recommended. Main courses $17–$29. AE, DC, DISC, MC, V. Mon–Thurs 11am–2pm and 5–9pm; Fri 11am–2pm and 5–10pm; Sat 5–10pm.

7 Only in San Antonio

Some of San Antonio's best and most popular places to eat have been reviewed in this chapter, but you can be sure you'll run into San Antonians who are passionate about other personal favorites I haven't written about in this book. Taquerias are one such animal: Everyone has a fave. A couple of high-ranking ones near downtown are **Estela's,** 2200 W. Martin St. (© **210/226-2979**), which has mariachi breakfasts on Saturday and Sunday from 9:30 to 11:30am, as well as a great conjunto/Tejano jukebox; and **Taco Haven,** 1032 S. Presa St. (© **210/533-2171**), where the breakfast *migas* or *chilaquiles* will kick-start your day. In Olmos Park, **Panchito's,** 4100 McCullough (© **210/821-5338**), has 'em lining up on weekend mornings for *barbacoa* plates, heaped with two eggs, potatoes, beans, and homemade tortillas, along with the Mexican-style barbecue.

You'll also find emotions rising when the talk runs to barbecue, with many locals insisting that their favorite is the best and most authentic joint in town. Maybe it's because the meat has been smoked the longest, or because the place uses the best smoking technique, or its sauce is the tangiest—the criteria are endless and often completely arcane to outsiders. Of San Antonio's more than 90 barbecue joints, a long-time local favorite that's spawned a Texas chain is

Rudy's, 24152 I-10 West at the Leon Springs/Boerne Stage Rd. exit (✆ **210/ 698-2141**). Cowboys, bicyclists, and other city folk come from miles around for what they insist are the best pork ribs, brisket, and turkey legs in town. There's a newer Rudy's near SeaWorld at 10623 Westover Hills, corner of Hwy. 151 (✆ **210/520-5552**). **County Line,** 111 W. Crockett St., Suite 104 (✆ **210/ 229-1941**), brings the menu and the signature 1940s Texas decor of a popular Austin-based restaurant to the River Walk, although its smoker is not actually on the premises. The recent arrival in Southtown of a **Bob's Smokehouse,** 1506 S. St. Mary's St. (✆ **210/532-5711**), brought an obscure San Antonio chain that elicits die-hard local testimonials to tourists for the first time. Other Bob's locations include 5145 Fredericksburg Rd. (✆ **210/344-8401**) and 3306 Roland Ave. (✆ **210/333-9338**).

San Antonians have been coming to **Bun 'N' Barrel,** 1150 Austin Hwy. (✆ **210/828-2829**), for more than 50 years to chaw barbecue and to check out each other's cool Chevys. Hang around on a Friday night and you might even see the occasional drag race down Austin Highway; winner gets the other guy's car! This joint is in a featureless area, but it's not far from the McNay Museum or the botanical gardens. If you're short on time, catch shots of this retro classic eatery in the film *Selena*.

6

Exploring San Antonio

San Antonio's dogged preservation of its past and avid development of its future guarantee that there's something in town to suit every visitor's taste. The biggest problem with sightseeing here is figuring out how to get it all in; you can spend days in the downtown area alone and still not cover everything. The itineraries below give some suggestions on how to organize your time. Walkers will love being able to hoof it from one downtown attraction to another, but the sedentary needn't despair—or drive. One of the most visitor-friendly cities imaginable, San Antonio has excellent and inexpensive tourist transportation lines, extending to such far-flung sights as SeaWorld San Antonio and Six Flags Fiesta Texas.

Before you visit any of the paid attractions, stop in at the **San Antonio Visitor Information Center,** 317 Alamo Plaza (© **210/207-6748**), across the street from the Alamo, and ask for their SAVE San Antonio discount book, including everything from the large theme parks to some city tours and museums. Many hotels also have a stash of discount coupons for their guests.

SUGGESTED ITINERARIES

If You Have 1 Day

If your time is very limited, it makes sense to stay downtown, where most of the prime attractions are concentrated. Start your day at the **Alamo,** which tends to get more crowded as the day goes on. When you finish touring the complex, take a streetcar from Alamo Square to **HemisFair Park;** from the observation deck at the Tower of the Americas, you can see everything there is to see in town from a bird's-eye view. You'll easily spot **La Villita,** just across the road, a good place to do some picturesque—and historic—crafts shopping. Then board the streetcar again and head to the nearby **King William Historic District,** where you can pick up a self-guided walking tour at the office of the San Antonio Conservation Society. Have lunch at the historic Guenther House or, if you're up for Mexican, at Rosario's, in nearby Southtown. Trolley back to downtown, do a quick tour of the **San Fernando Cathedral,** the **Spanish Governor's Palace,** and **Market Square,** then head over to the **River Walk,** where you might catch a riverboat tour before eating at one of the riverside restaurants (Boudro's would be my pick). Alternatively, if you can manage to get tickets to anything at either the Majestic or the Arneson River theaters, eat early (again, you'll have beaten the crowds) and enjoy the show.

If You Have 2 Days

Day 1 Follow the same itinerary outlined above.

Day 2 See the San Antonio **missions** in the morning (at the least, Mission San José). In the afternoon, go to **San Antonio Museum of Art** or the **McNay** or **Witte museums.**

If you're traveling with kids, you might want to visit the **Children's Museum** first thing in the morning, then go to **SeaWorld** or **Six Flags Fiesta Texas** in the afternoon (although the Witte is terrific for kids, too).

If You Have 3 Days

Day 1   Start at the **Alamo** and then tour the rest of the **missions;** that way, you'll see the military shrine in its historic context. Spend the late afternoon at one of the **theme parks** or at one of the **museums** (the San Antonio Museum of Art, the McNay, or the Witte).

Day 2   Go to **HemisFair Park** and visit the Tower of the Americas and the Institute of Texan Cultures, then stroll around nearby **La Villita.** Afterward, head down to the **King William Historic District** and take the tour of the **Steves Homestead.** (Those looking for a more contemporary experience might add—or substitute—**Southtown** and the **Blue Star Arts Complex**) In the afternoon, enjoy a **riverboat tour** and visit the **Southwest School of Art and Craft** and, if you like cutting-edge work, **ArtPace.**

Day 3   See the **Spanish Governor's Palace** and the **San Fernando Cathedral,** then shop and have lunch at **Market Square.** In the afternoon, go to one of the **museums** you haven't yet visited or to the **San Antonio Botanical Gardens.**

If You Have 4 Days

Days 1 to 3   Follow the itinerary outlined in "If You Have 3 Days," but eliminate the attractions in the Brackenridge Park area (the Witte and the McNay museums), substituting another downtown sight or a theme park.

Day 4   Visit the attractions in the **Brackenridge Park area,** including the Japanese Tea Garden, the Witte Museum, the McNay Museum, the zoo, and the San Antonio Botanical Gardens. Some of the best restaurants in San Antonio are in this part of town.

If You Have 5 Days or More

Days 1 to 4   Follow the above 4-day itinerary, but break it up with:

Day 5   A day trip through scenic ranch country to **Bandera,** a sleepy cowboy town that will remind you you're in the Wild West. An afternoon trail ride is great, but if you have more time, book a room at one of Bandera's many dude ranches; a 2-night minimum stay is usually required.

1 The Top Attractions

DOWNTOWN AREA

The Alamo ✦✦   Visiting San Antonio without going to the Alamo is like visiting New York and not going to the Statue of Liberty. You can do it, but it would be wrong. Don't expect something dramatic, however. If you've never been to the Alamo before, you'll likely be surprised to discover that Texas's most visited site—and the symbol of its turmoil-filled history—is not only rather small, but that it also sits smack in the heart of downtown San Antonio. Still, you'll immediately recognize the graceful mission church, if only from having seen endless images of it from the moment you land in any Texas airport. Here 188 Texas volunteers turned back a much larger army—its numbers vary depending on the Texas chauvinism of the teller—of Mexican dictator Santa Anna for 13 days in March 1836. Although all the men, including pioneers Davy Crockett and Jim Bowie, were killed, their deaths were used by Sam Houston in the cry "Remember the Alamo!" to rally his troops and defeat the Mexican army at the Battle of San Jacinto a month later, securing Texas's independence.

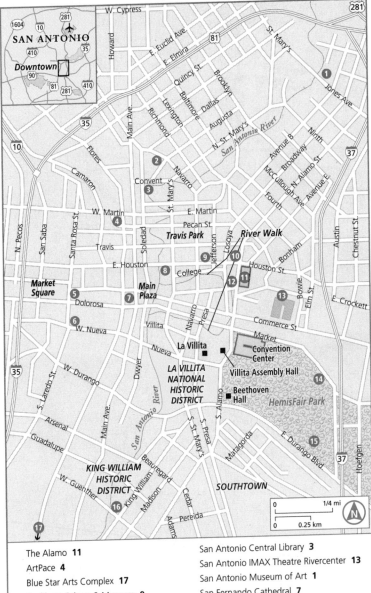

The Alamo **11**

ArtPace **4**

Blue Star Arts Complex **17**

Buckhorn Saloon & Museum **9**

Casa Navarro State Historical Park **6**

Institute of Texan Cultures **15**

Plaza Wax Museum &
    Ripley's Believe It or Not **12**

San Antonio Children's Museum **8**

San Antonio Central Library **3**

San Antonio IMAX Theatre Rivercenter **13**

San Antonio Museum of Art **1**

San Fernando Cathedral **7**

Southwest School of Art & Craft **2**

Spanish Governor's Palace **5**

Steves Homestead Museum **16**

The Texas Adventure **10**

Tower of the Americas **14**

Greater San Antonio Attractions

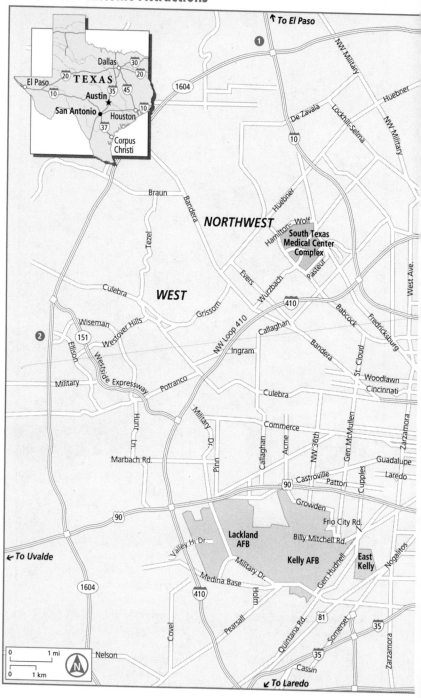

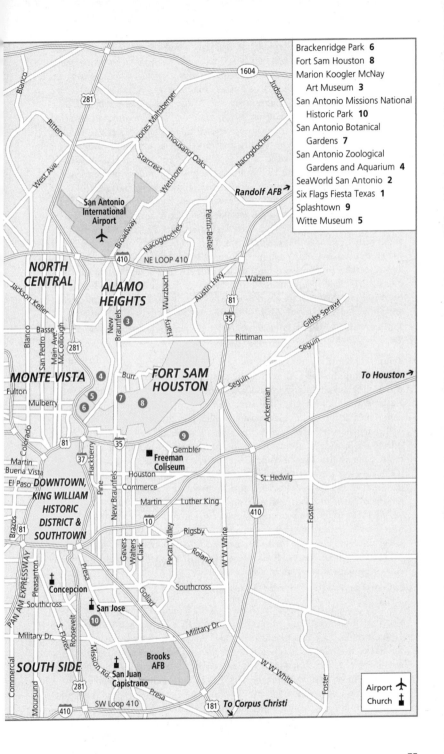

Brackenridge Park **6**
Fort Sam Houston **8**
Marion Koogler McNay
Art Museum **3**
San Antonio Missions National
Historic Park **10**
San Antonio Botanical
Gardens **7**
San Antonio Zoological
Gardens and Aquarium **4**
SeaWorld San Antonio **2**
Six Flags Fiesta Texas **1**
Splashtown **9**
Witte Museum **5**

1604

281

Bitters

Blanco

West Ave.

Jones Maltsberger

Thousand Oaks

Starcrest

Wetmore

Nacogdoches

Judson

Randolf AFB →

San Antonio
International
Airport
✈

Broadway

Nacogdoches

Perrin-Beitel

410 NE LOOP 410

**NORTH
CENTRAL**

Jackson Keller

**ALAMO
HEIGHTS**

New Braunfels

Wurzbach

Harry

Austin Hwy.

81

35

Walzem

Gibbs Sprawl

Blanco

Basse

San Pedro

Main Ave.
McCollough

281

❸

Rittiman

Seguin

MONTE VISTA

Fulton

Mulberry

❹

❺

❻

Burr

❼

❽

**FORT SAM
HOUSTON**

Seguin

Ackerman

Seguin

To Houston →

Colorado

81

37

Hackberry

35

❾

Gembler

**Freeman
Coliseum**

St. Hedwig

Foster

Martin
Buena Vista

El Paso

**DOWNTOWN,
KING WILLIAM
HISTORIC
DISTRICT &
SOUTHTOWN**

Pine

New Braunfels

Houston

Commerce

Martin   Luther King

410

Brazos

81

10

Gevers

Walters

Clark

Pecan Valley

Rigsby

Roland

W.W. White

PAN AM EXPRESSWAY

Pleasanton

Presa

Southcross

✝
Concepcion

Southcross

■ ✝ **San Jose**

❿

Military Dr.

S. Flores

Roosevelt

Goliad

Military Dr.

W.W. White

SOUTH SIDE

Commercial

Moursund

Mission Rd.

✝
■ **San Juan
Capistrano**

Presa

**Brooks
AFB**

281

410   SW Loop 410

181   **To Corpus Christi**
↘

Airport ✈
Church ■

75

The Daughters of the Republic of Texas, who saved the crumbling complex from being turned into a hotel by a New York syndicate in 1905, have long maintained it as a shrine to these fighters. More recently, however, additional emphasis has been placed on the Alamo's other historic roles, including as a Native American burial ground. Interestingly, the Alamo was actually founded on a nearby site in 1718 as the Mission San Antonio de Valero, and many converted Indians from a variety of tribes lived and died there. The complex was secularized by the end of the 18th century and leased out to a Spanish cavalry unit; by the time the famous battle took place, it had been abandoned. **A Wall of History,** erected in the late 1990s, provides a good chronology of these events.

Little remains of the original mission today; only the **Long Barrack** (formerly the *convento,* or living quarters for the missionaries) and the **mission church** are still here. The former houses a museum detailing the history of Texas in general and the battle in particular; the latter includes artifacts of the Alamo fighters, along with an information desk and small gift shop. A larger **museum** and gift shop are at the back of the complex. There's also a peaceful **garden** and an excellent **research library** (closed Sun) on the grounds. All in all, though, the complex is fairly small. You won't need to spend more than an hour here. Interesting historical presentations are given every half hour by Alamo staffers; for private, after-hour tours, phone ✆ **210/225-1391,** ext. 34.

300 Alamo Plaza. ✆ 210/225-1391. www.thealamo.org. Free admission (donations welcome). Mon–Sat 9am–5:30pm; Sun 10am–5:30pm. Closed Dec 24 and 25. Streetcar: Red and Blue lines.

King William Historic District ⭐   San Antonio's first suburb, King William was settled in the late 19th century by prosperous German merchants who displayed their wealth through extravagant homes and named the 25-block area after Kaiser Wilhelm of Prussia. (The other residents of San Antonio were rather less complimentary about this German area, which they dubbed "Sauerkraut Bend.")

The neighborhood fell into disrepair for a few decades, but you'd never know it from the pristine condition of most of the houses here today. The area has gotten so popular that tour buses have been restricted after certain hours. Anyway, it's much more pleasant to stroll up and down tree-shaded King William Street, gawking at the beautifully landscaped, magnificent mansions. Stop at the headquarters of the San Antonio Conservation Society, 107 King William St. (✆ **210/224-6163;** www.saconservation.org), and pick up a self-guided walking tour booklet outside the gate. If you go at a leisurely pace, the stroll should take about an hour. Only the Steves Homestead Museum (see "More Attractions," below) and the Guenther House (see chapter 5) are open to the public; figure two more hours if you plan to visit both.

East bank of the river just south of downtown. Streetcar: Blue line.

La Villita National Historic District ⭐   Developed by European settlers along the higher east bank of the San Antonio River in the late 18th and early 19th centuries, La Villita (the Little Village) was on the proverbial wrong side of the tracks until natural flooding of the west-bank settlements made it the fashionable place to live. It fell back into poverty by the beginning of the 20th century, only to be revitalized in the late 1930s by artists and craftspeople and the San Antonio Conservation Society. Now boutiques, crafts shops, and restaurants occupy this historic district, which resembles a Spanish/Mexican village, replete with shaded patios, plazas, brick-and-tile streets, and some of the settlement's original adobe structures. You can see (but not enter) the house of General Cós, the Mexican military leader who surrendered to the Texas revolutionary army in

1835, or attend a performance at the Arneson River Theatre (see "The Performing Arts," chapter 8). It'll only take you about 20 minutes to do a brisk walk-through, unless you're an inveterate shopper—in which case, all bets are off.

Bounded by Durango, Navarro, and Alamo sts. and the River Walk. ℂ 210/207-8610. www.lavillita.com. Free admission. Shops, daily 10am–6pm. Closed Thanksgiving, Dec 25, Jan 1. Bus: 40. Streetcar: Red, Purple, and Blue lines.

Market Square 𝕒   It may not be quite as colorful as it was when live chickens squawked around overflowing, makeshift vegetable stands, but Market Square will still transport you south of the border. Stalls in the indoor El Mercado sell everything from onyx paperweights and manufactured serapes to high-quality crafts from the interior of Mexico. Across the street, the Farmer's Market, which formerly housed the produce market, has carts with more modern goods. If you can tear yourself away from the merchandise, take a look around at the buildings in the complex; some date back to the late 1800s.

Bring your appetite along with your wallet: In addition to two Mexican restaurants (**La Margarita** and **Mi Tierra;** see chapter 5), almost every weekend sees the emergence of food stalls selling specialties such as gorditas (chubby corn cakes topped with a variety of goodies) or funnel cakes (fried dough sprinkled with powdered sugar). Most of the city's Hispanic festivals are held here, and mariachis usually stroll the square. The Alameda National Center for Latino Arts and Culture, a Smithsonian Institution affiliate scheduled to open in the Centro des Artes building in 2004, should provide a historic context to an area that can seem pretty touristy—though no more so than any Mexican border town.

Bounded by Commerce, Santa Rosa, Dolorosa, and I-35. ℂ 210/207-8600. Free admission. El Mercado and Farmer's Market Plaza, June–Aug daily 10am–8pm; Sept–May daily 10am–6pm; restaurants and some of the shops open later. Closed Thanksgiving, Dec 25, Jan 1, Easter. Streetcar: Red, Purple, and Yellow lines.

The River Walk (Paseo del Río) 𝕒𝕒𝕒   Just a few steps below the streets of downtown San Antonio is another world, alternately soothing and exhilarating, depending on where you venture. The quieter areas of the 2½ paved miles of winding riverbank, shaded by cypresses, oaks, and willows, exude a tropical, exotic aura; the River Square and South Bank sections, chock-a-block with sidewalk cafes, tony restaurants, bustling bars, high-rise hotels, and even a huge shopping mall, have a festive, sometimes frenetic feel. Tour boats, water taxis, and floating picnic barges regularly ply the river, and local parades and festivals fill its banks with revelers.

Although plans to cement over the river after a disastrous flood in 1921 were stymied, it wasn't until the late 1930s that the federal Works Project Administration (WPA) carried out architect Robert Hugman's designs for the waterway, installing cobblestone walks, arched bridges, and entrance steps from various street-level locations. And it wasn't until the late 1960s, when the River Walk proved to be one of the most popular attractions of the HemisFair exposition, that its commercial development began in earnest.

There's a real danger of the River Walk becoming overdeveloped—new restaurants, hotels, and entertainment complexes are opening at an alarming pace, and the crush of bodies along the busiest sections can be claustrophobic in the summer heat—but plenty of quieter spots still exist. And if you're caught up in the sparkling lights reflected on the water on a breeze-swept night, you might forget there was anyone else around.

All the streetcars stop somewhere along the river's route. The Riverwalk Streetcar Station at Commerce and Losoya is handicapped-accessible.

The Alamo: The Movie(s)

Volumes—well, at least *one* volume, Frank Thompson's *Alamo Movies*— have been devoted to the plethora of films featuring the events that occurred at San Antonio's most famous site. Some outtakes:

Most famous movie about the Alamo not actually shot at the Alamo: *The Alamo* (1959), starring John Wayne as Davy Crockett. Although it has no San Antonio presence, it was shot in Texas. Wayne had considered shooting the film in Mexico, but was told it wouldn't be distributed in Texas if he did.

Latest controversy-ridden attempt to tell the story of the Alamo: A 2003 Disney version with a script by John Sayles which may or may not be directed by Ron Howard. It's being filmed near Austin.

Most accurate celluloid depiction of the Alamo story (and also the largest): *Alamo—The Price of Freedom,* showing at the San Antonio IMAX Theater Rivercenter. According to writer and historian Stephen Harrigan in an interview on National Public Radio, it's "90% accurate."

Least controversial film featuring the Alamo: *Miss Congeniality,* starring Sandra Bullock and Benjamin Bratt. A beauty pageant moderated by William Shatner takes place in front of the shrine to the Texas martyrs.

San Antonio Museum of Art ★★   This attraction may not be top-listed by everyone, but I enjoy doable (read: not overwhelmingly large) museums with interesting architecture and collections related to the cities in which they're located—and this one definitely fits the bill on all those counts. Several castle-like buildings of the 1904 Lone Star Brewery were gutted, connected, and transformed into a visually exciting exhibition space in 1981; you also get terrific views of downtown from the multi-windowed crosswalk between the structures. Although holdings range from early Egyptian, Greek, Oceanic, and Asian (a new wing devoted to that genre will debut in the spring of 2004) to 19th- and 20th-century American, for me the prime reason to come is the $11 million Nelson A. Rockefeller Center for Latin American Art, opened in 1998. This 30,000-square-foot wing hosts the most comprehensive collection of Latin American art in the United States, with pre-Columbian, folk, Spanish colonial, and contemporary works. You'll see everything here from magnificently ornate altarpieces to a whimsical Day of the Dead tableau. Computer stations add historical perspective to the collection, which is a nationwide resource for Latino culture. If any of this sounds appealing to you, allot at least two hours for your visit.

200 W. Jones Ave. ⓒ 210/978-8100. www.sa-museum.org. Admission $6 adults, $5 seniors, $4 students with ID, $1.75 children 4–11; children under 4 free. General admission free on Tues 3–9pm. (fee for some special exhibits). Tues 10am–9pm; Wed–Sat 10am–5pm; Sun noon–5pm. Bus: 9, 11, and 14.

ALAMO HEIGHTS AREA

Marion Koogler McNay Art Museum ★★   Well worth a detour from downtown, this museum is one of my favorite places in the city to visit. It's got a knockout setting on a hill north of Brackenridge Park with a forever view of the city, and it's in a sprawling Spanish Mediterranean–style mansion (built 1929) so picturesque that it's constantly used as a backdrop for weddings and photo shoots. The McNay doesn't have a world-class art collection, but it has a good one, with at least one work by most American and European masters of the last two centuries. And the Tobin Collection of Theatre Arts, including costumes, set designs, and rare books, is outstanding. The McNay also hosts major traveling shows. It'll take you at least an hour to go through this place at a leisurely pace, longer if it's cool enough for you to stroll the beautiful 23-acre grounds dotted with sculpture and stunning landscaping. It's also well worth taking the time to view the 15-minute orientation film about oil heiress and artist Marion Koogler McNay, who established the museum. And, of course, there's a gift shop.

6000 N. New Braunfels Ave. ⓒ 210/824-5368. www.mcnayart.org. Free admission ($5 suggested donation; fee for special exhibits). Tues–Sat 10am–5pm; Sun noon–5pm. Docent tours Sun at 2pm Oct–May. Closed Jan 1, July 4, Thanksgiving, Dec 25. Bus: 11.

Witte Museum ⭐ *Kids*   A family museum that adults will enjoy as much as kids, the Witte focuses on Texas history, natural science, and anthropology, but often ranges as far afield as the Berlin Wall or the history of bridal gowns in the United States. Your senses will be engaged along with your intellect: You might hear animal cries as you crouch in south Texas thorn brush, or feel rough-hewn stone carved with Native American pictographs beneath your feet. Children especially like exhibits devoted to mummies and dinosaurs, as well as the EcoLab, where live Texas critters range from tarantulas to tortoises. But the biggest draw for kids is the terrific HEB Science Treehouse, a four-level, 15,000-square-foot science center that sits behind the museum on the banks of the San Antonio River; its hands-on activities are geared to all ages. Also on the grounds are a butterfly and hummingbird garden and three restored historic homes.

3801 Broadway (adjacent to Brackenridge Park). ⓒ 210/357-1900. www.wittemuseum.org. Admission $5.95 adults, $4.95 seniors, $3.95 children 4–11; children under 4 free. Free on Tues 3–9pm. Mon and Wed–Sat 10am–5pm (until 6pm June–Aug); Tues 10am–9pm; Sun noon–5pm (until 7pm June to early Aug). Closed Thanksgiving, Dec 25. Bus: 9.

SOUTH SIDE

San Antonio Missions National Historic Park ⭐⭐   Remember the Alamo? Well, it was originally just the first of five missions established by the Franciscans along the San Antonio River to Christianize the native population. The four missions that now fall under the aegis of the National Parks Department are still active parishes, run in cooperation with the Archdiocese of San Antonio. But the missions were more than churches; they were complex communities. The Parks Department has assigned each of them an interpretive theme to educate visitors about the roles they played in early San Antonio society. You can visit them separately, but if you have the time, see them all; they were built uncharacteristically close together and—now that you don't have to walk there or ride a horse—it shouldn't take you more than two or three hours to see them. Currently, you have to follow the brown signs that direct you from the Alamo to the 5½-mile mission trail that begins at Mission Concepción and winds its way south through the city streets to Mission Espada, but in the late 1990s ground was broken for the $17.7 million Mission Trails Project, designed to create a 12-mile hike-and-bike route along the San Antonio River and improve signage along the driving route. Parts of it are already operational, but the entire project won't be completed for many years.

The first of the missions you'll come to as you head south, **Concepción,** 807 Mission Rd. at Felisa, was built in 1731. The oldest unrestored Texas mission, Concepción looks much as it did 200 years ago. We tend to think of religious sites as somber and austere, but traces of color on the facade and restored wall paintings inside show how cheerful this one originally was.

San José ✦✦, 6539 San José Dr. at Mission Road, established in 1720, was the largest, best known, and most beautiful of the Texas missions. It was reconstructed to give visitors a complete picture of life in a mission community—right down to the granary, mill, and Indian pueblo. The beautiful Rose Window is a big attraction, and popular mariachi masses are held here every Sunday at noon (come early if you want a seat). This is also the site of the missions' excellent visitor center. If you're going to visit only one of the missions, this is it.

Moved from an earlier site in east Texas to its present location in 1731, **San Juan Capistrano**, 9102 Graf at Ashley, doesn't have the grandeur of the missions to the north—the larger church intended for it was never completed—but the original simple chapel and the wilder setting give it a peaceful, spiritual aura. A short (³⁄₁₀ mile) interpretive trail, with a number of overlook platforms, winds through the woods to the banks of the old river channel.

The southernmost mission in the San Antonio chain, **San Francisco de la Espada** ✦, 10040 Espada Rd., also has an ancient, isolated feel, although the beautifully maintained church shows just how vital it still is to the local community. Be sure to visit the Espada Aqueduct, part of the mission's original *acequia* (irrigation ditch) system, about 1 mile north of the mission. Dating from 1740, it's one of the oldest Spanish aqueducts in the United States.

Headquarters: 2202 Roosevelt Ave. ✆ 210/534-8833. Visitors Center: 6701 San José Dr. at Mission Rd. ✆ 210/932-1001. www.nps.gov/saan. Free admission (donations accepted). All the missions open daily 9am–5pm. Closed Thanksgiving, Dec 25, Jan 1. National Park Ranger tours daily. Bus: 42 stops at Mission San José (and near Concepción).

FAR NORTHWEST

Six Flags Fiesta Texas ✦ *Kids*   Every year brings another thrill ride to this theme park, set on 200-acres in an abandoned limestone quarry and surrounded by 100-foot cliffs. In 2002, the Scooby Doo Ghostblasters scarefest joined the Superman Krypton Coaster, nearly a mile of twisted steel with six inversions; the Rattler, the world's highest and fastest wooden roller coaster; the 60-mph-plus Poltergeist roller coaster; and Scream!, a 20-story space shot and turbo drop, to name just a few. Laser games and virtual reality simulators complete the technophile picture. Feeling more primal? Wet 'n' wild attractions include the Lone Star Lagoon, the state's largest wave pool; the Texas Treehouse, a five-story drenchfest whose surprises include a 1,000-gallon cowboy hat that tips over periodically to soak the unsuspecting; and Bugs' White Water Rapids.

If you want to avoid both sogginess and adrenaline overload, there are a vast variety of food booths, shops, crafts demonstrations, and live shows—everything from 1950s musical revues to big-name concerts (by the likes of Trisha Yearwood, Alabama, and the Beach Boys) in summer. This theme park still has some local character, dating back to the days when it was plain old Fiesta Texas: Themed areas include a Hispanic village, a western town, and a German town. But when it came under the aegis of Six Flags—a Time Warner company—such Looney Tunes cartoon characters as Tweety Bird became ubiquitous, especially in the endless souvenir shops.

17000 I-10W (corner of I-10W and Loop 1604). ✆ 800/473-4378 or 210/697-5050. www.sixflags.com. Admission $37 adults, $25 seniors, $23 children under 48 in., children under 3 free. Discounted 2-day and season passes available. Parking $7 per day. Opening hours are 8–10am to 10pm, depending on the season. The park is generally open daily late May to mid Aug; Sat–Sun from Mar–May and Sept–Oct; closed Nov–Feb. Call ahead or visit website for current information. Bus: 94. Take exit 555 on I-10W.

WEST SIDE

SeaWorld San Antonio ⊛ *Kids*   Leave it to Texas to provide Shamu, the performing killer whale, with his most spacious digs: At 250 acres, this SeaWorld is the largest of the Anheuser Busch–owned parks, which also makes it the largest marine theme park in the world. If you're a theme park fan (I'm not), you're likely to find the walk-through habitats where you can watch penguins, sea lions, sharks, tropical fish, and flamingos do their thing fascinating, but the aquatic acrobatics at such stadium shows as Shamu Visions (combining live action and video close-ups) might be even more fun. The humans hold their own with an impressive water-skiing exhibition on a 12½-acre lake.

You needn't get frustrated just looking at all that water: There are loads of places here to get wet. The Lost Lagoon has a huge wave pool and water slides aplenty, and the Texas Splashdown flume ride and the Rio Loco river-rapids ride also offer splashy fun. Younger children can cavort in Shamu's Happy Harbor and the "L'il Gators" section of the Lost Lagoon.

Nonaquatic activities abound, too. SeaWorld's latest addition is the multimillion-dollar Steel Eel, a huge "hypercoaster" that starts out with a 150-foot dive at 65 mph, followed by several bouts of weightlessness. It's a follow-up to The Great White, the Southwest's first inverted coaster—which means riders will go head-over-heels during 2,500 feet of loops (don't eat before either of them). It's well worth sticking around for the Summer Night Magic multimedia laser shows or one of the high-season concerts—if you're not too tuckered from the rides.

10500 SeaWorld Dr., 16 miles northwest of downtown San Antonio at Ellison Dr. and Westover Hills Blvd. ✆ 210/523-3611. www.seaworld.com. 1-day pass $38 adults, $3 off adult price for seniors (55 and over), $28 children 3–11; children under 3 free. Discounted 2-day and season passes available. Parking $7 per day. Open Mar–May, Fri 10am–6pm, Sat–Sun 10am–8pm; June to mid-Aug, daily 10am–9pm Mon–Sat, until 11pm Sun; mid-Aug to late Nov, Sat 10am–6pm, Sun 10am–8pm. Closed late Nov to early Mar. Call ahead or check website for current information. Bus: 64. From Loop 410 or from Hwy. 90W, exit Hwy. 151W to the park.

2 More Attractions

DOWNTOWN AREA

ArtPace   San Antonio's cutting-edge contemporary art gallery features rotating shows displaying the work of artists selected by a prestigious international panel for 3-month residencies at the facility. One artist must be from Texas, one from anywhere else in the United States, and one from anywhere else in the world. The result has been a fascinating mélange, including everything from conceptual pieces like a roof terrace covered with 600 sunflowers, a gallery piled with 5 tons of salt, and a refrigerator stocked with frozen snakes, to more or less representational photographs, paintings, and sculptures. Lecture series by the artists as well as public forums to discuss the work have also helped make this a very stimulating art space.

445 N. Main Ave. ✆ 210/212-4900. www.artpace.org. Free admission. Wed and Fri–Sun noon–5pm; Thurs noon–8pm. Check local listings or call for lectures and other special events. Streetcar: Purple line.

Blue Star Arts Complex ⊛   This huge former warehouse in Southtown hosts a collection of working studios and galleries, along with a performance space for the Jump-Start theater company. The 11,000-square-foot artist-run Contemporary Art Museum is its anchor. The style of work varies from gallery to gallery—you'll see everything from primitive-style folk art to feminist photography—but the level of professionalism is generally high. One of the most interesting spaces is SAY Si, featuring exhibitions by talented neighborhood high school students that might include collages or book art. A number of galleries are devoted to (or have sections purveying) arty gift items such as jewelry, picture frames, and crafts.

116 Blue Star (bordered by Probandt, Blue Star, and South Alamo sts. and the San Antonio River) ⓒ 210/227-6960. www.bluestarartspace.org. Free admission ($2 suggested donation). Hours vary from gallery to gallery; most are open Wed–Sun noon–6pm, with some opening at 10am. Streetcar: Blue line.

Buckhorn Saloon & Museum *Overrated*   If you like your educational experiences accompanied by a cold one, this is the place for you. With its huge stuffed animals, mounted fish, and wax museum version of history, this collection fulfills every out-of-stater's stereotype of what a Texas museum might be like. It's not nearly as funky as it was when it was in the old Lone Star brewery—all those dead animals seem out of place in this modern, new space—but it's still got exhibits like the church made out of 50,000 matchsticks and pictures designed from rattlesnake rattles. The facility includes a re-creation of the turn-of-the-century Buckhorn saloon, a curio shop, and a transported historic bar. Lots of people seem to like this place, but I think it's a bit pricey for what you get.

318 E. Houston St. ⓒ 210/247-4000. www.buckhornmuseum.com. Admission $10 adults, $9 seniors (55 and up), $7.50 children 3–11. Sun–Thurs 10am–5pm; Fri–Sat 10am–6pm (later hours in summer). Streetcar: Red and Blue lines.

Casa Navarro State Historic Site   A key player in Texas's transition from Spanish territory to American state, José Antonio Navarro was the Mexican mayor of San Antonio in 1821, a signer of the 1836 declaration of Texas independence, and the only native Texan to take part in the convention that ratified the annexation of Texas to the United States in 1845. His former living quarters, built around 1850, are an interesting amalgam of the architectural fashions of his time: The restored office, house, and separate kitchen, constructed of adobe and limestone, blend elements from Mexican, French, German, and pioneer styles. Guided tours and demonstrations are available; call ahead to inquire.

228 S. Laredo St. ⓒ 210/226-4801. www.tpwd.state.tx.us/park/jose. Admission $2 adults, $1 children 6–12; children under 6 free. Wed–Sun 10am–4pm. Streetcar: Purple line.

Institute of Texan Cultures *Kids*   It's the rare visitor who won't discover here that his or her ethnic group has contributed to the history of Texas: 26 different ethnic and cultural groups are represented in the imaginative, hands-on displays of this educational center, which is one of three campuses of the University of Texas at San Antonio. Outbuildings include a one-room schoolhouse and a windmill, and the multimedia Dome Theater presents images of Texas on 36 screens. There are always a variety of kid-friendly shows and events such as pioneer life re-enactments, holography exhibits, ghost tale storytellers at Halloween, and the like; phone or check the institute's website for a current schedule. An excellent photo archive here, open to the public by appointment, holds more than 3 million images. Call ⓒ 210/458-2298 for information on using it.

801 S. Bowie St. (at Durango St. in HemisFair Park). ⓒ 210/458-2300. www.texancultures.utsa.edu. Admission $5 adults, $2 seniors and children 3–12. Tues–Sun 9am–5pm. Dome shows presented at 10:15am, noon, 2pm, and 3:30pm. Closed Thanksgiving, Dec 25, Easter. Streetcar: Yellow and Purple lines.

Impressions

We have no city, except, perhaps, New Orleans, that can vie, in point of picturesque interest that attaches to odd and antiquated foreignness, with San Antonio.

—Frederick Law Olmsted, *A Journey Through Texas* (1853)

San Antonio Central Library   San Antonio's main library, opened in the mid-1990s at a cost of $38 million, has a number of important holdings (including part of the Hertzberg Circus Collection, scattered when it lost its museum home in 2001) but it is most notable for its architecture. Ricardo Legorreta, renowned for his buildings throughout Mexico, created a wildly colorful and whimsical public space that people apparently love to enter—by the second month after the library opened, circulation had gone up 95%. The boxy building, painted what has been called "enchilada red," is designed like a hacienda around an internal courtyard. A variety of skylights, windows, and wall colors (including bright purples and yellows) affords a different perspective from each of the six floors. A gallery offers monthly exhibits of paintings, photography, textiles, and more.

600 Soledad. (C) **210/207-2500.** www.santantonio.gov. Free admission. Mon–Thurs 9am–9pm; Fri–Sat 9am–5pm; Sun 11am–5pm. Streetcar: Blue line.

San Fernando Cathedral 🌟   Construction of a church on this site, overlooking what was once the town's central plaza, was begun in 1738 by San Antonio's original Canary Island settlers and completed in 1749. Part of the early structure—the oldest cathedral sanctuary in the United States and the oldest parish church in Texas—is incorporated into the magnificent Gothic revival–style cathedral built in 1868. Jim Bowie got married here, and General Santa Anna raised the flag of "no quarter" from the roof during the siege of the Alamo in 1836. The cathedral underwent major interior and exterior renovations in 2002; its most impressive new addition, a 24-foot-high gilded *retablo* (gradine), is slated to be unveiled sometime after Easter 2003.

115 Main Plaza. (C) **210/227-1297.** www.sfcathedral.org. Free admission. Daily 6am–7pm; gift shop Mon–Fri 9am–4:30pm; Sat until 5pm. Streetcar: Purple and Yellow lines.

Spanish Governor's Palace 🌟 *Finds*   Never actually a palace, this 1749 adobe structure formerly served as the residence and headquarters for the captain of the Spanish presidio. It became the seat of Texas government in 1772, when San Antonio was made capital of the Spanish province of Texas and, by the time it was purchased by the city in 1928, it had served as a tailor's shop, barroom, and schoolhouse. The building, with high ceilings crossed by protruding viga beams, is beautiful in its simplicity, and the 10 rooms crowded with period furnishings paint a vivid portrait of upper-class life in a rough-hewn society. It's interesting to see how the other half lived in an earlier era, and I love to sit out on the tree-shaded, cobblestone patio, listening to the burbling of the stone fountain.

105 Plaza de Armas. (C) **210/224-0601.** Admission $1.50 adults, 75¢ children 7–13; children under 7 free. Mon–Sat 9am–5pm; Sun 10am–5pm. Closed Dec 25, Thanksgiving, Jan 1, San Jacinto Day (during Fiesta week). Streetcar: Purple line.

Steves Homestead Museum   Built in 1876 for lumber magnate Edward Steves by prominent San Antonio architect Alfred Giles, this Victorian mansion was restored by the San Antonio Conservation Society, to whom it was willed by Steves's granddaughter. One of the only houses in the King William Historic District open to the public, it gives a fascinating glimpse into the lifestyles of the rich and locally famous of the late 19th century. You can't enter without taking a docent-led tour, which is fine: You wouldn't want to miss the great gossip about the Steves family that the Society's very knowledgeable volunteers pass along. The 30- to 45-minute tours are given when enough visitors arrive.

509 King William St. (C) **210/225-5924** or 210/227-9160. www.saconservation.org. Admission $3 adults; children under 12 free. Daily 10am–4:15pm (last tour at 3:30). Streetcar: Blue line.

Southwest School of Art and Craft ⚔   A stroll along the River Walk to the northern corner of downtown will lead you into another world: a rare French-designed cloister where contemporary crafts are now being created. An exhibition gallery and artist studios-cum-classrooms (not open to visitors) occupy the garden-filled grounds of the first girl's school in San Antonio, established by the Ursuline order in the mid–19th century. Learn about both the school and the historic site at the Visitors Center Museum, opened in 2001 in the First Academy Building. The Ursuline Sales Gallery carries unique crafts items, most made by the school's artists. You can enjoy a nice, light lunch in the Copper Kitchen Restaurant (weekdays 11:30am–2pm, closed national holidays). The adjacent Navarro Campus, built in the late 1990s, is not as architecturally interesting, but it's worth stopping there for its large contemporary art gallery.

300 Augusta. ✆ 210/224-1848. www.swschool.org. Free admission. Mon–Sat 9am–5pm (galleries); Mon–Sat 10–5 (gift shop and museum). Streetcar: Blue line.

Tower of the Americas ⚔   For a quick take on the lay of the land, just circle the eight panoramic panels on the observation level of the Tower of the Americas. The 750-foot-high tower was built for the HemisFair in 1968; the deck sits at the equivalent of 59 stories and is lit for spectacular night viewing. The tower also hosts a rotating restaurant with surprisingly decent food (for the revolving genre) as well as a thankfully stationary cocktail lounge.

600 HemisFair Park. ✆ 210/207-8616. Admission $3 adults, $2 seniors, $1 children 4–11; children under 4 free. Sun–Thurs 9am–10pm; Fri–Sat 9am–11pm. Streetcar: Yellow and Purple lines.

ALAMO HEIGHTS AREA

San Antonio Zoological Gardens and Aquarium *(Kids)*   I want to like this zoo, considered one of the top facilities in the country because of its conservation efforts and its successful breeding programs (it produced the first white rhino in the U.S.). Home to more than 700 species, it has one of the largest animal collections in the United States. But, although the zoo has expanded and upgraded its exhibits many times since it opened in 1914, the cages are small, the landscaping looks droopy, and some of the animals seem depressed. Still, kids who haven't recently been to SeaWorld or the San Diego Zoo will get a kick out of many critters (the Lory Encounter is especially popular), and parents will appreciate the fact that they won't run into an expensive gift shop around every corner.

3903 N. St. Mary's St. in Brackenridge Park. ✆ 210/734-7183. www.sazoo-aq.org. Admission $7 adults, $5 seniors 62 and over and children 3–11; children under 3 free. Boat rides $1. Daily 9am–5pm (until 6pm in summer). Bus: 8.

FORT SAM HOUSTON AREA

Fort Sam Houston   Since 1718, when the armed Presidio de Béxar was established to defend the Spanish missions, the military has played a key role in San Antonio's development; it remains one of the largest employers in town today. The 3,434-acre Fort Sam Houston affords visitors an unusual opportunity to view the city's military past (the first military flight in history took off from the fort's spacious parade grounds) in the context of its military present—the fort currently hosts the Army Medical Command and the headquarters of the Fifth Army. Most of its historic buildings are still in use and thus off-limits, but three are open to the public. The **Fort Sam Houston Museum,** 1210 Stanley Rd., Bldg. 123 (✆ **210/221-1311;** admission free, open Wed–Sun 10am–4pm),

details the history of the armed forces in Texas with a special focus on San Antonio. The **U.S. Army Medical Department Museum,** 2310 Stanley Rd., Bldg.
1046 (© **210/221-6277;** admission free; open Tues–Sun 10am–4pm), displays
army medical equipment and American prisoner-of-war memorabilia. Free
self-guided tour maps of the historic sites are available at the gift shop in the
Quadrangle ⭐, 1400 E. Grayson St. (© **210/221-0015;** admission free, open
Mon–Fri 8am–5pm, Sat–Sun noon–5pm). This impressive 1876 limestone
structure, the oldest on the base, is centered on a brick clock tower and encloses
a grassy square where peacocks, deer, and rabbits roam freely. The Apache chief
Geronimo was held captive here for 40 days in 1886.

Grayson St. and New Braunfels Ave., about 2½ miles northeast of downtown. © **210/221-1151** (public
affairs). http://fshtx.army.mil. Bus: 15 (Fort Sam Houston). Admission free; open Mon–Fri 8am–4pm, Sat–Sun
noon–5pm.

3 Parks & Gardens

Brackenridge Park ⭐   With its rustic stone bridges and winding walkways,
the city's main park, opened in 1899, has a charming, old-fashioned feel, and
serves as a popular center for such recreational activities as golf, polo, biking, and
picnicking. I especially like the **Japanese Tea Garden** ⭐ (also known as the
Japanese Sunken Garden), created in 1917 by prison labor to beautify an abandoned cement quarry, one of the largest in the world in the 1880s and 1890s.
(The same quarry furnished cement rock for the state capitol in Austin.) You can
still see a brick smokestack and a number of the old lime kilns among the beautiful flower arrangements, lusher than those in most Japanese gardens. After Pearl
Harbor, the site was officially renamed the Chinese Sunken Garden, and a Chi-
nese-style entryway added on; not until 1983 was the original name restored. Just
to the southwest, a bowl of limestone cliffs found to have natural acoustic properties was turned into the **Sunken Garden Theater** (see chapter 8, "The Performing Arts"). A 60-foot-high waterfall and water lily–laced ponds are among
its lures. Across from the entrance to the **San Antonio Zoological Gardens** (see
above), you can buy tickets for the **Brackenridge Eagle** (© **210/736-9534**), a
miniature train that replicates an 1863 model. The pleasant 2-mile ride through
the park takes about 20 minutes (tickets $2.25 for adults, $1.75 for children
3–11; opens 9:30 daily, closes a half hour after zoo gate closes).

Main entrance 2800 block of N. Broadway. © **210/207-3000.** Open daily dawn–dusk. Bus: 8.

HemisFair Park   Built for the 1968 HemisFair, an exposition celebrating the
250th anniversary of the founding of San Antonio, this urban oasis boasts **water
gardens** and a **wood-and-sand playground** constructed by children (near the

---

(Fun Fact **Did You Know?**

- Elmer Doolin, the original manufacturer of Fritos corn chips, bought
  the original recipe from a San Antonio restaurant in 1932 for $100. He
  sold the first batch from the back of his Model-T Ford.
- *Wings,* a silent World War I epic that won the first Academy Award for
  best picture in 1927, was filmed in San Antonio. The film marked the
  debut of Gary Cooper, who was on screen for a total of 102 seconds.
- Lyndon and Lady Bird Johnson were married in San Antonio's St. Mark's
  Episcopal Church.

Alamo St. entrance). Among its indoor diversions are the **Institute of Texan Cultures** and the **Tower of the Americas** (both detailed above). Be sure to walk over to the Henry B. Gonzales Convention Center and take a look at the striking mosaic **mural** by Mexican artist Juan O'Gorman. **The Schultze House Cottage Garden** ⟨★⟩, created and maintained by Master Gardeners of Bexar County, is also worth checking out for its heirloom plants, varietals, tropicals, and xeriscape area; it's located at 514 HemisFair Park, behind the Federal Building.

Bounded by Alamo, Bowie, Market, and Durango sts. No phone. Bus: 40. Streetcar: Blue, Yellow, and Purple lines.

San Antonio Botanical Gardens ⟨★⟩ Take a horticultural tour of Texas at this gracious 38-acre garden, encompassing everything from south Texas scrub to Hill Country wildflowers. Fountains, pools, paved paths, and examples of Texas architecture provide visual contrast to the flora. The formal gardens include a garden for the blind, a Japanese garden, an herb garden, a biblical garden, and a children's garden. Perhaps most outstanding is the $6.9 million Lucile Halsell Conservatory complex, a series of greenhouses replicating a variety of tropical and desert environments. The 1896 Sullivan Carriage House, built by Alfred Giles and moved stone-by-stone from its original downtown site, serves as the entryway to the gardens. It houses a gift shop (ⓒ **210/829-1227**) and a restaurant offering salads, quiches, sandwiches, and outrageously rich deserts, open Tues to Sun from 11am to 2pm.

555 Funston. ⓒ **210/207-3255**. www.sabot.org. Admission $4 adults, $2 seniors and military, $1 children 3–13, children under 3 free. Daily 9am–5pm. Closed Dec 25, Jan 1. Bus: 11.

4 Especially for Kids

Without a doubt, the prime spots for kids in San Antonio are **SeaWorld** and **Six Flags Fiesta Texas.** They'll also like the hands-on, interactive **Witte Museum** and the various ethnic pride kids' programs at the **Institute of Texas Cultures.** There's a children's area in the **zoo,** which vends food packets so people of all ages can feed the animals. The third floor of the main branch of the **San Antonio Public Library** is devoted to children, who get to use their own catalogs and search tools. Story hours are offered regularly, and there are occasional puppet shows.

In addition to these sights, detailed in "The Top Attractions" and "More Attractions" sections, above, and the **Magik Theatre** (p. 109) the following should also appeal to the sandbox set and up.

Plaza Wax Museum & Ripley's Believe It or Not ⟨★⟩ Adults may get the bigger charge out of the waxy stars—Dustin Hoffman and Dallas Cowboy coach Tom Landry are among the latest to be added to an impressive array—and some of the oddities collected by the globe-trotting Mr. Ripley, but there's plenty for kids to enjoy at this two-fer attraction. The walk-through wax Theater of Horrors, although tame compared to *Friday the Thirteenth*–type adventures, usually elicits some shudders. At Believe It Or Not, youngsters generally get a kick out of learning about people around the world whose habits—such as sticking nails through their noses—are even weirder than their own.

301 Alamo Plaza. ⓒ **210/224-9299**. www.plazawaxmuseum.com. Either attraction $12 adults, $4.95 children 4–12; both attractions $16 adults, $7.95 children 4–12. Memorial Day to Labor Day, daily 9am–10pm; remainder of the year, Sun–Thurs 9am–7pm, Fri–Sat 9am–10pm (ticket office closes 1 hr. before listed closing times). Streetcar: Red and Blue lines.

San Antonio Children's Museum ★★   San Antonio's children's museum offers a terrific, creative introduction to the city for the pint-sized and grown-up alike. San Antonio history, population, and geography are all explored through such features as a miniature River Walk, a multicultural grocery store, a bank where kids can use their own ATM, and even a teddy bear hospital. Activities range from crawl spaces and corn-grinding rocks to a weather station and radar room. Don't miss this place if you're traveling with children up to age 10.

305 E. Houston St. ✆ 210/21-CHILD. www.sakids.org. Admission $4; children under 2 free. Labor Day to Memorial Day Mon 9am–noon; Tues–Fri 9am–3:30pm; Sat 9am–6pm; Sun noon–4pm. Bus: 7 or 40. Streetcar: Red line.

San Antonio IMAX Theater Rivercenter ★   Having kids view this theater's main attraction, *Alamo—The Price of Freedom,* on a six-story-high screen with a stereo sound system is a sure-fire way of getting them psyched for the historical battle site (which, although it's just across the street, can't be reached without wending your way past lots and lots of Rivercenter shops). The theater also shows nature movies produced especially for the large screen, and occasionally commercial films (the redigitalized *Apollo 13,* for example). With the introduction in 2001 of a second, 50-foot-high screen with 3-D capability and a state-of-the-art sound system, this became first commercial IMAX theater in the country to double its big-screen pleasures. Your ticket also buys you entry into The Texas Adventure (see below).

849 E. Commerce St., in the Rivercenter Mall. ✆ 800/354-4629 or 210/247-4629. www.imax-sa.com. Admission $8.95 adults, $7.95 seniors, $5.50 children 3–11. Daily 8:30am–10:30pm. Streetcar: All lines.

Splashtown   Cool off at this 8-acre water park, which includes a huge wave pool, hydro tubes nearly 300 feet long, a Texas-size water bobsled ride, more than a dozen water slides, and a two-story playhouse for the smaller children. A variety of concerts, contests, and special events are held here.

3600 N. I-35 (exit 160, Splashtown Dr.). ✆ 210/227-1100. www.splashtownsa.com. Admission $22 adults, $17 children under 48 in. (after 5pm, $14 for any age); seniors over 65 and children under 2 free. Daily June–Aug; weekends May and Sept (call ahead or check website for exact times).

The Texas Adventure   San Antonio's foray into the high-tech history field, the world's first Encountarium F!X Theatre retells the battle for the Alamo with special effects that include life-size holographic images of the Alamo heroes and cannon fire roaring through a sophisticated sound system. The depiction of events is more accurate than in most such displays, but noise and smoke aside, this isn't terribly exciting, since the ghostly holograms do little more than hold forth about who they are. Still, it's included in the price of the IMAX theater (see above) and takes only 30 minutes.

307 Alamo Plaza. ✆ 210/227-8224. www.texas-adventure.com. Admission $8.95 adults, $7.95 seniors and military, $5.50 children 3–11 (includes IMAX theater admission), free for children under 3. Daily 10am–8pm in winter; 10am–10pm in summer. Streetcar: Red and Blue lines.

5 Special-Interest Sightseeing

FOR MILITARY HISTORY BUFFS

San Antonio's military installations are crucial to the city's economy, and testaments to their past abound. Those who aren't satisfied with touring Fort Sam Houston (see "More Attractions," above) can also visit the **Hangar 9/Edward H. White Museum** at Brooks Air Force Base, Southeast Military Drive at the junction of I-37 (✆ **210/536-2203,** www.brooks.af.mil). The history of flight medicine, among other things, is detailed via exhibits in the oldest aircraft hangar in the Air Force. Admission is free, and it's open Monday to Friday 9am to 2pm, except the last 2 weeks of December. Lackland Air Force Base (12 miles southwest of downtown off U.S. 90 at Southwest Military Dr. exit, www. lackland.af.mil) is home to the **Air Force History and Traditions Museum,** 2051 George Ave., Bldg. 5206 (© **210/671-3055**), which hosts a collection of rare aircraft and components dating back to World War II. Admission is free; it's open Monday to Friday 8am to 4:30pm. The hours and admission fees (or lack thereof) are the same for the **Security Police Museum,** about 3 blocks away at Bldg. 10501 (on Femoyer St., corner of Carswell Ave.) (© **210/671-2615**). Weapons, uniforms, and combat gear dating up to Desert Storm days are among the security police artifacts on display. Inquire at either museum about the 41 static aircraft on view throughout the base. With current security measures in place, the bases have been restricted to retired military, their families, and those sponsored by someone who works at the base. But it's worth calling to inquire about visitation status. In any case, phone ahead to find out if anyone is permitted on the base on the day you're planning to visit.

FOR THOSE INTERESTED IN HISPANIC HERITAGE

A Hispanic heritage tour is almost redundant in San Antonio, which is a living testament to the role Hispanics have played in shaping the city. **Casa Navarro State Historic Site, La Villita, Market Square, San Antonio Missions National Historical Park,** and the **Spanish Governor's Palace,** all detailed above, give visitors a feel for the city's Spanish colonial past, while the Nelson A. Rockefeller wing of the **San Antonio Museum of Art,** also discussed earlier, hosts this country's largest collection of Latin American art. The sixth floor of the main branch of the **San Antonio Public Library** (see above) hosts an excellent noncirculating Latino collection, featuring books about the Mexican-American experience in Texas and the rest of the Southwest. It's also the place to come to do genealogical research into your family's Hispanic roots.

The city's exploration of its own Hispanic roots is ongoing. It's part of the planned **Centro Alameda cultural zone** on downtown's west side, a project that will include a Smithsonian Institution affiliate, slated to debut in 2004. At 310 W. Houston St., you can see the spectacular 86-foot-high sign (lit by rare cold cathode technology, not neon) of the **Alameda Theater,** opened in 1949 as one of the last of the grand movie palaces—and the largest ever dedicated to Spanish-language entertainment. Among its many impressive features were private nursemaids for the patrons' children and gorgeous "Deco tropical" tilework hand-created in San Antonio. Described as being "to U.S. Latinos what Harlem's Apollo Theater is to African-Americans," the Alameda is scheduled to reopen as a multi-venue performance hall and teaching facility for Latino arts and culture by the end of this decade, when a multi-million restoration will be complete.

Cultural events and blowout festivals, many of them held at Market Square, abound. **The Guadalupe Cultural Arts Center,** which organizes many of them, is detailed in chapter 8. In HemisFair Park, the **Instituto Cultural Mexicano/ Casa Mexicana,** 600 HemisFair Plaza Way (© **210/227-0123**), sponsored by the Mexican Ministry of Foreign Affairs, hosts Latin American film series, concerts, conferences, performances, contests, and workshops—including ones on language, literature, and folklore as well as art. The institute also hosts shifting displays of art and artifacts relating to Mexican history and culture, from pre-Columbian to contemporary (Mon–Fri 10am–5pm; admission free).

For information on the various festivals and events, contact the **San Antonio Hispanic Chamber of Commerce** (© 210/225-0462). Another round-up resource for Latin *cultura* is the **"Guide to Puro San Antonio,"** available from the San Antonio Convention and Visitors Bureau (© 800/447-3372).

6 Strolling Around Downtown San Antonio

One of downtown San Antonio's great gifts to visitors on foot is its wonderfully meandering early pathways—not laid out by drunken cattle drivers as has been wryly suggested, but formed by the course of the San Antonio River and the various settlements that grew up around it. Turn any corner in this area and you'll come across some fascinating testament to the city's historically rich past.

Note: Stops 1, 5, 6, 7, 9, 11, 13, and 14 are described earlier in this chapter. Entrance hours and admission fees (if applicable) are listed there. See chapter 4 for additional information on stop no. 2 and chapter 7 for additional information on stop no. 3.

WALKING TOUR   DOWNTOWN

Start:	The Alamo.
Finish:	Market Square.
Time:	Approximately 1½ hours, not including stops at shops, restaurants, or attractions.
Best Times:	Early morning during the week, when the streets and attractions are less crowded. If you're willing to tour the Alamo museums and shrine another time, consider starting out before they open (9am).
Worst Times:	Weekend afternoons, especially in summer, when the crowds and the heat render this long stroll uncomfortable. (If you do get tired, you can always pick up a streetcar within a block or two of most parts of this route.)

Built to be within easy reach of each other, San Antonio's earliest military, religious, and civil settlements are concentrated in the downtown area. The city spread out quite a bit in the subsequent 2½ centuries, but downtown still functions as the seat of the municipal and county government, as well as the hub of tourist activities.

Start your tour at Alamo Plaza (bounded by E. Houston St. on the north); at the plaza's northeast corner, you'll come to the entrance for:

❶ The Alamo

Originally established in 1718 as the Mission San Antonio de Valero, the first of the city's five missions, the Alamo was moved twice before settling at this site. The heavy limestone walls of the church and its adjacent compound later proved to make an excellent fortress; in 1836, fighters for Texas's independence from Mexico took a heroic, if ultimately unsuccessful, stand against Mexican general Santa Anna here.

When you leave the walled complex, walk south along the plaza to:

❷ The Menger Hotel

This hotel was built by German immigrant William Menger in 1859 on the site of Texas's first brewery, which he had opened with partner Charles Deegan in 1855. Legend has it that Menger wanted a place to lodge hard-drinking friends who used to spend the night sleeping on his long bar. Far more prestigious guests—presidents,

Civil War generals, writers, stage actors, you name it—stayed here over the years, and the hotel turns up in several short stories by frequent guest William Sidney Porter (O. Henry). The Menger has been much expanded since it first opened, but retains its gorgeous, three-tiered Victorian lobby.

On the south side of the hotel, Alamo Plaza turns back into North Alamo Street. Take it south 1 block until you reach Commerce Street, where you'll spot:

❸ Joske's (now Dillard's)

This is San Antonio's oldest department store. The more modest retail emporium opened by the Joske Brothers in 1889 was swallowed up in 1939 by the huge modernist building you see now, distinctive for its intricate Spanish Renaissance–style details; look for the miniaturized versions of Mission San José's sacristy window on the building's ground-floor shadowboxes.

Walk a short way along the Commerce Street side of the building to:

❹ St. Joseph's Catholic Church

This church was built for San Antonio's German community in 1876. The Gothic revival–style house of worship is as notable for the intransigence of its congregation as it is for its beautiful stained-glass windows. The worshipers' refusal to move from the site when Joske's department store was rising up all around it earned the church the affectionate moniker "St. Joske's."

Head back to Alamo Street and continue south 2 blocks past the San Antonio Convention Center to reach:

❺ La Villita

Once the site of a Coahuiltecan Indian village, La Villita was settled over the centuries by Spanish, Germans, and, in the '30s and '40s, a community of artists. A number of the buildings have been continuously occupied for more than 200 years. The "Little Village" on the river was restored by a joint effort of the city and the San Antonio Conservation

Society, and now hosts a number of crafts shops and two upscale restaurants in addition to the historic General Cós House and the Arneson River Theatre.

Just south of La Villita, you'll see HemisFair Way and the large iron gates of:

❻ HemisFair Park

This park was built for the 1968 exposition held to celebrate the 250th anniversary of San Antonio's founding. The expansive former fairgrounds are home to two museums, a German heritage park, and an observation tower—the tallest structure in the city and a great reference point if you get lost downtown. The plaza is too large to explore even superficially on this tour, so come back another time.

Retrace your steps to Paseo de la Villita and walk 1 block west to Presa Street. Take it north for about half a block until you see the Presa Street Bridge, and descend from it to:

❼ The River Walk

You'll find yourself on a quiet section of the 2.6-mile paved walkway that lines the banks of the San Antonio River through a large part of downtown and the King William Historic District. The bustling cafe, restaurant, and hotel action is just behind you, on the stretch of the river that winds north of La Villita.

Stroll down this tree-shaded thoroughfare until you reach the St. Mary's Street Bridge (you'll pass only one other bridge, the Navarro St. Bridge, along the way) and ascend here. Then walk north half a block until you come to Market Street. Take it west 1 long block, where you'll find:

❽ Main Plaza (Plaza de Las Islas)

This is the heart of the city established in 1731 by 15 Canary Island families sent by King Philip V of Spain to settle his remote New World outpost. Much of the history of San Antonio—and of Texas—unfolded on this modest square. A peace treaty with the Apaches was signed (and later broken) on the plaza in 1749; in 1835,

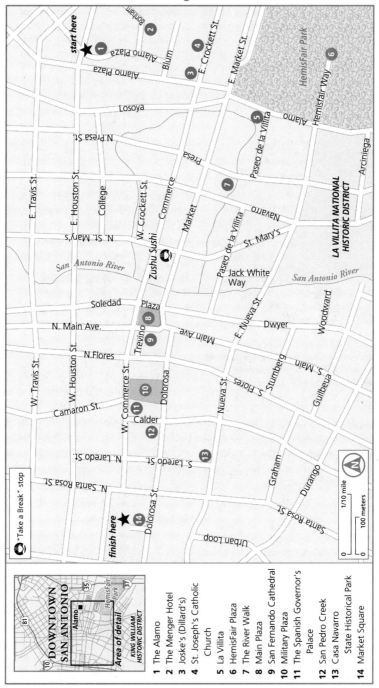

Walking Tour: Downtown San Antonio

Area of detail

DOWNTOWN SAN ANTONIO

KING WILLIAM HISTORIC DISTRICT

Alamo

HemisFair Park

start here

finish here

☕ "Take a Break" stop

LA VILLITA NATIONAL HISTORIC DISTRICT

San Antonio River

HemisFair Park

Zushu Sushi

Jack White Way

1 The Alamo
2 The Menger Hotel
3 Joske's (Dillard's)
4 St. Joseph's Catholic Church
5 La Villita
6 HemisFair Plaza
7 The River Walk
8 Main Plaza
9 San Fernando Cathedral
10 Military Plaza
11 The Spanish Governor's Palace
12 San Pedro Creek
13 Casa Navarro State Historical Park
14 Market Square

91

freedom fighters battled Santa Anna's troops here before barricading themselves in the Alamo across the river. Much calmer these days, the plaza still sees some action as home to the Romanesque-style Bexar County Courthouse, built out of native Texas granite and sandstone in 1892.

TAKE A BREAK
I know, it's not in keeping with the character of this area, but multiculturalism is San Antonio's trademark. And if you like Japanese food as much as I do, you'll enjoy cooling your heels at **Zushi Sushi** in the International Center, 203 S. St. Mary's St. at Market ((C) **210/472-2900**). You can get a quick raw fish fix at the sleek sushi bar (they're got lots of cooked and vegetarian rolls, too), or settle in at one of the tables for a bowl of soba noodles or some teppan grilled beef.

Walk along the south side of Main Plaza to the corner of Main Avenue. Across the street and just to the north you'll encounter:

❾ San Fernando Cathedral
This is the oldest parish church building in Texas and site of the earliest marked graves in San Antonio. Three walls of the original church started by the Canary Island settlers in 1738 can still be seen in the rear of the 1868 Gothic revival cathedral, which just underwent a massive renovation. Among those buried within the sanctuary walls are Eugenio Navarro, brother of José Antonio Navarro (see stop no. 13, below), and Don Manuel Muñoz, first governor of Texas when it was a province of a newly independent Mexico.

On the north side of the cathedral is Trevino Street; take it west to the next corner and cross the street to reach:

❿ Military Plaza (Plaza de Armas)
Once the drill ground for the Presidio San Antonio de Béxar, this garrison—

established in 1718 to protect the Mission San Antonio de Valero—was moved to this nearby site 4 years later. Military Plaza was one of the liveliest spots in Texas for the 50 years after Texas won its independence. In the 1860s, it was the site of vigilante lynchings, and after the Civil War it hosted a bustling outdoor market. At night, the townsfolk would come to its open-air booths to buy chili con carne from their favorite chili queen. The plaza remained completely open until 1889, when the ornate City Hall was built at its center.

The one-story white building you'll see directly across the street from the west side of the plaza is the:

⓫ Spanish Governor's Palace
This was the former residence and headquarters of the captain of the Presidio de Béxar (but not of any Spanish governors); from here, the commander could watch his troops drilling across the street. The source of the house's misnomer is not entirely clear; as the home of the highest local authority and thus the nicest digs in the area, the "palace" probably hosted important Spanish officials who came through town.

From the front of the Governor's Palace, walk south until you come to the crosswalk; just west across Dolorosa Street is a drainage ditch, the sad remains of:

⓬ San Pedro Creek
The west bank of this body of water, once lovely and flowing and now usually dry, was the original site of both Mission San Antonio de Valero and the Presidio de Béxar. At the creek's former headwaters, approximately 2 miles north of here, San Pedro Park was established in 1729 by a grant from the king of Spain; it's the second-oldest municipal park in the United States (the oldest being the Boston Common).

Continue west along Dolorosa Street to Laredo Street and take it south about three quarters of a block until you come to:

⓭ Casa Navarro State Historic Site

The life of José Antonio Navarro, for whom the park is named, traces the history of Texas itself: He was born in Spanish territory, fought for Mexico's independence from Spain, then worked to achieve Texas's freedom from Mexico. (He was one of only two Texas-born signatories to the 1836 Declaration of Independence.) In 1845, Navarro voted for Texas's annexation to the United States, and a year later, he became a senator in the new Texas State Legislature. He died here in 1871, at the age of 76.

Trace your steps back to Laredo and Dolorosa, and go west on Dolorosa Street; when you reach Santa Rosa, you'll be facing:

⓮ Market Square

This square was home to the city's Market House at the turn of the century. When the low, arcaded structure was converted to El Mercado in 1973, it switched from selling household goods and personal items to crafts, clothing, and other more tourist-oriented Mexican wares. Directly behind and west of this lively square, the former Haymarket Plaza has become the Farmer's Market, and now sells souvenirs instead of produce. If you haven't already stopped for sushi, you can enjoy a well-deserved lunch here at Mi Tierra or La Margarita, both reviewed in chapter 5.

7 Organized Tours

BUS TOURS

San Antonio City Tours   This company serves up a large menu of guided bus tours, covering everything from San Antonio's missions and museums to shopping forays south of the border and Hill Country excursions.

1331 N. Pine. © 800/868-7707 or 210/281-9900. www.sacitytours.net. Tours range from $18 adults, $12 children 4–10, children under 4 are free (3½ hr.) to $45 adults and $23 children 4–10 (full day). Lunch is included in the full day Grand Tour, not with other tours. Earliest tours depart at 8am, latest return is 6pm daily (including holidays).

TROLLEY TOURS

Alamo Trolley Tour ✦   This is a good way to sightsee without a car. One trolley tour touches on all the downtown highlights, plus two of the missions in the south; the second, Uptown tour goes north to the San Antonio Museum of Art, the botanical gardens, the zoo, and the McNay and Witte museums. If you want to get off at any of these sights, you can pick up another trolley (they run every 45 min.) after you're finished. At the least, you get oriented and learn some of the city's history.

216 Alamo Plaza (next to the Alamo). © 210/247-0238. www.sacitytours.net. Tickets for a 60-min. tour are $11 adults, 1 child 3–11 free with a paying adult; additional children are $4.95. ($2 more for an all day pass and the privilege to hop on and off at various stops; $20 for a 2-day pass). Daily 9:30am–4:15pm.

RIVER CRUISES

Yanaguana Cruises ✦   Maybe you've sat in a River Walk cafe looking out at people riding back and forth in open, flat-bottom barges. Go ahead—give in and join 'em. An amusing, informative tour, lasting from 35 to 40 minutes, will take you more than 2 miles down the most built-up sections of the Paseo del Río, with interesting sights pointed out along the way. You'll learn a lot about the river—and find out what all those folks you watched were laughing about. The company also runs a non-narrated shuttle (see "By River Taxi" in the "Getting Around" section of chapter 3 for details).

Ticket offices: Rivercenter Mall and River Walk, across the street from the Hilton Palacio del Rio Hotel. ℂ 210/244-5700. www.sarivercruise.com. Tickets $5.25 adults, $3.65 seniors and active military, $1 children under 6. Boats depart daily every 15–20 min. 10am–9:30pm (later in summer).

8 Staying Active

Most San Antonians head for the hills—that is, nearby Hill Country—for outdoor recreation. Some suggestions of sports in or around town follow; see chapter 17 for more.

BIKING   There aren't many scenic cycling trails within San Antonio itself—locals tend to ride in **Brackenridge Park;** in **McAllister Park** on the city's north side, 13102 Jones-Maltsberger (ℂ **210/207-PARK** or 210/207-3120); and around the area near **SeaWorld of Texas**—but there are a number of appealing places to bike in the vicinity. If you didn't bring your own two-wheeler, **Britton's Bicycles,** 4230 Thousand Oaks (ℂ **210/656-1655;** www.brittonbikes.com), can deliver one to your hotel. The store is a good resource, too, for cycling events around town. You might also log on to the San Antonio Wheelmen's website, www.sawheelmen.com, for details on organized rides in the area.

FISHING   Closest to town for good angling are **Braunig Lake,** a 1,350-acre, city-owned reservoir, a few miles southeast of San Antonio off I-37, and **Calaveras Lake,** one of Texas's great bass lakes, a few miles southeast of San Antonio off U.S. 181 South and Loop 1604. A bit farther afield (astream?) but still easy to reach from San Antonio are **Canyon Lake,** about 20 miles north of New Braunfels, and **Medina Lake,** just south of Bandera. Fishing licenses—sold at most sporting goods and tackle stores and sporting goods departments of large discount stores such as Wal-Mart or Kmart, as well as county courthouses and Parks and Wildlife Department offices—are required for all nonresidents; for current information, call ℂ **800/792-1112** (in Texas only) or 512/389-4800. **Tackle Box Outfitters,** 6330 N. New Braunfels (ℂ **210/821-5806**) offers referrals to private guides for fishing trips to area rivers and to the Gulf coast ($250–$400 per person).

GOLF   Golf has become a big deal in San Antonio, with more and more visitors coming to town expressly to tee off. Of the city's six municipal golf courses, two of the most notable are **Brackenridge,** 2315 Ave. B (ℂ **210/226-5612**), the oldest (1916) public course in Texas, featuring oak- and pecan-shaded fairways; and northwest San Antonio's $4.3 million **Cedar Creek,** 8250 Vista Colina (ℂ **210/695-5050**), repeatedly ranked as South Texas's best municipal course in golfing surveys. Other options for unaffiliated golfers include the 200-acre **Pecan Valley,** 4700 Pecan Valley Dr. (ℂ **210/333-9018;** www.thetexas golftrail.com), which crosses the Salado Creek seven times and has an 800-year-old oak near its 13th hole; the high-end **Quarry,** 444 E. Basse Rd. (ℂ **210/824-4500;** www.quarrygolf.com), on the sight of a former quarry and one of San Antonio's newest public courses; and **Canyon Springs,** 24400 Canyon Golf Rd. (ℂ **888/800-1511** or 210/497-1770; www.canyon springscc.com), at the north edge of town in the Texas Hill Country, lush with live oaks and dotted with historic rock formations. There aren't too many resort courses in San Antonio because there aren't too many resorts, but the two at **La Cantera,** 16401 La Cantera Pkwy. (ℂ **800/446-5387** or 210/558-4653)—the original one designed by Jay Morish and Tom Weiskopf, and the Arnold Palmer creation that debuted in early 2001—have knockout designs and dramatic hill-and-rock outcroppings to recommend them. Expect to pay $35 to $50 per person for an 18-hole round at a municipal course with a cart, from $70 to as much as $140 (on weekends) per person at a private resort's course. Twilight (afternoon) rates are often cheaper. To get a copy of the free San Antonio Golfing Guide, call © **800/447-3372** or log on to www.santoniovisit.com.

HIKING   **Friedrich Wilderness Park,** 21480 Milsa (© **210/698-1057**), operated by the city of San Antonio as a nature preserve, is crisscrossed by 5½ miles of trails that attract bird watchers as well as hikers; a 2-mile stretch is accessible to people with disabilities. The park offers free guided hikes, lasting about 2 hours, the first Saturday of every month at 9am. **Enchanted Rock State Natural Area,** near Fredericksburg, is the most popular spot for trekking out of town (see chapter 17).

RIVER SPORTS   For tubing, rafting, or canoeing along a cypress-lined river, San Antonio river rats head 35 miles northwest of downtown to the 2,000-acre **Guadalupe River State Park,** 3350 Park Rd. 31 (© **830/438-2656**; www. tpwd.state.tx.us). On Hwy. 46, just outside the park, you can rent tubes, rafts, and canoes at the **Bergheim Campground,** FM 3351 in Bergheim (© **830/ 336-2235**). Standard tubes run $6 per person (but the ones with a bottom for your cooler, at $7, are better), rafts are $15 per person (children 12 and under half-price), and canoes go for $25. The section of the Guadalupe River near Gruene is also extremely popular; see the "New Braunfels" section of chapter 17 for details.

SWIMMING/WATER PARKS   Most hotels have swimming pools, but if yours doesn't, the **Parks and Recreation Department** (© **210/207-3113**; www. ci.sat.tx.us/sapar) can direct you to the nearest municipal pool. Both **SeaWorld** and **Six Flags Fiesta Texas,** detailed in the "The Top Attractions" section, above, are prime places to get wet (the latter has a pool in the shape of Texas and a waterfall that descends from a cowboy hat). **Splashtown** water recreation park is described in the "Especially for Kids" section, above. Many San Antonians head out to New Braunfels to get wet at the **Schlitterbahn,** the largest water park in Texas; see the "New Braunfels" section of chapter 17 for additional information.

TENNIS   You can play at the lighted courts at the **Fairchild Tennis Center,** 1214 E. Crockett (© **210/226-6912**), and **McFarlin Tennis Center,** 1503 San Pedro Ave. (© **210/732-1223**), both municipal facilities. The former is free; the very reasonable fees for the latter are $1.50 per hour per person ($1 for students and seniors), $2.50 after 5pm.

9 Spectator Sports

AUTO RACING   The best local drag-race action March through October is at the **San Antonio Speedway,** 14901 S. Hwy. 16, 4 miles south of Loop 410 (© **210/628-1499**; www.sanantoniospeedway.com). Another good option is the **Alamo Dragway,** 15030 Watson Rd. (© **210/628-1371**; www.alamo dragway.com).

BASEBALL   From early April through early September, the minor league **San Antonio Missions** (who won the 2002 Texas League Championship) plays at the Nelson Wolff Stadium, 5757 Hwy. 90 West. Most home games for this Seattle Mariners farm club start at 7:05pm, except Sunday games, which start at 6:05pm. Tickets range from $4.50 for adult general admission to $8.50 for seats in the lower box. Call © **210/675-7275** for schedules and tickets, or check the website at www.samissions.com.

BASKETBALL   Spur madness hits San Antonio every year from mid-October through May, when the city's only major-league franchise, the **San Antonio Spurs,** shoot hoops. As of October 2002, the Spurs have a new home at the state-of-the-art SBC Center, One SBC Center Parkway, downtown; see "What's New in San Antonio & Austin" for details. Ticket prices range from $25 for seats behind the basket to $69 for seats on the corners of the court. Nosebleed-level seats, running from $9–$15, are also available. Tickets are available at the Spurs Ticket Office in the SBC Center (*C* **210/444-5819**) or via Ticketmaster San Antonio (*C* **210/224-9600;** www.ticketmaster.com). Get schedules, players' stats, promotional news—everything you might want to know or buy relating to the team—online at www.nba.com/spurs. It's also the place to get directions to the new stadium.

GOLF   The **SBC Championship,** an Official Senior PGA Tour Event, is held each October at the Oak Hills Country Club, 5403 Fredericksburg Rd. (*C* **210/698-3582;** www.pgatour.com). One of the oldest professional golf tournaments, now known as the **Westin Texas Open at La Cantera,** showcases the sport in September at 16401 La Cantera Pkwy. (*C* **201/558-4653**). Call the San Antonio Golf Association (*C* **800/TEX-OPEN** or 210/341-0823) for additional information.

HORSE RACING   **Retama Park,** some 15 minutes north of San Antonio in Selma (*C* **210/651-7119;** www.retamapark.com), is the hottest place to play the ponies; take exit 174-A from I-35, or the Lookout Road exit from Loop 1604. The five-level Spanish-style grandstand is impressive, and the variety of food courts, restaurants, and lounges is almost as diverting as the horses. Live racing is generally from mid-April through October on Wednesday or Thursday through Sunday. Call for thoroughbred and quarter horse schedules. Simulcasts from top tracks around the country are shown year-round. General admission is $2.50 adults, $1.50 seniors; clubhouse, $3.50 adults, $2.50 seniors; simulcast, $2. Kids 15 and under and members of the military, active or retired, can enter gratis. Call ahead for the dates of "Fifty-Cent Fridays," when parking, admission, programs, beer, soft drinks, and hot dogs cost only that much each.

ICE HOCKEY   The first hockey team in city history, started in 1994, the Central Hockey League's **San Antonio Iguanas** disbanded after the 2001–2002 season. They were replaced by an American Hockey League team, the **San Antonio Rampage,** who dropped their first puck at the new SBC Center (1 SBC Center Dr.) in November 2002. AHL tickets cost $9 to $20. Try *C* **210/227-GOAL** or www.sarampage.com for schedules and other information.

RODEO   If you're in town in early February, don't miss the chance to see 2 weeks of Wild West events like calf roping, steer wrestling, and bull riding at the annual **San Antonio Stock Show and Rodeo.** You can also hear major live country-and-western talent—Martina McBride, Toby Keith, George Jones, Alan Jackson, and Leann Womack were on the 2002 roster—and you're likely to find something to add to your luggage at the SBC Center's exposition hall, packed with Texas handcrafts. Contact the San Antonio Livestock Exposition Inc., P.O Box 200230, San Antonio, TX 78220 (*C* **210/225-5851;** www.sarodeo.com), for additional advance information. Smaller rodeos are held throughout the year in nearby **Bandera County,** the self-proclaimed "Cowboy Capital of the World." Contact the Bandera County Convention and Visitors Bureau (*C* **800/364-3833** or 830/796-3045; www.banderacowboycapital.com) for more information.

7

Shopping in San Antonio

San Antonio offers the retail-bound a nice balance of large malls and little enclaves of specialized shops. You'll find everything here from the utilitarian to the unusual: huge Sears and Kmart department stores, a Saks Fifth Avenue fronted by a 40-foot pair of cowboy boots, a mall with a river running through it, and some lively Mexican markets.

You can count on most shops around town being open from 9 or 10am until 5:30 or 6pm Monday through Saturday, with shorter hours on Sunday. Malls are generally open Monday through Saturday 10am to 9pm and on Sunday noon to 6pm. Sales tax in San Antonio is 7.875%.

1 The Shopping Scene

Most out-of-town shoppers will find all they need **downtown,** between the large Rivercenter Mall, the boutiques and crafts shops of La Villita, the colorful Mexican wares of Market Square, the Southwest School of Art and Craft, and assorted retailers and galleries on and around Alamo Plaza. More avant-garde boutiques and galleries, including Blue Star, can be found in the adjacent area known as Southtown.

San Antonians tend to shop the **Loop 410 malls**—especially North Star, Heubner Oaks, and Alamo Quarry Market near the airport—and cruise the upscale strip centers along Broadway in **Alamo Heights** (the posh Collection and Lincoln Heights are particularly noteworthy). Weekends might see locals poking around a number of terrific **flea markets.** For bargains on brand labels, they head out to New Braunfels and San Marcos, home to three large **factory outlet malls** (see chapter 17 for details).

2 Shopping A to Z

ANTIQUES

In addition to the places that follow, a number of antiques shops line Hildebrand between Blanco and San Pedro, and McCullough between Hildebrand and Basse.

AntiqueLand USA   San Antonio's largest antiques warehouse, with nearly 200 vendors and 47,000 square feet of space, is a link in a national antiques chain but it still has plenty of local character. You can find everything from Texas brewer-o-bilia to antique Mexican jewelry here. Alamo Hills Shopping Center, 1246 Austin Hwy. ✆ 210/822-7477. www.antiquelandusa.com.

Center for Antiques   Not quite as large as the newer AntiqueLand USA (see above), this is nevertheless another great place for an antiques forage. It's plenty huge and it has a slightly more convenient location near the airport. There are more than 115 vendors with specialties from knickknacks, records, and clothing to high-quality furniture for serious collectors. 8505 Broadway. © **210/804-6300.** www.centerforantiques.com.

The Land of Was   Every inch of space on the two floors of this shop is crammed with stuff—some of it strange and funky, more of it rare and pricey. The store is especially strong on Spanish-colonial and Mexican antiques; if you're seeking an altarpiece or a treasure chest, try here first. 3119 Broadway. © **210/ 822-5265.**

ART GALLERIES

ArtPace, in the northern part of downtown, and the **Blue Star Arts Complex,** in Southtown (see "More Attractions," in chapter 6, for details on both), are the best venues for cutting-edge art, but **Sala Díaz,** 517 Stieren St. in Southtown (© **210/325-5923**), and **Finesilver Gallery,** 816 Camaron St., Suites 1 and 2, just north of downtown (© **210/354-3333,** www.finesilver.com), are good alternative alternatives. Downtown is home to several galleries that show more established artists. Three of the top ones are **Galería Ortiz,** 102 Concho (in Market Sq.) (© **210/225-0731;** www.galeriaortiz.com), San Antonio's premier place to buy Southwestern art; **Nanette Richardson Fine Art,** 513 E. Houston St. (© **210/224-1550,** www.nanetterichardsonfineart.com), with a wide array of oils, watercolors, bronzes, ceramics, and handcrafted wood furnishings; and **Parchman Stremmel,** 203 N. Presa (© **210/266-8752**), featuring the work of contemporary artists who've made it big (or come close).

For more details on these and other galleries, pick up a copy of the **San Antonio Gallery Guide,** prepared by the San Antonio Art Gallery Association, at the San Antonio Convention and Visitors Bureau, 317 Alamo Plaza (© **800/ 447-3372** or 210/207-6700). You can also check out the art scene online at the Office of Cultural Affairs' website, **www.sanantonio.gov/art/website** with links to several local galleries, and schedules for events held during July's Contemporary Art Month (see chapter 2).

CRAFTS

See also Alamo Fiesta, Red Iguana, San Angel Folk Art, and Tienda Guadalupe in "Gifts/Souvenirs," below. Another top option is the Ursuline Sales Gallery in the Southwest School of Art and Craft (see chapter 6).

Glass Works *Finds*   If you've picked up an *Architectural Digest* lately, you've likely noticed that glass art is all the decorating rage. The goal of this Alamo Heights store and its larger counterpart in the northwest, at 18720 Stone Oak Parkway (© **210/545-1498**), is to show that in addition to being gorgeous, blown-glass can also be formed into items that are interesting—a golf putter, for example—affordable, and accessible. Everyone who walks into these stores is encouraged to touch the work ("It's all insured," owner/artist Judy Millspaugh declares cheerfully). 635 N. New Braunfels Ave. © **210/822-0146.**

Uriarte Talavera *Finds*   Aficionados of Mexican pottery know that the ceramics sold in the Uriarte Talavera workshop in Puebla, Mexico, are renowned for their artistry and high quality (see www.uriartetalavera.com for background and pictures). This San Antonio wholesaler owns the factory in Mexico and is the U.S. distributor for the pottery, so it has the country's largest selection and lowest prices, whether you buy a single mug or need to outfit a restaurant. 204 W. Olmos. © **210/930-5595.**

Downtown San Antonio Shopping

Boot Hill **3**
Chamade Jewelers **4**
Dillard's **3**
Paris Hatters **2**
The Red Iguana **5**
Rivercenter Mall **3**
San Angel Folk Art **8**
Southwest School of Art & Craft **1**
St. Jude's **7**
Tienda Guadalupe Folk Art & Gifts **6**

Greater San Antonio Shopping

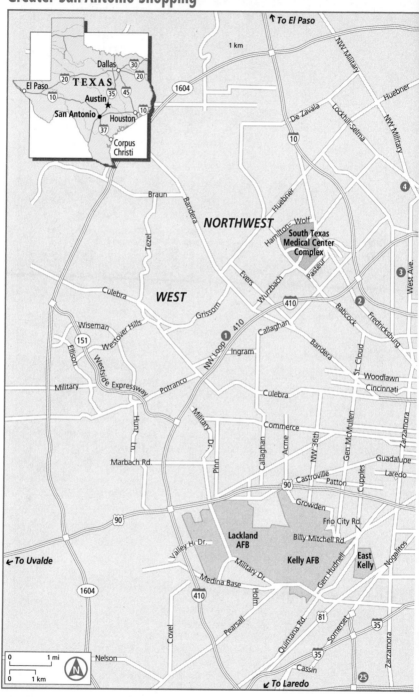

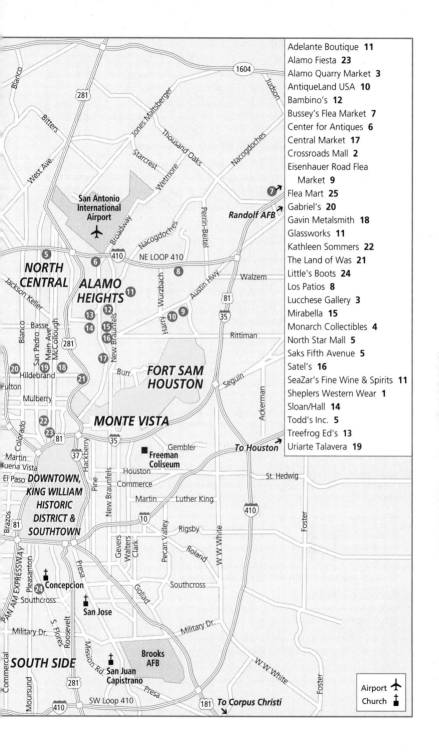

Adelante Boutique **11**
Alamo Fiesta **23**
Alamo Quarry Market **3**
AntiqueLand USA **10**
Bambino's **12**
Bussey's Flea Market **7**
Center for Antiques **6**
Central Market **17**
Crossroads Mall **2**
Eisenhauer Road Flea
 Market **9**
Flea Mart **25**
Gabriel's **20**
Gavin Metalsmith **18**
Glassworks **11**
Kathleen Sommers **22**
The Land of Was **21**
Little's Boots **24**
Los Patios **8**
Lucchese Gallery **3**
Mirabella **15**
Monarch Collectibles **4**
North Star Mall **5**
Saks Fifth Avenue **5**
Satel's **16**
SeaZar's Fine Wine & Spirits **11**
Sheplers Western Wear **1**
Sloan/Hall **14**
Todd's Inc. **5**
Treefrog Ed's **13**
Uriarte Talavera **19**

DEPARTMENT STORES

Dillard's You'll find branches of this Arkansas-based chain in many Southwestern cities and in a number of San Antonio malls (North Star, Ingram, and Rolling Oaks); all offer nice mid- to upper-range clothing and housewares, but the Dillard's in the Rivercenter Mall also has a section specializing in Western fashions. Enter or exit on Alamo Plaza so you can get a look at the historic building's ornate facade (see "Walking Tour: Downtown," in chapter 6, for details). 102 Alamo Plaza (Rivercenter Mall). (✆ 210/227-4343. www.dillards.com.

Saks Fifth Avenue Forget low-key and unobtrusive; this is Texas. Sure, this department store has the high-quality, upscale wares and attentive service one would expect from a Saks Fifth Avenue, but it also has a 40-foot-high pair of cowboy boots standing out front. 650 North Star Mall. (✆ 210/341-4111.

FASHIONS

The following stores offer clothing in a variety of styles; if you're keen on the cowpuncher look, see "Western Wear," below.

CHILDREN'S FASHION

Bambinos Whether your child goes in for the English Country look or veers more towards punk-rocker, you'll find something to suit his or her (okay—your) tastes at this delightful store, which also carries a great selection of kiddie room furnishings and toys. The focus is on the younger set: infants to age 7, that is. 5934 Broadway. (✆ 210/822-9595.

MEN'S FASHION

Satel's This family-run Alamo Heights store has been the place to shop for menswear in San Antonio since 1950; classic, high-quality clothing and personal service make it a standout. The neighborhood's most famous former resident, Tommy Lee Jones, has been spotted here. 5100 Broadway. (✆ 210/822-3376, www.satels.com.

Todd's Inc. Mexico's elite come to Todd's to buy their suits, casual wear, and accessories. Fine style doesn't come cheap, however; shop here only if you're prepared to part with some big bucks. 7400 San Pedro, Suite 722 (North Star Mall). (✆ 210/349-6464, www.toddshautecouture.com.

WOMEN'S FASHION

Adelante Boutique The focus here is on the ethnic and the handmade, with lots of colorful, natural fabrics and free-flowing lines. The store also offers a nice selection of leather belts and whimsical jewelry and gifts. 6414 N. New Braunfels Ave. (in Sunset Ridge). (✆ 210/826-6770, www.adelanteboutique.com.

Kathleen Sommers 🐾 This small shop on the corner of Main and Woodlawn has been setting trends for San Antonio women for years. Kathleen Sommers, who works mainly in linen and other natural fabrics, designs all the clothes, which bear her label. The store also carries great jewelry, bath items, books, fun housewares, and a selection of unusual gifts, including the San Antonio—originated Soular Therapy candles. 2417 N. Main. (✆ 210/732-8437.

Mirabella Super-stylish but friendly Mirabella owner Misti Riedel buys clothes according to the credo, "Girls just wanna have fun." If it's sexy, colorful, creative, and wearable, you'll find it here. Good looks never come cheap, but many of the designers represented on the racks of this cozy shop are not well known, which means costs are by no means prohibitive either. And if you're lucky, there'll be a sale on. 5910 Broadway. © **210/829-4435.**

FOOD

Central Market   Free valet parking at a supermarket? On Saturday and Sunday, so many locals converge here to take advantage of the huge array of delectable samples that it's easy to understand why the store is willing to alleviate parking stress. You'll feel as though you've died and gone to food heaven as you walk amid gorgeous mounds of produce (I've never seen so many types of chiles), cheeses and other dairy products, sauces, pastas, and more. If you don't want to just graze, there are freshly prepared hot and cold gourmet foods, including a soup and salad bar, and a seating area in which to enjoy them. Wine tastings and cooking classes draw crowds in the evenings. 4821 Broadway. © **210/ 368-8600.** www.centralmarket.com.

GIFTS/SOUVENIRS

Alamo Fiesta *(Finds*   Head just north of downtown to this two-level store near Monte Vista for a huge selection of Mexican folk art and handicrafts—everything from tinwork to colorful masks and piñatas—at extremely reasonable prices. Less touristy than most such shops, Alamo Fiesta is geared to local Hispanic families looking to celebrate special occasions. 2025 N. Main at Ashby. © **210/ 738-1188.** www.alamofiesta.com.

The Red Iguana   A high-quality array of Mexican arts and crafts—polished and painted gourds, shoemakers' forms covered with *milagros,* intricately

---

 Love Potion No. 9

Ask a proprietor of a **botanica,** "What kind of store is this?" and you'll hear anything from "a drugstore" to "a religious bookstore." But along with Christian artifacts (including glow-in-the-dark rosaries and dashboard icons), botanicas carry magic floor washes, candles designed to keep the law off your back, wolf skulls, amulets, herbal remedies, and, of course, love potions. The common theme is happiness enhancement, whether by self-improvement, prayer, or luck.

Many of San Antonio's countless small botanicas specialize in articles used by *curanderos:* traditional folk doctors or medicine men and women. Books directing laypersons in the use of medicinal herbs sit next to volumes that retell the lives of the saints. It's easy enough to figure out the use of the *santos* (saints), candles in tall glass jars to which are affixed such labels as "Peaceful Home," "Find Work," and "Bingo." *Milagros* (miracles) are small charms that represent parts of the body—or mind—that a person wishes to have healed. Don't worry that many of the labels are in Spanish; the person behind the counter will be happy to translate.

St. Jude's, 5630 S. Flores ((© **210/922-6665**), is the new name for Papa Jim's, the best known of all the botanicas (Papa Jim, who used to bless the various artifacts he sold, died recently). A mail-order catalog is in the works.

wrought silver jewelry (vintage and new), Spanish colonial–style paintings, and colorfully embroidered clothing, to name a few—have been gathered and/or created by Eduardo Tijerina, whose two-level gallery is one of Southtown's most interesting shops. You can find everything here from $15 T-shirts to paintings that run into four figures. 918 South Alamo St. ℂ 210/281-9667. www.therediguana.com.

San Angel Folk Art   Combing the crafts markets of Mexico might be more fun, but exploring this large store in the Blue Star Arts Complex is a pretty good substitute. Painted animals from Oaxaca, elaborate masks from the state of Guerrero—this place is chock-a-block with things colorful, whimsical, and well made. Of course, prices are better south of the border, but you're saving on airfare/gas and crossing time. 1404 S. Alamo, Suite 410 in the Blue Star Arts Complex. ℂ 210/226-6688. www.sanangelfolkart.com.

Sloan/Hall   A cross between The Body Shop, Sharper Image, and Borders, only more concentrated and more upscale, this addictive boutique carries an assortment of toiletries, gadgets, books, and those uncategorizable items that you probably don't need—but may find you desperately want. 5922 Broadway. ℂ 210/828-7738. www.sloanhall.com.

Tienda Guadalupe Folk Art & Gifts   This incense-scented shop in the Southtown/King William area is brimming with Hispanic items: painting and handicrafts from Latin America, Mexican antiques and religious items, and more. Come here to pick up a Day of the Dead T-shirt or anything else relating to the early November holiday celebrated with great fanfare in San Antonio. 1001 S. Alamo. ℂ 210/226-5873.

JEWELRY
See also "Crafts" and "Gifts/Souvenirs."

Chamade Jewelers   Expect the unexpected and the beautiful at this dazzling jewelry store, representing more than 30 U.S. and international artists. You'll find everything from classically designed gold rings with precious gemstones to funny sterling silver earrings encasing beans for one ear and rice for the other. Some of the creations are crafted by local and Southwest artisans, including Native Americans; others come from as far afield as France, Italy, China, and Indonesia. 504 Villita St. (La Villita). ℂ 210/224-7753. www.lavillita.com/chamade.html.

Gavin Metalsmith   For contemporary metal craft at its most creative, come to this small women's crafts gallery, where the exquisite original pieces range from wedding rings to salt-and-pepper shakers. The artists whose work is sold here incorporate lots of unusual stones into (mostly) silver and white gold settings. They also frequently do custom work for fair prices. 4024 McCullough St. ℂ 210/821-5254.

MALLS/SHOPPING COMPLEXES
Alamo Quarry Market   Alamo Quarry Market may be its official name, but no one ever calls this popular mall anything but "The Quarry" (from the early 1900s until 1985, the property was in fact a cement quarry). The four smokestacks, lit up dramatically at night, now signal play, not work. There are no anchoring department stores, but a series of large emporiums (Old Navy; Bed, Bath & Beyond; OfficeMax; and Borders) and smaller upscale boutiques (Laura Ashley, Aveda, and Lucchese Gallery—see "Western Wear," below) will keep you spending. A multiplex cinema and an array of refueling stations—Chili's and

Starbucks, as well as the more upscale Koi Kowa (see chapter 5) and Piatti's, an Italian eatery well liked by locals—complete this low-slung temple to self-indulgence. 255 E. Basse Rd. ℂ 210/225-1000. www.alamoquarry.com.

Crossroads of San Antonio Mall   Located near the South Texas Medical Center, this is San Antonio's bargain mall, featuring Burlington Coat Factory, and Stein Mart department stores alongside smaller discount shops; a Super Target is slated to open in March 2003. Some glitzier shops and Tuesday morning line dancing are part of an effort to draw San Antonians to this low-profile shopping destination. 4522 Fredericksburg Rd. (off Loop 410 and I-10). ℂ 210/735-9137.

Heubner Oaks Shopping Center   This upscale open-air mall in the north central part of town houses a variety of yuppie favorites, including Old Navy, Gap, Banana Republic, Victoria's Secret, and Eddie Bauer. When your energy flags, retreat to one of several casual dining spots like La Madeleine, serving good fast French food, or head straight to Starbucks for a caffeine boost. 11745 I-10. ℂ 210/697-8444.

Los Patios   The self-proclaimed "other River Walk" features about a dozen upscale specialty shops in a lovely 18-acre wooded setting. You'll find shops carrying imported clothing, crafts, jewelry, and antique furniture among other offerings here. 2015 NE Loop 410, at the Starcrest exit. ℂ 210/655-6171. www.lospatios.com.

North Star Mall   Starring Saks Fifth Avenue and upscale boutiques like Abercrombie & Fitch, Pappagallo, Aveda, Laura Ashley, and Williams-Sonoma, this is the crème de la crème of the San Antonio indoor malls. But there are many sensible shops here, too, including a Mervyn's department store. Food choices also climb up and down the scale, ranging from a Godiva Chocolatier to a Luby's Cafeteria. Loop 410, between McCullough and San Pedro. ℂ 210/340-6627. www.northstarmall.com.

Rivercenter Mall   There's a festive atmosphere at this bustling, light-filled mall, fostered, among other things, by its location on an extension of the San Antonio River. You can pick up a ferry from a downstairs dock or listen to bands play on a stage surrounded by water. Other entertainment options include the IMAX theater, the multiple-screen AMC, the Cyber Zone video arcade, and the Rivercenter Comedy Club. The shops—more than 130 of them, anchored by Dillard's and Foleys—run the price gamut, but tend toward upscale casual. Food picks similarly range from Dairy Queen and A&W Hot Dogs to Morton's of Chicago. This can be a great place to shop, but remember that it's thronged with teeny-boppers Friday and Saturday nights. 849 E. Commerce, between S. Alamo and Bowie. ℂ 210/225-0000. www.shoprivercenter.com.

MARKETS

Market Square   Two large indoor markets, El Mercado and the Farmer's Market—often just called, collectively, the Mexican market—occupy adjacent blocks on Market Square. Competing for your attention are more than 100 shops and pushcarts, eight restaurants, and an abundance of food stalls. The majority of the shopping booths are of the border town sort, filled with onyx chess sets, cheap sombreros, and the like, but you can also find a few higher quality boutiques, including Galería Ortiz (see above). Come here for a bit of local color, good people-watching, and food—in addition to the sit-down Mi Tierra and La Margarita, detailed in chapter 5, there are loads of primo places for street snacking. You'll often find yourself shopping to the beat of a mariachi band. 514 W. Commerce St. (near Dolorosa). © **210/207-8600.**

FLEA MARKETS

Bussey's Flea Market   Unless you're heading to New Braunfels or Austin, Bussey's is a bit out of the way. But these 20 acres of vendors selling goods from as far afield as Asia and Africa are definitely worth the drive (about ½-hour north of downtown). Crafts, jewelry, antiques, incense—besides perishables, it's hard to imagine anything you couldn't find at this market. 18738 I-35 North. © **210/651-6830.**

Eisenhauer Road Flea Market   The all-indoors, all air-conditioned Eisenhauer, complete with snack bar, is a good flea market to hit at the height of summer. You'll see lots of new stuff here—purses, jewelry, furniture, toys, shoes—and everything from houseplants to kinky leatherwear. Closed Monday and Tuesday. 3903 Eisenhauer Rd. © **210/653-7592.**

Flea Mart   On weekends, Mexican-American families make a day of this huge market, bringing the entire family to exchange gossip, listen to live bands, and eat freshly made tacos. There are always fruits and vegetables, electronics, crafts, and new and used clothing—and you never know what else. 12280 Hwy. 16 S. (about 1 mile south of Loop 410). © **210/624-2666.**

TOYS

The following stores (along with Bambinos—see "Fashions," above) carry unusual but often pricey toys. If your child is especially hard on playthings or your cash supply is running low, consider buying used toys at **Kids Junction Resale Shop,** 2267 NW Military Hwy. (© **210/340-5532**), or **Too Good to Be Threw,** 7115 Blanco (© **210/340-2422**).

Monarch Collectibles *(Kids)*   Welcome to doll heaven. Many of the models that fill Monarch's four rooms—about 3,000 dolls in all—are collectible and made from delicate materials like porcelain and baked clay, but others are cute and cuddly. Some come with real hair and eyelashes, and some are one of a kind. Doll furniture is also sold here—with a 6,000-square-foot dollhouse to showcase it—along with plates and a few stuffed animals. An entire room is devoted to Barbies. (Maybe the other dolls don't want to play with them.) 2012 NW Military Hwy. © 800/648-3655 or 210/341-3655. www.dollsdolls.com.

Treefrog Ed's *(Kids)*   More playful than an educational toy store and more educational than a traditional toy store, this small gem offers unique interactive toys for infants to (almost) teens. Some of the active learning items are more active than others: You'll also find bearded dragons, spiders, snakes, and frogs in the store (no, not loose, and no, not for sale). 5021 Broadway, behind Cappy's. © **210/821-7177.**

WESTERN WEAR

Boot Hill   This one-stop shopping center for all duds Western, from Tony Lama boots to Stetson hats and everything in between, is one of the few left in town that's locally owned. Arnold Schwarzenegger and Ashley Judd are among the stars who have been outfitted here. This is a great store with terrific goods, but as an Arizonan, I feel compelled to mention that the *real* Boot Hill is in Tombstone, in my home state. Boot Hill has another branch in the northwest, at 8023 Callaghan Rd. near I-10 West (© **210/341-4685**), as well as a major

presence on the Internet. Rivercenter Mall, 849 E. Commerce, Suite 213. ✆ **210/223-6634.**
www.boothillusa.com.

Little's Boots *Finds*   Lucchese (see below) is better known but this place—
established in 1915—uses as many esoteric leathers and creates fancier footwear
designs. You can get anything you like hand-customed for you if you're willing
to wait a while—possibly in line behind Reba McEntire and Tommy Lee Jones,
who have had boots handcrafted here. Purchase some just so you can tell your
friends back home, "Oh Lucchese is so commercial; Little's is still the real
thing." 110 Division Ave. ✆ **210/923-2221.** www.davelittleboots.com.

Lucchese Gallery   The name says it all: Footwear is raised to the level of art
at Lucchese. If it ever crawled, ran, hopped, or swam, these folks can probably
put it on your feet. The store carries boots made of alligator, elephant, ostrich,
kangaroo, stingray, and lizard. Come here for everything from executive to special-occasion boots, all handmade and expensive and all still serious Texas status
symbols. Lucchese also carries jackets, belts, and sterling silver belt buckles. 255
E. Basse, Suite 800. ✆ **210/828-9419.** www.lucchese.com.

Paris Hatters   What do Pope John Paul II, Prince Charles, Jimmy Smits, and
Dwight Yoakam have in common? They've all had headgear made for them by
Paris Hatters, in business since 1917 and still owned by the same family. About
half of the sales are special orders, but the shelves are stocked with high-quality
ready-to-wear hats, including Kangol caps from Britain, Panama hats from
Ecuador, and, of course, Stetson, Resistol, Dobbs, and other Western brands. A
lot of them can be adjusted to your liking while you wait. Check out the pictures and newspaper articles in the back of the store to see which other famous
heads have been covered here. 119 Broadway. ✆ **210/223-3453.**

Sheplers Western Wear   If you want instant (as in trying on the clothes)
gratification rather than waiting to get your duds in the mail from what has
turned into the world's largest online western store (www.sheplers.com), come
to this Super Store branch of the national chain founded in Wichita, Kansas,
during the 1950s. 6201 NW Loop 410. ✆ **210/681-8230.**

WINES
See also Central Market under "Food."

Gabriel's   A large, warehouse-style store, Gabriel's combines good selection
with good prices. You never know what oenological bargains you'll find on any
given day. The Hildebrand store is slightly north of downtown; there's also
another location near the airport at 7233 Blanco (✆ **210/349-7472**). 837 Hildebrand. ✆ **210/735-8329.**

SeaZar's Fine Wine & Spirits   A temperature-controlled wine cellar, a large
selection of beer and spirits, a cigar humidor, and a knowledgeable staff all make
this a good choice for aficionados of the various legal vices. 6422 N. New Braunfels,
in the Sunset Ridge Shopping Center. ✆ **210/822-6094.**

8

San Antonio After Dark

San Antonio has its symphony and its Broadway shows, and you can see both at one of the most beautiful old movie palaces in the country. But much of what the city has to offer is not quite so mainstream. Latin influences lend spice to some of the best local nightlife: San Antonio is America's capital for Tejano music, a unique blend of German polka and northern Mexico ranchero sounds (with a dose of pop added for good measure). You can sit on one side of the San Antonio River and watch colorful dance troupes like Ballet Folklórico perform on the other. And Southtown, with its many Hispanic-oriented shops and galleries, celebrates its art scene with the monthly First Friday, a kind of extended block party.

Keep in mind, too, that the Fiesta City throws big public parties year-round: Fiestas Navideñas and Las Posadas around Christmastime; Fiesta San Antonio and Cinco de Mayo events in spring; the Texas Folklife Festival in summer; and Oktoberfest events in autumn (see also "San Antonio Calendar of Events," in chapter 2).

For the most complete listings of what's on while you're visiting, pick up a free copy of the weekly alternative newspaper, the *Current,* or the Friday "Weekender" section of the *San Antonio Express-News.* You can also check out the **San Antonio Arts & Cultural Affairs Hot Line** at ✆ **210/222-ARTS** or log onto the website www.sanantonio.gov/art. There's no central office in town for tickets, discounted or otherwise. You'll need to reserve seats directly through the theaters or clubs, or, for large events, through **Ticketmaster** (✆ **210/224-9600;** www.ticketmaster.com). Generally, box office hours are Monday to Friday 10am to 5pm, and 1 to 2 hours before performance time. The Majestic and Empire also have hours on Saturday 10am to 3pm.

1 The Performing Arts

The San Antonio Symphony is the city's only resident performing arts company of national stature, but smaller, less professional groups keep the local arts scene lively, and cultural organizations draw world-renowned artists. The city provides them with some unique venues—everything from standout historic structures like the Majestic, Empire, Arneson, and Sunken Garden theaters to the new state-of-the-art SBC Center. Because, in some cases, the theater is the show and, in others, a single venue offers an eclectic array of performances, I've included a category called "Major Arts Venues," below.

CLASSICAL MUSIC

San Antonio Symphony   The city's symphony is one of the finest in the United States. Founded in 1939, the orchestra celebrated its 50th anniversary by moving into the Majestic Theatre, the reopening of which was planned to coincide with the event. The symphony offers two major annual series, classical and pops. The former showcases the talents of music director Christopher Wilkens emeritus and a variety of guest performers; for the latter, the orchestra plays second fiddle to the likes of Al Jarreau and Burt Bacharach. 222 E. Houston St. © 210/554-1000 or 210/554-1010 (box office). www.sasymphony.org. Tickets $18–$55.

THEATER

Most of San Antonio's major shows turn up at the Majestic or Empire theaters (see "Major Art Venues," below), but several smaller theaters are of interest too. The **Actors Theater of San Antonio at the Woodlawn,** 1920 Fredericksburg Rd. (© **210/738-2872**), uses local talent for its productions, which tend to be in the off-Broadway tradition. At the King William district's **Alamo Street Restaurant & Theatre,** 1150 S. Alamo (© **210/271-7791**; www.alamostreet restaurantandtheatre.com), interactive comedies and murder mysteries take place in the Green Room Dinner Theatre—the former choir rooms of a converted 1912 church—accompanied by buffet meals; upstairs, in the former sanctuary now called The Mainstage, there are lectures, concerts, musicals, comedies, and dramas, sans food. The community-based **Josephine Street Theater,** 339 W. Josephine St. (© **210/734-4646**), puts on an average of five productions a year—mostly musicals—at the Art Deco–style Josephine Street Theater, only 5 minutes from downtown. Whether it's an original piece by a member of the company or a work by a guest artist, anything you see at the **Jump-Start Performance Company,** 108 Blue Star Arts Complex (1400 S. Alamo; © **210/227-JUMP;** www.jump-start.org), is likely to push the social and political envelope. This is the place to find the big-name performance artists like Karen Finley or Holly Hughes who tour San Antonio. The only professional family theater in town, the popular **Magik Theatre,** Beethoven Hall, 420 S. Alamo in HemisFair Park (© **210/227-2751;** www.magiktheatre.org), features a daytime series with light fare for ages 3 and up, and evening performances, recommended for those 6 and older, that may include weightier plays. About half the plays are adaptations of published scripts, while the other half are originals, created especially for the theater. San Antonio's first public theater, the **San Pedro Playhouse,** 800 W. Ashby (© **210/733-7258;** http://members.tripod.com/san_pedro_playhouse), presents a wide range of plays in a neoclassical–style performance hall built in 1930. For information on other small theaters in San Antonio and links to many of those listed in this section, log on to the website of the **San Antonio Theater Coalition,** www.satheatre.com.

MAJOR ARTS VENUES

See also the "For Those Interested in Hispanic Heritage" section of chapter 6 for information on the Alameda Theater.

Arneson River Theatre If you're visiting San Antonio in the summer, be sure to see something at the Arneson. Built by the Works Project Administration in 1939 as part of architect Robert Hugman's design for the River Walk, this unique theater stages shows on one side of the river while the audience watches from an amphitheater on the other. Most of the year, performance schedules are erratic and include everything from opera to Tejano, but the summer brings a stricter calendar: the Fandango folkloric troupe perform every Tuesday and Thursday in June and July, and the Fiesta Noche del Río takes the stage on Friday and Saturday May through July. Both offer lively music and dance with a south-of-the-border flair. La Villita. © 210/207-8610. www.lavillita.com.

Beethoven Home and Garden San Antonio's German heritage is celebrated at this venue, a converted 1894 Victorian mansion in the King William

---

> ⌐ **Fun Fact**   **A Theater That Lives Up to Its Name**
>
> Everyone from Jack Benny to Mae West played the **Majestic,** one of the last "atmospheric" theaters to be built in America: The stock market crashed 4 months after its June 1929 debut, and no one could afford to build such expensive showplaces afterward. Designed in baroque Moorish/Spanish revival style by John Eberson, this former vaudeville and film palace features an elaborate village above the sides of the stage and, overhead, a magnificent night sky dome, replete with twinkling stars and scudding clouds. Designated a National Historic Landmark, the Majestic affords a rare glimpse into a gilded era (yes, there's genuine gold leaf detailing).

---

area. The season starts in April, with music and dance performances for the city-wide Fiesta. This is followed by monthly concerts with the Mannerchor (men's choir), which dates back to 1867, as well as brass bands, dancers, singers, and other choirs through September. Lots of traditional German food, drink, and revelry make Oktoberfest an autumn high point. The hall closes down after the first Saturday in December, when a Kristkrindle Markt welcomes the holiday season with an old country–style arts-and-crafts fair. 422 Pereida. ℂ 210/222-1521.

Carver Community Cultural Center   Located near the Alamodome on the east edge of downtown, the Carver's theater was built for the city's African-American community in 1929, and hosted the likes of Ella Fitzgerald, Charlie "Bird" Parker, and Dizzy Gillespie over the years. It continues to serve the community while providing a widely popular venue for an international array of performers in a variety of genres, including drama, music, and dance. The cultural center is undergoing a major renovation as part of a $12 million Carver Complex project, so some performances may be held at different San Antonio venues. 226 N. Hackberry. ℂ 210/207-7211 or 210/207-2234 (box office). www.thecarver.org. Tickets $22–$37.

The Empire Theatre   Among the celebrities who trod the boards of the Empire Theatre before its motion picture prime were Roy Rogers and Trigger; Mae West put in an appearance, too. Fallen into disrepair and shuttered for 2 decades, this 1914 opera house made its grand re-debut in 1998 after a massive renovation. Smaller than its former rival the Majestic (see below), just down the block, the Empire hosts a similarly eclectic array of acts, from rock to children's theater and shows like *Seussical the Musical with Kathy Rigby.* 226 N. St. Mary's St. ℂ 210/226-5700. www.majesticempire.com.

Guadalupe Cultural Arts Center   There's always something happening at the Guadalupe Center, the heart of Latino cultural activity in San Antonio. Visiting and local directors put on six or seven plays a year; the resident Guadalupe Dance Company might collaborate with the city's symphony or invite modern masters up from Mexico City. The Xicano Music Program celebrates the popular local conjunto and Tejano sounds; an annual book fair brings in Spanish-language literature from around the world; and the CineFestival, running since 1977, is one of the town's major film events. And then there are always the parties thrown to celebrate new installations at the theater's art gallery and its annex. 1300 Guadalupe. ℂ 210/271-3151. www.guadalupeculturalarts.org.

Laurie Auditorium   Some pretty high-powered people turn up at the Laurie Auditorium, on the Trinity University campus in the north-central part of town. Everyone from Margaret Thatcher to Colin Powell has taken part in the university's Distinguished Lecture Series, subsidized by grants and open to the public for free. The 2,700-seat hall also hosts major players in the popular and performing arts: Jay Leno and Bill Cosby were among those who took the stage in recent years. Dance recitals, jazz concerts, and plays, many with internationally renowned artists, are held here, too. Trinity University, 715 Stadium Dr. ℂ 210/999-8117 (taped box office information line) or 210/999-8119. www.trinity.edu/departments/Laurie.

Majestic Theatre   This theater introduced air-conditioning to San Antonio—the hall was billed beforehand as "an acre of cool, comfortable seats"—and society women wore fur coats to its opening, held on a warm June night in 1929. The Majestic hosts some of the best entertainment in town—the symphony, major Broadway productions, big-name solo performers—and, thanks to a wonderful restoration of this fabulous showplace, completed in 1989, coming here is still pretty cool. 230 E. Houston. ℂ 210/226-3333. www.majesticempire.com.

Sunken Garden Theater   Built by the WPA in 1936 in a natural acoustic bowl in Brackenridge Park, the Sunken Garden Theater boasts an open-air stage set against a wooded hillside; cut-limestone buildings in Greek revival style hold the wings and the dressing rooms. This appealing outdoor arena, open from March through October, offers a little bit of everything—rock, country, hip-hop, rap, jazz, Tejano, Cajun, and sometimes even the San Antonio Symphony. Annual events include Taste of New Orleans (a Fiesta event in Apr), the Margarita Pour-Off in August, and a biannual Bob Marley Reggae Festival. Brackenridge Park, 3975 N. St. Mary's St. (Mulberry Ave. entrance). ℂ 210/207-6000. www.sanantonio.gov.

2 The Club & Music Scene

The closest San Antonio comes to having a club district is the stretch of North St. Mary's between Josephine and Magnolia—just north of downtown and south of Brackenridge Park—known as the Strip. This area was hotter—or is that cooler?—about 15 years ago, but it still draws a young crowd to its restaurants and lounges on the weekend. The River Walk clubs tend to be touristy, and many of them close early because of noise restrictions. Downtown's **Sunset Station,** 1174 E. Commerce (ℂ 210/222-9481; www.sunset-station.com), a multi-venue entertainment complex in the city's original train station, has yet to take off when there are no events in the nearby Alamodome. When there are, you can get down at Studio 794, a high energy dance club with a 1916 steam engine in it, and Club Agave, where the movement has a Latin flavor.

In addition to the **Alamodome,** 100 Montana St. (ℂ 210/207-3663; www.sanantonio.gov/dome), the major concert venues in town include **Verizon Wireless Amphitheater,** 16765 Lookout Rd., north of San Antonio just beyond Loop 1604 (ℂ 210/657-8300; www.vwatx.com) and, when the Spurs aren't playing there, downtown's **SBC Center,** One SBC Center Parkway (ℂ 210/444-5000; www.nba.com/spurs/sbc_center), which opened in October 2002.

COUNTRY & WESTERN

Floores Country Store ℱℱ   John T. Floore, the first manager of the Majestic Theatre and an unsuccessful candidate for mayor of San Antonio, opened up this country store in 1942. A couple of years later, he added a cafe and a dance floor—at half an acre, the largest in south Texas. And not much has changed since then. Boots, hats, and antique farm equipment hang from the ceiling of this typical Texas roadhouse, and the walls are lined with pictures of Willie Nelson, Hank Williams, Sr., Conway Twitty, Ernest Tubb, and other country greats who have played here. There's always live music on weekends; Dwight Yoakum, Robert Earl Keen, and Lyle Lovett have all turned up along with Willie. The cafe still serves homemade bread, homemade tamales, old-fashioned sausage, and cold Texas beer. 14492 Old Bandera Rd./Hwy. 16, Helotes (2 miles north of Loop 1604). ℭ 210/ 695-8827. www.liveatfloores.com. Cover $5–$35.

Leon Springs Dancehall This lively 1880s-style dance hall can—and often does—pack some 1,200 people into its 18,000 square feet. Lots of people come with their kids when the place opens at 7pm; the crowd turns older (but not much) as the evening wears on. Some of the best local country-and-western talent is showcased here on Friday and Saturday nights, the only two nights the dance hall is open. Get a group of more than 10 together and you can order BBQ from the original Rudy's, just down the road. 24135 I-10 (Boerne Stage Rd. exit). ℭ 210/698-7072. www.leonspringsdancehall.com. Cover usually $5; kids under 12 free.

ROCK

Taco Land Loud and not much to look at—think low ceilings, red vinyl booths, garage pin-up calendars stapled to the ceiling—tiny Taco Land is nevertheless the hottest alternative music club in San Antonio, showcasing everything from mainstream rock to surf punk. Some of the bands that turn up may seem less than impressive, but, hey, you never know: Nirvana played here before they hit the big time (and before Taco Land actually began serving tacos). 103 W. Grayson St. ℭ 210/223-8406. Cover $3 Fri–Sat; free during the week.

White Rabbit One of the few alternative rock venues on the Strip—and one of the only ones large enough to have a raised stage—the Rabbit attracts a mostly young crowd to its black-lit recesses. Those 18 to 20 years old are allowed in for a higher cover. 2410 N. St. Mary's St. ℭ 210/737-2221. Cover varies.

ECLECTIC

Casbeers Opened in 1932, this is the real deal, an eclectic Texas dive bar/restaurant with so much local character that the Texas Tornadoes filmed their "Anybody Goin' to San Antone" video here. The venue may be old but the sounds are new. You can hear local, regional, national, and international artists (such as Grammy Award winner Dave Alvin) in a variety of genres, including roots, rock, blues, country, folk, and, for the monthly Sunday brunch to benefit the local homeless shelter, gospel. There's only beer and wine to accompany the hearty burgers and Tex-Mex chow. 1719 Blanco Rd. ℭ 210/732-3511. www. casbeers.com. No cover Tues–Wed, $5–$15 Thurs–Sat.

JAZZ & BLUES

The Landing 👫👫 You might have heard cornetist Jim Cullum on the airwaves: His American Public Radio program, *Riverwalk, Live from the Landing,* is now broadcast on more than 225 stations nationwide, and his band has backed some of the finest jazz players of our time. This is the best traditional jazz club in Texas; if you like big bands and Dixieland, there's no better place to listen to this music. The Landing Cafe features an eclectic menu with lots of New Orleans–style touches. Hyatt Regency Hotel, River Walk. ℭ 210/223-7266. www.landing. com. Cover $3.50 Mon–Thurs, $6.50 Fri–Sat, free Sun (outdoor stage only).

Conjuto: An American Classic

Cruise a San Antonio radio dial or go to any major city festival, and you'll most likely hear the happy, boisterous sound of conjunto. Never heard of it? Don't worry, you're not alone. Although conjunto is one of our country's original contributions to world music, for a long time few Americans outside Texas knew much about it.

Conjunto evolved at the end of the 19th century, when South Texas was swept by a wave of German immigrants who brought with them popular polkas and waltzes. These sounds were easily incorporated into—and transformed by—Mexican folk music; the newcomer accordion, cheap and able to mimic several instruments, was happily adopted, too. With the addition at the turn of the century of the *bajo sexto,* a 12-string guitarlike instrument used for rhythmic bass accompaniment, conjunto was born.

Tejano (Spanish for "Texan") is the 20th-century offspring of conjunto. The two most prominent instruments in Tejano remain the accordion and the *bajo sexto,* but the music incorporates more modern forms, including pop, jazz, and country-and-western, into the traditional conjunto repertoire. At clubs not exclusively devoted to Latino sounds, what you're likely to hear is Tejano.

Long ignored by the mainstream, conjunto and Tejano were brought into America's consciousness by the murder of Hispanic superstar **Selena.** Before she was killed, Selena had already been slotted for crossover success—she had done the title song and put in a cameo appearance in the film *Don Juan de Marco* with Johnny Depp—and the movie based on her life boosted awareness of her music even further.

San Antonio is to conjunto music what Nashville is to country. The most famous *bajo sextos,* used nationally by everyone who is anyone in conjunto and Tejano music, were created in San Antonio by the Macías family—the late Martín and now his son, Alberto. The undisputed king of conjunto, **Flaco Jiménez**—a mild-mannered triple-Grammy winner who has recorded with the Rolling Stones, Bob Dylan, and Willie Nelson, among others—lives in the city. And San Antonio's **Tejano Conjunto Festival,** held each May (see the "San Antonio Calendar of Events," in chapter 2), is the largest of its kind, drawing aficionados from around the world—there's even a conjunto band from Japan.

Most of the places to hear conjunto and Tejano are off the beaten tourist path, and they come and go fairly quickly. Those that have been around for a while—and are visitor friendly—include **Arturo's Sports Bar & Grill,** 3310 S. Zarzamora St. (© **210/923-0177**); **Cattleman's At Woodlake,** 3711 Roland Rd. (© **210/337-3880**); and **Cool Arrows,** 1025 Nogalitos St. (© **210/227-5130**). For live music schedules, check the Tejano/Conjunto section under "Entertainment" and "Music" of www.mysanantonio.com, the website of the *San Antonio-Express News.* You can also phone **Salute!** (see below) to find out which night of the week they're featuring a Tejano or conjunto band. Best yet, just attend one of San Antonio's many festivals—you're bound to hear these rousing sounds.

Salute!   The live jazz at this tiny club tends to have a Latin flavor, but you never know what you're going to hear—anything from synthesized '70s sounds to conjunto. 2801 N. St. Mary's St. ℂ 210/732-5307. Cover $3–$5 weekends; free during the week.

Tycoon Flats (_Kids_)   A friendly music garden, Tycoon Flats is a fun place to kick back and listen to blues, rock, acoustic, or jazz. The burgers are good, too. Bring the kids—an outdoor sandbox is larger than the dance floor. There's never any cover for the almost nightly live music. 2926 N. St. Mary's St. ℂ 210/737-1929. No cover.

DANCE CLUBS

Polly Esther's   Is it just a coincidence that the last four digits in the telephone number of this lively, three-level River Walk club match the year that the disco craze started to take hold? I think not. Even if you've sworn off strobe lights forever, you just can't help yourself once you hear that funky beat. That's especially true if you have indulged in one of the club's signature liqueur drinks, which sound innocuous (Peanut Butter 'n' Jelly, for example) and taste syrupy sweet but pack a major wallop. 212 College St. ℂ 210/220-1972. www.pollyesthers.com. Cover $3–$8.

COMEDY

Rivercenter Comedy Club   This club books big names in stand-up like Dennis Miller and Garry Shandling, but it also takes advantage of local talent on Mondays (Comedy Potpourri nights) and Fridays (open-mike night in the Ha!Lapeno Lounge 5–7:30pm; no cover). Also free: the late, late (12:20am) adult-oriented shows on Saturday nights. 849 E. Commerce St. (Rivercenter Mall, 3rd level). ℂ 210/229-1420. www.hotcomedy.com. Cover $9 Mon–Thurs, $12 Fri–Sun.

SALOONS

Howl at the Moon Saloon   It's hard to avoid having a good time at this rowdy River Walk bar; if you're shy, one of the dueling piano players will inevitably embarrass you into joining the crowd belting out off-key oldies from the '60s, '70s, and '80s. Don't worry. You're probably never going to see most of these people again. 111 W. Crockett St. ℂ 210/212-4695. www.howlatthemoon.com. Cover $4 Sun–Thurs, $6 Fri–Sat. 21 and older only.

THE GAY SCENE

In addition to the Bonham (see below), Main Street just north of downtown has three gay clubs in close proximity (it's been nicknamed the "gay bar mall"). **Pegasus,** 1402 N. Main (ℂ 210/299-4222; no cover), is your basic cruise bar. **The Silver Dollar,** 1418 N. Main (ℂ 210/227-2623; no cover), does the country-and-western thing. And **The Saint,** 1430 N. Main (ℂ 210/225-7330; www.thesaintshowbar.com; cover $4 for ages over 21, $5 ages 18–21), caters to dancing fools.

Bonham Exchange   Tina Turner, Deborah Harry, and LaToya Jackson—the real ones—have all played this high-tech dance club near the Alamo. While you may find an occasional cross-dressing show here, the mixed crowd of gays and straights, young and old, come mainly to move to the beat under wildly flashing lights. All the action—five bars, three dance floors, three levels—takes place in a restored German-style building dating back to the 1880s. Roll over, Beethoven. 411 Bonham. ℂ 210/271-3811. No cover for ages 21 and over before 10pm, then $5 ($3 on Wed).

3 The Bar Scene

Most bars close at 2am, although some alternative spots stay open until 3 or 4am.

Blue Star Brewing Company Restaurant & Bar   Preppies and gallery types don't often mingle, but the popularity of this brewpub in the Blue Star Arts Complex with college kids demonstrates the transcendent power of good beer. (The pale ale is especially fine.) And if a few folks who wouldn't know a Picasso from a piccolo happen to wander in and see some art after dinner, then the owners have performed a useful public service. The food's good, too. 1414 S. Alamo, no. 105 (Blue Star Arts Complex). ℂ **210/212-5506.** www.bluestarbrewing.com.

Cadillac Bar & Restaurant   During the week, lawyers and judges come to unwind at the Cadillac Bar, set in a historic stucco building near the Bexar County Courthouse and City Hall. On the weekends, singles take over the joint. A deejay spins on Saturday nights, but on Thursdays and Fridays, the sounds are live and local—anything from '70s disco to classic rock to pop. Full dinners are served on a patio out back. 212 S. Flores. ℂ **210/223-5533.**

Cappycino's   Although it's by no means deficient in the caffeine department, don't mistake Cappycino's for a coffee bar: The name derives from neighboring Cappy's restaurant (p. 65), of which it's an offshoot. The forte here is yuppie hard stuff, including classic cocktails, tequilas, and single-malt scotches. A skinny but high-ceilinged light-wood dining room and a plant-filled patio create a relaxed setting for drinking and dining off the stylish Southwest bistro menu. 5003 Broadway. ℂ **210/828-6860.**

Durty Nellie's Irish Pub   Chug a lager and lime, toss your peanut shells on the floor, and sing along with the piano player at this wonderfully corny version of an Irish pub. You've forgotten the words to "Danny Boy"? Not to worry— 18 old-time favorites are printed on the back of the menu. After a couple of Guinnesses, you'll be bellowing "H-A-double-R-I-G-A-N spells Harrigan!" as loud as the rest of 'em. 715 River Walk (Hilton Palacio del Rio Hotel). ℂ **210/222-1400.**

The Laboratory   One of the few microbreweries in San Antonio, and the only place in town that makes an "authentic" Bavarian *hefeweizen,* "The Lab" used to be the laboratory for the old Alamo Quarry cement factory. Stress tests were once conducted in the room where the beer is now brewed, but the only stress these days involves working up the nerve to walk up to that attractive stranger. For fortification, you can down dauntingly large sandwiches, nachos, and the like in the huge, two-level main room or on an outdoor patio, where trees do their best to hide the brightly lit Quarry shopping mall nearby. There's live music Friday and Saturday. 7310 Jones-Maltsberger. ℂ **210/824-1997.** www. labbrew.com.

Menger Bar   More than 100 years ago, Teddy Roosevelt recruited men for his Rough Riders unit at this dark, wooded bar; they were outfitted for the Spanish-American War at nearby Fort Sam Houston. Constructed in 1859 on the site of William Menger's earlier successful brewery and saloon, the bar was moved from its original location in the Victorian hotel lobby in 1956, but 90% of its historic furnishings remain intact. You can still see an "X" on the bar (modeled after the bar in the House of Lords in London) put there by prohibitionist Carrie Nation, and Spanish Civil War uniforms hang on the walls. It's still one of the prime spots in town to toss back a few. Menger Hotel, 204 Alamo Plaza. ℂ **210/223-4361.**

Polo's Lounge For a piano, bass, and sax trio in a high-tone atmosphere, come to Polo's on a Friday or Saturday night. You can sink into a plush leather couch or perch on a stool at the marble bar and enjoy some jazz, swing, or Broadway sounds. This romantic spot tends to draw an older crowd, who can afford the drinks. Fairmount Hotel, 401 S. Alamo St. ℂ 210/224-8800.

Saffron Come to this chic new Alamo Heights bar/restaurant for its *War and Peace*–size wine list and appealing tapas menu, featuring some selections rarely found outside Spain. The people-watching is good too: You can sit out on the front patio and watch the '09ers in their native habitat (the upscale Sunset Ridge shopping strip). 6450 N. New Braunfels. ℂ 210/930-8463.

Stone Werks Caffe and Bar Right next door to The Laboratory (see above), Stone Werks attracts a slightly older (30-something) crowd than its neighbor, but it's equally lively, with local cover bands getting the crowd moving on the dance floor from Wednesday through Saturday. It's also got an equally distinctive setting: It's housed in a 1920s building that used to be the Alamo Cement Company's office. An oak-shaded patio is surrounded by a fence hand-sculpted from cement by Mexican artist Dionicio Rodríguez. 7300 Jones-Maltsberger. ℂ 210/ 828-3508. www.stonewerks.com.

Swig Craving a chocolate martini? Belly up to the bar at the River Walk's latest nod to retro chic. Single-barrel bourbon, single-malt scotch, as well as a wide selection of beer and wines fill out the drinks menu, but James Bond's preferred poison is always the top seller. Nightly live jazz adds to the pizzazz. The catch (or draw) here is those big cigars. 111 W. Crockett, no. 205. ℂ 210/476-0005.

Tex's If you want to hang with the Spurs, come to Tex's, regularly voted San Antonio's best sports bar in the *Current* readers' polls. Three satellite dishes, two large-screen TVs, and 17 smaller sets keep the bleachers happy, as do the killer margaritas and giant burgers. Among Tex's major collection of exclusively Texas sports memorabilia are a signed Nolan Ryan jersey, a football used by the Dallas Cowboys in their 1977 Super Bowl victory, and one of George Gervin's basketball shoes (the other is at the newer Tex's on the River, at the Hilton Palacio del Rio). San Antonio Airport Hilton and Conference Center, 611 NW Loop 410. ℂ 210/340-6060.

Tower of the Americas No matter what, or how much, you have to drink, you'll get higher here than anywhere else in San Antonio—more than 700 feet high, in fact. Just below the observation-deck level, the bar at the Tower of the Americas Restaurant affords dazzling views of the city at night. Sample a Top of the Tower—light rum, vodka, apricot brandy, and fruit juices—and you might never want to come down. 600 HemisFair Park. ℂ 210/223-3101. www. toweroftheamericas.com.

(*Finds* **Mission Accomplished**

In 2001, the **Mission Drive-In,** 310 Roosevelt Ave. (ℂ 210/532-3258), celebrated its grand reopening. When it premiered in 1947, the movie screen was framed with a neon outline of nearby Mission San Jose, replete with moving bell, burro, and cacti. San Antonio's last remaining open-air movie house now has four screens and features first-run films. It's as much fun to come here for a family filmfest or romantic under-the-stars evening as it ever was.

Zinc This chic wine bar, open until 2am nightly, is perfect for a romantic after-hours glass of champagne. Hardwood floors, brick walls, and a cozy library make the space appealing; on temperate nights, head for the pretty back patio. 209 N. Presa St. ℂ **210/224-2900**. wwww.zincwine.com.

4 Movies

There's not that much of an alternative cinema scene in San Antonio. The one theater where art and foreign movies turned up most frequently closed in 2002, and so far hasn't been replaced. The good news: Several theaters in town offer 50¢ matinees for the first show of the day, and charge only $1.50 for the other shows—cheaper than renting a video and you get the big screen.

The **Guadalupe Cultural Arts Center** (see "Major Arts Venues," above) and the **McNay** and **Witte museums** (see chapter 6) often have interesting film series, and the **Esperanza Center,** 922 San Pedro (ℂ **210/228-0201**; www. esperanzacenter.org), usually offers an annual gay and lesbian cinema festival. In addition to *Alamo, the Price of Freedom,* the **San Antonio IMAX Theater Rivercenter,** 217 Alamo Plaza (ℂ **210/225-4629**; www.imax-sa.com), shows high-action films like *Spiderman* or *Into the Deep* suited to the big, big screen. Be on the lookout for a second-large screen theater on the River Walk, the Aztec Theater, which was still under construction in early 2003 with no opening date in sight.

9

The Best of Austin

Aah, Austin, laid-back city in the lake-laced hills, home to cyberpunks and environmentalists, high culture and haute cuisine. A leafy intellectual enclave lying well outside the realm of Lone Star stereotypes, Austin has been compared to Berkeley and Seattle, but it is at once its own place and entirely of Texas.

The University of Texas (UT), vastly expanded beyond the 40 acres deeded to it in 1883, is a key source of the city's cultural savvy. Its assets include a presidential library; theater, dance, and concert venues; major literary archives—UT was the model for the wealthy American university in A.S. Byatt's novel *Possession*—and an important art collection. But UT's funding comes from oil money, and Austinites display typical Texan fervor when it comes to rooting for the Longhorns.

Despite its growing concrete nexus of highways and business parks—many devoted to high-tech enterprises, like the one started by UT graduate Michael Dell—Austin's heart is green. It has a vast municipal system of parks and preserves, and a bustling hike-and-bike trail near downtown's Town Lake. And there isn't a species in the region, no matter how small or ugly, that isn't vociferously defended if its extinction is threatened.

When they're not exercising or espousing environmental causes—or even when they are—Austinites love music. Their obsession is large scale: The city has gigantic record stores, a shop devoted solely to music art, and more than 100 live music venues. One of the most appealing aspects of the local scene is the wide range of good sounds to be found at unexpected, completely original places: barbecue joints, Mexican restaurants, converted gas stations. The atmosphere almost everywhere is assiduously laid-back; legends like Bob Dylan and Joan Baez still perform at intimate spots like the Backyard, and covers in the smaller clubs are still relatively low.

Many Texans who live in faster-paced cities like Dallas or Houston dream of someday escaping to Austin, which, although it grew by 41% in the 1990s and passed the half-million population mark, still has a small-town feel. Meanwhile, they smile upon the city as they would on a beloved but eccentric younger sister; whenever an especially contrary story about her is told, they shrug, shake their heads, and fondly say, "Well, that's Austin."

1 Frommer's Favorite Austin Experiences

- **Having Coffee at Mozart's.** Caffeine and conversation on a deck overlooking Lake Austin—a great way to end the day. See p. 180.
- **Joining the Healthy Hordes on Austin's Hike & Bike Trails.** Head over to the shores of Town Lake to see why *Walking* magazine chose Austin as America's "Most Fit" city. Speed walkers, joggers, and in-line skaters share the turf with bicyclists and hikers on the many trails set up by the city for its urban athletes. See chapter 14.

Book your air, hotel, and transportation all in one place.

Hotel or hostel? Cruise or canoe? Car? Plane? Camel? Wherever you're going, visit Yahoo! Travel and get total control over your arrangements. Even choose your seat assignment. So. One hump or two? travel.yahoo.com

powered by COMPAQ

YAHOO!
Travel

Do You YAHOO!?

© 2002 Yahoo! Inc.

- **Splashing around Barton Springs Pool.** The bracing waters of this natural pool have been drawing Austinites to its banks for more than 100 years. If there's one thing that everyone in town can agree on, it's that there's no better plunge pond on a hot day than this one. See p. 186.

- **Going Batty.** From late March through November, thousands of bats emerge in smoky clouds from under the Congress Avenue Bridge, heading west for dinner. It's a mind-boggling sight, and you can thank each of the little mammals for keeping the air pest-free—a single bat can eat as many as 600 mosquitoes in an hour. See chapter 14.

- **Playing in the Water at Lake Travis.** The longest of the seven Highland Lakes, Travis offers the most opportunities for watery cavorting, including Jet-Skiing, snorkeling, and angling. See chapter 14.

- **Touring the Capitol.** The country's largest state capitol was pretty impressive even in its run-down state, but after a massive face-lift at the end of the last century, visitors can really see that it's a legislative center fit for Texas. See p. 186.

- **Smelling the Bluebonnets at the Lady Bird Johnson Wildflower Center.** Spring is prime viewing time for the flowers, but Austin's mild winters ensure that there will always be bursts of color at Lady Bird Johnson's pet project. See p. 188.

- ✗ **Chuckling over Tall Tales at the LBJ Library.** At the largest and most visited of the country's presidential libraries, a surprisingly lifelike animatronic figure of LBJ, dressed in the actual clothes of the late president and speaking (via recording) in his famed slow drawl, regales visitors with terrific Texas stories. See p. 187.

- ✗ **Ascending Mount Bonnell.** Sure, the 100-odd steps are steep, but the climb is far more rewarding than a StairMaster: When you reach the top, the view of the city will take away whatever breath you have left. See chapter 14.

- **Taking a Visitors Center Walking Tour.** I wouldn't ordinarily suggest herding activities, but these historic excursions provided free by the city are superb. See chapter 14.

- **Visiting Stevie Ray Vaughan at Town Lake.** The late rock guitarist looks uncharacteristically stiff in his bronze incarnation, but he has a great view of Austin across the lake, and it's fun to see what kind of stuff his fans have left him. See chapter 14.

- **Touring the Austin City Limits Studio.** C'mon, admit it, you've always wanted to play air guitar on the stage where Lyle Lovett and Mary Chapin Carpenter performed. The logistics for getting tickets to the live taping sessions is a bit more complicated than the regular tours, but it's worth a shot to take part in PBS's longest running show. See chapter 16.

- **Listening to the Blues at Antone's.** Antone's may have moved to the trendy Warehouse District, but the music is as timeless as ever. Major blues stars coming through town always end up doing a few sets at Clifford Antone's institution. See p. 229.

- **Drinking in Some History at Scholz Garten.** The oldest biergarten in Texas has loads of atmosphere—not to mention an up-to-date sound system. Just don't come here after the University of Texas Longhorns have won (or lost) a game; the place will be packed with singing (or sulking) UT fans. See p. 232.

2 Best Austin Hotel Bets

- **Best for Conducting Business:** Located near a lot of the high-tech companies in northwest Austin, the **Renaissance Austin Hotel,** 9721 Arboretum Blvd. (© **800/ HOTELS-1** or 512/343-2626), has top-notch meeting and schmoozing spaces, not to mention fine close-the-deal-and-party spots. See p. 156.

- **Best Hotel Lobby for Pretending You're Rich:** Settle in at the lobby lounge at the posh **Four Seasons Austin,** 98 San Jacinto Blvd. (© **800/332-3442** or 512/ 478-4500), overlooking Town Lake, and for the price of a Dubonnet, you can act like you stay here every time you fly in on your Lear jet. See p. 145.

- **Best Place to Play Cattle Baron.** If you want to imagine you've acquired your fortune in an earlier era, bed down at **The Driskill,** 604 Brazos St. (© **800/252-9367** or 512/474-5911), where big meat mogul Jesse Driskill still surveys (via stone image) the opulent 1886 hotel that bears his name. See p. 148.

- **Hippest Budget Hotel:** Look for the classic neon sign for the **Austin Motel,** 1220 S. Congress St. (© **512/441-1157**), in Austin's cool SoCo district. The rooms have been individually furnished, many in fun and funky styles, but the place retains its 1950s character and its retro prices. See p. 150.

- **Best New Arrival:** The **Austin Folk House** bed-and-breakfast, 506 West 22nd St. (© **866/472-6700** or 512/472-6700), has a great location near the University of Texas, lovely rooms far better equipped than those in most B&Bs (or hotels for that matter), and reasonable rates. See p. 151.

- **Best View of Town Lake:** Lots of downtown properties have nice water views, but the **Hyatt Regency**'s location, 208 Barton Springs Rd. (© **800/233-1234** or 512/477-1234), on the lake's south shore, gives it the edge. You get a panoramic spread of the city with the capitol as a backdrop. See p. 146.

- **Best Health Club:** All those high-tech ways to sweat, and all those massage rooms to soothe sore muscles afterward—the **Barton Creek Resort,** 8212 Barton Club Dr. (© **800/336-6158** or 512/ 329-4000), raises exercise to an art form. See p. 157.

- **Greenest Hotel:** Several hotels in Austin take eco-consciousness beyond the old "we-won't-wash-your-towels" option, but no one takes it nearly as far as **Habitat Suites,** 500 E. Highland Mall Blvd. (© **800/535-4663** or 512/ 467-6000). Almost everything here is eco-friendly. See p. 153.

- **Best for Forgetting Your Troubles:** Stress? That's a dirty word at the **Lake Austin Spa Resort,** 1705 S. Quinlan Park Rd. (© **800/ 847-5637,** or 512/372-7300). After a few days at this lovely, ultrarelaxing spot, you'll be ready to face the world again, even if you don't especially want to. See p. 157.

3 Best Austin Dining Bets

- **Best Restaurant for Making a Good Impression:** At **Emilia's,** 600 E. 3rd St. (© **512/469-9722**), the New American cuisine is first-rate, the setting—a beautiful historic house with good acoustics—is impeccable, and the wine list is literally the best in

Netting the Best of the Austin Web

Austin is such a plugged-in city that it's tough to select just a few websites. However, some do stand out for their depth and breadth:

www.austin360.com: Movie times, traffic reports, restaurant picks, homes, jobs, cars . . . this site, sponsored in part by the *Austin-American Statesman,* the city's daily newspaper, is a one-stop clicking center for a variety of essentials. It's easy to navigate, too.

www.austinchronicle.com: The online version of Austin's excellent alternative tabloid, the *Austin Chronicle,* has everything you would expect: muckraking stories; hard-hitting book, movies and restaurant reviews; personal ads; and above all, attitude. And it looks a lot better online than it does on paper.

www.ci.austin.tx.us: Talk about big government. **Austin City Connection** is proof positive that practically everything in Austin falls under the aegis of its municipal system, from air quality to bus schedules and parks and recreation. A surprising number of museums (including the one devoted to O. Henry) are covered on this site, too.

www.utexas.edu: After the city government, the University of Texas might have the largest network of influence in town. In addition to giving info about the many on-campus museums, entertainment venues, and sports teams, this website links to such visitor-oriented sites as the *Austin Chronicle* Restaurant Guide and the Guide to Texas Outside's description of scenic overlooks in the area. Wouldn't want the students—or their visiting parents—to get hungry or bored, right?

Texas. Whether it's a romance or business deal you want to consummate, you can't do better than to conduct the wooing ritual here. See p. 164.

- **Best Place to Pretend You're in Italy:** It's not only the menu—great cappuccino, delicious thin-crust pizzas, focaccia sandwiches and the like—that make **Cipollina,** 1213 West Lynn (© 512/477-5211), feel European. This deli also has a cosmopolitan atmosphere that makes you want to settle in with a copy of Umberto Eco's latest book. See p. 173.

- **Best Vegetarian Cuisine:** The **West Lynn Cafe,** 1110 W. Lynn (© 512/482-0950), has a huge meatless selection prepared in the most innovative ways. Vegetarians

of all stripes leave here completely sated. See p. 171.

- **Best Place to Spot Celebrities:** You can expect to see the likes of Quentin Tarantino, Emilio Estevez, and Richard Linklater lounging in one of the back booths or hugging a bar stool up front at ultrahip **Güero's,** 1412 S. Congress (© 512/447-7688). The "Presidential" plate refers to the selection made by Bill Clinton when he dined here. See p. 174.

- **Most Quintessentially Austin:** Its laid-back Texas menu, huge outdoor patio, and "unplugged" music series all make **Shady Grove,** 1624 Barton Springs Rd. (© 512/474-9991), the Platonic ideal of The Austin Restaurant. See p. 169.

- **Best Brunch:** It's a tie between the Sunday buffet at **Green Pastures,** 811 W. Live Oak Rd. (© **512/444-4747**), where Austinites have been imbibing milk punch, liberally dosed with bourbon, rum, brandy, ice cream, and nutmeg, for years, and the one at **Fonda San Miguel,** 2330 W. North Loop (© **512/459-4121**), where the spread runs deliciously toward Mexico. See p. 170.

- **Best Melding of Old and New Worlds:** The **Driskill Grill,** 600 E. 3rd St. (© **512/391-7162**), has the grace and tone that befits the historic hotel it serves, but there's nothing dated about the New American cuisine that dazzles this era's culinarily demanding guests. See p. 162

- **Best if You're Game for Game:** It's a bit of a drive and more than a bit of a wallet bite, but if you want to see how tasty venison or bison can be, you can't beat **Hudson's on the Bend,** 3509 Hwy. 620 North (© **512/266-1369**). See p. 177.

- **Best View:** The easy winner is **The Oasis,** 6550 Comanche Trail, near Lake Travis (© **512/266-2441**), whose multiple decks afford stunning views of Lake Travis and the Texas Hill Country. See p. 178.

- **Sweetest Contribution to the Dining Scene:** Austin's home-grown brand of ice cream, **Amy's,** is wonderfully rich and creamy, and watching the colorfully clad servers juggling the scoops is always a kick. Amy's has eight Austin locations, including one on the west side of downtown, 1012 W. Sixth St. at Lamar Boulevard (© **512/480-0673**), and one at the Arboretum, 10000 Research Blvd., (© **512/345-1006**). If you don't get a chance to try it in town, hit the airport Amy's as you leave town. See p. 174.

Planning Your Trip to Austin

Planning a trip is not only half the fun of getting there; it also helps ensure your enjoyment when you arrive. See chapter 2 for additional information about planning your trip: The "Money" section discusses ATM networks and traveler's check agencies; "Insurance" talks about trip cancellation, medical, and lost luggage insurance; and "Planning Your Trip Online" describes Internet resources.

1 Visitor Information

Austin is one of the country's most wired cities, and I'm not talking caffeine. If you're not e-oriented, call the **Austin Convention and Visitors Bureau,** 201 E. Second St., Austin, TX 78701 (© **800/926-2282**), to receive a general information packet in the mail; otherwise log on to www. austintexas.org. The Austin municipal site, www.ci.austin.tx.us, is a good source for learning about several aspects of the city, not just the airport, roads, police and the like; you'd be surprised how many attractions fall under the aegis of the Department of Parks and Recreation. The site also provides several useful links, for example to the University of Texas. To read the entertainment listings and reviews in *The Austin-American Statesman,* the city's mainstream newspaper, log on to www.austin360.com; for the daily news, go to www.austin360.com/aas. You'll find the *Austin Chronicle,* the city's alternative newspaper, at www. auschron.com.

See this same section in chapter 2 for suggestions on getting information about other parts of Texas.

2 When to Go

Although Austin's supply of hotel rooms has increased, it's still important to book ahead of time. Summer season is typically busy, but legislative sessions (the first half of odd-numbered years) and University of Texas events (graduation, say, or home-team games) can also fill up the town's lodgings quickly.

CLIMATE

May showers follow April flowers in the Austin/Texas Hill Country area; by the time the late spring rains set in, the bluebonnets and most of the other wildflowers have already peaked. Mother Nature thoughtfully arranges mild, generally dry weather in which to enjoy her glorious floral arrangements in early spring—an ideal and deservedly popular time to visit. Summers can be steamy—the past several summers have seen atypically long stretches of triple-digit temperatures—but Austin offers plenty of great places to cool off, among them the Highland Lakes and Barton Springs. Fall foliage in this leafy area is another treat, and it's hard to beat a Texas evening by a cozy fireplace—admittedly more for show than for warmth in Austin, which generally enjoys mild winters.

What Things Cost in Austin	U.S. $	U.K. £
Taxi from the airport to downtown	$24.00–$26.00	£15–£16.25
Bus ride between any two downtown points	Free	Free
Local telephone call	35¢	20p
Double at the Four Seasons (very expensive)	$250.00–$350.00	£156.25–£218.75
Double at the Holiday Inn Austin Town Lake (moderate)	$129.00–$139.00	£80.60–£86.90
Double at the Austin Motel (inexpensive)	$70.00–$90.00	£43.75–£56.25
Lunch for one at the Shoreline Grill (expensive)	$16.00	£10.00
Lunch for one at Las Manitas (inexpensive)	$6.00	£3.75
Dinner for one, without drinks, at Jeffrey's (very expensive)	$60.00	£37.50
Dinner for one, without drinks, at Manuel's (moderate)	$18.00	£11.25
Dinner for one, without drinks, at The Iron Works (inexpensive)	$8.50	£5.30
Pint of beer at brewpub	$4.00	£2.50
Coca-Cola	$1.50	95p
Cup of espresso	$2.50	£1.55
Admission to Austin Museum of Art–Downtown	$5.00	£3.10
Roll of ASA 100 Kodacolor film, 36 exposures	$7.25	£4.55
Movie ticket	$3.50–$7.50	£2.20–4.70
Austin Symphony ticket	$19.00–$35.00	£11.90–£21.90

Austin's Average Monthly Temperature & Rainfall

	Jan	Feb	Mar	Apr	May	June	July	Aug	Sept	Oct	Nov	Dec
Avg. Temp. (°F)	52	55	61	68	75	82	84	84	80	71	60	53
Avg. Temp (°C)	11	13	16	20	24	28	29	29	26	21	15	12
Rainfall (in.)	1.66	2.06	1.54	2.54	3.07	2.79	1.69	2.41	3.71	2.84	1.77	1.46

AUSTIN CALENDAR OF EVENTS

Many of Austin's festivals capitalize on its large community of local musicians and/or on the great outdoors. The major annual events are listed here. See also chapter 16 for information on the various free concerts and other cultural events held every summer, and call ② 866-GO-AUSTIN for additional events information.

January

Red Eye Regatta, Austin Yacht Club, Lake Travis. The bracing lake air at this keelboat race should help cure what ails you from the night before. ② **512/266-1336;** www. austinyachtclub.org. New Year's Day.

February

Carnival Brasileiro, Palmer Events Center. Conga lines, elaborate costumes, samba bands, and confetti are all part of this sizzling Carnavale-style event, started in 1975 by homesick Brazilian students at the University of Texas. ℂ 512/452-6832; www.sambaparty.com. First or second Saturday of February.

March

Kite Festival, Zilker Park. Colorful handmade kites fill the sky during this popular annual contest, one of the oldest of its kind in the country. ℂ 512/478-0905. First Sunday in March.

South by Southwest (S×SW) Music and Media Conference & Festival. The Austin Music Awards kick off this huge conference, which organizes hundreds of concerts at more than two dozen city venues. Aspiring music industry and high-tech professionals sign up months in advance. ℂ 512/467-7979; www.sxsw.com. Usually around third week in March (during University of Texas's spring break).

Jerry Jeff Walker's Birthday Weekend, various locations. Each year, singer/songwriter Walker performs at such venues as the Broken Spoke and the Paramount Theatre, and takes part in a golf tournament with other musicians. The man knows how to throw a party. ℂ 512/477-0036; www.jerryjeff.com. Last weekend of March.

Capitol 10,000. Texas's largest 10K race winds its way from the state capitol through West Austin, ending up at Town Lake. ℂ 512/445-3598; www.runtex.com. Late March.

Star of Texas Fair and Rodeo, Travis County Exposition Center. This two-week Wild West extravaganza features rodeos, cattle auctions, a youth fair, a parade down Congress Avenue, and lots of live country music. ℂ 512/919-3000; www.staroftexas.org. Late March/early April.

April

Austin Fine Arts Festival, Republic Square. The major fundraiser for the Austin Museum of Art, this show features a large juried art show, local musicians, and lots of kids' activities. ℂ 512/458-6073; www.austinfineartsfestival.org. Second weekend in April.

Texas Hill Country Wine and Food Festival (most events at the Four Seasons Hotel). Book a month in advance for the cooking demonstrations; beer, wine, and food tastings; and celebrity chef dinners. For the food fair, just turn up with an appetite. ℂ 512/542-WINE; www.texaswineandfood.org. First weekend after Easter.

Old Settlers Music Festival, Salt Lick BBQ Pavilion. More than 30 bluegrass bands descend on nearby Dripping Springs to take part in this Americana roots music fest, which also includes songwriter workshops, arts and crafts booths, and children's entertainment. ℂ 512/346-1629; www.bluegrassfestival.com. Mid-April.

Austin ParksFest. Inaugurated in 2002, with a BBQ Cook-Off, several races, and a series of concerts, including one starring Travis Tritt, this benefit event for the park system is likely to become an annual institution. ℂ 512/477-1566; www.austinparksfest.org. Weekend after Earth Day (Apr 22).

May

O. Henry Pun-Off, O. Henry Museum. One of the punniest events around, this annual battle of the wits is for a wordy cause—the upkeep of the O. Henry Museum.

© 512/472-1903; http://home. attbi.com/~ohenrypunoff/right. html. First Sunday in May.

Old Pecan Street Spring Arts and Crafts Festival, Sixth Street. Eat and shop your way along Austin's restored Victorian main street while bands play in the background. © 512/441-9015; www.roadstar productions.com. First weekend in May.

Cinco de Mayo, Fiesta Gardens and other locations. Mariachis, flamenco dancers, Tejano music, tacos, and tamales are all part of the traditional Mexican freedom celebration. © 512/499-6720; www. austin-cincodemayo.com. May 5.

June

Juneteenth, various venues, mostly in East Austin. The celebration of African-American emancipation, which became a Texas state holiday in 1980, generally includes a parade, gospel singing, and many children's events. The best source of information is the Carver Library branch. © 512/989-1539. June 19.

July

Austin Symphony Orchestra, Auditorium Shores. Cannons, fireworks, and of course a rousing rendition of the "1812 Overture" contribute to the fun at this noisy freedom celebration. © 512/476-6064; www.austinsymphony.org. July 4.

August

Austin Chronicle **Hot Sauce Festival,** Waterloo Park. The largest hot sauce contest in the world features more than 300 salsa entries, judged by celebrity chefs and food editors. The bands that play this super party are hot, too. © 512/454-5766; www.austinchronicle.com. Last Sunday in August.

Fall Creek Vineyards Celebration & Grape Stomp, Lake Buchanan.

Grape squishing, footprint T-shirts, and wine tastings are all part of the fun. © 915/379-5361; www.fcv. com. Third and fourth Saturdays in August.

September

Diez y Seis, Plaza Saltillo and other sites. Mariachis and folk dancers, conjunto and Tejano music, as well as fajitas, piñatas, and clowns help celebrate Mexico's independence from Spain. The highlight is the crowning of the Fiestas Patrias Queen. © 512/476-7502. Four days usually starting around September 16.

Fall Jazz Festival, Zilker Hillside Theater. Zilker Park swings with 2 days of free concerts by top local jazz acts. © 512/442-2263. Second weekend of September.

Austin City Limits Music Festival, Zilker Park. Yet more evidence of Austin's devotion to live music, this 2-day music extravaganza kicked off in 2002. If the first year was any indication, expect a super lineup of musical talent. © 512/478-4811 or 512/478-7211; www. aclfestival.com. Late September.

October

Austin Film Festival, Paramount Theatre and other venues. If you like the idea of sitting in the dark and watching 80 films in 8 days—everything from classic recuts to new indie releases—or are an aspiring screenwriter or filmmaker, this one's for you. © 800/310-FEST or 512/478-4795; www.austinfilm festival.com. 8 days in mid-October.

Halloween, Sixth Street. 100,000 costumed revelers take over 7 blocks of historic Sixth Street. © 800/926-2282. October 31.

November

Día de los Muertos (Day of the Dead), Congress Avenue. Death is embraced as part of the life cycle in this Hispanic festival, involving Latino music, a parade, and, of course, food. © **512/480-9373;** www.main.org/mexic-arte. November 2 (All Soul's Day).

December

Zilker Park Tree Lighting. The lighting of a magnificent 165-foot tree is followed by the Trail of Lights, a mile-long display of life-size holiday scenes. First Sunday of the month (tree lighting); second Sunday through December 23 (Trail of Lights). This being Austin, a 5K run is also involved. © **512/974-6700;** www.cityofaustin.org/tol.

Christmas at the French Legation Museum. Père Noël (the French Santa Claus) and costumed guides help host this lively gift bazaar, held in an 1840 historic house. © **512/472-8180.** First weekend of December.

Armadillo Christmas Bazaar, Austin Music Hall. Revel in Tex-Mex food, live music, and a full bar at this high-quality art, craft, and gift show. © **512/447-1605;** www.armadillobazaar.com. Begins approximately 2 weeks before Christmas.

3 Tips for Travelers with Special Needs

FOR TRAVELERS WITH DISABILITIES

See this section in chapter 2 for details on **Mobility International USA** and on the **Access-Able Travel Source** website. There's an active **Americans with Disabilities (ADA)** office in Austin. Its website, www.ci.austin.tx. us/ada, has lots of useful links. You can also call © **512/974-3256** or **512/974-1897** if you have questions about whether any of the hotels or other facilities you're interested in are in compliance with the Act.

FOR GAY & LESBIAN TRAVELERS

A university town and probably the most left-leaning enclave in Texas, Austin is generally gay-friendly. To find out about clubs in addition to those listed in chapter 16 (Oilcan Harry's and Rainbow Cattle Co.), log on to http://austin.about.com/cs/gaynightlife. **Book Woman,** 918 W. 12th St., at Lamar (© **512/472-2785;** www.ebookwoman.com), and **Lobo,** 3204-A Guadalupe St. (© **512/454-5406**), are the best places to find gay and lesbian books and magazines, as

well as the free *Austin Gay-Friendly Resource Directory,* published annually, and *Q Texas,* a resource for the whole state. The website of the Lesbian, Bisexual, and Gay Students Association (LBGSA) at the University of Texas, www.lbgsa.org, provides links to these and every other gay and lesbian resource in the city.

FOR SENIORS

The **Old Bakery and Emporium,** 1006 Congress Ave. (© **512/477-5961**), not only sells crafts and baked goods made by senior citizens, but also serves as a volunteer center for people over 50. It's a good place to find out about any senior activities in town. Another excellent resource is the monthly *Senior Advocate* newspaper, 3710 Cedar St., Box 17, Austin, TX 78705 (© **512/451-7433**), which you can pick up, gratis, at HEB supermarkets, libraries, hospitals, and many other places. You can also call or write in advance for a subscription ($15 per year).

See chapter 2 for information about the **AARP** (formerly the American Association of Retired Persons) and

Elderhostel. Elderhostel classes in Austin often focus on the natural beauties of the region; there's usually a seminar at the Lady Bird Johnson Wildflower Center.

FOR FAMILIES

Austin's free monthly publication **"Our Kids,"** which can be found at libraries, bookstores, children's clothing stores, The Children's Museum, Hollywood Video, Wal-Mart, and HEB and Sun Harvest grocery stores, gives a detailed day-by-day calendar of children-oriented events in town, as well as recommendations for local attractions that youngsters would enjoy. For a subscription ($15 per year), contact Our Kids, 500 San Marcos St., Suite 200-D, Austin, TX 78702 (© **512/236-8417;** www. parenthood.com). Not as up to date as "Our Kids," but still a good general resource, *Kidding Around Austin,* by Drew D. Johnson and Cynthia Brantley Johnson (John Muir Publications), is available at most local bookstores for $7.95. See also this section of chapter 2 for information about the

Family Travel Times newsletter, "Travel with Your Children."

FOR STUDENTS

There are endless resources for students in this university town. Just stop by the **University of Texas Student Union Building** (see map in chapter 14) to check out the scene. Austin's oldest institution of higher learning, **Huston Tillotson College,** 600 Chicon St. (© **512/505-3000**), in east Austin, is especially helpful for getting African-American students oriented. The **Hostelling International–Austin** (see chapter 12) is another great repository of information for students.

One of the best sources for information and bookings of discounted airfares, rail fares, and lodgings is **STA Travel** (© **800/777-0112;** www. statravel.com), with offices throughout the United States. In Austin, there's an STA Travel retail office at 2116 Guadalupe St., Austin, TX 78705 (© **512/472-2900**). See this section of chapter 2 for details on **Hostelling International–American Youth Hostels (HI-AYH).**

4 Getting There

BY PLANE

THE MAJOR AIRLINES   America West (© 800/235-9292; www.america west.com), **American** (© 800/433-7300; www.aa.com), **Continental** (© 800/525-0280; www.fly continental.com), **Delta** (© 800/221-1212; www.delta.com), **Frontier** (© 800/432-1359; www.frontier airlines.com), **Midwest Express** (© 800/452-2022; www.midwest express.com), **Northwest** (© 800/225-2525; www.nwa.com), **Southwest** (© 800/435-9792; www.ifly swa.com), and **United** (© 800/241-6522; www.united.com) all fly into Austin. There are currently nonstop flights to 30 destinations including (outside of Texas) Atlanta; Baltimore/

Washington; Chicago; Cincinnati; Denver; Houston; Kansas City; Las Vegas; Los Angeles; Memphis; Minneapolis/St. Paul; Nashville; New York/Newark; Orlando; Phoenix; Raleigh-Durham; St. Louis; Salt Lake City; San Diego; San Jose; and Tampa.

FINDING THE BEST AIRFARE All the airlines run seasonal specials that can lower fares considerably. If your dates of travel don't coincide with these promotions, however, the least expensive way to travel is to purchase tickets 21 days in advance, stay over Saturday night, and travel during the week. (See chapter 2 for more advice on fighting, and winning, the airfare wars.)

BY CAR

I-35 is the north–south approach to Austin; it intersects with **Hwy. 290,** a major east–west thoroughfare, and **Hwy. 183,** which also runs roughly north–south through town. If you're staying on the west side of Austin, hook up with **Loop 1,** almost always called Mo-Pac by locals.

Stay on I-35 north and you'll get to Dallas/Fort Worth in about 4 hours. Hwy. 290 leads east to Houston, approximately 2½ hours away, and west via a scenic Hill Country route to I-10, the main east–west thoroughfare. I-10 can also be picked up by heading south to San Antonio, some 80 miles away on I-35.

In case you're planning a state capital tour, it's 896 miles from Austin to Atlanta; 1,911 miles to Boston; 921 miles to Springfield, Illinois; 671 miles to Santa Fe; 963 miles to Phoenix; and 1,745 miles to Sacramento.

BY TRAIN

To get to points east or west of Austin on the Sunset Limited by **Amtrak,** 250 N. Lamar Blvd. (© **800/872-7245** or 512/476-5684; www.amtrak.com), you'll have to pass through San Antonio (see "By Train," in chapter 2). Trains depart from Austin to San Antonio nightly. The Texas Eagle runs from Austin to Chicago daily.

BY BUS

You'll also be going through San Antonio if you're traveling east or west to Austin via **Greyhound,** 916 E. Koenig Lane (© **800/231-2222** or 512/458-4463; www.greyhound.com); see chapter 2 for details. There are approximately 15 buses between the two cities each day, with one-way fares running around $13.

5 Recommended Reading

The foibles of the Texas "lege"—along with those of Congress and the rest of Washington—are hilariously pilloried by Molly Ivins, Austin's resident scourge, in two collections of her syndicated newspaper columns: *Molly Ivins Can't Say That, Can She?* and *Nothing But Good Times Ahead.* George W. Bush was a more recent target in *Shrub.* For background into the city's unique music scene, try Jan Reid's *The Improbable Rise of Red Neck Rock.* It's been followed more recently by Barry Shank's scholarly tome, *Dissonant Identities: The Rock 'n' Roll Scene in Austin, Texas.* Serious history buffs might want to dip into Robert Caro's excellent multivolume biography of Lyndon B. Johnson, the consummate Texas politician, who had a profound effect on the Austin area. (Volume 3 of the proposed four-volume series was published in 2002.)

William Sydney Porter, better known as O. Henry, published a satirical newspaper in Austin in the late 19th century. Among the many short tales he wrote about the area—collected in *O. Henry's Texas Stories*—are four inspired by his stint as a draftsman in the General Land Office. Set largely in Austin, Billy Lee Brammer's *The Gay Place* is a fictional portrait of a political figure loosely based on LBJ.

The city's most famous resident scribe, the late James Michener, placed his historical epic *Texas* in the frame of a governor's task force operating out of Austin. The city is also the locus of several of Austin resident Mary Willis Walker's mysteries, including *Zero at the Bone* and *All the Dead Lie Down;* it is also the setting for *The Boyfriend School,* a humorous novel by San Antonian Sarah Bird.

It's only logical that the king of cyberpunk writers, Bruce Sterling, should live in Austin; he gets megabytes of fan mail each week for such books as *Islands in the Net, The Difference Engine* (with William Gibson), and *Holy Fire*. His nonfiction work, *The Hacker Crackdown,* details a failed antihacker raid in Austin.

11

Getting to Know Austin

With thousands of acres of parks, preserves, and lakes set aside for public enjoyment, Austin is unusually nature-friendly. It's easy to miss that, however, when you're busy negotiating the city's freeways. As soon as possible, get out of your car and smell the flowers: Just a few blocks south of downtown's office towers lie the green shores of Town Lake, where you'll begin to see the real Austin.

Central Austin is, very roughly, bounded by Town Lake to the south, Hwy. 290 to the north, I-35 to the east, and Mo-Pac (Loop 1) to the west. South Austin, east of Mo-Pac, tends to be blue-collar residential, although its northern sections have been gentrified, and hotels have been cropping up like mushrooms since an airport opened in this area in the late 1990s. Although the tech boom–driven development in north Austin is on hold for the time being, residential growth is not showing much sign of slowing down. What was once flat farmland in the old section of east Austin has become home to many Hispanic and African-American communities, while some of the city's most opulent mansions now perch on the lakeshores and hills of west Austin.

1 Orientation

ARRIVING

BY PLANE The $581 million **Austin-Bergstrom International Airport** (© 512/530-ABIA), opened in 1999 on the site of the former Bergstrom Air Force Base, just off Hwy. 71 (Ben White Blvd.) and only 8 miles southwest of the capitol, is the town's transportation darling.

Not only did the airy glass-and-granite structure replace an outdated facility with an expanded new one, but also it was designed to capture the spirit of Austin from the moment you step off the plane. The passenger terminal, named after the late Texas Congresswoman Barbara Jordan, boasts a stage area for performances by Austin musicians (see sidebar), hosts local businesses like BookPeople and an Austin City Limits gift shop, and features Austin food concessions such as Amy's Ice Cream, Matt's El Rancho, and The Salt Lick—with prices comparable to those in town. This was also the first airport in the country to go wireless: Anyone with a Wayport card can access data, unplugged. Since Austin is such a hotbed of high-tech, the airport's even got a geek's dream of a website, www.ci.austin.tx.us/austinairport, featuring a virtual reality tour of the terminal, flight schedules, links to airlines and car-rental companies, descriptions of concessions, the latest bulletins on noise-pollution control, and more. For those wanting nonvirtual data, there's an information booth on the lower level of the terminal open daily from 7am to 11pm.

Taxis from the major companies in town usually form a line outside the terminal, though occasionally you'll find nobody waiting. To ensure off-hour pickup in advance, phone **American Yellow Checker Cab** (© 512/542-9999)

Fun Fact **Leaving on a Jet Plane? Tuneful Take-Offs**

Who could have predicted that musicians would scramble for an airport gig? But with music lovers flying into town from all over, the Austin airport's stage has turned out to be a great place for local bands to get national exposure—who knows what record company exec might be fortuitously stranded? The music mirrors the eclecticism of Austin's scene, including R&B, honky-tonk, jazz, conjunto, world, pop, Western retro—you name it. Don't expect to be entertained every time you fly in or depart, though. Performances generally take place on weekdays from 3:30 to 5pm. Check the airport's website to find out what bands might fit in with your flight plans.

---

before you leave home. The ride between the airport and downtown generally costs around $25. The flag-drop charge is $1.50, and it's $1.75 for each mile after that.

If you're not in a huge rush to get to your hotel, **SuperShuttle** (© **800-BLUE VAN** or 512/258-3826; www.supershuttle.com) is a less-expensive alternative to cabbing it, offering comfortable minivan service to hotels and residences. Prices range from $10 one-way ($18 round-trip) for trips to a downtown hotel to $12 ($20 round-trip) for trips to a central hotel and $15 ($26) for trips to a hotel in the northwestern part of town. The drawback is that you often must share your ride with several others, who may be dropped off first—at various points around town nowhere near your destination. You don't have to book in advance for pickups at the airport, but you do need to phone 24 hours ahead of time to arrange for a pickup if you're leaving town.

For details about public transportation from the airport, phone **Capital Metro Transit** (© **512/474-1200** or TTY 512/385-5872), or click on the "Parking-Transportation" section of the airport website. See also the "By Bus" section, below, and "By Public Transportation" in "Getting Around," later in this chapter, for additional information.

Most of the major car-rental companies—Advantage, Alamo, Avis, Budget, Dollar, Hertz, National, and Thrifty—have outlets at the airport, and you can now stroll across the road from the terminal building to pick up (and drop off) your car; see "Car Rentals" in the "Getting Around" section, below, for details. The trip from the airport to downtown by car or taxi can take anywhere from 25 minutes to an hour, depending on the time of day and the current state of highway repairs; during rush hour, there are often backups all along Hwy. 71. Be sure to slot in extra time when you need to catch a flight.

BY TRAIN The **Amtrak** station (© **512/476-5684**) is at Lamar and West First Street, in the southwest part of downtown. There are generally a few cabs around to meet the trains, but if you don't see one, you'll find a list of phone numbers of taxi companies posted near the pay phones. Some of the downtown hotels offer courtesy pickup from the train station. A cab ride shouldn't run more than $4 or $5 (there's a $3 minimum charge).

BY BUS The **bus terminal** is near Highland Mall, about 10 minutes north of downtown and just south of the I-35 motel zone. There are some hotels within walking distance, and many others a short cab ride away; a few taxis usually wait outside the station. If you want to go downtown, you can catch either bus no.

and west, merges with I-35 where it comes in on the north side of town, briefly reestablishing its separate identity on the south side of town before merging with Hwy. 71 (which is called Ben White Blvd. between 183 and Lamar Blvd.). Highways 290 and 171 split up again in Oak Hill, on the west side of town. Not confused enough yet? Hwy 2222 changes its name from Koenig to Northland and, west of Loop 360, to Bullcreek, while, in the north, Hwy 183 is called Research Blvd. (Looking at a map should make all this clear as mud). Important north–south city streets include Lamar, Guadalupe, and Burnet. If you want to get across town north of the river, use Cesar Chavez (once known as First St.), 15th Street (which turns into Enfield west of Lamar), Martin Luther King Jr. Boulevard (the equivalent of 19th St., and often just called MLK), 38th Street, and 45th Street.

FINDING AN ADDRESS   Congress Avenue was the earliest dividing line between east and west, while the Colorado River marked the north and south border of the city. Addresses were designed to move in increments of 100 per block, so that 1500 N. Guadalupe, say, would be 15 blocks north of the river. This system still works reasonably well in the older sections of town, but breaks down where the neat street grid does (look at a street map to see where the right angles end). All the east–west streets were originally named after trees native to the city (for example, Sixth St. was once Pecan St.); many that run north and south, such as San Jacinto, Lavaca, and Guadalupe, retain their original Texas river monikers.

STREET MAPS   The surprisingly detailed free maps available at the Austin Convention and Visitor's Bureau, as well as at many car-rental companies at the airport, should help you find any place you're likely to want to locate. Alternatively, I'd recommend the **Gousha** city maps, available at most convenience stores, drugstores, newsstands, and bookstores.

THE NEIGHBORHOODS IN BRIEF

Although Austin, designed to be the capital of the independent Republic of Texas, has a planned, grand city center similar to that of Washington, D.C., the city has spread out far beyond those original boundaries. These days, with a few exceptions, detailed below, locals tend to speak in terms of landmarks (the University of Texas) or geographical areas (east Austin) rather than neighborhoods. The following designations are just rough approximations. Like pretty much everything else in Austin, they're open to discussion.

Downtown   The original city, laid out by Edwin Waller in 1839, runs roughly north–south from the river (Cesar Chavez) to Martin Luther King Boulevard (around 20th St.) and east–west between I-35 and Lamar. This prime sightseeing (it includes the Capitol and several historic districts) and hotel area has seen a resurgence in the past 3 decades, with music clubs, restaurants, shops, and galleries thriving on and around **Sixth Street,** and businesses returning to the beautiful old office buildings on and around **Congress Avenue.** The

latest subsection of downtown to take off is the **Warehouse District,** centered on Third and Fourth streets just west of Congress; new restaurants and watering holes seem to pop up there every time you turn around. Although this area technically ends at Town Lake, most people would consider the lake's south shore and its hike-and-bike trail to be part of downtown.

South Austin   For a long time, not a lot was happening south of Barton Springs Road/East Riverside Drive. Then in the 1990s, **South Congress,** the once-derelict stretch

7 (Duval) or bus no. 15 (Red River) from the bus stop across the street. A cab ride downtown—about 10 minutes away on the freeway—should cost from $8 to $10.

VISITOR INFORMATION

The **Austin Convention and Visitors Bureau,** 201 E. Second St. (© **800/ 926-2282;** www.austintexas.org), down the street from the Convention Center in the southeast section of downtown, is open Monday through Friday 8:30am to 5pm, Saturday 9am to 5pm, Sunday noon to 5pm (extended hours Memorial Day through Labor Day; closed Thanksgiving and Christmas). You can pick up tourist information pamphlets downtown at the **Old Bakery and Emporium,** 1006 Congress Ave. (© 512/477-5961), open Monday to Friday 9am to 4pm, and the first two Saturdays in December 10am to 3pm. In the **Capitol Visitors Center,** 112 E. 11th St. (© **512/305-8400;** www.texascapitolvisitorscenter.com), open daily 9am to 5pm, a Texas Department of Transportation travel center dispenses information on the entire state. Other sources of local information include the **Capital City African American Chamber of Commerce,** 5407 N. I-35, Suite 304 (© 512/459-1181), and the **Hispanic Chamber of Commerce of Austin/Travis County,** 3000 S. I-35 (© **512/476-7502,** www.Hispanic austin.com).

For entertainment listings, pick up the free alternative newspaper the *Chronicle,* distributed to stores, hotels, and restaurants around town every Thursday. It's got a close rival in *XLent,* the free weekend entertainment guide put out by the *Austin-American Statesman,* which also turns up on Thursday at most of the same places that carry the *Chronicle.*

Inside Line (© **512/416-5700**) can clue you in on Austin information from the essential to the esoteric—everything from weather forecasts and restaurant reviews to financial news and bat facts. Punch extension 4636 for instructions on how to use the system.

CITY LAYOUT

In 1839, Austin was laid out in a grid on the northern shore of the Colorado River, bounded by Shoal Creek to the west and Waller Creek to the east. The section of the river abutting the original settlement is now known as Town Lake, and the city has spread far beyond its original borders in all directions. The land to the east is flat Texas prairie; the rolling Hill Country begins on the west side of town.

MAIN ARTERIES & STREETS   I-35, forming the border between central and east Austin (and straddling the Balcones Fault Line), is the main north–south thoroughfare; Loop 1, usually called Mo-Pac (it follows the course of the Missouri-Pacific railroad, although some people like to say it got its name because it's "mo' packed"), is the westside equivalent. Hwy. 290, running east

> **Tips   The Quickest Route**
>
> If you're heading downtown from the airport, you're best off taking Riverside Drive—one of the first exits on Hwy. 71—and then Congress Avenue north rather than staying on Hwy. 71 and using I-35. If you want to get to the northwest, take Hwy. 183 all the way, again avoiding often-congested I-35.

Austin at a Glance

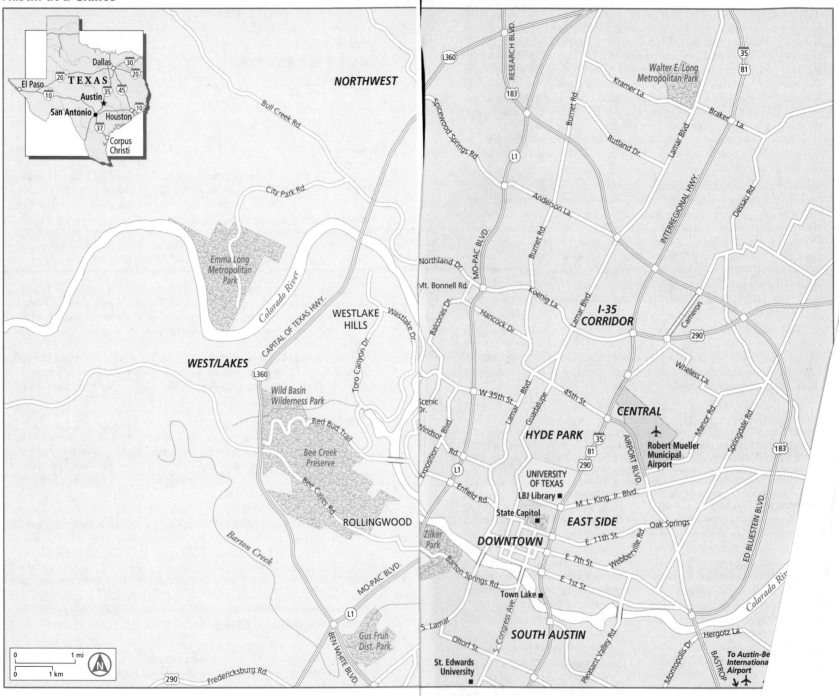

TEXAS

El Paso
Dallas
Austin
San Antonio
Houston
Corpus Christi

0   1 mi
0   1 km

NORTHWEST

Bull Creek Rd.

City Park Rd.

Colorado River

Emma Long
Metropolitan
Park

CAPITAL OF TEXAS HWY.

WESTLAKE
HILLS

Westlake Dr.

WEST/LAKES

L360

Wild Basin
Wilderness Park

Toro Canyon Dr.

Red Bud Trail

Bee Creek
Preserve

Bee Caves Rd.

ROLLINGWOOD

Barton Creek

MO-PAC BLVD.

BEN WHITE BLVD.

L1

Gus Fruh
Dist. Park

290   Fredericksburg Rd.

L360

RESEARCH BLVD.

183

Walter E. Long
Metropolitan Park

Kramer La.

Braker La.

Burnet Rd.

Rutland Dr.

Lamar Blvd.

INTERREGIONAL HWY.

Dessau Rd.

35

81

Spicewood Springs Rd.

L1

Anderson La.

MO-PAC BLVD.

Northland Dr.

Mt. Bonnell Rd.

Balcones Dr.

Hancock Dr.

Koenig La.

Burnet Rd.

Lamar Blvd.

I-35
CORRIDOR

Cameron

290

Wheless La.

W 35th St.

Scenic Dr.

Windsor Rd.

Exposition Blvd.

Enfield Rd.

L1

Lamar Blvd.

Guadalupe

45th St.

CENTRAL

HYDE PARK

81
290

35

AIRPORT BLVD.

Manor Rd.

Springdale Rd.

183

Robert Mueller
Municipal
Airport

UNIVERSITY
OF TEXAS

LBJ Library

State Capitol

Zilker
Park

DOWNTOWN

Barton Springs Rd.

M. L. King, Jr. Blvd.

EAST SIDE

Oak Springs

E. 11th St.

Webberville Rd.

E. 7th St.

Town Lake

E. 1st St.

S. Lamar

Oltorf St.

S. Congress Ave.

SOUTH AUSTIN

Colorado River

ED BLUESTEIN BLVD.

Pleasant Valley Rd.

Montopolis Dr.

Hergotz La.

BASTROP

St. Edwards
University

To Austin-Be
International
Airport

of Congress Avenue that extends (presently) to Oltorf Street, started becoming gentrified—or at least trendified. It's now lined with cutting-edge art galleries, antiques boutiques, and retro clothing shops, and has, naturally, been nicknamed "SoCo." **Fairview Park** and **Travis Heights,** adjoining neighborhoods between Congress and I-35 from Town Lake to Oltorf Street, were Austin's first settlements south of the river. At the end of the 19th century, these bluffs became desirable as Austin residents realized they were not as likely to be flooded as the lower-ground areas north of the Colorado. Many mansions in what had become a working-class district have lately been reclaimed by the newly rich kids and boomers who are helping to develop South Congress Avenue. And since the 1999 debut of the **airport** at Ben White Blvd., just east of Hwy. 183, hotels and services have started cropping up in an area once dominated by faceless residential developments. It's not until you head farther south and west, towards the Lady Bird Johnson Wildflower Center and the Austin Zoo, that south Austin begins to reassert its rural roots.

Central Austin Consisting roughly of the area north of Barton Springs Road/East Riverside Drive up until 45th Street, bordered by I-35 on the east and Mo-Pac on the west, Central Austin includes **Downtown** (see above) as well as several neighborhoods on its fringes. Just north of the capitol, the original 40 acres allotted for the **University of Texas** have expanded to 357, and Guadalupe Street, along the west side of the campus, is now a popular shopping strip known as the Drag. North of the university between 38th and 45th streets, **Hyde Park** got its start in 1891 as

one of Austin's first planned suburbs; renovation of its Victorian and early craftsman houses began in the 1970s, and now there's a real neighborhood feel to this pretty, tree-lined area. One of the neighborhoods that developed as downtown Austin expanded beyond Shoal Creek, **Clarksville,** just east of Mo-Pac, was founded by a former slave in 1871 as a utopian community for freed blacks; it's now an artists' enclave—but definitely not for the starving types. Directly to the north, from about West 15th to West 24th streets, **Enfield** boasts a number of beautiful homes and upscale restaurants. Larger mansions line the northern shores of Lake Austin, in the section known as **Tarrytown;** it's just south of Mount Bonnell and a beautiful stretch of land where, some historians say, Stephen F. Austin himself planned to retire.

East Side The section east of I-35 between Cesar Chavez and Manor Road is home to many of Austin's Latino and African-American residents. Mexican restaurants and markets dot the area, which also hosts a number of African-American heritage sites, including Huston-Tillotson College, Metropolitan African Methodist Episcopal Church, and the George Washington Carver Museum; the French Legation Museum and state cemetery are also in this area. The quiet, tree-lined **French Place,** just east of I-35 between Manor and 38½ streets, is beginning to vie with South Congress for yuppie/artist ingress, and art galleries are beginning to crop up in the warehouses near MLK.

I-35 Corridor Austin has grown around the heavily traveled connector area between Central and the Northwest, where the airport used to be located. Lined with chain hotels and restaurants, it's as charmless as it sounds, but it's convenient to both downtown and the north.

West/Lakes It's been said that the higher you rise in Austin's financial ranks, the farther west you move. As you head along Lake Austin and Lake Travis into Hill Country, you'll encounter such affluent residential developments as **Westlake Hills** (where Michael Dell lives) and **Lakeway,** as well as the more charming, low-key **Bee Cave.** But you don't have to live here to play here: This is also where those who

live in Central Austin come to splash around and kick back on nice weekends.

Northwest This high-growth area, Austin's version of the suburbs, consists largely of upscale business, shopping, and residential complexes; The Arboretum is this area's retail heart. The northwest has been described as extending north from Hwy. 2222 to Dallas, but Parmer Lane is probably the real northern boundary. Farther north are such bedroom communities as Round Rock and Cedar Park.

2 Getting Around

BY PUBLIC TRANSPORTATION

Austin's public transportation system, **Capital Metropolitan Transportation Authority** (www.capmetro.austin.tx.us), is excellent, including more than 50 bus lines and featuring low to nonexistent fares. The regular adult one-way fare on Metro routes is 50¢; express service from various Park & Ride lots costs $1.

Best of all, the five downtown 'Dillo routes—Red, Orange, Yellow, Blue, and Silver—are free. You'll need exact change or fare tickets (see below) to board the bus; free transfers are good for 3 hours on weekdays, 4 hours on weekends. Call ℘ 800/474-1201 or 512/474-1200 (TTY 512/385-5872) from local pay phones for point-to-point routing information. You can also pick up a schedule booklet at any HEB, Fiesta, or Albertsons grocery store or at the Capital Metro Information Center, 106 E. Eighth St., just off Congress.

DISCOUNT FARES 'Dillos aren't the only free ride in Austin. With the exception of Special Transit Service and Public Event shuttles, passengers 65 and older or those with mobility impairments may ride all fixed bus routes for free upon presenting a Capital Metro ID card to the driver. Cards are available for $3 from the Capital Metro Information Center (open Mon–Fri 7:30am–5:30pm). University of Texas students also ride for free upon presentation of a UT ID card; all other students who get a Capital Metro ID card pay half-price. If you buy a Ticket Book, available at the same place as schedule booklets (see above), you can get 20 50¢ tickets for only $5—a 50% savings. Children 5 years or younger ride free when accompanied by adults.

BY CAR

Between its long-standing traffic oddities and the more recent—but rampant—construction, driving in Austin is, to put it mildly, a challenge. Don't fall into a driver's daze anywhere in town; you need to be as vigilant on the city streets as you are on highways. The former are rife with signs that suddenly insist LEFT LANE MUST TURN LEFT or RIGHT LANE MUST TURN RIGHT—generally positioned so they're noticeable only when it's too late to switch. A number of major downtown streets are one-way; many don't have street signs or have signs so covered with foliage they're impossible to read. Driving is particularly confusing in the university area, where streets like "32½" suddenly turn up. Multiply the difficulties at night, when you need x-ray vision to read the ill-lit street indicators.

The highways are no more pleasant. I-35—nicknamed "the NAFTA highway" because of the big rigs speeding up it from Mexico—is mined with tricky on-and-off ramps and, around downtown, a confusing complex of upper and lower levels; it's easy to miss your exit or find yourself exiting when you don't want to. The rapidly developing area to the northwest, where Hwy. 183 connects I-35 with Mo-Pac and the Capital of Texas Highway, requires particular vigilance, as the connections occur very rapidly. There are regular lane mergings and sudden, precipitous turnoffs.

Nervous? Good. Better a bit edgy than lost or injured. Consult maps in advance and, when driving around the university or downtown, try to gauge the number of blocks before turns so you won't have to be completely dependent on street signs. You can also check the Texas Department of Transportation's (TXDoT) website, www.dot.state.tx.us, for the latest information on road conditions, including highway diversions, construction, and closures.

CAR RENTALS   If you're planning to travel at a popular time, it's a good idea to book as far in advance as you can, both to secure the quoted rates and to ensure that you get a car. Some of the companies I phoned in early October to inquire about the winter holiday season were already filled up for Christmas.

Advantage (© 800/777-5500; www.arac.com), **Alamo** (© 800/327-9633; www.goalamo.com), **Avis** (© 800/831-2847; www.avis.com), **Budget** (© 800/527-0700; www.budgetrentacar.com), **Dollar** (© 800/800-4000; www.dollarcar.com), **Hertz** (© 800/654-3131; www.hertz.com), **National** (© 800/227-7368; www.nationalcar.com), and **Thrifty** (© 800/367-2277; www.thrifty.com) all have representatives at the airport.

Lower prices are usually available for those who are flexible about dates of travel or who are members of frequent-flyer or frequent hotel stay programs or of organizations such as AAA or AARP. Car-rental companies are eager to get your business, so they're as likely as not to ask whether you belong to any group that will snag you a discount, but if the clerk doesn't inquire, it can't hurt to mention every travel-related program you're a member of; you'd be surprised at the bargains you might turn up. See chapter 3 for more tips about car rental.

PARKING   Unless you have congressional plates, you're likely to find the selection of parking spots downtown extremely limited during the week (construction isn't making the situation any better); as a result, lots of downtown restaurants offer valet parking (with rates ranging $4–$6). There are a number of lots around the area, costing anywhere from $5 to $7, but the most convenient ones tend to fill up quickly. If you're lucky enough to find a metered spot, it'll run you 75¢ per hour, with a two-hour limit, so bring change. Although there's virtually no street parking available near the capitol before 5pm during the week, there is a free visitor garage on 15th and San Jacinto (2-hr. time limit). *Tip:* If you're willing to forgo your own wheels for a bit, park in one of the free Park-and-Ride lots serviced by the Red, Gold, and Silver 'Dillo lines and take advantage of Austin's excellent free public transport (see "By Public Transportation," above).

In the university area, trying to find a spot near the shopping strip known as the Drag can be just that. Cruise the side streets; you're eventually bound to find a lot that's not filled. The two most convenient on-campus parking garages are located near San Jacinto and East 26th streets and off 25th Street between San

---

(*Fun Fact* **So Much for Safety**

Austinites were so up in arms about a helmet law passed in 1996, they forced its repeal a year later. Go figure; you'd think all those techies would want to keep their heads intact.

Antonio and Nueces; there's also a (free!) parking lot near the LBJ Library, but it's far from the central campus. Log on to **www.utexas.edu/business/parking/ resources** for additional places to drop off your car.

DRIVING RULES   Unless indicated, right turns are permitted on red after coming to a full stop. Seat belts and child-restraint seats are mandatory in Texas.

BY TAXI

Among the major cab companies in Austin are **Austin Cab** (✆ **512/478-2222**), **Roy's Taxi** (✆ **512/482-0000**), and **American Yellow Checker Cab** (✆ **512/ 452-9999**). Rates are regulated by the city; rides cost $1.50 plus $1.75 for each additional mile.

BY BIKE

Although an increase in traffic has rendered Austin's streets less bicycle-friendly than they once were, the city is still pretty good for two-wheelers. Many city streets have separate bicycle lanes, and lots of scenic areas have been set aside for hiking and biking; see the "Staying Active" section of chapter 14 for details.

ON FOOT

Crossing wide avenues such as Congress is not as easy as it should be, because lights tend to be geared toward motorists rather than pedestrians. Still, downtown Austin and other old sections of the city are generally quite walkable. Austin is also dotted with lovely, tree-shaded spots for everything from strolling to in-line skating. The city's jaywalking laws are not usually enforced, except occasionally downtown.

 ***FAST FACTS:* Austin**

American Express   The branch at 2943 W. Anderson Lane (✆ **512/452-8166**; www.americanexpress.com) is open Monday to Friday 9am to 6pm.

Area Code   The telephone area code in Austin is **512**.

Business Hours   Banks and offices are generally open Monday to Friday 8 or 9am to 5pm. Some banks offer drive-through service on Saturday 9am to noon or 1pm. Specialty shops and malls tend to open around 9 or 10am, Monday to Saturday; the former close at about 5 or 6pm, the latter at around 9 or 10pm. You can also shop at most malls and boutiques on Sunday from noon until 6pm. Bars and clubs tend to stay open until midnight during the week, 2am on weekends.

Car Rentals   See "By Car," earlier in this section.

Climate   See "When to Go," in chapter 9.

Dentist   Call the Dental Referral Service at ✆ **800/917-6453**.

Doctor The Medical Exchange (© **512/458-1121**) and Seton Hospital (© **512/324-4450**) both have physician referral services.

Driving Rules See "By Car," earlier in this section.

Drugstores See "Pharmacies," below.

Embassies/Consulates See "Fast Facts: For the International Traveler," in Appendix B.

Emergencies Call © **911** if you need the police, the fire department, or an ambulance.

Hospitals Brackenridge, 601 E. 15th St. (© **512/324-7000**), St. David's, 919 E. 32nd St. at I-35 (© **512/397-4240**), and Seton Medical Center, 1201 W. 38th St. (© **512/324-1000**) have good and convenient emergency-care facilities.

Hot Lines Suicide Hot Line (© **512/472-4357**); Poison Center (© **800/764-7661**); Domestic Violence Crisis Hot Line (© **512/928-9070**); Sexual Assault Crisis Hot Line (© **512/440-7273**).

Information See "Visitor Information," earlier in this chapter.

Internet Schlotzky's Deli, a chain that originated in Austin, usually offers free Internet access via computer stations; you're limited to 20 minutes but that should give you enough time to check your e-mail. Several Schlotzky's also offer free wireless network access, though these require that you come with your own computer outfitted with an access card (if you have one, you'll know it). Of the 17 Schlotkzy's in Austin, the two locations most convenient to the majority of visitors are those at 106 E. Sixth St., downtown, © **512/473-2867**, and at 1915 Guadalupe © **512/457-1129**, near the University of Texas. See the Austin Yellow Pages for the other locations or log on to www.cooldeli.com.

Laundry/Dry Cleaners Reliable dry cleaners in the downtown area include Ace Cleaners, 1117 S. Congress Ave. (© **512/444-2332**); Washburn's Town & Country, 1423 S. Congress Ave (© **512/442-1467**); and Sweet Cleaner's, 613 Congress (© **512/477-4083**). The only laundromat anywhere near downtown is Kwik Wash, 1000 W. Lynn (© **512/473-3725**); it's not within walking distance of any city hotels, but it's a short drive away from some of them.

Libraries Downtown's Faulk Central Library, 800 Guadalupe St. (© **512/974-7400**), and adjoining Austin History Center, 810 Guadalupe St. (© **512/974-7480**), are excellent information resources. To find the closest local branch, log on to **www.ci.austin.tx.us/library**.

Liquor Laws See this section in chapter 3. Briefly, you have to be 21 to drink in Texas, it's illegal to have an open container in your car, and liquor cannot be served before noon on Sunday except at brunches (if it's billed as complimentary).

Lost Property You can check with the police to find out whether something you've lost has been turned in by calling © **512/974-5000**. If you leave something on a city bus, call © **512/389-7454**; on a train heading for Austin or at the Amtrak station, © **512/476-5684**; on a Greyhound bus or at the station, © **512/458-4463**; at the airport, © **512/530-760** (Mon–Fri 7am–5pm) or © **512/530-COPS** (weekends and after hours).

Luggage Storage/Lockers At the Greyhound station, there's only one size locker; the price is $2 per 6 hours. You can check your luggage at the Amtrak station for $1.50 per bag per 24 hours. As we went to press, lockers had not yet been installed at Austin's airport.

Maps See "City Layout," earlier in this chapter.

Newspapers/Magazines The daily *Austin American-Statesman* (www. austin360.com) is the only large-circulation, mainstream newspaper in town. The *Austin Chronicle* (www.auschron.com), a free alternative weekly, focuses on the arts, entertainment, and politics. Monday through Thursday, the University of Texas publishes the surprisingly sophisticated *Daily Texan* (www.dailytexanonline.com) newspaper, covering everything from on-campus news to international events.

Pharmacies You'll find many Walgreens, Eckerd, and Randalls drugstores around the city; most HEB grocery stores also have pharmacies. Several Walgreens are open 24 hours. Have your zip code ready and call ⓒ **800/ 925-4733** to find the Walgreens branch nearest you.

Police The non-emergency number for the Austin Police Department is ⓒ **512/974-5000.**

Post Office The city's main post office is located at 8225 Cross Park Dr. (ⓒ **512/342-1252**); more convenient to tourist sights are the Capitol Station, 111 E. 17th St., in the LBJ Building, and the Downtown Station, 510 Guadalupe St. For information on other locations, phone ⓒ **800/ 275-8777.** You can also find post offices on line at www.mapsonus.com/db/USPS.

Radio On the FM dial, turn to KMFA (89.5) for classical music, KUT (90.5) for National Public Radio talk programming and eclectic music, KASE (100.7) for country, KUTZ (98.9) for contemporary rock, and KGSR (107.1) for folk, reggae, rock, blues, and jazz. AM stations include KVET (1300) for news and talk, and KJCE (1300) for soul and Motown oldies.

Safety Austin has been ranked one of the five safest cities in the United States, but that doesn't mean you can throw common sense to the wind. It's never a good idea to walk down dark streets alone at night, and major tourist areas always attract pickpockets; keep your purse or wallet in a safe place. Although Sixth Street itself tends to be busy, use caution on the side streets in the area.

Taxes The tax on hotel rooms is 15%. Sales tax, added to restaurant bills as well as to other purchases, is 8.25%.

Taxis See "By Taxi," earlier in this section.

Television You'll find CBS (KEYE) on Channel 5, ABC (KVUE) on Channel 3, NBC (KXAN) on Channel 4, Fox (KTBC) on Channel 2, and PBS (KLRU) on Channel 9. Austin cable channels include Channel 8, with nonstop local news (interspersed with updates of state and international news), and Channel 15, the city-run Austin Music Network, featuring a variety of sounds but emphasizing Austin and Texas artists.

Time Zone Austin is on Central Standard Time and observes daylight saving time.

Transit Information Call Capital Metro Transit (© **800/474-1201** or 512/474-1200 from local pay phones; TTY 512/385-5872).

Useful Telephone Numbers Get the time and temperature by dialing © **512/973-3555**.

Weather Check the weather at © **512/451-2424** or www.kvue.com/weather.

12

Where to Stay in Austin

The room shortage that long plagued Austin has finally abated: Motels have cropped up like mushrooms near Bergstrom International Airport, some excellent historic restorations have been completed in the downtown area, and several new hotels designed to serve the expanded convention center should all be open by 2004. Still, finding a room in Austin isn't always easy: You can't predict when a major microchip convention is going to be in town.

To plan your stay, keep two things in mind: the state legislature and the University of Texas (enrollment more than 50,000). Lawmakers and lobbyists converge on the capital for 140-day sessions at the start of odd-numbered years, so you can expect very tight bookings during the first half of both 2003 and 2005. The beginning of fall term, graduation week, and weekends of important University of Texas football games—UT's football stadium seats nearly 80,000—also draw visitors en masse. During the third week of March, record label execs and aspiring artists attending the huge annual S×SW music conference take up all the town's rooms. It's always a good idea to book as far in advance as possible, but it's essential if your trip coincides with any of these events.

Low rates and quick freeway access to both downtown and the northwest help fill the chain motels that line I-35 near the old airport; those along I-35 to the south are convenient to the new airport and downtown. But you'll get a far better feel for what makes Austin special if you stay in the verdant Town Lake area, which includes both the historic downtown area near the capitol and the newly resurgent South Congress area. The leafy enclaves near the University of Texas, especially the Hyde Park neighborhood, are ideal for those willing to trade some modern perks for hominess and character. Those with a penchant for playing on the water or putting around should consider holing up near the lakes and golf courses to the west.

Austin has some glitzy high-rises but only a few historic hotels and motels; if it's character you're after, you might opt for one of the town's bed-and-breakfasts. For Austin inns that belong to Historic Accommodations of Texas, check the website at www.hat.org or contact the organization at P.O. Box 139, Fredericksburg, TX 78624 (© **800/HAT-0368**).

The prices listed below are based on full rack rates, the officially established, undiscounted tariffs that you should never have to pay. Most hotels catering to business travelers offer substantially lower prices on weekends, while some bed-and-breakfasts offer reduced rates Sunday through Thursday. If you don't mind changing rooms once, you can get the best of both discount worlds. You'll find lots of Austin room deals on the Internet (see chapter 2), but don't stop there. Be sure to phone and ask about packages—which might include extras like breakfast or champagne—reduced rates for senior citizens, families, active-duty military personnel . . . whatever you can think of. In fact, it's a good idea to call both the 800 number and the hotel itself; sometimes the central reservation agent doesn't know about local deals. Sure, calling is not as impersonal as the Internet, but don't be afraid of being a pain. What are the odds that you'll ever see these people again?

Note that rates listed below do not include the city's 15% hotel sales tax.

Incidentally, wherever you bunk (except in some of the B&Bs) in Austin, you're likely to be in high-tech heaven; I've never been in a city where I've connected at higher speeds, or more easily, from hotel and motel rooms than here. Many hotels even have WebTV, enabling you to retrieve e-mail and cruise the Internet via the television.

1 Downtown

VERY EXPENSIVE

The Driskill ★★   Talk about historic cachet. Lyndon Johnson holed up here during the final days of his presidential campaign, anxiously awaiting election results. Ann Richards held her inaugural ball at The Driskill when she became governor. This is where the Daughters of the Republic of Texas gathered to decide the fate of the Alamo, and Texas lawmen met to set an ambush for Bonnie and Clyde.

Of course, opening in 1886 has its downside: It's hard to stay gorgeous and up-to-date when you're more than a century old. But old hotels tend to fare far better in their makeovers than old people do. A $35 million renovation, celebrated with the new millennium, restored The Driskill's former sheen—and then some. The public areas, dripping with marble and crystal, are dazzling. Although you're near all the prime tourist spots (the hotel is one of them), you've got plenty of reasons to hang around: The 1886 Café (opened in 2002), with good breakfast selections; the Driskill Grill for dinner (p. 162); a cushy piano bar (p. 232); and a small but well equipped spa, added in 2001.

The guest rooms—100 of them in a 1929 addition, the rest in the original structure—feature beautiful reproductions of the original 19th-century furnishings, plus the latest in high-tech connectivity. Some of the king rooms are quite small, though, and so dominated by the large bed that there's little room to move about. (At least sinks and mirrors are outside the tiny bathrooms.) It's a good idea to check room size before settling in.

604 Brazos St. (at E. 6th St.), Austin, TX 78701. ☎ 800/252-9367 or 512/474-5911. Fax 512/474-2214. www.driskillhotel.com. 188 units. $270–$290 double; suites from $450. AE, DC, DISC, MC, V. Valet parking $17. Pets under 20 lb. accepted; $50 fee per pet per stay. **Amenities:** 2 restaurants; bar; health club; spa; concierge; business center; 24-hr. room service; laundry service; dry cleaning. *In room:* A/C, TV, dataport, hair dryer, safe.

Four Seasons Austin ★★★ *Kids*   When someone else is footing the bill, this is the best place to stay in Austin. It's got a great location on Town Lake, near all the downtown attractions; large, comfortable rooms; an excellent restaurant (which is also the toniest roost in town for watching bats stream out of the Congress Ave. Bridge); and the best health club and spa in the downtown area. And the service . . . Queen Elizabeth, Prince Charles, and King Philip of Spain have all bedded down here, but even peons get the royal treatment. The Posture Luxe beds, custom-made for the hotel, are so comfortable that many guests arrange to buy them for their homes. Allergic to feathers? Plush pillows without any animal affiliation will be provided.

Polished sandstone floors, a cowhide sofa, horn lamps, and an elk head hanging over the fireplace in the lobby remind you you're in Texas, but the guest rooms are European country-manse elegant, with light florals, wood, and live plants. The city views are fine, but the ones of the lake are prime.

98 San Jacinto Blvd. (at 1st/Cesar Chavez St.), Austin, TX 78701. © **800/332-3442** or 512/478-4500. Fax 512/478-3117. www.fourseasons.com. 291 units. $250–$360 double; $395–$1400 suite. Lower rates on weekends, bed-and-breakfast and romance packages available. AE, DC, MC, V. Self-parking $10; valet parking $15. Pets beagle size or smaller accepted; advance notice to reservations department required. **Amenities:** Restaurant; bar; outdoor pool; health club; spa; bike rentals; concierge; car-rental desk; secretarial services; 24-hr. room service; same-day laundry service; dry cleaning. *In room:* A/C, TV w/pay movies, dataport, minibar, hair dryer, iron, safe.

Hyatt Regency Austin on Town Lake ★★

Austin's Hyatt Regency brings the outdoors indoors, with a signature atrium lobby anchored by a Hill Country tableau of a limestone-banked flowing stream, waterfalls, and oak trees. It's impressive, but the genuine article outside is more striking still: Because the hotel sits on Town Lake's south shore, its watery vistas have stunning city backdrops.

Although the Hyatt is just minutes from downtown, outdoor recreation makes this hotel tick. Bat tours and other Town Lake excursions depart from a private dock, where you can also rent paddleboats and canoes. In addition, guests can rent mountain bikes to ride on the hike-and-bike trail outside the door. All rooms are decorated in vibrant Southwest tones and rich woods; those on higher floors facing Town Lake are most coveted.

208 Barton Springs Rd. (at S. Congress), Austin, TX 78704. © **800/233-1234** or 512/477-1234. Fax 512/480-2069. www.hyatt.com. 447 units. $260–$300 double; $345–$650 suite. Weekend specials, corporate and state-government rates available. AE, DC, DISC, MC, V. Self-parking $8; valet parking $12. **Amenities:** Restaurant; bar; outdoor pool; health club; Jacuzzi; bike rentals; business center; laundry service; dry cleaning; limited room service; club-level rooms. *In room:* A/C TV, hair dryer, iron.

EXPENSIVE

Austin Marriott at the Capitol

For those who want to be in the northwest part of downtown, which puts you within walking distance of the University of Texas (if you're energetic), this is a good pick. The hotel itself isn't exciting, just your basic blocky high-rise, but for a business-oriented place it's got a relaxed, comfortable atmosphere, enhanced by a good sports lounge with broadcasts of international games—not to mention Krispy Kreme and Starbucks kiosks in the lobby. The walls of windows on the hotel's atrium levels give its public areas an open, airy feel, and the rooms—done in nondescript but light style—also feel unconfined; those on the higher floors have terrific city views, and those on the west side all look out on the state capitol, 4 blocks away.

701 E. 11th St. (at Red River), Austin, TX 78701. © **800/228-9290** or 512/478-1111. Fax 512/478-3700. www.marriott.com. 365 units. $169 double; suites from $275. Weekend discounts, holiday rates. AE, DC, DISC, MC, V. Self-parking $10; valet parking $15. Pets under 30 lb. accepted; $50 deposit required. **Amenities:** Restaurant; bar; indoor pool; outdoor pool; health club; Jacuzzi; sauna; concierge; business center; secretarial services; 24-hr. room service; babysitting; dry cleaning. *In room:* A/C, TV w/pay movies, dataport, coffeemaker, hair dryer, iron.

Doubletree Guest Suites ★ *Kids*

Lobbyists sock in for winter legislative sessions at this tony all-suites high-rise, a stone's throw from the state capitol. It would be hard to find more comfortable temporary quarters: At 625 square feet, the standard one-bedroom suites are larger than a typical New York City apartment. All are decorated in attractive Western style with Texas details, and offer cushy foldout sofas and large mirrored closets; bathrooms are spacious, too. Many rooms have balconies with capital capitol views. Full-sized refrigerators, toasters, stoves, coffeemakers, and cookware allow guests to prepare meals in

Downtown Austin Accommodations

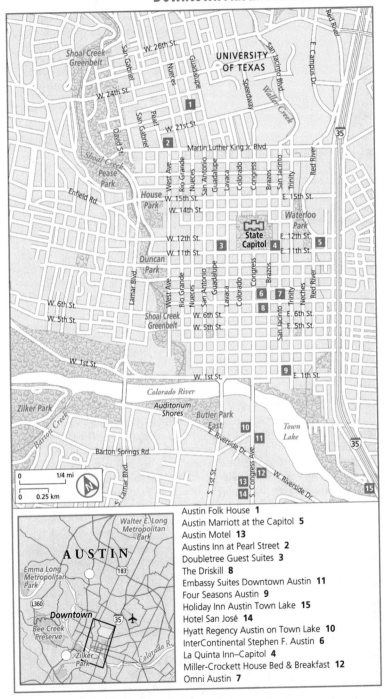

Austin Folk House **1**
Austin Marriott at the Capitol **5**
Austin Motel **13**
Austins Inn at Pearl Street **2**
Doubletree Guest Suites **3**
The Driskill **8**
Embassy Suites Downtown Austin **11**
Four Seasons Austin **9**
Holiday Inn Austin Town Lake **15**
Hotel San José **14**
Hyatt Regency Austin on Town Lake **10**
InterContinental Stephen F. Austin **6**
La Quinta Inn–Capitol **4**
Miller-Crockett House Bed & Breakfast **12**
Omni Austin **7**

comfort and, unlike kitchens in many all-suite hotels, the ones here are separate—you don't have to stare at dirty dishes after you eat. (The maid washes them every day, anyway.)

303 W. 15th St. (at Guadalupe), Austin, TX 78701. © **800/222-TREE** or 512/478-7000. Fax 512/478-3562. www.doubletreehotelaustin.com. 189 units. 1-bedroom suite $164–$194; 2-bedroom suite $209–$269. Corporate, extended-stay, Internet, and other discounts available. AE, DC, DISC, MC, V. Self- or valet parking $15. Pets under 25 lb. accepted; $100 deposit required plus $25 per day. Children stay free. **Amenities:** Restaurant; outdoor pool; health club; Jacuzzi; sauna; concierge; business center; secretarial services; 24-hr. room service; babysitting. *In room:* A/C, TV, dataport, kitchen, hair dryer, iron.

Embassy Suites Downtown Austin (Kids)

Embassy Suites are generally a good deal for those traveling on business or with families, and this link in the national chain has a great location to boot. It's convenient to the airport, and it's a straight shot south of the state capitol and only a few blocks west of the row of restaurants on Barton Springs Road. When you step outside the hotel's door, you're only a few minutes on foot from the Town Lake hike-and-bike trail.

All the attractive, modern suites here have two TVs, two 2-line telephones, microwaves, refrigerators, and a living room with a queen-size sleeper sofa. The large breakfasts and afternoon snacks, both gratis, help cut costs. About a third of the suites look out on downtown, the lake, and the hills. The open atrium arrangement of the rooms is its own security system, but the hotel also offers a nighttime security escort service around the grounds, making it a good bet for single travelers.

300 S. Congress Ave. (at Barton Springs Rd.) Austin, TX 78704. © **800/EMBASSY** or 512/469-9000. Fax 512/480-9164. www.embassysuites.com. 262 units. $159–$209 double. Rates include full breakfast, complimentary afternoon cocktails and snacks. AE, DC, DISC, MC, V. Free indoor parking; valet parking $10. Children 18 and under stay free. **Amenities:** Restaurant; indoor pool; health club; Jacuzzi; sauna; video arcade; limited room service; dry cleaning; club-level rooms. *In room:* A/C, TV w/pay movies, dataport, kitchen, fridge, coffeemaker, hair dryer, iron.

InterContinental Stephen F. Austin ★

Built in 1924 to compete with The Driskill (see above) a block away, the Stephen F. Austin was another favorite power center for state legislators, along with celebrities like Babe Ruth and Frank Sinatra. Closed in 1987 and reopened in 2000 after being gutted and built from the ground up, the hotel is once again welcoming movers and shakers, although now they're most likely to be high-tech and music industry execs. Everyone's made to feel like a power broker, with such perks as a packing and unpacking service (only if you want it) and complimentary umbrellas for guest use (not that it rains all that often).

The public areas are elegant, if not quite as grand as those in The Driskill. The tradeoff is the more spacious, less fussy rooms here, done in soothing earth tones. Luxe amenities include down duvets, alarm clock/CD players, in-room safes large enough to fit a laptop in—and every type of in-room business perk that one could desire, including ergonomic chairs. Beware the sensitive, sensor-operated minibar, however, which may register a charge for jellybeans if you simply move, rather than consume, the contents of the jar. Anyway, it's better to take your drinks in the second-story terrace of the Stephen F bar, before great views of Congress Avenue and the capitol.

701 Congress Ave. (at E. 7th St.), Austin, TX 78701. © **800/327-0200** or 512/457-8800. Fax 512/457-8896. www.intercontinental.com. 189 units. $229–$289 double; $340–$2,000 suite. Weekend discounts. AE, DC, DISC, MC, V. Valet parking $18. **Amenities:** Restaurant; bar; heated pool; health club; spa; concierge; business center; 24-hr. room service; dry cleaning; club-level rooms. *In room:* A/C, TV, dataport, minibar, hair dryer, iron, safe.

Omni Austin   Part of the posh Austin Center office and retail complex, the Omni's spectacular 200-foot rise of sun-struck glass and steel leaves you feeling simultaneously dwarfed and exhilarated. Rooms are far less overwhelming—they're not especially large, and ceilings tend to be low. But they're attractive enough, in a bland contemporary way, and well equipped. If you need to hole up for a while and your company is footing the bill, your best bet is one of the condominium rooms—studio efficiencies with full kitchens, walk-in closets, and jetted tubs. If you're here on vacation, you're not going to be spending that much time indoors, what with the hotel's proximity to all the downtown sights, but the Omni's rooftop pool, sun deck, and Jacuzzi (with terrific city views) is an inducement to lounge around.

700 San Jacinto Blvd. (at E. 8th St.), Austin, TX 78701. (C) **800/THE-OMNI** or 512/476-3700. Fax 512/320-5882. www.omnihotels.com. 375 units. $219–$249 double; $319–$399 suite. AE, DC, DISC, MC, V. Self-parking $8; valet parking $12. **Amenities:** Restaurant; bar; outdoor pool; health club; Jacuzzi; sauna; car-rental desk; shopping arcade; salon; limited room service; business center; secretarial services; dry cleaning; club-level rooms. *In room.* A/C, TV, hair dryer, iron.

MODERATE

Holiday Inn Austin Town Lake (Value) (Kids)   The most upscale Holiday Inn in Austin, this high-rise is also the best situated: It's on the north shore of Town Lake, at the edge of downtown and just off I-35. Guest rooms are unexpectedly stylish, with simulated brick walls, light wood furniture, and Southwest patterns; it won't cost you much more to get one that looks out on Town Lake. Fifty of the units have additional sofa sleepers, which can translate into real family savings, especially since kids stay free (and if they're under 12, eat free at the hotel restaurant too). Amenities are a cut above the usual chain offerings, with a rooftop pool big enough to swim laps, happy-hour specials, and a big-screen TV in the lounge.

20 N. I-35 (exit 233, Riverside Dr./Town Lake), Austin, TX 78701. (C) **800/HOLIDAY** or 512/472-8211. Fax 512/472-4636. www.holiday-inn.com./austintownlake. 322 units. $129–$139 double. Weekend and holiday rates, corporate discounts. Children under 18 stay free. AE, DC, DISC, MC, V. Free parking. Pets under 25 lb. accepted; $125 deposit plus $25 fee. **Amenities:** Restaurant; bar; outdoor pool; health club; Jacuzzi; secretarial services; dry cleaning; club-level rooms. *In room:* AC, TV w/pay movies, dataport, coffeemaker, hair dryer, iron.

Hotel San José ⊛   Opened in the late 1990s, this revamped 1930s motor court in trendy SoCo quickly became the darling of hip travelers. It's not hard to see why: It's got retro appeal, with small porches and a small pool, it's right across the street from the famed Continental Club, and the staff has the requisite semi-haughty attitude (except to musicians and their handlers). There are nods to local design—red Spanish tile roofs, cowhide throw rugs, and Texas pine beds—but the dominant theme is Zen, with Japanese-style outdoor landscaping and rooms so stripped down they border on the stark. Of course, being in Austin requires high-tech basics like high-speed Internet access plus VCRs and CD players. Try to get a room in the back to avoid the Congress Avenue traffic noise.

1316 S. Congress Ave. (south of Nelly, about ½ mile south of Riverside), Austin, TX 78704. (C) **800/574-8897** or 512/444-7322. Fax 512/444-7362. www.sanjosehotel.com. 40 units. $75–$145 double; $165–$200 suite. Corporate and entertainment discounts available. AE, DC, MC, V. Free parking. Dogs accepted; $100 deposit plus $10 per day. **Amenities:** Bar, outdoor pool, bike rentals, dry cleaning, limited room service. *In room:* TV/VCR, dataport.

La Quinta Inn–Capitol (Finds)   Practically on the grounds of the state capitol, this is a great bargain for both business and leisure travelers. Rooms are more attractive than those in your typical motel: TVs are large, the rich-toned furnishings are far from cheesy, and there are perks such as free local phone calls (on dataport phones with voice mail) and free continental breakfasts to keep annoying extras off your bill. The sole drawback is that there's no restaurant on the premises, and there aren't that many places to eat in the area on weekends if you don't feel like getting in your car.

300 E. 11th St. (at San Jacinto), Austin, TX 78701. © **800/NU-ROOMS** or 512/476-1166. Fax 512/476-6044. www.laquinta.com. 145 units. $89–$119 double; $150 suite. Rates include continental breakfast. Children under 18 stay free with parents. AE, DC, DISC, MC, V. Valet parking $10. **Amenities:** Outdoor pool; laundry service; dry cleaning; secretarial services. *In room:* A/C, TV w/pay movies, dataport, coffeemaker, hair dryer, iron.

The Miller-Crockett House Bed & Breakfast ⭐ *(Finds)* Sure, it's got all the B&B accouterments, including gracious veranda-wrapped quarters dating back to 1888, 1½-acre grounds spread with ancient live oaks, the requisite generous gourmet breakfasts, and there are lovely antiques in several of the rooms. But don't expect ducks and gingham—or even your typical B&B guests. The cast and crew for the *Newton Boys,* including Matthew McConnaughey, stayed here, as have members of several bands, including Barenaked Ladies; depending on who's visiting, the music at breakfast could range from the Buena Vista Social Club to Jimi Hendrix. If you want to escape the B&B experience entirely, you can hole up in one of the appealing Southwest-decor bungalows, with separate kitchens. You can't beat the location, near all the Town Lake and SoCo action, but far quieter than the lodgings that sit right on Congress Avenue.

112 Academy Dr. (1 block east of Congress Ave.), Austin, TX 78704. © **888/441-1641** or 512/441-1600. Fax 512/474-5910. www.millercrockett.com. 5 units. Sun–Thurs $139 double; $159 suite; $149 bungalow. Lower weekday rates. Rates include full breakfast. AE, MC, V. Free off-street parking. **Amenities:** Bikes (free). *In room:* A/C, TV/VCR, dataport, kitchen (in bungalows), iron.

INEXPENSIVE

Austin Motel ⭐ *(Value)* It's not only nostalgia that draws repeat guests to this Austin institution, established in 1938 on what used to be the old San Antonio Highway and in the current owner's family since the 1950s. A convenient (but not quiet) location on nouveau chic South Congress Avenue and reasonable rates help, too. Other assets are a classic kidney-shaped pool, a great neon sign,

It Pays to Stay

If you're planning to settle in for a spell, two downtown accommodations at prime locations will save you major bucks. You'll pay $409 a week to bunk at the **Extended Stay America Downtown,** 600 Guadalupe (at Sixth), Austin, TX 78701 (© **800/EXT-STAY** or 512/ 457-9994; www.extstay.com), within easy walking distance of both the Warehouse District and the Lamar and 6th shops. Seven days at **Homestead Village Downtown/Town Lake,** 507 S. 1st St. (at Barton Springs) Austin, TX 78704 (© **888/782-9473** or 512/476-1818; www.homestead hotel.com), near the Barton Springs restaurant row, the hike-and-bike trail, and the new Long Performing Arts Center, will run you $385 (less if you book through the Internet). Full kitchens and coin-op laundries at both bring your costs down even more.

free HBO, free coffee (donuts, too, on Sun) in the lobby, and El Sol y La Luna, a good Latin restaurant that's popular with Town Lake athletes on weekend mornings. Ask to see the room—all are different and some are more recently renovated—before settling in.

1220 S. Congress St. (south of Nelly, about ½ mile south of Riverside), Austin, TX 78704. **②** **512/441-1157.** Fax 512/441-1157. www.austinmotel.com. 41 units. $70–$99 double; $140 suite. AE, DC, DISC, MC, V. Free parking. Limited number of rooms for pets; $10 fee. **Amenities:** Outdoor pool. *In room:* A/C, TV, fridge (some), coffeemaker, hair dryer, iron, safe.

Hostelling International–Austin *(Value)* Youth- and nature-oriented Austin goes all out for its hostelers at this winning facility, located on the hike-and-bike trail, with views of Town Lake that many would pay through the nose to get. In addition to being an excellent all-around resource for visitors, the hostel organizes various daytime and nighttime activities, including live music several nights each week. Facilities include a laundry room and kitchen. The building, which once served as a boathouse, is solar paneled.

2200 S. Lakeshore Blvd. (East of I-35, on the southern shore of Town Lake), Austin, TX 78741. **②** **800/ 725-2331** or 512/444-2294. Fax 512/444-2309. www.hiaustin.org. 39 beds in 4 dorms. $17 for AYH members, $3 additional for nonmembers. AE, MC, V. Free parking. **Amenities:** Kayak rentals; bike rentals. *In room:* A/C, no phone.

2 Central

MODERATE

Austin Folk House *★★ (Value)* You get the best of both worlds at this appealing B&B: old time charm and new plumbing. When it was transformed from a tired apartment complex in 2001, this 1880s house near the University of Texas got a complete interior overhaul, but maintained such integral traditional assets as the comfy front porch. The sunny rooms have newly painted walls and the wiring to accommodate megachannel cable TVs, private phone lines, and radio/alarms with white noise machines. At the same time, nice antiques and such amenities as fancy bedding and towels, candles, robes, expensive lotions, and soaps make you feel like you're in a small luxury inn. The lavish breakfast buffet served in a dining room decorated with the folk art for which the B&B is named—it doubles as a space for folk performances sometimes—does nothing to dispel that idea. Come to think of it, book a room before the young owner realizes what a bargain her place is and raises rates to the level they warrant. The free off-street parking, near the heart of The Drag, puts this place at a premium all by itself.

506 West 22nd St. (between San Antonio and Nueces) Austin, TX 78705 ((**②** **866/472-6700** or 512/472-6700). 9 units. $85–$125 double. Rates include breakfast. Pets accepted. AE, DISC, MC, V. Free off-street parking. *In room:* TV/VCR, dataport, hair dryer, iron.

Austins Inn at Pearl Street *★* Located on a rise above one of Austin's busier streets, this 1896 Greek revival–style house manages to preserve the peace. Although it's unassuming on the outside, the home is an interior decorator's dream. You'll be ogling all the public areas, with their silk wallpaper and Oriental rugs, and asking other guests for a peek in their rooms (or at least wanting to). The Gothic suite features a medieval-style draped canopy bed, as well as its own marble bathroom with a Jacuzzi tub. It adjoins a mint-green sun porch. The Far East room, resplendent in red, gold, and black, has a gorgeous inlaid chest and other Asian treasures. On nice days, you can enjoy breakfast on a tree-shaded deck. Although this place appeals to vacationers, business travelers also like the direct phone line with voice mail in every room, as well as the weekday morning breakfast buffet (it's quick and easy, but don't expect gourmet).

Also on the grounds are a carriage house and three rooms in the tri-level Burton House next door. Rooms in the latter, like those in the main house, have exotic themes (Italian, safari, and Oxford); two offer private balconies. A Texas motif dominates in the carriage house.

809 W. MLK, Jr. Blvd. (at Pearl St., east of Lamar), Austin, TX 78701. © **800/494-2261** or 512/477-2233. Fax 512/478-0033. www.innpearl.com. 9 units. $125–$160 double; $175 suite; $175–$200 cottage. Lower weekday rates. Rates include continental breakfast weekdays, full breakfast weekends. Packages available. 2-night minimum most weekends. AE, DC, DISC, MC, V. Free off-street parking. *In room:* A/C TV/VCR, kitchenette (some), fridge (some), hair dryer, iron.

Woodburn House Herb and Sandra Dickson's late Victorian home couldn't look more firmly rooted. You'd never guess that, in danger of being bulldozed in 1980, it was jacked up, loaded on a flatbed trailer, and shifted from its original location 6 blocks away. Now settled in as the first bed-and-breakfast in Hyde Park, the Woodburn House is not only a delightful place to stay, but also a prime source of information about the historic neighborhood.

The inn's turn-of-the-century origins are apparent: Lustrous moldings made of Louisiana long-leaf pine, hardwood floors, and a built-in corner cabinet recall an age of meticulous attention to detail. Such original attributes are complemented throughout by American period antiques handed down over the years by the Dickson family. The bedrooms are similarly filled with delicate antiques. Breakfasts are designed to be heart healthy, but you can't tell the difference: Strawberry-filled crêpes topped with yogurt, apple-cinnamon pancakes, or a Mexican casserole might turn up on any given morning, along with delicious home-baked bread.

4401 Ave. D (between 44th and 45th sts.), Austin, TX 78751. © **888/690-9763** or 512/458-4335. Fax 512/458-4319. www.woodburnhouse.com. 5 units. $98–$100 double; $138 suite. Rates include breakfast. Corporate and monthly rates available. No children under 12. AE, MC, V. Free parking. *In room:* A/C, dataport.

INEXPENSIVE

The Adams House *(Value)* Monroe Shipe, the developer of Hyde Park, designed his homes to be both attractive and affordable to the middle class. This B&B, built as a single-story bungalow, expanded into a more grandiose colonial revival in 1931, and restored in the 1990s by a preservation architect, honors Shipe's egalitarian spirit. Although the house is beautifully furnished, it has a friendly, open feel to it—in part because of its 12-foot ceilings and in part because of the hospitable Lock family, who own and run it with their adorable cocker spaniel, Dulce. All the rooms are lovely, but the nicest is the suite with a king-size four-poster bed and a sun porch with a fold-out couch. If you're looking for a home-away-from-home with good rates rather than high-tech extras (or even your own TV), this is your place.

4300 Ave. G (at 43rd St.), Austin, TX 85751. © **512/453-7696.** Fax 512/453-2616. www.theadamshouse. com. 4 units. $80–90 double; $125 suite. Rates include breakfast. AE, MC, V. Free off-street parking. No children under 12. *In room:* A/C.

Brook House *(Value)* This 1922 colonial revival–style on a quiet block just north of the University of Texas used to be a crash pad; chances are that Janis Joplin, who lived in the area in the 1960s, dropped in now and then. Although it's been a respectable bed-and-breakfast since 1985, the Brook House still has good vibes. The main house contains three lovely but unfussy rooms, two with their own screened porches, and all with antique furnishings. A romantic private cottage has its own kitchen and sitting deck, as does the lower of the two bedrooms in the separate carriage house. On nice days, a full breakfast—lots of fresh-baked goods, fruit, juices, and a hot dish—is served outside on the peaceful covered patio. A convenient location and extensive in-room features clinch the fact that this place gives you excellent value for your money.

609 W. 33rd St. (at Guadalupe), Austin, TX 78705. ☎ **800/871-8908** or 512/459-0534. www.austinbedand breakfast. 6 units. $79–$119 double. Rates include breakfast. AE, DC, DISC, MC, V. Free parking. Some pets accepted. **Amenities:** Dry cleaning. *In room:* A/C, TV/VCR, dataport, fridge (some), coffeemaker, hair dryer, iron.

3 I-35 Corridor

MODERATE

Austin North Hilton and Towers   Austin's first convention hotel, this Hilton is a nice surprise: A blocky, nondescript exterior gives no hint of the gracious public areas inside. The lobby, a favorite gathering spot for business travelers, is decorated in a Lone Star Texas theme, including hardwood floors and cowhide chairs. The pool area is a tree-shaded oasis in a concrete desert— a desert where you can drop a lot of dough. The Hilton adjoins the shops, restaurants, and movie theaters of the Highland Mall and is within walking distance of the tonier Lincoln Village. Rooms combine the Lone Star theme with cheerful florals and light wood furnishings; all are large, and some have vaulted ceilings.

6000 Middle Fiskville Rd. (1 block west of the intersection of I-35 and Hwy. 290), Austin, TX 78752. ☎ **800/ HILTONS** (reservations), 800/347-0330, or 512/451-5757. Fax 512/467-7644. 240 units. $119–$149 double. Weekend and seasonal specials available. AE, DC, DISC, MC, V. Free parking. Pets under 25 lb. accepted; $50 non-refundable fee required. **Amenities:** Restaurant; outdoor pool; health club; concierge; business center; limited room service; club-level rooms. *In room:* AC, TV w/pay movies, dataport, coffeemaker, hair dryer, iron.

Doubletree Hotel Austin ⭐   Leisure travelers should take advantage of the plummeting weekend rates at this tony business-oriented hotel. Once you step inside, you'll feel as though you're in a private luxury property rather than a chain lodging just off the freeway. The reception area has polished Mexican-tile floors and carved-wood ceiling beams, while an adjoining colonnade boasts a massive cherry hutch and other antiques from Mexico, along with 19th-century English wall tapestries. In keeping with the hacienda theme, rooms are arranged around a lushly landscaped courtyard, dotted with umbrella-shaded tables. Although decorated in fairly dark tones, the guest quarters are airy and spacious. Wherever you stay, you needn't walk very far to reach your car; all the sleeping floors have direct access, via room key, to the parking garage.

6505 N. I-35, Austin (between Hwy. 290 E. and St. Johns Ave.), TX 78752. ☎ **800/222-TREE** or 512/454-3737. Fax 512/454-6915. 350 units. $139 double; $194–$224 suite. Corporate, weekend rates; romance package available. AE, DC, DISC, MC, V. Self-parking $7; valet parking $9. Pets under 20 lb. accepted; $50 non-refundable fee required. **Amenities:** Restaurant; bar; outdoor pool; health club; Jacuzzi; concierge; business center; limited room service; babysitting; concierge-level rooms. *In room:* A/C, TV, dataport, coffeemaker, hair dryer, iron.

Habitat Suites ⭐⭐ *(Finds* *(Kids*   Only in Austin would you find an "ecotel" that offers Kukicha twig tea, at least one vegan and macrobiotic entree at breakfast, a swimming pool that uses ionized water, and a book of Buddha's teaching in the bedside-table drawer. Don't be put off by the generic name and nondescript location on the outskirts of Highland Mall; lush gardens (tended without

Greater Austin Accommodations & Dining

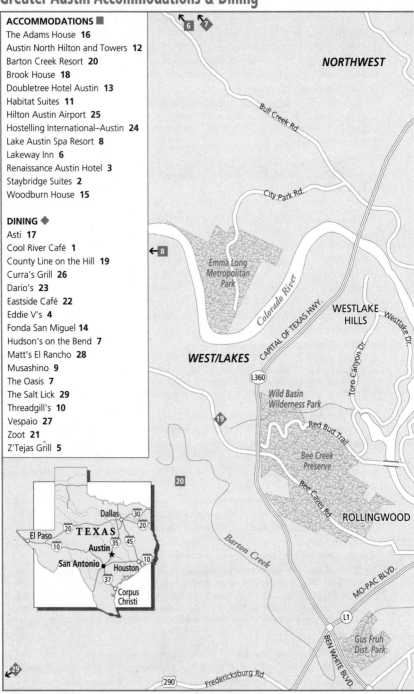

NORTHWEST

Bull Creek Rd.

City Park Rd.

Emma Long
Metropolitan
Park

Colorado River

CAPITAL OF TEXAS HWY.

WESTLAKE
HILLS

Westlake Dr.

WEST/LAKES

Toro Canyon Dr.

L360

Wild Basin
Wilderness Park

Red Bud Trail

Bee Creek
Preserve

Bee Caves Rd.

ROLLINGWOOD

Barton Creek

Dallas
30
20
El Paso
20
TEXAS
10
35
45
Austin
San Antonio
Houston
10
37
Corpus
Christi

MO-PAC BLVD.

L1

Gus Fruh
Dist. Park

BEN WHITE BLVD.

290
Fredericksburg Rd.

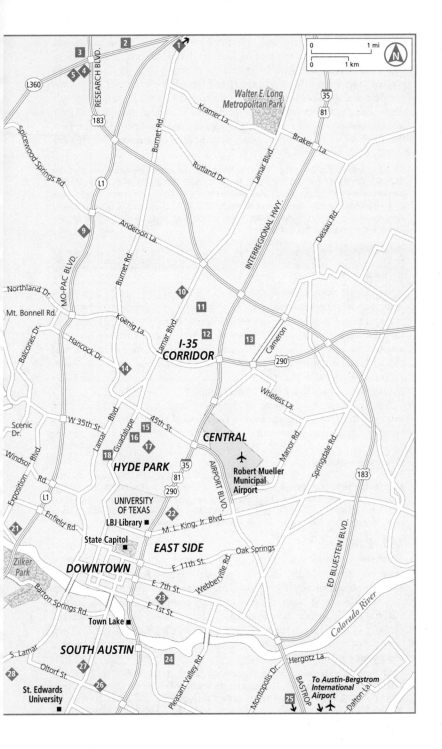

chemical fertilizers, natch) and little front porches or decks, are among the many details that make this lodging far from cookie cutter. The rooms themselves don't have much character, but they're extremely large (the two-bedroom duplex suites have separate entrances) and offer full kitchens, as well as real fireplaces and windows that actually open. Suites for chemically sensitive people are available at no extra charge. The "quiet hours" in effect from 9pm to 9am, and the general marriage of eco-consciousness and friendliness with function, make this an unusually soothing and pleasant place to stay, whether for work or play.

500 E. Highland Mall Blvd. (take exit 222 off I-35 to Airport Blvd., take a right to Highland Mall Blvd.), Austin, TX 78752. ✆ 800/535-4663 or 512/467-6000. Fax 512/467-6000. www.habitatsuites.com. 97 units. $127 1-bedroom suite; $187 2-bedroom suite. Lower weekend rates; extended stay rates available. Rates include full breakfast and (Mon–Sat) afternoon wine and snacks. AE, DC, DISC, MC, V. Free parking. Dogs and cats 2 years and up accepted; $50 fee required. **Amenities:** Outdoor pool; Jacuzzi. *In room:* A/C, TV, dataport, kitchen, fridge, coffeemaker, hair dryer, iron.

4 Northwest

EXPENSIVE

Renaissance Austin Hotel ★★ *Value* Anchoring the upscale Arboretum mall on Austin's northwest side, the toney Renaissance caters to executives visiting nearby computer firms. But on weekends, when rates are slashed, even underlings can afford to take advantage of the hotel's many amenities, including an excellent health club, a nightclub, and direct access to the myriad allures of the mall (movie theaters among them). Guests buzz around the eateries, elevator banks, and lounges in the nine-story-high atrium lobby, but the space is sufficiently large to avoid any sense of crowding.

Silk wallpaper, lacquer chests, and Japanese-design draperies and bedspreads, in muted tones, add an Asian flavor to the oversized guest rooms, all with comfortable sitting areas. Suites add on such extras as wet bars and electric shoe buffers.

9721 Arboretum Blvd. (off Loop 360, near Research Blvd.), Austin, TX 78759. ✆ 800/HOTELS-1 or 512/343-2626. Fax 512/346-7945. www.renaissancehotels.com. 478 units. $199–$239 double; suites from $249. Weekend packages available. AE, DC, DISC, MC, V. Free self-parking; valet parking $10. Pets under 20 lb. accepted. **Amenities:** 2 restaurants; indoor pool; outdoor pool; health club; Jacuzzi; sauna; concierge; business center; secretarial services; 24-hr. room service; babysitting; laundry service; dry cleaning; club-level rooms. *In room:* A/C, TV w/pay movies, dataport, coffeemaker, fridge (some), hair dryer, iron.

MODERATE

Staybridge Suites *Kids* Although it's designed with business travelers in mind, this cheery Holiday Inn property is also ideal for families, who can take advantage of the kitchen in every suite, the multiple TVs (with VCR), the complimentary breakfast buffet, the pool in a leafy courtyard, and the free laundry facilities that adjoin the exercise room (the latter is small but has the latest in cardio machines). Both types of travelers appreciate the proximity to the Arboretum and other upscale shopping complexes, as well as the many restaurants in this burgeoning area.

10201 Stonelake Blvd (between Great Hills Trail and Braker Lane), Austin, TX 78759. ✆ 800/238-8000 or 512/349-0809. www.staybridge.com. 121 units. $119 studio suite; $139 1-bedroom suite; $179 2-bedroom suite. Rates include breakfast. Extended stay and weekend discounts. AE, DC, DISC, MC, V. Free parking. Pets accepted; $12 fee per night, extended stay requires refundable deposit. **Amenities:** Outdoor pool; tennis court; health club; business center. *In room:* A/C, TV/VCR w/pay movies, dataport, kitchen, coffeemaker, hair dryer, iron.

5 West/Lakes

VERY EXPENSIVE

Barton Creek Resort ★★ *(Kids)*   Sure it's a conference resort, but with four 18-hole championship golf courses (two designed by Tom Fazio, the other two by Ben Crenshaw and Arnold Palmer), a plethora of pools and tennis courts, and a state-of-the-art European-style spa and fitness center, how much work do you suppose actually gets done here, anyway? If you don't happen to be employed by a generous company, book a room on your own; Barton Creek's many golf-and-spa packages are designed to draw leisure travelers. There's plenty to occupy their offspring, too. And if you're an A-type who's driven to self-improvement, even on vacation, that's not a problem. You've got a Golf Advantage School and a tennis clinic to keep your adrenaline flowing.

This place is gorgeous. Spread out over 4,000 gently rolling and wooded acres in west Austin, the hotel complex includes two main buildings resembling European châteaux and a nine-story tower connecting the spa and the conference center. All three structures house accommodations as large and high-toned as one might expect, with 10-foot ceilings, custom-made Drexel Heritage pieces, and marble-topped sinks and vanities. Some have balconies, and rooms in the back offer superb views of the Texas Hill Country.

8212 Barton Club Dr. (1 mile west of the intersection of Loop 36 and RR 2240), Austin, TX 78735. ☎ **800/ 336-6158** or 512/329-4000. Fax 512/329-4597. www.bartoncreek.com. 316 units. $230–$280 double; suites from $450. Seasonal discounts Spa and golf packages available. AE, DC, MC, V. Free self- or valet parking. **Amenities:** 2 restaurants; bar; indoor pool; outdoor pool; 4 golf courses; 12 tennis courts; health club; spa; children's center; business center; salon; limited room service; massage; babysitting; laundry service; dry cleaning. *In room:* A/C, TV, dataport, minibar, coffeemaker, hair dryer, iron.

Lake Austin Spa Resort ★★★   If you had to create the quintessential Austin spa, it would be laid-back, located on a serene body of water, offer lots of outdoor activities, and feature super-healthy food that lives up to the locals' high culinary standards—in short, this place. You'll sign off on every item of that wish list here. The spa takes advantage of its proximity to the lovely Hill Country by offering such activities as combination canoe/hiking trips and excursions to view the wildflowers. The aromatic ingredients for soothing spa treatments like a honey-mango scrub are grown in the resort's garden, which is also the source for the herbs used at mealtimes. Guest rooms, many in cottages with private gardens, fireplaces, and hot tubs, are casually elegant, with all natural fabrics, locally crafted furniture, and Saltillo tile floors. And whereas some spas create their own stress by inspiring style competitions among guests; here, single travelers are likely to bond with each other at the communal breakfast table while lounging around in bathrobes.

It would be hard to imagine an interest or activity you couldn't indulge here, from the kick-butt kind like aerobics and circuit training to the gentler yoga, tai chi, and Pilates. Then there are the cooking classes, trips to Central Market, one-on-one consults with a gardener—you get the idea. The only thing that's not quite up to snuff is the spa, which is fairly small. That should be remedied by early 2004, when a new, larger facility is slated to be completed.

1705 S. Quinlan Park Rd (5 miles south of Hwy. 620)., Austin, TX 78732. ☎ **800/847-5637** or 512/372-7300. Fax 512/266-1572. www.lakeaustin.com. 40 units. $390 per person for 1 night, double occupancy (standard room); $450 per person (luxury room). Rates include all meals, classes, and activities. 3-, 4-, and 7-night packages, seasonal specials and a variety of theme packages available. Pets under 30 lb. accepted in Garden Cottage rooms; $250 pet guest fee. Children 14 and up only. AE, MC, DISC, V. Free parking. **Amenities:**

Kids Family-Friendly Hotels

Four Seasons Austin (p. 145)   Tell the reservations clerk that you're traveling with kids, and you'll be automatically enrolled in the free amenities program: Age-appropriate snacks—cookies and milk for children under 10, popcorn and soda for those older—along with various toys and games will be waiting for you when you arrive. And you don't have to travel with all your gear: The hotel will provide you with such items as a car seat, stroller, playpen, bedrails, disposable pacifiers, a baby bathtub, shampoo, powder and lotions, bib, bottle warmers, and disposable diapers.

Holiday Inn Austin Town Lake (p. 149)   You're near lots of the outdoor play areas at Town Lake, and kids stay and (under 12) eat free. Hard to beat that.

Embassy Suites Downtown Austin (p. 148), **Doubletree Guest Suites** (p. 146), **Habitat Suites** (p. 153), and **Staybridge Suites** (p 156)   That "suites" in the name of these properties says it all. These guest quarters all offer spacious, *not* in-your-face quarters, plus the convenience (and economy) of kitchen facilities, so you don't have to eat out all the time.

Barton Creek Resort (p. 157)   In addition to the great recreational activities here (including a basketball court), this resort also has an activity room for ages 6 months to 8 years, open from morning 'til night. It's a small fee to drop your kids off here for a maximum of 4½ hours.

Lakeway Inn (below)   There's plenty for kids to do here, and this property offers a Family Playday Package, which includes a $100 credit towards recreational activities (such as boat rentals and tennis), plus a free meal and dessert for children 12 and under. Prices vary depending on the time of year.

Restaurant; indoor pool; outdoor pool; 2 lighted tennis courts; health club; spa; kayaks; canoes; bikes; sports equipment; limited room service; laundry service. *In room:* A/C, TV/VCR, dataport, hair dryer.

EXPENSIVE

Lakeway Inn (Value (Kids   Not as glitzy as Barton Creek nor as New Age-y as the Lake Austin Spa, this conference resort in a planned community on Lake Travis is great for those seeking traditional recreation at prices that won't break the bank.

There's something for everyone in the family. At the resort's marina, you can rent pontoons, ski boats, sculls, sailboats, water-skis, WaveRunners, fishing gear and guides—just about everything but fish that promise to bite. Lakeway's lovely 32-court tennis complex, designed for indoor or outdoor, day or night games, has a pro shop with trainers and even a racquet-shaped swimming pool. Duffers can tee off from 36 holes of golf on the property, get privileges at other courses nearby, or brush up on their game at the Jack Nicklaus–designed Academy of Golf. Just want to kick back and be pampered? In addition to Lakeway's small spa, guests can book treatments at the excellent Millennium day spa nearby.

The main lodge of this older property was razed and rebuilt at the end of the 1990s, but, oddly, the rooms were reincarnated with a rather dark and staid 1970s look. Still, they're spacious and comfortable, with all the requisite conference attendee business amenities and, best of all, lake views.

101 Lakeway Dr., Austin, TX 78734. *C* **800/LAKEWAY** or 512/261-6600. Fax 512/261-7322. www. lakeway inn.com. 239 units. $125–$240 double. Romance, golf, spa, and holiday packages available. Pets permitted in some rooms. AE, DC, DISC, MC, V. Free self-parking; valet parking $8. **Amenities:** Restaurant; bar; outdoor pool; 32 tennis courts; 2 golf courses; health club; spa; watersports rentals; concierge; business center; limited room service; babysitting. *In room:* A/C, TV w/pay movies, dataport, coffeemaker, hair dryer, iron.

6 South (Airport)

EXPENSIVE

Hilton Austin Airport   Beam me up, Scotty. Austin's only full-service airport hotel, located in the former administrative center of Bergstrom Air Force Base, has a distinctively spacey look. For one thing, it's round. And although the underground tunnels and fallout shelters designed to protect the Commander in Chief in Texas's capital were capped off during the Hilton's construction, the building remains rock-solid—and blissfully soundproof. But there's nothing cold looking about this place inside. Centered under a skylit dome, the lobby is light and airy. The theme throughout is Texas Hill Country: Think limestone and wood, with lots of live plants for good measure. Large, comfortable rooms are equipped with all the amenities.

9515 New Airport Dr. (½ mile from the airport, 2 miles east of the intersection of Hwy. 183 and Hwy. 71), Austin TX 78719. *C* **800/445-8667** or 512/385-6767. Fax 512/385-6763. www.hilton.com. 262 units. $189 double. Weekend discounts. AE, DC, DISC, MC, V. Self-parking $8; valet parking $12. **Amenities:** Restaurant; lounge; outdoor pool; health club; business center; 24-hr. room service; laundry service; dry cleaning; club-level rooms. *In room:* A/C, TV w/pay movies, dataport, minibar, coffeemaker, hair dryer, iron.

13

Where to Dine in Austin

You would expect to eat well in a town where lawmakers schmooze power brokers, academics can be tough culinary graders, and techies and musicians require high-grade fuel. Austin doesn't disappoint. Chic industrial spaces vie for diners' dollars with gracious 100-year-old houses and plant-filled hippie shacks. Inside, the food ranges from upscale New American to the stylish but reasonably priced cuisine once dubbed "Nouveau Grub" by *Texas Monthly* magazine to tofu burgers, barbecue, and enchiladas. Many of these dining rooms are Austin originals, but in recent years such high-end chains as Sullivan's, Flemings, Ruth's Chris, P.F. Chang, and Roy's have also established a local presence. (Since you're likely to be familiar with those chains, I'm not going to review them here.)

The hippest areas to eat are downtown's West End/Warehouse district, near Fourth and Colorado streets, and South Congress Avenue, less than a mile away. If you prefer a view of Town Lake to a view of black-clad young people, several more established restaurants in the same general vicinity—one conveniently near most tourist attractions—should appeal. Many popular downtown eateries have branches in the northwest, near the Arboretum mall. Sprawling with new-growth apartment and business complexes, this area doesn't have a lot of character, but those living and doing business around here keep the top dining rooms hopping.

Fast-food joints tend to be concentrated to the north, along the I-35 corridor. If you're looking for authentic Mexican, the East Side is the place. Barton Springs Road, near Zilker Park; the Enfield area around Mo-Pac; Lake Austin, near the Tom Miller Dam; and the tiny town of Bee Cave to the far west are also popular dining enclaves, but there's good food to be found in almost every part of town. (To locate restaurants outside of Downtown, see the map on p. 154.) Wherever you eat, think casual. There isn't a restaurant in Austin that requires men to put on a tie and jacket, and many upscale dining rooms are far better turned out than their wealthy techno-geek clientele.

It's a good idea to eat at off-hours, either early or late, if the restaurant you're interested in doesn't take reservations. If you arrive at a popular place at prime time—around 7:30pm—you may find yourself waiting an hour or more for a table. Make reservations whenever you can, and make them as far in advance as possible. Dining out can be a competitive sport in Austin.

In addition, at some of the hottest restaurants, the buzz is literal. Many Austin eateries, especially those in converted homes, have terrible acoustics, and the rooms are LOUD. At the height of the dinner rush, you're likely to find yourself shouting to your companion. Quiet, romantic eateries are hard to come by—but at least you can argue in complete privacy, because no one's likely to hear a thing.

Note, too, that the downtown area still tends to be underserved on the weekend; many restaurants popular with businesspeople during the week are closed for lunch on Saturday and for both lunch and dinner on Sunday.

Finally, if you're staying in the downtown or University of Texas area, consider taking a cab when you go out to dinner. It's hard to find a metered spot for your car, and you won't pay much more for a taxi than you would for valet parking or an independent lot. And of course the value of not having to drive around unfamiliar, often confusing streets in the dark after having had a few cocktails is incalculable.

See chapter 5 for an explanation of culinary categories.

1 Restaurants by Cuisine

AMERICAN
Cool River Café (Northwest, $$$, p. 176)
Eastside Café ⭐ (East Austin, $$, p. 175)
Shady Grove ⭐ (Downtown/ Capitol, $, p. 169)
Threadgill's (Central, $, p. 173)
The Oasis (West/Lakes, $$, p. 178)

ASIAN
Noodle-ism ⭐ (Downtown/ Capitol, $, p. 169)

BARBECUE
County Line on the Hill ⭐ (West/Lakes, $$, p. 178)
The Iron Works ⭐ (Downtown/ Capitol, $, p. 168)
The Salt Lick ⭐ (South Austin, $$, p. 175)

CAJUN/CREOLE
Gumbo's ⭐ (Downtown/Capitol, $$$, p. 165)

CARIBBEAN
Gilligan's ⭐ (Downtown/Capitol, $$$, p. 165)

CONTINENTAL
Green Pastures ⭐ (South Austin, $$$, p. 173)

DELI
Cipollina ⭐ (Central, $, p. 173)
Katz's (Downtown/Capitol, $, p. 168)

FRENCH
Aquarelle ⭐⭐ (Downtown/ Capitol, $$$, p. 164)
Chez Nous (Downtown/Capitol, $$$, p. 165)

FUSION
Noodle-ism ⭐ (Downtown/ Capitol, $, p. 169)
Saba Blue Water Café (Downtown/Capitol, $$, p. 168)

INDIAN
Clay Pit ⭐ (Downtown/Capitol, $$, p. 167)

ITALIAN
Asti ⭐ (Central, $$, p. 172)
Basil's ⭐ (Downtown/Capitol, $$$, p. 164)
La Traviata ⭐⭐ (Downtown/ Capitol, $$$, p. 166)
Mezzaluna ⭐ (Downtown/Capitol, $$$, p. 166)
Pizza Nizza (Downtown/Capitol, $, p. 169)
Vespaio ⭐ (South Austin, $$$, p. 174)

JAPANESE
Musashino (Northwest, $$, p. 177)
Noodle-ism (Downtown/Capitol, $, p. 169)

MEDITERRANEAN
Louie's 106 (Downtown/Capitol, $$$, p. 166)

Key to Abbreviations: $$$$ = Very Expensive $$$ = Expensive $$ = Moderate $ = Inexpensive

MEXICAN (NORTHERN & TEX-MEX)

Chuy's (Downtown/Capitol, $, p. 168)

Dario's (East Austin, $, p. 176)

Güero's ✪✪ (South Austin, $$, p. 174)

Las Manitas ✪ (Downtown/Capitol, $, p. 169)

Manuel's (Downtown/Capitol, $$, p. 167)

Matt's El Rancho (South Austin, $$, p. 175)

The Oasis (West/Lakes, $$, p. 178)

NEW AMERICAN

Castle Hill Café ✪ (Downtown/Capitol, $$$, p. 165)

Driskill Grill ✪✪ (Downtown/Capitol, $$$$, p. 162)

Emilia's ✪✪✪ (Downtown/Capitol, $$$$, p. 164)

Hudson's on the Bend ✪✪ (West/Lakes, $$$$, p. 177)

Jeffrey's ✪✪ (Central, $$$$, p. 170)

Shoreline Grill ✪ (Downtown/Capitol, $$$, p. 167)

Wink ✪ (Central, $$$, p. 171)

Zoot ✪✪ (Central, $$$, p. 172)

PIZZA

Pizza Nizza (Downtown/Capitol, $, p. 169)

REGIONAL MEXICAN

Curra's Grill ✪ (South Austin, $$, p. 174)

Güero's ✪✪ (South Austin, $$, p. 174)

Fonda San Miguel ✪✪ (Central, $$, p. 170)

Manuel's (Downtown/Capitol, $$, p. 167)

SEAFOOD

Eddie V's Edgewater Grill ✪ (Northwest, $$$$, p. 176)

Gilligan's ✪ (Downtown/Capitol, $$$, p. 165)

Shoreline Grill ✪ (Downtown/Capitol, $$$, p. 167)

SOUTHWEST

Cool River Café (Northwest, $$$, p. 176)

Z'Tejas Grill ✪ (Northwest, $$, p. 177)

STEAKS

Eddie V's Edgewater Grill ✪ (Northwest, $$$$, p. 176)

2 Downtown/Capitol

VERY EXPENSIVE

Driskill Grill ✪✪ NEW AMERICAN   Don't be misled by the gracious, Old World atmosphere of the Driskell Hotel's fine dining room—all that dim lighting, the etched glass, those cushy banquettes. The cuisine that emerges from the kitchen of chef David Bull (the youngest sous chef ever to toil at Dallas's famed Mansion on Turtle Creek) is totally up to date. Sure, you'll find some classics here such as Caesar salad and, as befits a hotel founded by a cattle baron, prime cuts of beef. But they've been reinvigorated—the Caesar incorporates boursin cheese and focaccia croutons, for example—mingling on the menu with interesting appetizers like barbecued duck burrito with spicy corn cakes and entrees such as Chilean sea bass and crab spring roll over a soba noodle stir fry. It's New American cooking at its best: Ingredients that initially seem discordant turn out to be terrifically complementary. Save room for dessert—perhaps the caramelized cappuccino semifreddo in vanilla cream, swirled with espresso. A nice bonus: If you want to sample your companion's food (and you will), you

Downtown Austin Dining

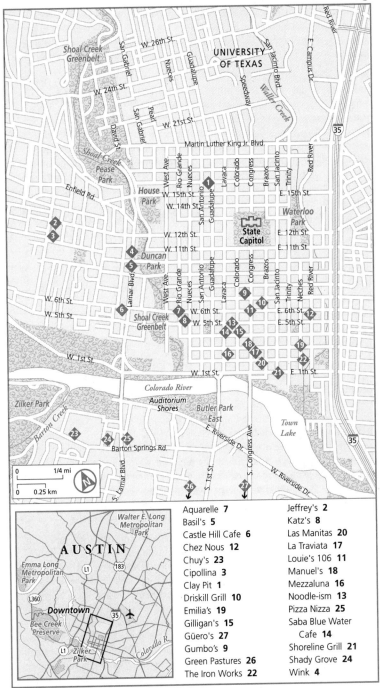

Aquarelle **7**
Basil's **5**
Castle Hill Cafe **6**
Chez Nous **12**
Chuy's **23**
Cipollina **3**
Clay Pit **1**
Driskill Grill **10**
Emilia's **19**
Gilligan's **15**
Güero's **27**
Gumbo's **9**
Green Pastures **26**
The Iron Works **22**

Jeffrey's **2**
Katz's **8**
Las Manitas **20**
La Traviata **17**
Louie's 106 **11**
Manuel's **18**
Mezzaluna **16**
Noodle-ism **13**
Pizza Nizza **25**
Saba Blue Water
    Cafe **14**
Shoreline Grill **21**
Shady Grove **24**
Wink **4**

don't have to shout above the din to ask permission. This is one of the quietest dining rooms in town.

604 Brazos St., The Driskill. ℂ 512/391-7162. Reservations recommended. Main courses $24–$38. AE, DC, DISC, MC, V. Tues–Sat 5:30–10:30pm.

Emilia's ★★★ NEW AMERICAN   Arguably the best restaurant in Austin, and definitely the best to arrive on the local dining scene in recent years, Emilia's is neither inexpensive (no surprise) nor easy to find (a little odder, since it's right near the convention center). But it's well worth both the expense and the reconnaissance effort. You can't go wrong with anything on the menu; the specialty is seafood, with dishes such as a delicate and flavorful loup de mer. The prelude, a selection of buttery smooth patés made on the premises, was dazzling, nor have I have ever tasted better vegetables—a succulent and tasty array of tiny artichokes, fennel, and carrots. The two dining rooms, in a converted 1850s limestone building, are elegant without being ostentatious, and this is Austin's only restaurant to win *Wine Spectator*'s top Best of Award of Excellence (2002). You can have a more casual dining experience (charcûterie, burgers, and the like) in the pleasant courtyard or Carriage House Bar, though it seems a waste to lounge around heaven's gate instead of entering.

600 E. 3rd St. ℂ 512/469-9722. Reservations recommended. Main courses $18–$34. AE, DC, DISC, MC, V. Dining room Mon–Thurs 6–10pm; Fri–Sat 6–11pm; Carriage House Mon–Thurs 5pm–midnight; Fri–Sat 5pm–1am.

EXPENSIVE

Aquarelle ★★ FRENCH   Isn't it romantic? A converted neoclassical house with gilded mirrors, fresh flowers, tiny candle lamps flickering on the tables, strains of "La Vie en Rose" floating in the background—you get the picture. Aquarelle is a traditional and pretty Francophile haven. The food also stays traditionally Gallic; Jacques Richard, the Loire-born chef, doesn't believe in messing with success. All the prix-fixe menus are a good bet, but such dishes as the warm foie gras over red-wine poached pears or rainbow trout with sorrel cream cooked in parchment paper are worth going a la carte. Prepare to make an evening of dinner here: In classic French fashion, you're likely to spend at least three hours slowly savoring the experience. Cap the night off with a chocolate soufflé cake with a molten center, and you're likely to keep savoring the memory days later.

606 Rio Grande. ℂ 512/479-8117. Reservations recommended. Main courses $18–$29; prix-fixe $25 (3-course market menu/$35 with wine), $45 (4-course tasting menu/$55 with wine), $70 (6-course menu gourmand/$100 with wine). AE, DC, DISC, MC, V. Tues–Thurs 6–9:30pm; Fri–Sat 6–10:15pm.

Basil's ★ ITALIAN   Pretty in pink, with lace curtains, oak trim, and lazily swirling ceiling fans, Basil's dining room sets a duly festive tone for its fine northern Italian cuisine. You'll find the traditional dishes here, but turned out with innovative touches. For example, the pasta with which the manicotti is made is infused with carrots; its stuffing includes hazelnuts and four cheeses.

Consider sharing the rotollo alla salmone—pinwheels of layered egg pasta, salmon, and ricotta with peppers and spinach—so you can get your carb fix before moving on to one of specialty fish dishes: the catch of the day sautéed with crab and artichokes in a mustard cream sauce, perhaps. Heartier appetites might appreciate the beef tenderloin in port wine over portobello mushrooms with a small Gorgonzola wedge on the side.

900 W. 10th St. ℂ 512/477-5576. Reservations recommended. Pastas $13–$16; main courses $19–$30. AE, DC, DISC, MC, V. Daily 6–10:30pm (sometimes closes earlier weekdays).

Castle Hill Café ★ *Value* NEW AMERICAN   Surrounded on three sides by trees, Castle Hill feels tucked away somewhere remote, but it's just a block beyond downtown's western border, near two major thoroughfares. With its dark-wood tables, rich Southwestern tones, and abundant Oaxacan folk art, this favored yuppie haunt balances comfort and creativity. The empanadas filled with curried lamb and raisins—and topped with a cilantro-yogurt sauce—make a superb appetizer, as do the crab-crayfish cakes with apple-rosemary vinaigrette. Imaginatively conceived and beautifully arranged dinners might include roasted pork tenderloin Cubano served with saffron-chorizo grits, or linguini with garlic shrimp in crab-brie sauce.

Entree prices have crept up in recent years, so at first glance this no longer appears like the dinner bargain it once was. But main courses come with salads, and the low-priced starters are huge. If you really want to keep costs down, go for one of the entree salads such as the grilled chicken with guacamole relish and two blue corn empanadas, perhaps preceded by a cup of spicy duck and sausage gumbo. You won't go away hungry.

1101 W. Fifth St. ✆ 512/476-0728. Reservations accepted for parties of 6 or more only. Main courses $11–$20. AE, DISC, MC, V. Mon–Fri 11am–2:30pm; Mon–Sat 6–10pm.

Chez Nous *Value* FRENCH   With its lace curtains, fresh flowers in anisette bottles, and Folies Bergère posters, this intimate restaurant feels closer to Paris, France than to Paris, Texas. Items on the a la carte dinner menu are reasonably priced, but the real bargain is the menu du jour, which includes a choice of soup, salad, or pâté; one of three designated entrees; and crème caramel, chocolate mousse, or Brie for dessert. The main courses might include an *poisson poivre vert* (fresh fish of the day with a green-peppercorn sauce) or a simple but delicious roast chicken.

Chez Nous's friendly French owners opened their bistro in 1982, and perhaps 20 years in the business have taken their toll: There are reports lately that the food is tired. The restaurant is around the corner from Sixth Street, prime downtown touring territory; try it at lunch, when prices are lower than in the evening.

510 Neches St. ✆ 512/473-2413. Reservations accepted for parties of 6 or more only. Main courses $17–$26; menu du jour $22. AE, DC, DISC, MC, V. Tues–Fri 11:45am–2pm; Tues–Sun 6–10:30pm.

Gilligan's ★ CARIBBEAN/SEAFOOD   If you like your seafood with a kick, get yourself to Gilligan's, located in one of the converted buildings in the warehouse district. You might start with calamari with Cajun seasonings and move on from there to tuna mignon with pineapple-mango salsa or macadamia-crusted mahimahi. There's also a selection of Caribbean-style nonfish dishes, including wild boar potstickers and Jamaican jerk chicken. Portions are huge, and many entrees come with a delicious coconut rice; accompaniments like New World slaw and West Indies black beans are winners, too. Don't be misled by the name: This is no collegiate meat mart, but a skylit, sophisticated place of colorful tropical murals and weekend music, including terrific reggae bands.

407 Colorado St. ✆ 512/474-7474. Reservations recommended on weekends. Main courses $15–$21. AE, DC, DISC, MC, V. Mon–Thurs 6–9:30pm; Fri–Sat 6–10pm.

Gumbo's ★ CAJUN/CREOLE   When it come to culinary geography, Texas is mostly associated with Mexico and the West (all that meat, don't you know). Here's a nice reminder that the state also borders Louisiana. Come here for blackened catfish with dirty rice and sausage jambalaya, some rich shrimp Creole, or, at lunch, a crispy oyster Po'Boy. The menu tends more towards casual

Cajun than fancy Creole, but no matter what their level of formality, the dishes never wuss out, spice-wise. The high-ceiling dining room, with a black-and-white tiled floor, lots of gleaming wood, and canned jazz piped in, successfully re-creates the atmosphere of a Louisiana café, and it's nice to be able to dine in the recently renovated art deco Brown Building (1938), where LBJ used to have an office.

701 Colorado. ⓒ 512/480-8053. Reservations recommended on weekends. Main courses $13–$28. AE, DC, DISC, MC, V. Mon–Thurs 11am–2pm and 5:30–10pm; Fri 11am–2pm and 5:30–11pm; Sat 5:30–11pm; Sun 11am–2pm (brunch) and 5:30–10pm.

La Traviata ⟨★★⟩ ITALIAN   When I lunched at this intimate Italian bistro, I immediately loved the Euro-chic atmosphere, the way the textured limestone walls of the 1890s building complemented the hardwood floors, sleek bar, and sunny yellow walls. I loved my simple but delicious seared salmon salad, an Italian spin on the French salade niçoise; the taste I had of my companion's chicken parmesan, which bore little resemblance to the boring dish I've avoided for years; and the tiramisù dessert, wonderfully light with toasted hazelnuts and topped by a dusting of espresso. So when I learned that chef Marion Gilchrist had come to Austin to open a place with her brother after cooking at Geronimo, my favorite Santa Fe restaurant, I wasn't surprised. At dinner, try the crispy polenta with Gorgonzola sauce or the divers scallops with couscous and smoked bacon; I've heard they're incredible. *Note:* On Friday and Saturday evenings, reservations are only accepted for times between 5:30 and 6:30pm. If you want to eat at a more civilized hour without having to wait, book a table here for a weekday evening.

314 Congress Ave. ⓒ 512/479-8131. Reservations accepted (and recommended for dinner) Mon–Thurs and 5:30–6:30pm Fri and Sat. Pasta $9.50–$16. Main courses $15–$25. AE, MC, V. Mon–Thurs 11am–2pm and 5:30–10pm; Fri 11am–2pm and 5:30–10:30pm; Sat 5:30–10:30pm.

Louie's 106 MEDITERRANEAN   Some downtown restaurants popular with a business crowd don't draw many customers after dark, but Louie's successfully straddles the business/pleasure divide. The lunchtime business types who find the tony, private club atmosphere of the restored Littlefield building congenial for schmoozing clients return after work to kick back with a glass of wine (Louie's has an impressive list) and updated versions of traditional Spanish tapas—portobello mushroom–potato blini, say, or beef carpaccio with capers. (Some also come to escape the onus against smoking in Austin in the separate cigar room.) But, lights dimmed, the high-ceiling dining room can be romantic too, and the pre- and post-theater crowds enjoy the Mediterranean menu, including appetizer-size tapas and such entrees as a classic paella Valencia or the pork chop with garlic mashed potatoes. The hefty portion sizes don't hurt business, either.

106 E. Sixth St. ⓒ 512/476-1997. Reservations recommended for dinner. Tapas $2.50–$7; main courses $15–$25. AE, DC, DISC, MC, V. Mon–Thurs 11:30am–10:30pm; Fri 11:30am–11pm; Sat 6–11pm; Sun 6–9:30pm.

Mezzaluna ⟨★⟩ ITALIAN   One of the first restaurants to open in the now chic warehouse district, the dimly lit, buzzy Mezzaluna is still ahead of the pack (and always packed). The menu is a tad trendy—goat cheese and white truffle essence turn up several times—but mostly mixes fairly familiar Italian dishes with some you won't see on many menus: a starter of *carciofini al forno*, herb-baked artichoke hearts, say, or lasagna made with smoked chicken rather than the traditional chopped beef. The wood-fired pizzas make a nice light meal; heartier specialties range from a rich fusilli del Nonna with grilled chicken and Gorgonzola cream to a beef tenderloin done in a Chianti reduction. An exclusively Italian selection of wines by the glass introduces diners to interesting bottles, too.

310 Colorado St. ℭ **512/472-6770.** Reservations recommended. Pizzas and pastas $8–$18; main courses $19–$27. AE, DC, DISC, MC, V. Mon–Thurs 11:30am–10:30pm; Fri 11:30am–11pm; Sat 5–11pm; Sun 4–9pm.

Shoreline Grill ★ SEAFOOD/NEW AMERICAN   Fish is the prime bait at this tony grill, which looks out over Town Lake and the Congress Avenue Bridge, but in late spring through early fall, bats run a close second. During this period, when thousands of Mexican free-tailed bats emerge in unison from under the bridge at dusk, patio tables for viewing the phenomenon are at a premium.

When they're not going batty, diners focus on such starters as semolina-crusted oysters or venison chorizo quesadillas. Drum, a moist, meaty fish from the Gulf, is worth trying however it's prepared; the cinnamon-glazed salmon with red chile polenta is excellent, too. Non-aquatic dishes include Parmesan-crusted chicken with penne pasta and prime rib with goat cheese potatoes. Menus change seasonally; in summer, entree-sized salads are offered. A nice cocktail menu—mojito, anyone?—complements a wine list with a good by-the-glass selection.

98 San Jacinto Blvd. ℭ **512/477-3300.** Reservations recommended (patio is first-come, first-served). Main courses $16–$29. AE, DC, DISC, MC, V. Mon–Fri 11am–10pm; Sat 5–10pm; Sun 5–9pm.

MODERATE

Clay Pit ★ *Value* INDIAN   An elegant setting—a historic building with wood floors and exposed limestone walls, lit with soft lamps and votive candles—and sumptuous recipes, including creative curries and other sauces rich with nuts, raisins, and exotic spices, raise this brainchild of a husband-and-wife team and a New Delhi–trained chef to gourmet status. The starter of perfectly cooked coriander calamari is served with a piquant cilantro aioli. For an entree, consider *khuroos-e-tursh,* baked chicken breast stuffed with nuts, mushrooms, and onions and smothered in a cashew-almond cream sauce, or one of the dazzling vegetarian dishes. A bargain buffet and a variety of wraps made with nan make this a great lunch stop while touring the nearby Capitol.

1601 Guadalupe St. ℭ **512/322-5131.** Reservations recommended. $6.50 lunch buffet. Main courses $8.95–$16. AE, DC, DISC, MC, V. Mon–Thurs 11am–2pm and 5–10pm; Fri 11am–2pm and 5–11pm; Sat 5–11pm; Sun 5–10pm.

Manuel's MEXICAN/REGIONAL MEXICAN   One of the few moderate holdouts in a downtown dining scene that's rapidly heading uptown, price-wise, Manuel's is sleek, chic, and lively. Downtown executives are among the many who come to unwind at Manuel's lively happy hour (daily 4–7pm), with half-price hors d'oeuvres and salsa music (see "Only in Austin," later in this chapter, for the musical Sun brunch).

The food, which includes dishes from the interior of Mexico, is a creative cut above many Tex-Mex places. You can get well-prepared versions of the standards, but Manuel's also offers hard-to-find specialties such as the *chiles rellenos en nogada,* stuffed with pork and topped with walnut–cream brandy sauce. The excellent *enchiladas banderas* are arrayed in the colors of the Mexican flag: a green *tomatillo verde* sauce; a white sour-creamy *suiza;* and a red *adobada,* made with ancho chiles. A northwest branch, in Great Hills, 10201 Jollyville Rd. (© 512/345-1042), lays on live music Thursday and Saturday nights.

310 Congress Ave. © 512/472-7555. Reservations accepted for 8 or more only. Main courses $7.25–$18. AE, DISC, MC, V. Mon–Thurs 11am–10pm; Fri–Sat 11am–11pm, Sun 11am–9pm.

Saba Blue Water Café FUSION   An aquatic-oriented color scheme, ocean-inspired artwork, and a menu heavy on seafood make for a hip, tropical dining experience far from any beach. Right on the main strip of downtown's popular warehouse district, this bar and restaurant boasts distinctive Asian/Caribbean/Mexican fusion fare, with an emphasis on light "bites." You can graze your way through the likes of seaweed-wrapped tuna pieces flash-fried and served with a delightful honey-wasabi sauce, cilantro-pork-and-shrimp potstickers, or masa-fried oyster tostadas. Not satisfied with smaller dishes? Saba also serves up enticing entrees like mahimahi with lemon grass cream and pineapple rice or calypso pork tenderloin with roasted sweet potatoes. The drinks tend towards the tropical, too. The mojitos are excellent but don't have too many of them, lest you find yourself getting overenthusiastic about the tapas; too many can easily move your tab into the expensive range.

208D W. Fourth St. © 512/478-7222. Reservations accepted for parties of 6 or more. Tapas $6–$9; main courses $10–$19. AE, DC, DISC, MC, V. Mon–Tues 4pm–midnight; Wed–Fri 4pm–2am; Sat 5pm–2am. Food served until midnight Thurs–Sat, until 10pm Mon–Wed.

INEXPENSIVE

Chuy's *Kids* MEXICAN   One of the row of low-priced, friendly restaurants that line Barton Springs Road just east of Zilker Park, Chuy's stands out for its determinedly wacky decor—hubcaps lining the ceiling, Elvis memorabilia galore—and its sauce-smothered Tex-Mex food. You're not likely to leave hungry after specials like Southwest enchiladas, piled high with smoked chicken and cheese and topped with a fried egg; or a huge sopapilla stuffed with grilled sirloin. This has been a local landmark since 2001, when Jenna Bush got busted here for underage drinking. There are two other Chuy's in town, one in the north on 10520 N. Lamar Blvd. (© 512/836-3218), the other in the northwest on 11680 N. Research Blvd. (© 512/342-0011).

1728 Barton Springs Rd. © 512/474-4452. Reservations not accepted. Main courses $6–$9. AE, DC, DISC, MC, V. Sun–Thurs 11am–10pm; Fri–Sat 11am–11pm.

The Iron Works ★ *Kids* BARBECUE   Some of the best barbecue in Austin is served in one of the most unusual settings. Until 1977, this building housed the ironworks of the Weigl family, who came over from Germany in 1913. You can see their ornamental craft all around town, including the State Capitol. Cattle brands created for Jack Benny ("Lasting 39"), Lucille Ball, and Bob Hope are displayed in front of the restaurant. The fall-off-the-bones-tender beef ribs are the most popular order, with the brisket running a close second. Lean turkey breast and juicy chicken are also smoked to perfection.

Red River and E. First sts. © 800/669-3602 or 512/478-4855. Reservations accepted for large parties only. Sandwiches $2–$4.10; plates $5.90–$10; by the lb. $6–$11. AE, DC, MC, V. Mon–Sat 11am–9pm.

Katz's *Kids* DELI   Even if it doesn't quite achieve New York deli status—for one thing, the staff is not nearly rude enough, and for another, you can get jalapeños in your omelets—Katz's is as close as you'll come in Austin. The matzo balls are as light and the cheesecake as dense as they're supposed to be, and the corned beef sandwiches come in the requisite gargantuan portions. Katz's is a great place to come after hitting the Sixth Street clubs, whether you're craving challah French toast or *kasha varnishkas* at 4am.

618 W. Sixth St. C **512/472-2037**. Reservations not accepted. Sandwiches $4.25–$9 main courses $7.50–$12. AE, DISC, MC, V. Daily 24 hr.

Las Manitas ✦ MEXICAN   This funky family-owned Mexican diner, decked out with local artwork and colorful booths and tables, is an Austin classic; don't leave town without checking it out. A rack of alternative newspapers at the door sets the political tone, but businesspeople and slackers alike pile into this small place for breakfasts of *migas con queso* (eggs scrambled with corn tortillas, cheddar cheese, and ranchero sauce) or *chilaquiles verdes* (tortilla strips topped with green tomatillo sauce, Jack cheese, and onions). The delicious refried beans are prepared with bacon but, this being Austin, most of the rest of the food is cooked in canola or olive oil; vegetarian items are highlighted, and smoothies as well as Mexican soft drinks and beers share the menu.

211 Congress Ave. C **512/472-9357**. Reservations not accepted. Breakfast $2.95–$5.95; lunch $2.95–$7.95. AE, DISC, MC, V. Mon–Fri 7am–4pm; Sat–Sun 7am–2:30pm.

Noodle-ism ✦ ASIAN/FUSION   The Warehouse District is chock-a-block with expensive, trendy restaurants, so it's nice to have a newcomer on the scene that's only trendy. As the name suggests, noodles are the focus at this Zen-spare but attractive spot, where you order at a counter and the food is brought to you (fairly quickly, I should add): noodle soups, noodle bowls, even noodles that are better known as pasta (for example, a delicious three-cabbage ravioli). The preparations are mostly Japanese, but Thai, Chinese, and even Italian are also influences. Salads and even a burger fill out the offerings. Expect whatever you order to be tasty and beautifully presented.

107 W. 5th St. C **512/275-9988**. Reservations not accepted. $5.95–$8.95. AE, DISC, MC, V. Mon–Thurs 11am–10pm; Fri 11am–11pm; Sat noon–11pm; Sun noon–9pm.

Pizza Nizza *Value* ITALIAN/PIZZA   This pizzeria does a thriving delivery business, but unless the place where you're staying has a large pecan tree growing in its center, it's a lot more interesting to place your order at the counter and then eat at one of the colorful glass-topped tables painted in Roman mosaic style. Pastas such as cannelloni stuffed with chicken, Italian sausage, ricotta, mozzarella, and provolone, and doused in tomato cream sauce are not only delicious, but also bargain priced. The pizzas are billed as offering "the most toppings in Austin," and with selections like hamburger, jalapeno pesto, and smoked bacon, who would doubt it? The lunch specials—a dinner salad plus a large slice with three toppings—are a real deal at $5.50 ($6.50 if you want your salad to speak Greek).

1608 Barton Springs Rd. C **512/474-7070**. Reservations not accepted. Main courses $7.50–$8.95; pizza $14–$19. AE, DC, DISC, MC, V. Mon–Thurs 11am–10pm; Fri 11am–11pm; Sat noon–11pm; Sun noon–10pm.

Shady Grove ✦ AMERICAN   If your idea of comfort food involves chiles, don't pass up Shady Grove. The inside dining area, with its Texas kitsch roadhouse decor and cushy booths, is plenty comfortable, but most people head for the large, tree-shaded patio when the weather permits. After a day of fresh air at nearby Zilker Park, a hearty bowl of Freddie's Airstream chili might be just the thing. All the burgers are made with high-grade ground sirloin, and if you've never had a Frito pie (Fritos topped with Airstream chili and cheese), this is the place to try one. Large salads—among them, noodles with Asian vegetables—or the hippie sandwich (grilled eggplant, veggies, and cheese with pesto mayonnaise) will satisfy the less carnivorous. The quintessential laid-back Austin restaurant, it naturally has live music on the patio from April through October (except during Aug).

1624 Barton Springs Rd. ✆ 512/474-9991. Reservations not accepted. Main courses $7.25–$11. AE, DC, DISC, MC, V. Sun–Thurs 11am–10pm; Fri–Sat 11am–11pm.

3 Central

VERY EXPENSIVE

Jeffrey's ⭐⭐ NEW AMERICAN   Jeffrey's has been garnering local acclaim since 1975, but it wasn't until 1991, when David Garrido came on board, that it became a celebrity chef restaurant. Garrido's enthusiasm about food is boundless; on any given day you might catch him excitedly explaining to an admiring patron how he went out at dawn to buy just the right mushrooms for one of his daily specials. But Garrido isn't always around now—when a certain Texan who liked the restaurant went to the White House, it seemed like a propitious time to open a branch in D.C.—and both chefs and customers familiar with the concept of tailoring fresh ingredients to daily specials have become more common in town.

That said, eating in Jeffrey's is an Austin experience you shouldn't miss: Politicos (Dems as well as Republicans), celebs, and regular folks turn up at this former storefront in artsy Clarksville wearing everything from T-shirts to tuxes. And the food is often dazzling, with flavors and textures that dance wildly together without tripping. Appetizers might include the likes of a morel mushroom soufflé with pistachios and Armagnac chervil cream and—a signature dish that never leaves the menu—crispy oysters topped with habanero honey aioli. Venison and foie gras in puff pastry with chestnut sherry sauce was among the entree successes on a recent menu. Desserts such as Chocolate Intemperance live up to their diet-destroying promise, and the wine list is outstanding.

1204 W. Lynn. ✆ 512/477-5584. Reservations strongly recommended. Main courses $25–$39. AE, DC, DISC, MC, V. Mon–Thurs 6–10pm; Fri–Sat 5:30–10:30pm; Sun 5:30–9:30pm.

EXPENSIVE

Fonda San Miguel ⭐⭐ REGIONAL MEXICAN   Like American Southwest chefs who look to Native American staples such as blue corn for inspiration, Mexico City chefs have had their own back-to-the-roots movement. Such trends as using ancient Aztec ingredients have been carefully tracked and artfully translated since 1975 at Fonda San Miguel, one of America's top fine-dining spots for Mexican regional cuisine. Eat here and you'll discover that food from the northern Mexico state of Sonora, on which most Tex-Mex fare is based, represents Mexico in the same limited way that hearty Midwestern cooking represents the United States.

The huge dining room, with its carved wooden doors, colorful paintings (many by famed Mexico artists), and live ficus tree, is a gorgeous backdrop to such appetizers as Veracruz-style ceviche or quesadillas with *huitlacoche,* a corn fungus as rare as French truffles. *Cochinita pibil,* pork baked in banana leaves, is one of the Yucatán offerings. Those with more traditional tastes will find familiar northern Mexican fare, extremely well prepared, on the menu.

2330 W. North Loop. ✆ 512/459-4121. Reservations recommended. Main courses $13–$20. AE, DC, DISC, MC, V. Mon–Thurs 5:30–9:30pm; Fri–Sat 5:30–10:30pm (bar opens 30 min. earlier); Sun brunch 11am–2pm.

Veggie Heaven

Visitors to Austin who want to go meatless won't have to play second fiddle in the culinary orchestra. Not only do most fine dining rooms in town offer at least one good veggie option—not just the typical boring pasta dish, either—but the restaurants solely dedicated to vegetarians are a cut above those in most towns. These top picks all fall into the Inexpensive range:

Mother's Cafe & Garden The Save the Earth crowd that frequents this Hyde Park cafe enjoys an international array of veggie dishes, with heavy south-of-the-border representation. You'll find classic chiles rellenos, burritos, and nachos, along with more unusual tofu enchiladas. The tropical shack–style back garden is appealing, and the young staff is friendly, but not nauseatingly so. There's a good, inexpensive selection of local beers and wines. 4215 Duval St. ✆ **512/451-3994.**

Mr Natural Only on Austin's East Side would you find a health food store/restaurant/bakery with an all Mexican-American staff, and dishes such as tofu pipian, vegetarian chorizo, and zucchini poblana. Richard Linklater, Robert Rodriguez, and other successful hipsters are often spotted grazing at the lunchtime buffet. Question is, will they defect to the South Austin branch at 2414 S. Lamar (✆ **512/916-9223**), opened in November 2002? Stay tuned. 1901 E. 1st St. ✆ **512/477-5228.**

West Lynn Cafe Although this sunny, soaring-ceiling restaurant, part homey, part techno-chic, is totally vegetarian, it doesn't attract only the Birkenstocks-with-socks set. Health-conscious sophisticates and artsy locals in the West Lynn neighborhood (just northwest of Downtown) also come to enjoy well-prepared dishes that range over the world's cuisine—everything from Thai red pepper curry and Szechuan stir-fry to pesto primavera, mushroom stroganoff, spanakopita, and artichoke enchiladas—accompanied by nice, reasonably priced wine. 1110 W. Lynn. ✆ **512/482-0950.**

Wink ⋆ *Finds* NEW AMERICAN   One of the latest darlings of the local foodie scene is a spare but attractive 17-table eatery in an unlikely strip center. Chef/owners Stewart Scruggs and Mark Paul are fresh ingredient fanatics and they train their staff well. Your server should be able to fill you in on every detail of the menu, down to the organic farm where the arugula and fennel in your rabbit confit salad came from. You never know what dishes will turn up unless—this being Austin—you check the daily listings on the Internet at www.winkrestaurant.com, but expect a mix of such typical New American suspects as ahi tuna with bok choy and more adventurous dishes like veal sweetbreads on grilled apples. The five-course tasting menu, which includes some chef's off-menu surprises ($40 food only, $70 paired with wine), is worth the splurge. This restaurant is just north of the Lamar/Sixth St. retail mecca; save some room (and dough) for desserts like chocolate soup with milk chocolate-ginger mousse.

1014 N. Lamar. ✆ **512/482-8868.** Reservations strongly suggested. Main courses $17–$24. AE, DC, DISC, MC, V. Mon–Sat 6–11pm.

Zoot ★★ NEW AMERICAN   Texas chauvinism and eco-consciousness come together at Zoot to produce a cuisine that's creative, fresh, and delicious. This cozy Enfield restaurant, set in a 1920s cottage, was one of the first in Austin to use only organic vegetables and to design its dishes around ingredients grown in the local area. Appetizers such as the orange-sesame marinated beef satay show an Asian influence, but the backbone of the menu, which changes seasonally, is its new takes on American standards. Comfort food here might be anything from Moroccan-style chicken breast to a more standard seared filet mignon with grilled onions and spinach. Vegetarian offerings are equally interesting—perhaps vegetable samosas on basmati rice in a mint-and-cumin yogurt sauce or cabbage stuffed with quinoa, pine nuts, and raisins. The presentations are always gorgeous and the setting is soothing, but the prices don't reflect the fact that the tech boom is over. Eating here was once a weekend treat, but now it's likely to call for an occasion more special than Friday's arrival.

509 Hearn. © **512/477-6535.** Reservations recommended, especially on weekends. Main courses $18–$36; six-course tasting menu $50. AE, DC, DISC, MC, V. Daily 5:30–10pm.

MODERATE

Asti ★ *Value* ITALIAN   This is the Italian place everyone wants in their neighborhood: casual, consistently good, and reasonably priced. An open kitchen and retro Formica-topped tables create a hip, upbeat atmosphere. The designer pizzas make a nice light meal, and northern Italian specialties such as the Calabrese-style trout and the pan-seared halibut with green beans are winners. Skip the unexciting risotto choices, though, and save room for such desserts as the creamy espresso sorbet or the amazing chocolate mousse cannoli.

408C E. 43rd St. © **512/451-1218.** Reservations recommended on weekends. Pizzas, pastas $8–$16; main courses $15–$16. AE, DC, DISC, MC, V. Mon–Thurs 11am–10pm; Fri 11am–11pm; Sat 5–11pm.

⌒ *Kids* **Family-Friendly Restaurants**

Chuy's (p. 168)   Teens and aspiring teens will enjoy this colorful, inexpensive restaurant, with its cool T-shirts, Elvis kitsch, and green iguanas crawling up the walls. And it provides a cautionary tale about underage drinking (or at least the perils of being related to the president).

Cool River Café (p. 176)   The noise level, super-sized menu, and opportunity to observe grown-up singles acting silly all make this place kid-compatible.

Güero's (p. 174)   As family friendly as it is hip, this is a great place to introduce kids to really good Mexican food; you're sure to find something on the huge menu to please even picky eaters. Special plates are available for kids under 12.

Katz's (p. 168)   The Kid's Club Menu here not only has small fry–friendly items such as chicken fingers and peanut-butter-and-sliced-banana sandwiches, but it also includes connect-the-dot, maze, and word games to keep youngsters occupied.

Threadgill's (p. 173)   This bustling, cheerful diner has an impressive music history—surely your kids have heard of Janis Joplin?—and an inexpensive "miniature" menu for ages 12 and under.

INEXPENSIVE   *Great!*

Cipollina *Finds* ITALIAN/DELI   It's worth the short drive from downtown to have lunch or a light dinner at this casual chic neighborhood favorite, a large, open room with a deli case that could as easily be in Italy as in Clarksville. Everything's delicious: the thin-crust pizzas (I loved the simple margherita, topped with mozzarella tomato, and basil); creative grilled sandwiches such as lamb and sweet onion; and salads like the Mediterranean, with romaine, feta, olives and oregano. Good coffee, a nice selection of wines by the glass, and excellent pastries round out the menu; there's a hot entree special every lunch and dinner, too. Come on your own with a good book or a newspaper; this is the kind of place where you'll immediately feel comfortable anyway.

1213 West Lynn. ⒞ **512/477-5211.** Reservations not accepted. Pizzas $7–$13; sandwiches $4.75–$6.50; salads $3.25–$4.95. AE, DC, DISC, MC, V. Sun–Thurs 7am–9:30pm; Fri and Sat 7am–10pm.

Threadgill's *Kids* AMERICAN   If you want a hit of music history along with heaping plates of down-home food at good prices, this Austin institution is for you. When Kenneth Threadgill obtained Travis County's first legal liquor license after the repeal of Prohibition in 1933, he turned his Gulf gas station into a club. His Wednesday night hootenannies were legendary in the 1960s, with performers like Janis Joplin turning up regularly. In turn, the Southern-style diner that was added on in 1980 became renowned for its huge chicken-fried steaks, as well as its vegetables. You can get fried okra, broccoli-rice casserole, garlic-cheese grits, and black-eyed peas in combination plates or as sides—and seconds are free.

Eddie Wilson, the current owner of Threadgill's, was the founder of the now defunct Armadillo World Headquarters, Austin's most famous music venue; the downtown branch at 301 W. Riverside (⒞ **512/472-9304**) is called Threadgill's World Headquarters. Across the street from the old Armadillo, it's filled with music memorabilia from the club and a state-of-the-art sound system. Both still double as live music venues.

6416 N. Lamar Blvd. ⒞ **512/451-5440.** Reservations not accepted. Sandwiches and burgers $5.95–$7.95; main courses $5.95–$13. DISC, MC, V. Mon–Sat 11am–10pm; Sun 11am–9pm.

4 South Austin

EXPENSIVE

Green Pastures CONTINENTAL   Peacocks strut their stuff among 225 live oaks surrounding this 1894 mansion, which has remained in the hands of the same renowned Austin family since 1916, and which the current owner's mother converted into a restaurant in 1945. The Southern graciousness and impeccable service have been retained over the years, but the new millennium brought a new chef, who gently moved the menu away from the Old World towards New America.

Still, the food tends more towards creative classic than trendy. Although a grilled tofu entree and the requisite wasabi mashed potatoes are likely to turn up on the seasonally changing menu, you're equally likely to encounter smoked prime rib eye with crab and avocado, or sautéed pheasant breast with chanterelles. And the desserts have remained decidedly retro, including a Texas pecan ball (vanilla ice cream rolled in nuts and dripping fudge) and bananas Foster.

811 W. Live Oak Rd. ⒞ **512/444-4747.** Reservations advised. Main courses $14–$32; Sunday brunch $28. AE, DISC, MC, V. Daily 11am–2pm and 6–10pm (Sun brunch buffet 11am–2pm).

Tips **Sweet Tooth**

Austin's homegrown brand of ice cream, **Amy's,** is not only wonderfully rich and creamy, but watching the colorfully clad servers juggling the scoops is a kick. Amy's has seven Austin locations, including one on the west side of downtown, 1012 W. Sixth St. at Lamar Boulevard (② **512/480-0673**), and one at the Arboretum, 10000 Research Blvd. (② **512/345-1006**). And if you don't have a chance to try it in town, you can catch this tasty treat at the airport.

Vespaio ⊛ ITALIAN   Still one of Austin's trendiest restaurants, Vespaio doesn't quite draw the long lines that it did when it first opened in the late 1990s, but the weird policy for reservations—they're accepted only for early hours on off-days—ensures that the see-and-be-seen bar is always packed. The swanked-up old storefront with lots of exposed brick and glass is a fun setting, and the food is worth waiting for, but you can drop quite a bit of dough on expensive wines while you're doing so. Best bet: Get an order (they're huge) of the crispy calamari while you're waiting for a table. The spaghetti alla carbonara is super, as is the veal scallopine with mushrooms. In the mood for a go-for-baroque pizza? Try the boscaiola, topped with wild boar sausage and Cambozola cheese.

1610 S. Congress Ave. ② **512/441-6100.** Reservations accepted only for Tues–Thurs, and Sun 5:30–6:30pm. Pizzas and pastas $8–$19; main courses $14–$27. AE, DC, DISC, MC, V. Tues–Sun 5:30–10:30pm (bar open 5pm–midnight).

MODERATE

Curra's Grill ⊛ REGIONAL MEXICAN   You're likely to find this funky, colorful restaurant packed at any time of day, but it's worth the wait for the best interior Mexican food in South Austin (and, in the moderate price range, in the city). A couple of breakfast tacos and a cup of special Oaxacan dark roast coffee are a great way to jump-start your day. For lunch, consider the octopus ceviche and the *crema de calabaza* (cream of zucchini) soup, or perhaps the tacos *al pastor,* stuffed with chile-grilled pork. The chiles rellenos topped with cream pecan sauce make a super dinner entree, but if you're sharing, the tamale platter lets you sample from the five kinds available, including veggie and pecan-pineapple-coconut. The avocado and mango margaritas are tops in the potent potables department.

A newer Curras in the northwest, 6801 Burnet Rd. (② **512/451-2560**) is not open for breakfast during the week and only open from 9am on the weekends.

614 E. Oltorf. ② **512/444-0012.** Reservations accepted for 12 or more only. Main courses $5.95–$16. AE, DISC, MC, V. Sun–Thurs 7am–10pm; Fri and Sat 7am–11pm

Güero's ⊛⊛ *Kids* MEXICAN/REGIONAL MEXICAN   Although the menu listings at this sprawling converted feed store, which serves as the unofficial center of the newly hip SoCo scene, are stylishly tongue-in-cheek—the entry for one pork dish describes it as being the same as the beef version "except piggish"—the food is seriously good. You can enjoy health-conscious versions of Tex-Mex standards as well as dishes from the interior of Mexico: snapper *a la veracruzana* (with tomatoes, green olives, and jalapeños), say, or Michoacán-style tamales. Lots of plates come topped with cheese, guacamole, and sour cream, but you can also get delicious, low-fat entrees like the chicken *al carbón* (breast meat grilled in *achiote,* a Yucatán spice), served with whole-wheat tortillas and beans. Come Sunday afternoon for a live music bonus.

1412 S. Congress. (✆ **512/447-7688.** Reservations not accepted. Main courses $7–$13. AE, DC, DISC, MC, V. Mon–Fri 11am–11pm; Sat–Sun 8am–11pm.

Matt's El Rancho MEXICAN   An oldie but a goodie. Lyndon Johnson hadn't been serving in the U.S. Senate very long when Matt's El Rancho first opened its doors. Although owner Matt Martinez outlived LBJ and other early customers, plenty of his original patrons followed when he moved his restaurant south of downtown in 1986. They came not out of habit, but because Matt (and now his son, Matt, Jr.) has been dishing up consistently tasty food since 1952.

Some of the items show the regulars' influence. For instance, you can thank former land commissioner Bob Armstrong for the tasty cheese, guacamole, and spiced-meat dip that bears his name. Chiles rellenos and grilled shrimp seasoned with garlic and soy are perennial favorites. Although the place can seat almost 500, you might still have to wait for an hour on weekend nights. Just lounge out on the terrace, sip a fresh lime margarita, and chill. The new branch at the Austin airport is not as atmospheric, nor is the menu as extensive, but you'll get a taste of what draws the crowds to this relatively untouristy (for the time being, anyway) part of town.

2613 S. Lamar Blvd. (✆ **512/462-9333.** Reservations not accepted after 5pm on weekends, except for large groups. Main courses $8–$18. AE, DC, DISC, MC, V. Sun–Mon and Wed–Thurs 11am–10pm; Fri–Sat 11am–11pm.

The Salt Lick ⭐ *(Kids* BARBECUE   It's 11½ miles from the junction of 290 West and FM 1826 (turn right) to The Salt Lick, but you'll start smelling the smoke during the last 5 miles of your trip. Moist chicken, beef, and pork, as well as terrific homemade pickles—not to mention the pretty, verdant setting—more than justify the drive. You're faced with a tough decision here: If you indulge in the all-you-can-eat family-style platter of beef, sausage, and pork ribs, you might have to pass on the fresh-baked peach cobbler, which would be a pity. In warm weather, seating is outside at picnic tables under oak trees; in winter, fireplaces blaze in a series of large, rustic rooms. Unlike many Texas barbecue places, The Salt Lick prides itself on its sauce, which has a sweet-and-sour tang. If you like your barbecue with a brew, you'll need to tote your own in a cooler; Hays County is dry.

But you don't have to drive all the way out to the country for a smoked meat fix. It's not quite as atmospheric as the original, but the Salt Lick's airport branch is convenient and quick (if you happen to be flying in or out of town). If you get hooked on the barbecue at either place, you can ship some brisket or smoked turkey back home.

18300 FM 1826, Driftwood. (✆ **512/858-4959** or 888/SALT-LICK (mail order). Reservations for large parties only. Sandwiches $5.95–$7.95; plates $7–$14. No credit cards. Daily 11am–10pm.

5 East Side

MODERATE

Eastside Café ⭐ AMERICAN   Located in a trendifying area just east of the university and northeast of the capitol, Eastside Café is hugely popular with student herbivores and congressional carnivores alike. Diners enjoy eating on a tree-shaded patio or in one of a series of cheery, intimate rooms in a classic turn-of-the-century bungalow.

This restaurant gears its menu to all appetites; you can get half orders of many of the pasta dishes, including an excellent artichoke manicotti, and of some salads, such as the mixed field greens topped with warm goat cheese. Many of the main courses have a Southern comfort orientation—sesame-breaded catfish, say, or pork tenderloin with cornbread stuffing—and all come with soup or salad and a vegetable. Each morning, the gardener informs the head chef which of the vegetables in the restaurant's large organic garden are ready for active duty. An adjoining store carries gardening tools, cookware, and the cafe's salad dressings.

2113 Manor Rd. © 512/476-5858. Reservations recommended. Pastas $13–$17, main courses $12–$20. AE, DC, DISC, MC, V. Mon–Thurs 11am–10pm; Fri 11am–11pm; Sat 10am–11pm; Sun 10am–10pm (brunch Sat–Sun 10am–3pm).

INEXPENSIVE

Dario's MEXICAN   One of the most enduring of the many family-run Mexican restaurants in Hispanic East Austin, Dario's is nothing to look at: Tables are Formica, walls are pseudo-wood paneled, and the decor is pretty much nonexistent. But most of the people who gather here concentrate on what's on their plates—combinations such as the Dario's #1: one taco, one cheese enchilada, one tamale with chili con carne, guacamole, Spanish rice, refried beans, and two tortillas. On Sunday, the place is packed with post-Mass parishioners and post-Saturday night revelers, who come for the reputed hangover cure: a large bowl of *menudo* (if you don't know the ingredients, don't ask; the info won't make you feel any better).

1800 E. Sixth St. © 512/479-8105. Reservations for large parties only. Main courses $4.50–$7.50. DC, DISC, MC, V. Tues–Thurs 7am–4pm; Fri–Sat 7am–10pm, Sun 7am–3pm.

6 Northwest

VERY EXPENSIVE

Eddie V's Edgewater Grill ⚛ SEAFOOD/STEAK   A recent Arboretum shopping complex arrival, Eddie V's quickly became one of the hottest dinner tickets in the Northwest. The swank supper club–style atmosphere—white tablecloths, lots of black accents, live jazz in the lounge—is a contributing factor, but the main hook is the top-notch seafood. The crispy calamari appetizer and lump crab cake make great starters, but you might be better off going for the less filling oysters-on-the-half-shell; this place doesn't stint on portion sizes, and grilled mahimahi filet with blue crab fritters or smoked salmon with horseradish crust might not cut it as breakfast the next day. Besides, you want to leave room for the hot bread pudding soufflé, large enough for a table so long as you're not dining with an entourage. The downtown Eddie V's, 301 E. 5th St. (© 512/472-1860), has the same menu, same decor, and the same see-and-be-seen (sea-and-be-seen?) cachet, but it doesn't have this room's Hill Country views at sunset.

9400B Arboretum Blvd. © 512/342-6242. Reservations recommended. Main courses $19–$29. AE, DC, DISC, MC, V. Mon–Sat 5pm–11pm; Sun 5–10pm.

EXPENSIVE

Cool River Café *Kids* AMERICAN/SOUTHWEST   Cool River has something for everyone, from families to prowling singles. The food at this gigantic, self-styled "multi-functional entertainment facility" is good, although not quite as adventurous as the descriptions of the Southwestern dishes might lead one to expect. Stick with the certified Angus beef or simple chicken and fish preparations, and you won't go wrong.

But eating is almost beside the point. You come for the scene, which moves from the high-ceilinged, Alpine-style dining rooms through a cushy cigar lounge and past a bar to pool tables, a live music stage, an outdoor patio . . . this place is endless. There's been an attempt to make this a dress-up destination, so cut-offs and shorts are discouraged, but during my last visit the crowd was the typical "anything-goes" Austin mix.

4001 Parmer Lane. ℂ 512/835-0010 or 512/835-8629 (reservations). Reservations recommended Thurs–Sat. Main courses $13–$33. AE, DISC, MC, V. Mon–Sat 11am–11pm (bar Mon–Wed to 1am, Thurs–Sat to 2am; light food served until 12:30am).

MODERATE

Musashino ✮ JAPANESE   This place has the freshest, best prepared sushi in town and every Austin aficionado knows it—which is why, in spite of its inauspicious location (on the southbound access road of Mo-Pac in northwest Austin) and less-than-stunning setting (beneath a Chinese restaurant called Chinatown), it's always jammed. A combination of Musashino's local star status and its policy of not accepting reservations means you're likely to have to wait awhile for a table, especially on Friday and Saturday nights. If you don't mind not having the entire menu at your disposal, the cozy upstairs area, which has a sushi bar and table service, but a shorter menu, is a good substitute. Be sure to ask your server what's special before you order; delicacies not listed on the regular menu are often flown in.

3407 Greystone Dr. ℂ 512/795-8593. Reservations not accepted. Sushi $2–$10; main courses $15–$40. AE, DC, DISC, MC, V. Tues–Thurs 5:30–10pm; Fri–Sat 5:30–10:30pm.

Z'Tejas Grill ✮ (Value) SOUTHWEST   An offshoot of a popular downtown eatery, this northwest location improves a bit on the original. Not that the food is different here—both share a terrifically zippy Southwestern menu—but the room is a lot more open, with floor-to-ceiling windows, a soaring ceiling, sophisticated Santa Fe–style decor, and, in cool weather, a roaring fireplace. Grilled shrimp and guacamole tostada bites make a great starter, and if you see it on a specials menu, go for the smoked chiles rellenos—they're made with apricots and goat cheese. Entrees include a delicious horseradish-crusted salmon and a pork tenderloin stuffed with chorizo, cheese, onions, and poblano chiles. Even if you think you can't eat another bite, order a piece of ancho chile fudge pie, too. It will miraculously disappear.

If you can't make it to the northwest, try the original Z'Tejas at 1110 W. Sixth St. (ℂ 512/478-5355).

9400-A Arboretum Blvd. ℂ 512/346-3506. Reservations recommended. Main courses $8.95–$18. AE, DISC, MC, V. Mon–Thurs 11am–10pm; Fri 11am–11pm; Sat 10am–11pm; Sun 10am–10pm.

7 West/Lakes

VERY EXPENSIVE

Hudson's on the Bend ✮✮ NEW AMERICAN   If you're game for game, served in a very civilized setting, come to Hudson's. Soft candlelight, fresh flowers, fine china, and attentive service combine with outstanding and out-of-the-ordinary cuisine to make this worth a special-occasion splurge. Sparkling lights draped over a cluster of oak trees draw you into a series of romantic dining rooms, set in an old house some 1½ miles southwest of the Mansfield Dam, near Lake Travis. The chipotle cream sauce was sufficiently spicy so that it was hard to tell whether Omar's rattlesnake cakes tasted like chicken. But they were very good, as were the duck and liver pâté starters. Pecan-smoked prime rib and a mixed grill of venison, rabbit, quail, and buffalo are among the excellent entrees I've sampled; there's also a superb trout served with tangy mango-habanero butter. Although portions are more than generous, a slice of Key lime pie with graham-cracker crust is a good finisher.

One caveat: The charming but acoustically poor setting can make Hudson's indoor dining rooms noisy on weekends. Opt for the terrace if the weather's good.

3509 Hwy. 620 N. © 512/266-1369. Reservations recommended, essential on weekends. Main courses $28–$35. AE, DC, MC, V. Sun–Mon 6–9pm; Tues–Thurs 6–10pm; Fri–Sat 5:30–10pm (closing times may be earlier in winter; call ahead).

MODERATE

County Line on the Hill ⊛ *Kids* BARBECUE   This is a bit of local history, the original of the County Line chain, opened in 1975. Some critics deride these smoked meat outlets for their "suburban" barbecue, but Austinites have voted with their feet (or, rather, their cars). The crowds have lessened somewhat since this restaurant started opening for lunch, but if you don't get here before 6pm for dinner, you can wait as long as an hour to eat. Should this happen, sit out on the deck and soak in the views of the Hill Country, or look at the old advertising signs hung on the knotty-pine planks of this 1920s roadhouse, formerly a speakeasy and a brothel. In addition to the barbecue—oh-so-slowly-smoked ribs, brisket, chicken, or sausage—skewered meat or vegetable plates are available. County Line on the Lake, near Lake Austin, 5204 FM 2222 (© **512/346-3664**), offers the same menu, and is also open for lunch and dinner.

6500 W. Bee Cave Rd. © 512/327-1742. Reservations not accepted. Plates $9–$18. AE, DC, DISC, MC, V. Mon–Fri 11:30am–2pm and 5–9pm; Sat–Sun 11:30am–10pm; closes a ½ hour earlier in winter.

The Oasis AMERICAN/MEXICAN   This is where Austinites like to take out-of-town guests at sunset: From the 40 multilevel decks nestled into the hillside hundreds of feet above Lake Travis, visitors and locals alike cheer—with toasts and applause—as the fiery orb descends behind the hills on the opposite bank. No one ever leaves unimpressed—by the sunset. Food is another matter entirely; don't let anyone tell you that it has improved. Although different owners have tried over the years, so far no one has succeeded. Keep it simple—nachos, burgers—and you'll be okay. Then add a margarita, and kick back. It doesn't get much mellower than this.

6550 Comanche Trail, near Lake Travis. © 512/266-2441. Reservations not accepted. Main courses $10–$25. AE, DISC, MC, V. Mon–Thurs 11:30am–10pm; Fri 11:30am–11pm; Sat 11am–11pm; Sun 11am–10pm (brunch 11am–2pm).

8 Only in Austin

For information on Austin's funky, original cafe scene, see "Late-Night Bites" in chapter 15.

A BAT'S-EYE VIEW

From late March through mid-November, the most coveted seats in town are the ones with a view of the thousands of bats that fly out from under the Congress Avenue Bridge in search of a hearty bug dinner at dusk. The **Shoreline Grill** (see above) and the **Cafe at the Four Seasons,** 98 San Jacinto Blvd. (© **512/478-4500**), are the two toniest spots for observing this astounding phenomenon.

Reel Barbecue

Forget cheap labor and right-to-work laws: One of the less-publicized inducements for filmmakers to come to Austin is the barbecue—slow-cooked over a wood-fueled fire, and so tasty it doesn't need sauce. Think in terms of an "Austin Barbecue Loop," a circle with a roughly 30-mile radius from the state capitol where hungry crews make the rounds. Sometimes the meat in joints within this loop comes on butcher paper rather than plates, and there's usually little ceremony in the service—if there's any service at all. But who cares about amenities when you're dealing with this kind of flavor and aroma?

Gary Bond, film liaison for the Austin Convention and Visitors Bureau, has the skinny on the celluloid-barbecue connection. According to Bond, the eastern portion of the Loop—where rolling prairies, farmland, and small towns conveniently pass for Everywhere, USA—has received rave reviews from location scouts, stars, and producers alike. **Rudy Mikeska's** (✆ 512/352-5561), in downtown Taylor, was featured in *The Hot Spot* as The Yellow Rose, the racy hangout of the Don Johnson character, while less than a block away, **Louie Mueller Barbecue** (✆ 512/352-6206) served as a location for *Flesh and Bone,* starring Dennis Quaid and James Caan. To the south, in Elgin, crews from movie segments, music videos, and commercials happily hit **Southside Market & BBQ** (✆ 512/281-4650) on breaks. Still farther south, three hot meat purveyors in Lockhart have Hollywood dealmakers bickering about which is best: **Kreutz Market** (in either of its two incarnations, one of which is called Smitty's; ✆ 512/398-2361), **Black's Barbecue** (✆ 512/398-2712), or **Chisholm Trail** (✆ 512/398-6027).

As for the western part of the loop, the guys scouting for *Lolita* loved **Cooper's** (✆ 915/247-5713) open pit in Llano, while **The Salt Lick,** near Driftwood (p. 175), has hosted lots of wrap parties. In Austin itself, Nora Ephron couldn't tear herself away from **The Green Mesquite** (✆ 512/335-9885; various locations).

TGIF's at the Radisson Hotel on Town Lake, 11 E. First St. (✆ **512/478-9611**), and **La Vista** at the Hyatt Regency Austin on Town Lake, 208 Barton Springs Rd. (✆ **512/477-1234**), offer more casual, collegial roosts.

MUSICAL BRUNCHES

For a religious experience on Sunday morning that doesn't require entering a church or temple, check out the gospel brunch at **Stubb's Bar-B-Q,** 801 Red River St. (✆ **512/480-8341**). The singing is heavenly, the pork ribs divine. At **Threadgill's World Headquarters** (p. 173), you can graze at a Southern-style buffet while listening to live inspirational sounds; find out who's playing on www.threadgills.com. If you worship at the altar of the likes of Miles Davis, the Sunday jazz brunches at both locations of **Manuel's** (p. 167) let you enjoy eggs with venison chorizo or corn gorditas with garlic and cilantro while listening to hot live jazz or Latin sounds. Log on to www.manuels.com to find out who's gonna be sizzling while you're visiting.

COFFEEHOUSES

Austin has often been compared to Seattle for its music scene and its green, college-town atmosphere. Although the city isn't quite up to, er, speed when it comes to coffeehouses, there are enough homegrown versions these days to constitute a respectable presence around downtown and the university.

Little City, 916 Congress Ave. (© **512/476-2489**), with its ultra-chic design, is close to the downtown tourist sights, and the only local place to get a java fix near the capitol on Sunday. Another location, at 3403 Guadalupe, near the UT campus (© **512/467-2326**), roasts its own beans. Also near UT and also a roaster/grinder, **Mojo,** 2714 Guadalupe, (© **512/477-6656**), provides java, pastry, broadband access, and attitude 24/7. At **Flipnotics,** 1601 Barton Springs Road (© **512/322-9750**), a two-story, indoor/outdoor "coffeespace," you can sip great caffeine drinks or beer while listening to acoustic singer/songwriters most nights. You don't have to get wired at **Spider House,** 2908 Fruth St. (© **512/480-9562**), just north of the UT campus, where the likes of tempeh chili, Frito pie, great smoothies, and beer complement the coffee portion of the menu. The large, tree-shaded patio should get you mellow, too. Still, in the chill-out department, it's impossible to beat **Mozart's,** 3825 Lake Austin Blvd. (© **512/477-2900**), with killer views of Lake Austin and great white-chocolate-almond croissants.

14

Exploring Austin

Stroll up Congress Avenue and you'll see much the same sight visitors to Austin did more than 100 years ago: a broad thoroughfare, gently rising to the grandest of all state capitols. Long obsessed with its place in history, the city continues to honor that place today. The capitol underwent a complete overhaul in the 1990s; a grand new state history museum opened its doors near the capitol in 2001; and downtown's historic Sixth Street is turning back the clock with ongoing restorations. Austin is also on a cultural mission: Two multimillion-dollar complexes are being built to house the city's top art collections, and new galleries are opening all over town.

But it is Austin's myriad natural attractions that put the city on all the "most livable" lists. From bats and birds to Barton Springs, from the Highland Lakes to the hike-and-bike trails, Austin lays out the green carpet for its visitors. You'd be hard-pressed to find a city that has more to offer fresh-air enthusiasts.

It's also easy to sightsee here, even if you don't have a car. There's no charge for transportation on the city's five 'Dillo lines, which cover most of the downtown tourist sites and the University of Texas. Other freebies include the Convention and Visitors Bureau's excellent guided walks and the state-sponsored tours of the governor's mansion and the state capitol.

SUGGESTED ITINERARIES
If You Have 1 Day

You'll see much of what makes Austin unique if you spend a day downtown. You might start out with a cup of coffee and a pastry at the **Little City Café,** then head over to the **Capitol Visitors Center,** a historic building that's interesting and an ideal place to begin your tour of the capitol complex. The **Capitol** and newer extension are next; you'll be impressed by the results of the costly restoration. You can either go from here to the **governor's mansion** (keep in mind that the day's last tour begins at 11:40am, and tours are given Mon–Thurs only) and the nearby historic **Bremond block** district for a taste of how the other half lived during the 19th century. Or visit the **Bob Bullock Texas State History Museum,** where you'll get the big picture (both figuratively and literally, via an IMAX theater).

Now head south, having lunch at one of the restaurants along Congress Avenue (La Traviata if you're up for Italian, Las Manitas if you prefer Mexican) or one on Riverside Drive (I'd vote for Shady Grove) near the shore of **Town Lake,** where you can rest under an oak tree or join the athletic hordes in perpetual motion on the hike-and-bike trail. Or, in fair weather, wait an hour and take a swim in **Barton Springs Pool.** If you're in town from late March through October, book a table for dinner at the Shoreline Grill and **watch the bats** take off at dusk from under the Congress Avenue Bridge. Devote any energy you have left to hitting one—or several—of Austin's **live music** spots, perhaps the Continental Club or Antone's.

If You Have 2 Days

Day 1   Follow the itinerary outlined in "If You Have 1 Day," above.

Day 2   In the morning, head out to the **Lady Bird Johnson Wildflower Center** to see Texas's bountiful natural blooms. In the afternoon, visit the **LBJ Library** and **Harry Ransom Humanities Research Center** (or, if it has reopened, the **Jack S. Blanton Museum of Art**) on the University of Texas campus; weekends, you can also tour the **UT Tower.** If you're traveling with youngsters, substitute the excellent **Children's Museum** or the **Jourdan Bachman Pioneer Farm.** At night, visit a different **live music club**—maybe the Broken Spoke, Stubb's, or La Zona Rosa.

If You Have 3 Days

Days 1 to 2   Same as Days 1 and 2 in "If You Have 2 Days."

Day 3   Scope out the cityscape from **Mount Bonnell,** the highest point in Austin; then visit the historic **Hyde Park neighborhood,** including the **Elisabet Ney**

museum. If the weather is nice, have lunch at one of the restaurants along Barton Springs Road, then spend the afternoon in **Zilker Park,** perhaps going for a stroll at the lovely Botanical Gardens. Or if you're interested in history, substitute the sights on Austin's East Side—the **George Washington Carver Museum,** the **State Cemetery,** and the **French Legation Museum.** There are a number of good, inexpensive Mexican restaurants in the area too. Alternatively, after Mt. Bonnell you could head for **Lake Travis** and some serious waterplay. Just be sure to make it to **The Oasis** in time to applaud the sunset.

If You Have 4 Days

Days 1 to 3   Same as Days 1 to 3 in "If You Have 3 Days."

Day 4   Take a day trip to Fredericksburg or New Braunfels in the **Hill Country** (see chapter 17). Fredericksburg lays on the Germanic charm a bit more, but New Braunfels competes with a discount mall and lots of river-rafting options.

If You Have 5 Days or More

Days 1 to 3   Follow the strategy in "If You Have 3 Days," above.

Days 4 to 5   Stay overnight at a bed-and-breakfast in **Fredericksburg** and visit the **LBJ Ranch, Enchanted Rock State Park,** and some nearby **Hill Country** towns (see chapter 17).

1 The Top Attractions

DOWNTOWN

The Bob Bullock Texas State History Museum ★ *(Value) (Kids)*   You'll get a quick course in Texas 101 at this museum, opened near the state capitol in 2001 and designed to echo some of its elements: Three floors of exhibits are arrayed around a huge rotunda centered by a 50-foot, polished granite map of Texas. It's an impressive building, and the permanent displays—everything from Stephen F. Austin's diary to Neil Armstrong's space suit—and rotating exhibits are interesting enough but, for all the interactive video clips and engaging designs (lots

Downtown Austin Attractions

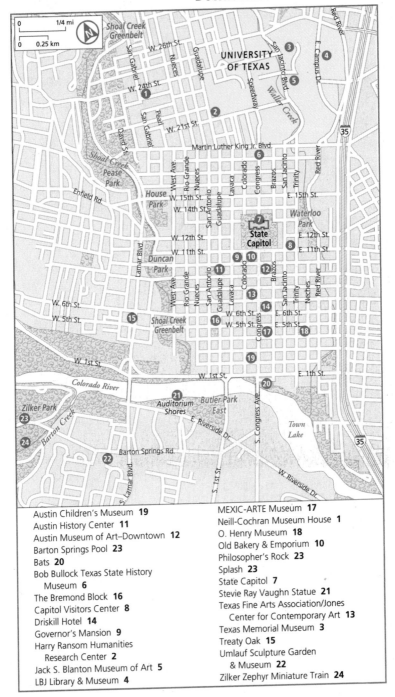

Austin Children's Museum **19**
Austin History Center **11**
Austin Museum of Art–Downtown **12**
Barton Springs Pool **23**
Bats **20**
Bob Bullock Texas State History
   Museum **6**
The Bremond Block **16**
Capitol Visitors Center **8**
Driskill Hotel **14**
Governor's Mansion **9**
Harry Ransom Humanities
   Research Center **2**
Jack S. Blanton Museum of Art **5**
LBJ Library & Museum **4**

MEXIC-ARTE Museum **17**
Neill-Cochran Museum House **1**
O. Henry Museum **18**
Old Bakery & Emporium **10**
Philosopher's Rock **23**
Splash **23**
State Capitol **7**
Stevie Ray Vaughn Statue **21**
Texas Fine Arts Association/Jones
   Center for Contemporary Art **13**
Texas Memorial Museum **3**
Treaty Oak **15**
Umlauf Sculpture Garden
   & Museum **22**
Zilker Zephyr Miniature Train **24**

Greater Austin Attractions

Austin Museum of Art–
  Laguna Gloria **3**
Austin Nature & Science Center **7**
Austin Zoo **12**
Elisabet Ney Museum **5**
French Legation Museum **9**
Hyde Park **4**
Lady Bird Johnson Wildflower Center **11**
Jourdan Bachman Pioneer Farm **1**
Moore/Andersson Compound **6**
Mt. Bonnell **2**
Texas State Cemetery **10**
Zilker Botanical Garden **8**

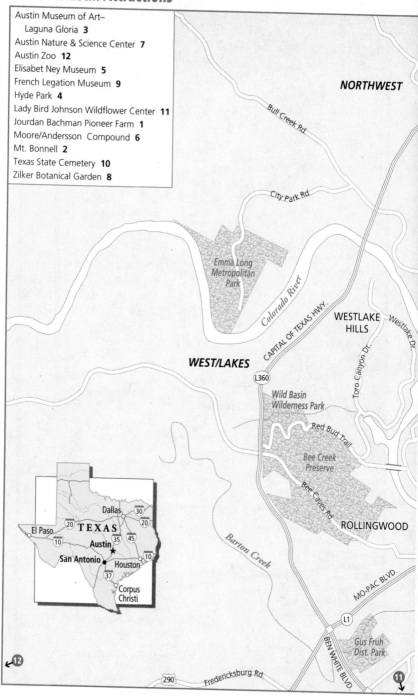

NORTHWEST

Bull Creek Rd.

City Park Rd.

Emma Long
Metropolitan
Park

Colorado River

CAPITAL OF TEXAS HWY.

WESTLAKE
HILLS

Westlake Dr.

WEST/LAKES

L360

Toro Canyon Dr.

Wild Basin
Wilderness Park

Red Bud Trail

Bee Creek
Preserve

Bee Caves Rd.

ROLLINGWOOD

Barton Creek

TEXAS

Dallas

30

El Paso

20

20

35

45

Austin

10

San Antonio

Houston

10

37

Corpus
Christi

MO-PAC BLVD.

L1

Gus Fruh
Dist. Park

BEN WHITE BLVD.

12

290

Fredericksburg Rd.

11

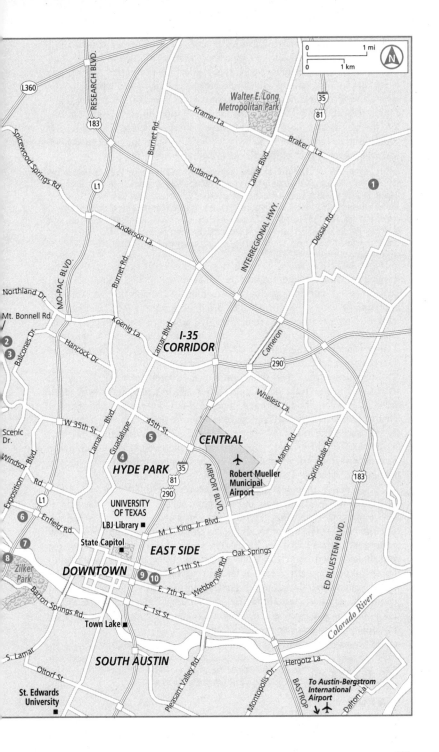

of different rooms to duck into, varied floor surfaces), the presentations didn't strike me as dramatically different from those in history museums I toured as a kid. The real treat is the multimedia, special-effects Spirit Theater, the only one of its kind in Texas, where you can experience the high-speed whoosh of the great Galveston hurricane and feel your seats rattle as an East Texas oil well hits a gusher. Austin's only IMAX theater, with 3-D capabilities, is pretty dazzling too, though the films don't necessarily have a direct relation to Texas history. If you do everything (and at just $6 for a combination ticket for visitors under 19, you really should), plan to spend at least 2½ to 3 hours here.

1800 N. Congress Ave. © 512/936-8746. www.TheStoryofTexas.com. Exhibit areas: $5 adults, $4.25 seniors 65 and over, free for ages 18 and under. IMAX theater: $6.50 adults, $5.50 seniors, $4.50 youth. Texas Spirit Theater: $5 adult, $4 senior, $3.50 youth. Combination tickets: Exhibits and IMAX, $9/$7.50/$4.50; exhibits and Spirit Theater $8/$6.50/$3.50; exhibits and both theaters $13/$10/$6 (under 3 free to theaters if they sit in a parent's lap). Parking $3 with $5 minimum museum purchase, $8 otherwise (IMAX parking free after 6pm). Mon–Sat 9am–6pm; Sun noon–6pm. Phone or check website for additional IMAX evening hours. Closed Jan 1, Easter, Thanksgiving, Dec 24, and Dec 25. Bus: Orange and Blue 'Dillo.

State Capitol ★★ *Value*   The history of Texas's legislative center is as turbulent and dramatic as that of the state itself. The current 1888 capitol replaced an 1852 limestone statehouse that burned down in 1881; a land-rich but otherwise impecunious Texas government traded 3 million acres of public lands to contractors to finance its construction. Gleaming pink granite was donated to the cause, but a railroad had to be built to transport the material some 75 miles from Granite Mountain, near Marble Falls, to Austin. Texas convicts labored on the project alongside 62 stonecutters brought in from Scotland.

The result was the largest state capitol in the country, covering 3 acres and second only in size to the U.S. Capitol—but still, in typical Texas style, measuring 7 feet taller. The cornerstone alone weighs 16,000 pounds, and the total length of the wooden wainscoting runs approximately 7 miles. A splendid rotunda and dome lie at the intersection of the main corridors; the House and Senate chambers are located at opposite ends of the second level. Go up to the third-floor visitors' balcony during the legislative sessions if you want see how politics are conducted, Texas-style.

The building had become dingy and its offices warren-like over the last century, but a massive renovation and expansion in the 1990s—to the tune of $187.6 million—restored its grandeur. The expansion process itself is fascinating: Almost 700,000 tons of rock were chiseled from the ground to make way for an annex (often called the "inside-out, upside-down capitol"), constructed with similar materials and connected to the capitol and four other state buildings by tunnels. You can either opt for a 30- to 45-minute free guided tour or walk around on your own using self-guided tour pamphlets (one for the capitol, one for the grounds). Include the Capitol Visitors Center (see "More Attractions," below), and figure on spending a minimum of two hours here. Wear comfortable shoes; you'll be doing a lot of walking.

11th and Congress sts. © 512/463-0063. www.tspb.state.tx.us. Free admission. Mon–Fri 7am–10pm; Sat–Sun 9am–8pm; 24 hr. a day during legislative sessions (held in odd years, starting in Jan, for 140 straight days; 30-day special sessions are also sometimes called). Free guided tours. Mon–Fri 8:30am–4:30pm; Sat–Sun 9:30am–4:30pm. Bus: Orange, Red, Gold and Blue 'Dillos, multiple bus lines.

CENTRAL

Barton Springs Pool ★★ *Kids*   If the University of Texas is the seat of Austin's intellect, and the state capitol is its political pulse, Barton Springs is the

(Kids) Going Batty

Austin has the largest urban bat population in North America—much to the delight of Austinites. Some visitors are dubious at first, but it's impossible not to be impressed by the sight of 1.5 million of the creatures emerging en masse from under the Congress Avenue Bridge.

Each March, free-tailed bats migrate from central Mexico to various roost sites in the Southwest. In 1980, when a deck reconstruction of Austin's bridge created an ideal environment for bringing up babies, some 750,000 pregnant females began settling in every year. Each bat gives birth to a single pup; by August, these offspring take part in nightly forays west for bugs, usually around dusk. Depending on the size of the group, they might collectively munch on anywhere from 10,000 to 30,000 pounds of insects a night—one of the things that makes them so popular with Austinites. By November, these youngsters are old enough to hitch rides back south with the group on the winds of an early cold front.

While the bats are in town, an educational kiosk designed to dispel some of the more popular myths about them is set up each evening on the north bank of the river, just east of the bridge. You'll learn, for example, that bats are not rodents; that they're not blind; and that they're not in the least interested in getting in your hair. **Bat Conservation International** (© **512/327-9721;** www.batcon.org), based in Austin, has lots of information, and you can call the *Austin American-Statesman* **Bat Hot Line** (© **512/416-5700,** category 3636) to find out when the bats are going to emerge from the bridge.

city's soul. The Native Americans who settled near here believed these waters had spiritual powers, and today's residents still place their faith in the abilities of the spring-fed pool to soothe and cool.

Each day, approximately 32 million gallons of water from the underground Edwards Aquifer bubble to the surface here; at one time, this force powered several Austin mills. Although the original limestone bottom remains, concrete was added to the banks to form uniform sides to what is now a swimming pool of about 1,000 feet by 125 feet. Maintaining a constant 68°F (20°C) temperature, the amazingly clear water is bracing in summer and warming in winter, when many hearty souls brave the cold for a dip. Lifeguards are on duty for most of the day, and a large bathhouse operated by the Parks and Recreation Department offers changing facilities and a gift shop. For details about the Splash! environmental information center, see "Especially for Kids," below.

Zilker Park, 2201 Barton Springs Rd. © 512/476-9044. www.ci.austin.tx.us/parks. Admission $2.50 Mon–Fri, $2.75 Sat–Sun adults; $1 ages 12–17; 50¢ children 11 and under. Daily 5am–10pm except during pool maintenance (Thurs 8am–7pm). Lifeguard on duty Apr–Sept 8am–10pm; Oct to early Nov 8am–8pm; mid-Nov to Mar 9am–6pm. Gift shop and Splash!, Tues–Fri noon–6pm; Sat–Sun 10am–6pm. Bus: 30 (Barton Creek Sq.).

LBJ Library and Museum ★ *Value*   A presidential library may sound like a big yawn, but this one's almost as interesting as the 36th president to whom it's devoted. Lyndon Baines Johnson's popularity in Texas and his many successes in

Washington are often forgotten in the wake of his involvement in the Vietnam War. The story of Johnson's long political career, starting with his early days as a state representative and continuing through to the Kennedy assassination and the groundbreaking Great Society legislation, is told through a variety of documents, mementos, and photographs. Johnson loved political cartoons, even when he was their butt; examples from his large collection are among the museum's most interesting rotating exhibits. Other exhibits might include anything from photographs from the American Civil Rights era to a display of presidential holiday cards. Adults and kids alike are riveted by the animatronic version of LBJ. Dressed in his clothes and speaking with a tape recording of his voice, the life-size, gesticulating figure seems eerily alive from afar. From 1971, when it was dedicated, until his death in 1973, Johnson himself kept an office in this building, which commands an impressive campus view. A large, free parking lot next to the library makes it one of the few UT campus sights that's easy to drive up to.

University of Texas, 2313 Red River. ℂ **512/916-5136.** www.lbjlib.utexas.edu. Free admission. Daily 9am–5pm. Closed Dec 25. Bus: 15, Blue and Orange 'Dillos, UT Shuttle.

SOUTH AUSTIN

Lady Bird Johnson Wildflower Center ★★★   Talk about fieldwork: The researchers at this lovely, colorful complex have 178 acres of wildflowers for their personal laboratory. Founded by Lady Bird Johnson in 1982, the center is dedicated to the study and preservation of native plants—and where better to survey them than in the Texas Hill Country, famous for its glorious spring blossoms?

The main attractions are naturally the display gardens—among them, one designed to attract butterflies—and the wildflower-filled meadow, but the native stone architecture of the visitors center and observation tower is attention grabbing, too. Included among the interesting indoor displays is one of Lady Bird's wide-brimmed gardening hats and a talking lawnmower with a British accent. There are usually free lectures and guided walks on the weekends; phone or check the website for current programs. The facility's research library is the largest in the United States for the study of native plants. The excellent gift shop sells packets of information about the species that are indigenous to your home state, as well as plant books and many creative botanical-related items. And you'll be buying for a good cause: Gift shop proceeds (as well as admission fees) all help fund the nonprofit organization. It'll take you at least half an hour to drive here from central Austin, so plan to eat lunch here and spend a leisurely half-day.

4801 La Crosse Ave. ℂ **512/292-4200.** www.wildflower.org. Admission $5 adults, $4 students and seniors 60 and up, under 5 free. Tues–Sun 9am–5:30 (Mar–Apr rates go up to $7/$5 and grounds are open Mon). Take Loop 1 (Mo-Pac) south to Slaughter Lane; drive ¾ mile to La Crosse Ave.

2 More Attractions

DOWNTOWN

Austin History Center/Austin Public Library   Built in 1933, this Renaissance revival–style public library not only embodies some of the finest architecture, ironwork, and stone carving of its era, but also serves as the best resource for information about Austin from before the city's founding in 1839 to the present. The center also often hosts exhibitions drawn from its vast archives of historical photographs and sketches. And, of course, it's full of good books.

810 Guadalupe St. ⓒ **512/974-7480**. www.ci.austin.tx.us/library. Free admission. Mon–Thurs 9am–9pm; Sat 9am–6pm; Sun noon–6pm. Closed Fri and most holidays. Bus: 171, Blue or Silver'Dillo.

Austin Museum of Art–Downtown   Plans for a major downtown museum of art have been in the works for two decades. This high-ceiling one-story space isn't it—architect Richard Gluckman is designing a multimillion-dollar facility slated to open a few blocks away sometime in this decade—but will still do nicely for the time being. Major name shows—for example, the small paintings of Alex Katz in early 2003—are complemented by exhibits of lesser known local artists, of consistently high quality.

823 Congress Ave. (at 9th St.) ⓒ **512/495-9224**. www.amoa.org. Admission $5 adults, $4 seniors and students, $1 for everyone on Thurs, children under 12 free. Tues–Wed and Fri–Sat 10am–6pm; Thurs 10am–8pm; Sun noon–5pm. Bus: Red, Gold, and Orange 'Dillos.

Bremond Block ⚞   "The family that builds together, bonds together" might have been the slogan of Eugene Bremond, an early Austin banker who established a mini real-estate monopoly for his own kin in the downtown area. In the mid-1860s, he started investing in land on what was once Block 80 of the original city plan. In 1874, he moved into a Greek revival home made by master builder Abner Cook. By the time he was through, he had created a family compound, purchasing and enlarging homes for himself, two sisters, a daughter, a son, and a brother-in-law. Some were destroyed, but those that remain on what is now known as the Bremond Block are exquisite examples of elaborate late-19th-century homes.

Between Seventh and Eighth, San Antonio and Guadalupe sts. Bus: Silver 'Dillo.

Capitol Visitors Center ⚞   The capitol wasn't the only important member of the state complex to undergo a face-lift: Texas also spent $4 million to gussy up its oldest surviving office building, the 1857 General Land Office. If the imposing German Romanesque structure looks a bit grand for the headquarters of an administrative agency, keep in mind that land has long been the state's most important resource. Among the employees of this important—and very political—office, charged with maintaining records and surveying holdings, was the writer O. Henry, who worked as a draftsman from 1887 to 1891; he based two short stories on his experiences here.

The building was rededicated as a visitors center for the Capitol Complex in the mid-1990s; the Texas Department of Transportation also distributes state travel information here. A Walter Cronkite–narrated video tells the history of the complex, and changing exhibits on the first floor highlight the Capitol Preservation Project; upstairs, displays focus on the Land Office and other aspects of Texas's past. A good gift shop carries lots of historical books and souvenirs.

112 E. 11th St. (southeast corner of Capitol grounds). ⓒ **512/305-8400**. www.texascapitolvisitorscenter. com. Free admission. Daily 9am–5pm. Bus: Gold, Orange, Red, and Blue 'Dillos.

The Driskill   Colonel Jesse Driskill was not a modest man. When he opened a hotel in 1886, he named it after himself, put busts of himself and his two sons over the entrances, and installed bas-relief sculptures of longhorn steers—to remind folks how he had made his fortune. Nor did he build a modest property: The ornate four-story structure, which originally boasted a skylit rotunda, has the largest arched doorway in Texas over its east entrance. So posh that the state legislature met here while the 1888 capitol was being built, the hotel has had its ups and downs over the years, but it was restored to its former glory in the late

1990s. You can pick up a history of the hotel at the front desk; if the concierge has time, he'll be happy to help orient you.

604 Brazos St. ℂ 512/474-5911. Bus: Silver, Blue, and Red 'Dillos.

Governor's Mansion ✦ Although this is one of the oldest buildings in the city (1856), this opulent house is far from a mere symbol or museum piece: State law requires that the governor live here whenever he or she is in Austin. If the governor happens to be hosting a luncheon, you might notice warm smells wafting from the kitchen if you're on the last mansion tour of the day.

Living in the mansion isn't exactly a hardship, although it was originally built by Abner Cook without any indoor toilets (there are now seven). The house was beautifully restored in 1979, but you can still see the scars of nails that were hammered into the banister of the spiral staircase to break Governor Hogg's young son Tom of the habit of sliding down it. The nation's first female governor, Miriam "Ma" Ferguson, entertained her friend Will Rogers in the mansion, and Governor John Connally recuperated here from gunshot wounds received when he accompanied John F. Kennedy on his fatal motorcade through Dallas. Among the many historical artifacts on display are a desk belonging to Stephen F. Austin and portraits of Davy Crockett and Sam Houston.

Tip: Come as close to opening time as you can; only a limited number of visitors are allowed to tour the mansion during the few hours it's open to the public. If you arrive later, you might have a long wait—or not get in at all.

1010 Colorado St. ℂ 512/463-5516 (recording). www.txfgm.org. Free admission. Tours offered every 20 min. Mon–Thurs 10–noon (last tour starts 11:40am). Closed Fri, weekends, some holidays, and at the discretion of the governor; call the 24-hr. information line to see if tours are offered the day you want to visit. Bus: Red, Blue, Gold, and Orange 'Dillos

MEXIC-ARTE Museum The first organization in Austin to promote multicultural contemporary art when it was formed in 1983, MEXIC-ARTE has a small permanent collection of 20th-century Mexican art, including photographs from the Mexican revolution and a fascinating array of masks from the state of Guerrero. It's supplemented by visiting shows—including some from Mexico such as colonial art treasures from a cathedral in Saltillo—and a back gallery of works of local Latino artists.

419 Congress Ave. ℂ 512/480-9373. www.main.org/mexic-arte. Admission $5 adults, $2 seniors and students, under 13 free. Mon–Thurs 10am–6pm; Fri–Sat 10am–5pm; Sun 1–4pm for special exhibitions. Bus: Red 'Dillo.

O. Henry Museum When William Sidney Porter, better known as O. Henry, lived in Austin (1884–98), he published a popular satirical newspaper called *Rolling Stone.* He also held down an odd string of jobs, including a stint as a teller at the First National Bank of Austin, where he was later accused of embezzling funds. It was while he was serving time for this crime that he wrote the 13 short stories that established his literary reputation. The modest Victorian cottage in which O. Henry lived with his wife and daughter from 1893 to 1895 showcases the family's bedroom furniture, silverware, and china, as well as the desk at which the author wrote copy for his failed publication. Temporary exhibits, which change throughout the year, include displays of O. Henry letters. Visitors are asked to wear flat, soft-soled shoes to prevent damage to the original pine floors.

409 E. Fifth St. ℂ 512/472-1903. www.ci.austin.tx.us/parks/ohenry.htm. Free admission. Wed–Sun noon–5pm. Closed Thanksgiving, Dec 25, and Jan 1. Bus: Blue 'Dillo.

Old Bakery and Emporium   On the National Register of Historic Landmarks, the Old Bakery was built in 1876 by Charles Lundberg, a Swedish master baker, and continuously operated until 1936. You can still see the giant oven and wooden baker's spade inside. Rescued from demolition by the Austin Heritage Society, and now owned and operated by Austin's Parks and Recreation Department, the brick-and-limestone building is one of the few unaltered structures on Congress Avenue. It houses a gift shop, selling crafts handmade by seniors, a reasonably priced lunch-room, and a hospitality desk with visitors' brochures.

1006 Congress Ave. ⓒ 512/477-5961. www.ci.austin.tx.us/parks/bakery1.htm. Free admission. Mon–Fri 9am–4pm; first 3 Sat in Dec 10am–2pm. Closed most holidays. Bus: Red, Gold, and Orange 'Dillos.

Sixth Street   Formerly known as Pecan Street—all the east–west thorough-fares in Austin were originally named for trees—Sixth Street was once the main connecting road to the older settlements east of Austin. During the Reconstruc-tion boom of the 1870s, the wooden wagon yards and saloons of the 1850s and 1860s began to be replaced by the more solid masonry structures you see today. After the new state capitol was built in 1888, the center of commercial activity began shifting toward Congress Avenue, and by the middle of the next century, Sixth Street had become a skid row.

Restoration of the 9 blocks designated a National Register District began in the late 1960s. In the 1970s, the street blossomed into a live-music center. Austin's former main street is now lined with restaurants, galleries, theaters, nightspots, and shops. The section east of Congress is still somewhat deserted during the day, when the roots of its sleazy past show in tattoo parlors and S&M leather shops. But that's changing, as wrecking balls seem to be swinging on every square inch of downtown. The streets west of Congress are seeing an increase in upscale business activity, and on weekend nights a mostly young crowd throngs the sidewalks of the entire stretch for club crawls.

Between Lavaca Ave. and I-35. Bus: Silver 'Dillo.

Texas Fine Arts Association/Jones Center for Contemporary Art   A recent addition to downtown's art scene, the Jones Center is home to, and the exhibition venue for, the Texas Fine Arts Association (TFAA), which has promoted visual art in Texas since 1911. But this ain't full of purty pictures of bluebonnets, darlin'; the only blue hair here is the spiked variety. Genres range from represen-tational to performance, and artists of all ethnicities are represented.

700 Congress Ave. ⓒ 512/453-5312. www.tfaa.org. Free admission. Tues–Wed and Fri 11am–7pm; Thurs 11am–9pm; Sat 10am–5pm; Sun 1–5pm. Bus: Red 'Dillo.

(*Fun Fact* **Did You Know?**

- Austin is the only city in the world to preserve its first public electric lights—17 of the original 31 "moonlight towers" are still operating around the city. (A special moonlight tower was erected for scenes in the movie *Dazed and Confused* when it was filmed in Austin.)
- The University of Texas's Buford H. Jester Center, which hosts many of the college dormitories, has the largest kitchen in Texas, capable of feeding more than 13,000 students a day.
- The world's first photograph, created by Joseph Nicèphore Nièpce in 1826, is at UT's Harry Ransom Humanities Research Center.

Treaty Oak   Legend has it that Stephen F. Austin signed the first boundary treaty with the Comanches under the spreading branches of this 500-year-old live oak, which once served as the symbolic border between Anglo and Indian territory. Whatever the case, this is the sole remaining tree in what was once a grove of Council Oaks—which made the well-publicized attempt on its life in 1989 especially shocking. But almost as dramatic as the story of the tree's deliberate poisoning by an attention-seeking Austinite is the tale of its rescue by an international team of foresters. The dried wood from major limbs that they removed was allocated to local artists, whose works were auctioned off for the tree's 500th anniversary in 1993. Now such items as pen sets, gavels, and clocks made out of the tree's severed limbs are for sale, with proceeds going to plant additional trees throughout public areas of Austin.

503 Baylor St., between W. Fifth and Sixth sts. Ⓒ **512/440-5194**. www.ci.austin.tx.us/treatyoak. Bus: Silver 'Dillo.

CENTRAL

Austin Museum of Art–Laguna Gloria   The reopening of this museum will be something to look forward to; the intimate institution sits on 28 palm- and pecan-shaded acres overlooking Lake Austin, believed by some to be part of a claim staked out for his retirement by Stephen F. Austin, who didn't live to enjoy the view. The lovely Mediterranean-style villa housing the exhibits here was built in 1916 by Austin newspaper publisher Hal Sevier and his wife, Clara Driscoll, best known for her successful crusade to save the Alamo from commercial development. The buildings and exhibition spaces have been shuttered as part of a multi-million renovation project, but the grounds and sculpture gardens remain open. Check the website for the current state of the renovations.

3809 W. 35th St. Ⓒ **512/458-8191**. www.amoa.org. 1 mile past west end of 35th St. at the foot of Mt. Bonnell. Buildings closed for renovations until 2004.

Jack S. Blanton Museum of Art   The good news: The Blanton is ranked among the top 10 university art museums in the United States, featuring some of the most important art in the country. Most notable is the Suida-Manning Collection, a superb gathering of Renaissance works by such masters as Veronese, Rubens, and Tiepolo that was sought after by the Metropolitan museum, among others. Other permanent holdings include the Mari and James Michener collection of 20th-century American masters, the largest gathering of Latin American art in the United States, and a rare display of 19th-century plaster casts of monumental Greek and Roman sculpture.

   The bad news: A new structure planned to highlight these impressive works isn't open yet. Scheduled to debut in 2005 on MLK and Speedway (across from the Bob Bullock History Center), the new Blanton art space will help connect the university with the capitol complex. Meantime, you can still view portions of its impressive collection—albeit in a less than optimum setting inside a University of Texas building.

University of Texas, Art Building, 23rd St. and San Jacinto Blvd. Ⓒ **512/471-7324**. www.blantonmuseum. org. Free admission. Mon–Fri 9am–5pm (Thurs until 9pm); Sat–Sun 1–5pm. Closed university holidays. Bus: Blue 'Dillo, UT Shuttle.

Elisabet Ney Museum ⭐   Strong-willed and eccentric, German-born sculptor Elisabet Ney nevertheless charmed Austin society in the late 19th century. When she died, her admirers turned her Hyde Park studio into a museum. In the former loft and working area—part Greek temple, part medieval battlement—visitors can view plaster replicas of many of her pieces. Drawn toward the larger-than-life figures of her age, Ney had created busts of Schopenhauer, Garibaldi, and Bismarck by the time she was commissioned to make models of Texas heroes Stephen F. Austin and Sam Houston for an 1893 Chicago exposition. William Jennings Bryan, Enrico Caruso, Jan Paderewski, and four Texas governors were among the many visitors to her Austin studio.

304 E. 44th St. ℂ **512/458-2255.** www.ci.austin.tx.us/elisabetney. Free admission. Wed–Sat 10am–5pm; Sun noon–5pm. Bus: 1 or 5.

Harry Ransom Humanities Research Center ✪   The special collections of the Harry Ransom Center (HRC) contain approximately one million rare books (including a Gutenberg Bible, one of only five complete copies in the U.S.); 30 million literary manuscripts (including those by James Joyce and Ernest Hemingway); 5 million photographs, including the world's first; and more than 100,000 works of art, with several pieces by Diego Rivera and Frida Kahlo. Most of this wealth is the domain of scholars, although anyone can request a look at it, but permanent and rotating exhibits of HRC holdings are held in two buildings: the Harry Ransom Center and the Leeds Gallery of the Flawn Academic Center. You never know what you might see: costumes from *Gone With the Wind*, the original manuscript of *Death of a Salesman*, or letters written by novelist Isaac Bashevis Singer. Highlights of the permanent collection will be featured in the spring 2003 debut of two new exhibition galleries here.

University of Texas. Harry Ransom Center, 21st and Guadalupe sts; Flawn Academic Center, west of the main tower. ℂ **512/471-8944.** www.hrc.utexas.edu. Free admission. Exhibitions Mon–Fri 9am–5pm. (Ransom Center), 8:30am–4:30pm (Leeds Gallery). Closed university holidays. Bus: Blue 'Dillo, UT Shuttle.

Hyde Park   Unlike Eugene Bremond (see "Downtown," above), developer Monroe Martin Shipe built homes for the middle, not upper, classes. In the 1890s, he created—and tirelessly promoted—a complex-cum-resort at the southwest edge of Austin. He even built an electric streetcar system to connect it with the rest of the city. By the middle of this century, Austin's first planned suburb had become somewhat shabby, but recent decades of gentrification have turned the tide. Now visitors can amble along pecan-shaded streets and look at beautifully restored residences, many in pleasing combinations of late Queen Anne and early craftsman styles. Shipe's own architecturally eclectic home, at 3816 Ave. G, is a bit grander than some of the others, but not much.

Between E. 38th and E. 45th, Duval and Guadalupe sts. Bus: 1.

Moore/Andersson Compound   Architecture buffs won't want to miss the hacienda-like compound where Charles Moore spent the last decade of his life—when he wasn't traveling, that is. The peripatetic American architect, who kept a low profile but had a great influence on postmodernism, built five homes; this one, which he designed with Arthur Andersson, perfectly demonstrates his combination of controlled freedom, whimsical imagination, and connection to the environment. The wildly colorful rooms are filled with folk art from around the world; odd angles, bunks, and dividers render every inch of space fascinating. In the evening, the compound is now used as a conference and lecture center. Tours are led by enthusiastic graduate students in historic preservation at the University of Texas, where Moore held his last chair in architecture.

2102 Quarry Rd. ℂ **512/477-4557.** www.charlesmoore.org. Tours $10 adults, $4 students. By appointment only.

Neill-Cochran Museum House Abner Cook, the architect-contractor responsible for the governor's mansion and many of Austin's other gracious Greek revival mansions, built this home in 1855. It bears his trademark portico with six Doric columns and a balustrade designed with crossed sheaves of wheat. Almost all its doors, windows, shutters, and hinges are original—which is rather astonishing when you consider that the house was used as the city's first Blind Institute in 1856 and then as a hospital for Union prisoners near the end of the Civil War. The beautifully maintained 18th- and 19th-century furnishings are interesting, but many people come just to see the painting of bluebonnets that helped convince legislators to designate these native blooms the state flower.

2310 San Gabriel St. ℂ 512/478-2335. Admission $2 adults, children under 10 free. Wed–Sun 2–5pm; free 20-min. tours given. Bus: Gold 'Dillo, UT shuttle.

Texas Memorial Museum *Kids* This museum, opened in 1936 to guard the natural and cultural treasures of the state, is undergoing a shift of focus: Until recently, history vied with science for visitors' attention, but now the natural sciences will rule alone. Throughout 2003, only two of the museum's four floors will remain open. On the second floor, the Treasures exhibit will highlight never-before displayed specimens from the permanent collection, such as rare fossils of saber tooth tiger kittens. The third floor will continue to be devoted to Texas wildlife, past and present, including bugs and reptiles. For the 2004 reopening, the first floor will house a Hall of Geology, complete with dinosaur displays and an on-site paleontologist who will answer questions. The 4th floor will feature a high-tech visualization lab that will let visitors examine fossils with 3-D technology resembling that used in medical CT scans. Not to worry: The museum won't be dino-deficient in 2003. Kids can still check out the dinosaur footsteps right outside the building.

University of Texas, 2400 Trinity St. ℂ 512/471-1604. www.texasmemorialmuseum.org. Free admission (donations appreciated). Mon–Fri 9am–5pm; Sat 10am–5pm; Sun 1–5pm. Closed major holidays. Bus: Orange 'Dillo, Bus 7.

Umlauf Sculpture Garden & Museum This is a very user-friendly museum, one for people who don't enjoy being cooped up in a stuffy, hushed space. An art instructor at the University of Texas for 40 years, Charles Umlauf donated his home, studio, and more than 250 pieces of artwork to the city of Austin, which maintains the lovely native garden where much of the sculpture is displayed. Umlauf, whose pieces reside in such places as the Smithsonian Institution and New York's Metropolitan Museum, worked in many media and styles. He also used a variety of models; you'll probably recognize the portrait of Umlauf's most famous UT student, Farrah Fawcett. The museum video is captioned for those who are hearing impaired, and with advance notice, "touch tours" can be arranged for the blind or visually impaired.

605 Robert E. Lee Rd. ℂ 512/445-5582. www.umlaufsculpture.org. Admission $3.50 adults, $2.50 seniors, $1 students, children under 7 free. Wed–Fri 10am–4:30pm; Sat–Sun 1–4:30pm (Sat 10am–4:30pm June–Aug). Bus: 29 or 30.

University of Texas at Austin In 1883, the 221 students and 8 teachers who made up the newly established University of Texas in Austin had to meet in makeshift classrooms in the town's temporary capitol. At the time, the two million acres of dry west Texas land that the higher educational system had been granted barely brought in 40¢ an acre for grazing. Now, nearly 50,000 students occupy 120 buildings on UT's main campus alone, and that arid west Texas land, which blew a gusher in 1923, has raked in more than $4 billion in oil money—two-thirds of it directed to the UT school system.

The Texas Union Information Center, at 24th and Guadalupe (© **512-475-6636**) is the best place to get information about the campus; it's open Monday through Friday from 7am to 3am (really), Saturday from 10am to 3am, and Sunday from noon to 3am. In addition, you can pick up campus maps and other UT Austin–related materials at the ground floor of the Main building/UT Tower (near 24th and Whitis), which is also the point of departure for free campus tours—they're designed for prospective students and their families, but anyone can come. These leave weekdays at 11am and 2pm (only at 2pm in Dec and May) and Saturday at 2pm. Call © **512/475-7399**, option 3, for recorded details. It's a lot tougher to get on the free Moonlight Prowl Tours, packed with amusing anecdotes of student life and campus lore, because they're only held a few evenings a month and they fill up quickly, but if you want to give it a try, log on to www.utexas.edu/tours/prowl and fill out the registration form.

See also "The Top Attractions," above, for more on the LBJ Library and Museum; listings earlier in this section for the Harry Ransom Humanities Research Center, Jack S. Blanton Museum of Art, and Texas Memorial Museum; the Walking Tour of university sights section, below; and information on visiting the UT Tower in the "Organized Tours" section.

Guadalupe and I-35, Martin Luther King Jr. Blvd. and 26th St. © 512/471-3434. www.utexas.edu.

EAST SIDE

French Legation Museum   The oldest residence still standing in Austin was built in 1841 for Count Alphonse Dubois de Saligny, France's representative to the fledgling Republic of Texas. Although his home was very extravagant for the then primitive capital, the flamboyant de Saligny didn't stay around to enjoy it for very long; he left town in a huff after his servant was beaten in retaliation for making bacon out of some pigs that had dined on the diplomat's linens. In the back of the house, considered the best example of French colonial–style architecture outside Louisiana, is a re-creation of the only known authentic Creole kitchen in the United States.

802 San Marcos. © 512/472-8180. www.frenchlegationmuseum.org. Admission $4 adults, $3 seniors, $2 students/teachers, 5 and under free. Tours Tues–Sun 1–5pm. Go east on Seventh St., then turn left on San Marcos St.; the parking lot is behind the museum on Embassy and Ninth sts. Bus: Silver 'Dillo and Bus 4/18 stop nearby (at San Marcos and 7th sts.).

Texas State Cemetery ✦   The city's namesake, Stephen F. Austin, is the best-known resident of this East Side cemetery, established by the state in 1851. Judge Edwin Waller, who laid out the grid plan for Austin's streets and later served as the city's mayor, also rests here, as do eight former Texas governors, various fighters in Texas's battles for independence, a woman who lived to tell the tale of the Alamo, and Barbara Jordan, the first black woman from the South elected to the U.S. Congress (in 1996, she became the first African American to gain admittance to these grounds). Perhaps the most striking monument, sculpted by Elisabet Ney (see "Central," above), commemorates Confederate General Albert Sidney Johnston, who died at the Battle of Shiloh.

A multimillion-dollar revamp in the mid-1990s added much-needed pedestrian walkways and a visitors center, designed to suggest the long barracks at the Alamo. Two self-guided tour pamphlets are available. The one published by the cemetery details the new features and sketches the histories of some of the most important residents, while the one created by the Austin Convention and Visitors Bureau offers a wider historical context and gives some headstone highlights.

909 Navasota St. ℭ **512/463-0605.** www.cemetery.state.tx.us. Free admission. Grounds, daily 8am–5pm; visitors center, Mon–Fri 8am–5pm. Bus: 4 and 18 stop nearby.

AUSTIN OUTDOORS
LAKES
Highland Lakes The six dams built by the Lower Colorado River Authority in the late 1930s through the early 1950s not only controlled the flooding that had plagued the areas surrounding Texas's Colorado River (not to be confused with the more famous river of the same name to the north), but also transformed the waterway into a sparkling chain of lakes, stretching some 150 miles northwest of Austin. The narrowest of them, Town Lake, is also the closest to downtown. The heart of urban recreation in Austin, it boasts a shoreline park and adjacent hike-and-bike trail. Lake Austin, the next in line, is more residential, but offers Emma Long Park (see "Parks and Gardens," below) as a public shore. Serious aquatic enthusiasts go all the way to Lake Travis, the longest lake in the chain, which offers the most possibilities for playing in the water. Together with the other Highland Lakes—Marble Falls, LBJ, Inks, and Buchanan—these compose the largest concentration of freshwater lakes in Texas. See also "Staying Active," below, for activity and equipment rental suggestions.

MOUNTAINS
Mount Bonnell ⍟ For the best views of the city and Hill Country, ascend this mountaintop park, at 785 feet the highest point in Austin (and the oldest tourist attraction in town). It has long been a favorite spot for romantic trysts; rumor had it that any couple who climbed the 106 stone steps to the top together would fall in love (an emotion often confused with exhaustion). The peak was named for George W. Bonnell, Sam Houston's commissioner of Indian affairs in 1836.

3800 Mt. Bonnell Rd. No phone. Free admission. Daily 5am–10pm. Take Mt. Bonnell Road 1 mile past the west end of W. 35th St.

NATURE PRESERVES
For information on **Wild Basin Wilderness Preserve,** see "Organized Tours," below.

City of Austin Nature Preserves Highlights of the remarkably diverse group of natural habitats Austin boasts in its city-run nature preserves include **Blunn Creek** (1100 block of St. Edward's Dr.), 40 acres of upland woods and meadows traversed by a spring-fed creek; one of the two lookout areas is made of compacted volcanic ash. Spelunkers will like **Goat Cave** (3900 Deer Lane), which is honeycombed with limestone caves and sinkholes; you can arrange for cave tours by phoning the **Austin Nature Center** (ℭ **512/327-8181**). Lovely **Mayfield Park** (3505 W. 35th St.) directly abuts the Barrow Brook Cove of Lake Austin. Peacocks and hens roam freely around lily ponds, and trails cross over bridges in oak and juniper woods. Visitors to the rock-walled ramada (a shaded shelter) at the **Zilker Preserve** (Barton Springs Rd. and Loop 1), with its meadows, streams, and cliff, can look out over downtown Austin. All the preserves are maintained in a primitive state with natural surface trails and no restrooms. The preserves are free, and open daily from dawn to dusk. To locate these preserves, phone *©* **512/372-7723** or log on to www.ci.austin.tx.us/cepreserves.

Westcave Preserve   If you don't like the weather in one part of Westcave Preserve, you might like it better in another: Up to a 25°F (−4°C) difference in temperature has been recorded between the highest area of this beautiful natural habitat, an arid Hill Country scrub, and the lowest, a lush woodland spread across a canyon floor. Because the ecosystem here is so delicate, the 30 acres on the Pedernales River may be entered only by guided tour. No reservations are taken; the first 30 people to show up at the allotted times are allowed in.

Star Rte. 1, Dripping Springs. *©* **830/825-3442**. www.westcave.org. Free admission Sat–Sun for tours at 10am, noon, 2, and 4pm (weather permitting). Take Hwy. 71 to Ranch Rd. 3238. Follow the signs 15 miles to Hamilton Pool, across the Pedernales River Bridge from the preserve.

OUTDOOR ART

Philosophers' Rock   Glenna Goodacre's wonderfully witty bronze sculpture of three of Austin's most recognized personalities from mid-century—naturalist Roy Bedichek, humorist J. Frank Dobie, and historian Walter Prescott Webb—captures the essence of the three friends who used to schmooze together at Barton Springs Pool. No heroic posing here: Two of the three are wearing bathing trunks, which reveal potbellies, wrinkles, and sagging muscles, and all three are sitting down in mid-discussion. But the intelligence of their expressions and the casual friendliness of their pose have made this piece, installed in 1994, an Austin favorite.

Zilker Park, 2201 Barton Springs Rd., just outside the entrance to Barton Springs Pool.

Stevie Ray Vaughan Statue   In contrast to the Philosophers' Rock (see above), Ralph Roehming's bronze tribute to Austin singer/songwriter Stevie Ray Vaughan is artificial and awkward. Although he's wearing his habitual flat-brimmed hat and poncho, the stiffly posed Stevie Ray looks more like a frontiersman with a gun than a rock star with a guitar. But his devoted fans don't care; flowers and messages can almost always be found at the foot of the statue.

South side of Town Lake, adjacent to Auditorium Shores.

PARKS & GARDENS

Emma Long Metropolitan Park   More than 1,100 acres of woodland and a mile of shore along Lake Austin make Emma Long Park—named after the first woman to sit on Austin's city council—a most appealing metropolitan space. Water activities revolve around two boat ramps, a fishing dock, and a protected swimming area, guarded by lifeguards on summer weekends. This is the only city park to offer camping, with permits ($6 for open camping, $15 hookups in addition to entry fee) available on a first-come, first-served basis. If you hike through the stands of oak, ash, and juniper to an elevation of 1,000 feet, you'll get a view of the city spread out before you. Note that the park closes whenever its maximum capacity is reached.

1706 City Park Rd. *©* **512/346-1831** or 512/346-3807. Admission $5 per vehicle Mon–Thurs; $8 Fri–Sun and holidays. Daily 7am–10pm. Exit I-35 at 290W, then go west (street names will change to Koenig, Allendale, Northland, and FM 2222) to City Park Rd. (near Loop 360). Turn south (left) and drive 6¼ miles to park entrance.

Zilker Botanical Garden ⋇ *Kids*   There's bound to be something blooming at the Zilker Botanical Garden from March to October, but no matter what time of year you visit, you'll find this a soothing spot. The Oriental Garden created by Isamu Taniguchi is particularly peaceful; ask someone at the garden center to point out how Taniguchi landscaped the word "Austin" into his design. A butterfly garden attracts gorgeous winged visitors during April and October migrations, and you can poke and prod the plants in the herb garden to get them to yield their fragrances. One-hundred-million-year-old dinosaur tracks, discovered on the grounds in the early 1990s, were opened to the public in 2002 as part of the 1.5-acre Hartman Prehistoric Garden, which includes plants from the Cretaceous period and a 13-foot bronze sculpture of an Ornithomimus dinosaur.

2220 Barton Springs Rd. ℂ 512/477-8672. www.zilker-garden.org. Free admission. Grounds open dawn–dusk. Garden center open Mon–Fri 8:30am–4pm; Sat 10am–5pm (Jan–Feb, 1–5pm); Sun 1–5pm (sometimes open earlier on weekends for special garden shows; phone ahead). Bus: 30.

Zilker Park ⭐ (Kids)   Comprising 347 acres, the first 40 of which were donated to the city by the wealthy German immigrant for whom the park is named, this is Austin's favorite public playground. Its centerpiece is Barton Springs Pool (see "The Top Attractions," above), but visitors and locals also flock to the Zilker Botanical Garden, the Austin Nature Preserves, and the Umlauf Sculpture Garden and Museum, all described in this chapter. See also the "Especially for Kids" and "Staying Active" sections for details about the Austin Nature and Science Center, the Zilker Zephyr Miniature Train, and Town Lake canoe rentals. In addition to its athletic fields (eight for soccer, two for softball, and one for rugby), the park also hosts a nine-hole disk (Frisbee) golf course.

2201 Barton Springs Rd. ℂ 512/476-9044. www.ci.austin.tx.us/zilker. Free admission. Daily 5am–10pm. Bus: 30.

3 Especially for Kids

The Bob Bullock Texas State History Museum and the **Texas Memorial Museum,** both described in earlier sections, are child-friendly, but outdoor attractions are still Austin's biggest kiddie draw. There's lots of room for children to splash around at **Barton Springs,** and even youngsters who thought **bats** were creepy are likely to be converted on further acquaintance with the critters. In addition, the following attractions are especially geared toward children.

Austin Children's Museum ⭐   Located in a large, state-of-the-art facility, this excellent children's museum has something for all ages. Tots enjoy low-key but creative playscapes, in-betweens take on a variety of "creation stations" and grown-up environments like a studio sound stage, and the Loft section challenges teens from 12 to 18 with workshops in different arts and media. Parents will get a kick out of the replica Austin cityscapes, including a model of the Congress Avenue Bridge and its bats. Visiting exhibits, such as one on bridges (which involves building them as well as contemplating them) in early 2003, keep the museum continuously interesting.

Dell Discovery Center, 201 Colorado St. ℂ 512/472-2499. www.austinkids.org. Admission $4.50, children under 2 free. Tues–Sat 10am–5pm, Sun noon–5pm;. Free Wed 5–8pm, Sun 4–5pm. Closed Mon and some holidays. Bus: 2, 10, 12, 15, 16, 64, Red and Orange 'Dillo lines.

Austin Nature and Science Center ⭐   Bats, bees, and crystal caverns are among the subjects of the Discovery Boxes at this museum in the 80-acre Nature Center, which features lots of interactive exhibits. The tortoises, lizards, porcupine, and vultures in the Wildlife Exhibit—among more than 50 orphaned or injured creatures brought here from the wild—also hold kids' attention. An

Eco-Detective trail highlights pond-life awareness. The Dino Pit, slated to open early 2003, is sure to lure budding paleontologists. A variety of specialty camps, focusing on everything from caving to astronomy, are offered from late May through August.

Zilker Park, 301 Nature Center Dr. (C) **512/327-8181.** www.ci.austin.tx.us/nature_science. Donations requested; occasional special exhibits charge separately. Mon–Sat 9am–5pm; Sun noon–5pm. Closed July 4, Thanksgiving, and Dec 25. Bus: 30.

Austin Zoo   This small zoo, some 14 miles southwest of downtown, may not feature the state-of-the-jungle habitats of larger facilities, but it's easy to get up close and personal with the critters here. Most of the animal residents, who range from turkeys and pot-bellied pigs to marmosets and tigers, were mistreated, abandoned, or illegally imported before they found a home here. It costs $2 to board the 1.5-mile miniature train for a scenic Hill Country ride, which lets you peer at some of the shyer animals. There are no food concessions here, just plenty of picnic tables.

10807 Rawhide Trail. (C) **512/288-1490.** www.austinzoo.org. Admission $6 adults, $5 seniors, $4 children 2–12, children under 2 free. Daily 10am–6pm. Closed Thanksgiving and Dec 25. Take Hwy. 290W to Circle Dr., turn right, go 1.5 miles to Rawhide Trail, and turn right.

Jourdan Bachman Pioneer Farm 🖈   A glimpse of what life was like in the rural 1880s might help kids appreciate the simplicity (or absence) of their own chores—at least for a while. When Harriet Bachman and Frederic Jourdan set up housekeeping in northeast Austin in 1852, cattle herders drove past their property on the Chisholm Trail. Today's visitors to their farm can enter into the worlds of three typical late 19th-century Texas families: wealthy cotton farmers, homesteaders from Appalachia, and freed slaves turned tenant farmers. The costumed interpreters clearly relish playing their historic roles, and their enthusiasm is contagious. On Sunday afternoon, there's always something interactive for kids to do, from making sausage to milking cows.

11418 Sprinkle Cut Off Rd. (C) **512/837-1215.** www.pioneerfarm.org. Admission $5 adults, $4 children 3 and older, free for children under 3. Mon–Wed 9:30am–1pm (Thurs 9:30am–1pm June–Aug); Sun 1–5pm. Take exit 243 east off I-35 to Dessau Rd., turn left, go ½ mile and take a right on Sprinkle Cut Off Rd.

Splash! Into the Edwards Aquifer   The Edwards Aquifer, Austin's main source of water, is fed by a variety of underground creeks filtered through a large layer of limestone. You'll feel as though you're entering one of this vast ecosystem's sinkholes when you walk into the dimly lit enclosure—formerly the bathhouse at Barton Springs pool—where a variety of interactive displays grab kids' attention. Young visitors can make it rain on the city, identify water bugs, or peer through a periscope at swimmers. Although the focus is on the evils of pollution, the agenda is by no means heavy-handed.

Zilker Park, 2201 Barton Springs Rd. (C) **512/481-1466.** www.ci.austin.tx.us./splash. Free admission. Tues–Sat 10am–5pm; Sun noon–5pm. Bus: 30 (Barton Creek Sq.).

Zilker Zephyr Miniature Train   Take a scenic 25-minute ride through Zilker Park on a narrow-gauge, light-rail miniature train, which takes you at a leisurely pace along Barton Creek and Town Lake. The train departs approximately every hour on the hour during the week and every half hour on the half hour on the weekend, weather permitting.

Zilker Park, 2100 Barton Springs Rd. (just across from the Barton Springs Pool). (C) **512/478-8286.** Admission $2.75 ages 12 and over, $1.75 children under 12, free for infants (under 1) on guardian's lap. Daily 10am–5pm. Bus: 30.

4 Special-Interest Sightseeing

AFRICAN-AMERICAN HERITAGE

The many contributions of Austin's African-American community are high-lighted at **George Washington Carver Branch Library and Museum,** 1165 Angelina St. (© **512/472-4809;** www.carvermuseum.org), the first in Texas devoted to black history. Rotating exhibits of contemporary artwork share the space with photographs, videos, oral histories, and other artifacts from the community's past. A number of other sites on the East Side are worth visiting, too. Less than 2 blocks from the Carver, on the corner of Hackberry and San Bernard streets, stands the **Wesley United Methodist Church.** Established at the end of the Civil War, it was one of the leading black churches in Texas. Diagonally across the street, the **Zeta Phi Beta Sorority,** Austin's first black Greek letter house, occupies the Thompson House, built in 1877; it's also the archival center for the Texas chapter of the sorority. Nearby, at the **State Ceme-tery** (see "More Attractions," above), you can visit the gravesite of congress-woman and civil rights leader Barbara Jordan, the first African American to be buried here.

About a half-mile away, the sparsely furnished **Henry G. Madison Cabin** was built around 1863 by a black homesteader. When it was donated to the city in 1873, it was relocated to the grounds of the **Rosewood Park and Recreation Center,** 2300 Rosewood Ave. (© **512/472-6838**). The cabin is under renova-tion; phone to find out if it's reopened for public visits. You'll have to go across town, to the near west side, to explore the neighborhood known as **Clarksville,** founded by a former slave in 1871 as a utopian community for freed blacks; it's an almost entirely white artists' enclave now, however.

For a more up-to-date look at the Austin scene, visit **Mitchie's Fine Black Art & Gift Gallery,** 5706 Manor Rd., Suite B1 (© **512/323-6901;** www.mitchie. com), and **Bydee Arts & Gifts,** 412 E. Sixth St. (© **512/474-4343;** www. bydee.com), both offering a good selection of African-American painting and sculpture.

5 Strolling Around the University of Texas

No ivory tower (although it has several of them), the University of Texas is as integral to Austin's identity as it is to its economy. To explore the vast main campus is to glimpse the city's future as well as its past: Here, state-of-the-art structures—including information kiosks that can play the school's team songs—sit cheek by jowl with elegant examples of 19th-century architecture. The following tour points out many of the most interesting spots on campus. Unless you regularly trek the Himalaya, however, you'll probably want to drive or take a bus between some of the first seven sights. (Parking limitations were taken into account in this initial portion of the circuit.) For a walking-only tour, begin at stop 8; also note that stops 2, 5, 6, 12, and 20 are discussed earlier in this chapter, and stop 9 is detailed in the "Organized Tours" section, below.

WALKING TOUR   UT AUSTIN

Start:	The Arno Nowotny Building.
Finish:	The Littlefield Fountain.
Time:	1 hour, not including food breaks or museum visits.

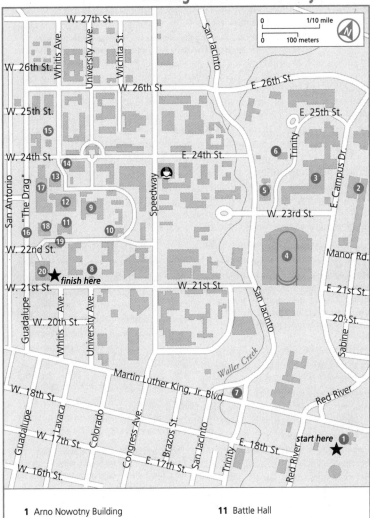

1 Arno Nowotny Building
2 LBJ Library and Museum
3 Performing Arts Center
4 Darrell K. Royal/Texas Memorial Stadium
5 Art Building
6 Texas Memorial Museum
7 Santa Rita No. 1
8 Littlefield Memorial Fountain
9 Main Building and Tower
10 Garrison Hall

11 Battle Hall
12 Flawn Academic Center
13 Hogg Auditorium
14 Battle Oaks
15 Littlefield Home
16 The Drag
17 Texas Union Building
18 Goldsmith Hall
19 Sutton Hall
20 Harry Ransom Center

 Take a Break

Best Times: On the weekends, when the campus is less crowded, more parking is available, and the Tower is open.

Worst Times: Morning and midday during the week when classes are in session and parking is impossible to find. (**Beware:** Those tow-away zone signs mean business.)

In 1839, the Congress of the Republic of Texas ordered a site set aside for the establishment of a "university of the first class" in Austin. Some 40 years later, when the flagship of the new University of Texas system opened, its first two buildings went up on that original 40-acre plot, dubbed College Hill. Although there were attempts to establish master-design plans for the university from the turn of the century onward, they were only carried out in bits and pieces until 1930, when money from an earlier oil strike on UT land allowed the school to begin building in earnest. Between 1930 and 1945, consulting architect Paul Cret put his mark on 19 university buildings, most showing the influence of his education at Paris's Ecole des Beaux-Arts. If the entire 357-acre campus will never achieve stylistic unity, its earliest section has a grace and cohesion that make it a delight to stroll.

Though it begins at the oldest building owned by the university, this tour begins far from the original campus. At the frontage road of I-35 and the corner of Martin Luther King Jr. Boulevard, pull into the parking lot of:

❶ **The Arno Nowotny Building**

In the 1850s, several state-run asylums for the mentally ill and the physically handicapped arose on the outskirts of Austin. One of these was the State Asylum for the Blind, built by Abner Cook around 1856. The ornate Italianate-style structure soon became better known as the headquarters and barracks of General Custer, who had been sent to Austin in 1865 to reestablish order after the Civil War. Incorporated into the university and restored for its centennial celebration, the building is now used for administration.

Take Martin Luther King Jr. Boulevard to Red River, then drive north to the:

❷ **LBJ Library and Museum**

This library and museum offers another rare on-campus parking lot. (You'll want to leave your car here while you see sights 3–6.) The first presidential library to be built on a university campus, the huge travertine marble structure oversees a beautifully landscaped 14-acre complex. Among the museum's exhibits is a seven-eighths scale replica of the Oval Office as it looked when the Johnsons occupied the White House. In the adjoining Sid Richardson Hall are the Lyndon B. Johnson School of Public Affairs and the Barker Texas History Center, housing the world's most extensive collection of Texana.

Stroll down the library steps across East Campus Drive to 23rd Street, where, next to the large Burleson bells on your right, you'll see the university's $41 million:

❸ **Performing Arts Center**

This arts center includes the 3,000-seat Bass Concert Hall, the 700-seat Bates Recital Hall, and other College of the Fine Arts auditoriums. The state-of-the-art acoustics at the Bass Concert Hall enhance the sounds of the largest tracker organ in the United States. Linking contemporary computer technology with a design that goes back some 2,000 years, it has 5,315 pipes—some of them 16 feet tall—and weighs 48,000 pounds.

From the same vantage point to the left looms the huge:

❹ Darrell K. Royal/Texas Memorial Stadium

The first of the annual UT–Texas A&M Thanksgiving Day games was played here in 1924. The upper deck directly facing you was added in 1972. In a drive to finance the original stadium, female students sold their hair, male students sold their blood, and UT alum Lutcher Stark matched every $10,000 they raised with $1,000 of his own funds. The stadium's mid-1990s name change to honor legendary Longhorns football coach Darrell K. Royal angered some who wanted the stadium to remain a memorial to Texas veterans, and confused others who wondered if Royal is still alive (he is).

Continue west on 23rd; at the corner of San Jacinto, a long staircase marks the entrance to the:

❺ Art Building

At press time, this was temporary home to the Jack S. Blanton Museum of Art (see "More Attractions," earlier in this chapter), until its larger facility is completed on MLK and Speedway.

Walk a short distance north on San Jacinto. A stampeding group of bronze mustangs will herald your arrival at the:

❻ Texas Memorial Museum

This monumental art moderne building was designed by Paul Cret; ground was broken for the institution by Franklin Roosevelt in 1936. Once home to the Capitol's original zinc goddess of liberty, which was moved to the Bob Bullock Texas State History Museum along with other historic treasures, this museum now focuses solely on the natural sciences.

Exit the building and take Trinity, which, curving into 25th Street, will bring you back to the parking lot of the LBJ Library and your car. Retrace your original route along Red River until you reach Martin Luther King

Jr. Boulevard. Drive west; at the corner of San Jacinto, you'll see:

❼ Santa Rita No. 1

No. 1 is an oil rig transported here from west Texas, where liquid wealth first spewed forth from it on land belonging to the university in 1923. The money was distributed between the University of Texas system, which got the heftier two thirds, and the Texas A&M system. Although not its main source of income, this windfall has helped make UT the second richest university in the country, after Harvard.

Continue on to University Avenue and turn left. There are public parking spaces around 21st Street and University, where you'll begin your walking tour at the:

❽ Littlefield Memorial Fountain

This fountain was built in 1933. Pompeo Coppini, sculptor of the magnificent bronze centerpiece, believed that the rallying together of the nation during World War I marked the final healing of the wounds caused by the Civil War. He depicted the winged goddess Columbia riding on the bow of a battleship sailing across the ocean—represented by three rearing sea horses—to aid the Allies. The two figures on the deck represent the Army and the Navy. This three-tiered fountain graces the most dramatic entrance to the university's original 40 acres. Behind you stands the state Capitol.

Directly ahead of you, across an oak-shaded mall lined with statues, is the:

❾ Main Building and Tower

The university's first academic building was built here in 1884. The 307-foot-high structure that now rises above the university was created by Paul Cret in 1937. It's a fine example of the Beaux Arts style, particularly stunning when lit to celebrate a Longhorn victory. Sadly, the clock tower's many notable features—the small classical temple on top, say, or the 17-bell carillon—will always be dogged by the shadow of the carnage committed by Charles Whitman, who in August 1966 shot and killed 16 people and wounded 31 more from the tower before he was gunned down by a sharpshooter. Closed off to the public in 1975 after a series of suicide leaps from its observation deck, the tower reopened for supervised ascensions in 1999 (see "Organized Tours," below). If you climb the staircase on the east (right) side of the tower to the stone balustrade, you can see the dramatic sweep of the entire eastern section of campus, including the LBJ Library.

The first building in your direct line of vision is:

⑩ Garrison Hall

Garrison Hall is named for one of the earliest members of the UT faculty, and home to the department of history. Important names from Texas's past—Austin, Travis, Houston, and Lamar—are set here in stone. The walls just under the building's eaves are decorated with cattle brands; look for the carved cow skulls and cactuses on the balcony window on the north side.

If you retrace your steps to the western (left) side o f the Main Building, you'll see:

⑪ Battle Hall

This building is regarded by many as the campus's most beautiful building. Designed in 1911 by Cass Gilbert, architect of the U.S. Supreme Court building, the hall was the first to be done in the Spanish Renaissance style that came to characterize so many of the structures on this section of campus; note the terra-cotta-tiled roof and broadly arched windows. On the second floor, you can see the grand reading room of what is now the Architecture and Planning Library.

Exit Battle Hall; go left to the northern door, which faces the much newer:

⑫ Flawn Academic Center

A 200,000-volume undergraduate library shares space here with exhibits from the archives of the Humanities

Research Center (see stop 20, below). Among the permanent displays in the Academic Center's Leeds Gallery is a cabin furnished with the effects of Erle Stanley Gardner, Perry Mason's creator. In front of the building, Charles Umlauf's *The Torch Bearers* symbolizes the passing of knowledge from one generation to the next.

Continue along the eastern side of the Academic Center, where you'll pass:

⑬ The Hogg Auditorium

This auditorium is another Paul Cret building, designed in the same monumental art moderne mode as his earlier Texas Memorial Museum, and recently renovated.

A few steps farther along, you'll come to the trees known as the:

⑭ Battle Oaks

The three oldest members of this small grove are said to predate the city of Austin itself. They survived the destruction of most of the grove to build a Civil War fortress and a later attempt to displace them with a new Biology Building. It was this last, near-fatal skirmish that earned them their name. Legend has it that Dr. W. J. Battle, a professor of classics and an early university president, holed up in the largest oak with a rifle to protect the three ancient trees.

Look across the street. At the corner of 24th and Whitis, you'll see the:

⑮ Littlefield Home

This home was built in high Victorian style in 1894. Major George W. Littlefield, a wealthy developer, cattle rancher, and banker, bequeathed more than $1 million to the university on the condition that its campus not be moved to land that his rival, George W. Brackenridge, had donated. During the week, when the UT Development Office is open, you can enter through the east carriage driveway to see the house's gorgeous gold-and-white parlors, griffin-decorated fireplace, and other ornate details.

TAKE A BREAK
O's Campus Cafe, in the A.C.E.S. building on 24th St. and Speedway (© 512/232-9060), is brought to you by the same folks who created Jeffrey's and Cippolina (see chapter 13 for both) so you know it's going to be a notch up from standard campus fare. Its gourmet sandwiches, pizzas, and muffins don't disappoint. If you haven't stopped here en route to the central campus from stop #7, head east to Speedway along 24th Street.

Backtrack to #15 and walk west about a block to Guadalupe to reach:

⑯ The Drag

As its name suggests, the Drag is Austin's main off-campus action strip. Bookstores, fast-food restaurants, and shops line the thoroughfare, which is usually crammed with students trying to grab a bite or a book between classes. On weekends, the pedestrian mall set aside for the 23rd Street Renaissance Market overflows with crafts vendors.

To get back to the university, cross Guadalupe at the traffic light in front of the huge Co-op, between 24th and 22nd streets. You'll now be facing the west mall.

On your left is the:

⑰ Texas Union Building

UT's student union building is yet another Paul Cret creation. A beautifully tiled staircase leads up to the second level where, through the massive carved wooden doors, you'll see the Cactus Cafe, a popular coffeehouse and music venue (see chapter 16). This bustling student center hosts everything from a bowling alley to a formal ballroom.

Immediately across the mall to the right stands:

⑱ Goldsmith Hall

This is one of two adjacent buildings where architecture classes are held. Also designed by Paul Cret, this hall has beautifully worn slate floors and a palm tree–dotted central courtyard.

Walk through the courtyard and go down a few steps; to your right is:

⑲ Sutton Hall

This hall was designed by Cass Gilbert in 1918 and part of School of Architecture. Like his Battle Hall, it is gracefully Mediterranean, with terracotta moldings, a red-tile roof, and large Palladian windows.

Enter Sutton Hall through double doors at the front and exit straight through the back. You are now facing the:

⑳ Harry Ransom Center

The Humanities Research Center (HRC) is housed here. The satirical portrait of a rich American literary archive in A. S. Byatt's best-selling novel *Possession* is widely acknowledged to have been based on HRC. On the first floor of this building, you can view the center's extremely rare Gutenberg Bible, one of just five complete copies in the U.S.

Exit the building to 21st Street and the fountain where the tour began.

6 Organized Tours

See also chapter 16 for details on touring the Austin City Limits studio.

AN AMPHIBIOUS TOUR

Austin Duck Adventures   It's a hoot—or should I say a quack? Whether or not you opt to shell out for a duck call whistle to blow at the folks you pass in the street, you'll get a kick out of this combination land and sea tour. You'll be transported in a six-wheel-drive amphibious vehicle (originally created for NATO troops) through Austin's historic downtown and the scenic west side before splashing into Lake Travis. Comedy writers helped devise the script for this 1½-hour tour, so it's amusing as well as informative.

Boarding in front of the Austin Convention and Visitors Bureau, 201 E. 2nd St. © **512/4-SPLASH.** www. austinducks.com. Tours $19 adults, $17 seniors and students, $13 children under 13. Daily tours; times change seasonally; call to check schedule.

BOAT TOURS

Capital Cruises   From March through October, Capital Cruises plies Town Lake with electric-powered boats heading out on a number of popular tours. The bat cruises are especially big in summer, when warm nights are perfect for the enjoyable and educational hour-long excursions; the high point is seeing thousands of bats stream out from under their Congress Avenue Bridge roost. Dinner cruises, featuring fajitas from the Hyatt Regency's La Vista restaurant, are also fun on a balmy evening, and the afternoon sightseeing tours are a nice way to while away an hour on the weekend.

Hyatt Regency Town Lake boat dock. © **512/480-9264.** www.capitalcruises.com. Bat and sightseeing cruises $8 adults, $6.50 seniors, $5 children 4–12; dinner cruises (including tax and tip) $30 adults, $20 children. Bat cruise daily ½ hour before sunset (call ahead for exact time), weather permitting; sightseeing cruise Sat–Sun at 1pm; dinner cruise Fri–Sun at 6pm. Reservations required for dinner cruises; for bat and sightseeing cruises, show up at the dock a minimum of 30 min. in advance.

Lone Star River Boat   You'll set out against a backdrop of Austin's skyline and the state capitol on this riverboat cruise and move upstream past Barton Creek and Zilker Park. Along the way, you'll glimpse 100-foot-high cliffs and million-dollar estates. These scenic tours, accompanied by knowledgeable narrators, last 1½ hours. Slightly shorter bat-watching tours leave around half an hour before sunset, so call ahead to check.

South shore of Town Lake, between the Congress Ave. and S. First St. bridges, just next to the Hyatt. © **512/ 327-1388.** www.lonestar.austin.citysearch.com. Scenic tours $9 adults, $7 seniors, $6 children under 12; bat tours $8 adults, $6 seniors, $5 children under 12. Scenic tours Sat–Sun 3pm Mar–Oct only. Bat tours nightly Apr–Oct only; call for exact times.

WALKING TOURS

Whatever price you pay, you won't find better guided walks than the informative and entertaining ones offered free of charge by the **Austin Convention and Visitors Bureau (ACVB),** 201 E. Second St. (© **800/926-2282** or 512/454-1545), from March through November. Ninety-minute tours of the historic Bremond Block leave every Saturday and Sunday at 11am; Congress Avenue/East Sixth Street is explored for an hour and a half on Thursday, Friday, and Saturday starting at 9am, Sunday at 2pm. The hour-long Capitol Grounds tour is conducted on Saturday at 2pm and Sunday at 9am. All tours depart promptly from the south entrance of the capitol, weather permitting; come even a few minutes late, and you'll miss out.

Austin Ghost Tours   If you favor activities that are likely to keep you from sleeping, these tours are for you. Not only are the three outings offered by Jeanine Plumer held in the evening, but they're all concerned with ghouls. The Ghosts of Austin tour explores the stories of those that didn't want to depart downtown, even after they died; the Haunted Sixth Street Pub Crawl capitalizes on the spirits that liked their spirits (and those who like spirits and spirits); and The Serial Killings of 1885 takes you on the route of the Servant Girl Annihilator, who terrorized the town three years before Jack the Ripper was around. Pleasant dreams.

All tours depart from The Hideout Coffeehouse & Theater, 617 Congress Ave. *©* **512/695-7297.** www. austinghosttours.com. 90-minute Ghosts of Austin and Serial Killings tours: $13 per person; 2-hour Pub Crawl: $15 per person (participants must be 21). Tours are held mostly on weekends, but schedules vary. Call or check the website.

University of Texas Tower Observation Deck Tour Off-limits to the public for nearly a quarter of a century, the observation deck of the UT Tower (see "Strolling Around the University of Texas," above) was remodeled with a webbed dome and reopened in late 1999. Billed as tours, these excursions to the top of the tower are really supervised visits, although a guide gives a short, informative spiel and stays on hand to answer questions. You're permitted to bring a camera, binoculars, or videocam to take advantage of the spectacular, 360-degree view of Austin, but must leave behind everything else, including purses, camera bags, tripods, strollers, and so on. (Lockers are available at the Texas Union for $1.)

Deck tours are available by reservation only. They may be made in person at the Texas Union Information Center in the Texas Union building, corner of 24th Street and Guadalupe, or by phoning the numbers listed below on Monday to Friday 8am to 5pm. Arrive 20 minutes before your reserved tour time to claim your ticket; otherwise, you'll forfeit your reservation. If you haven't booked, come by an hour before a scheduled tour and put your name on a waiting list for the next ascent. Unclaimed tickets are sold to standby patrons 10 minutes before the starting time for each tour.

UT Campus, Texas Union Building. *©* **512/475-6633** or 877/475-6633 (outside Austin). Tours $3. Usually Sat–Sun on the hour 1–7pm in fall and winter, 11am–5pm in spring; additional hours late May to late Aug Thurs–Fri at 6, 7, 8pm, Sat hourly 1–8pm; no tours on Sun.

Wild Basin Wilderness Preserve The varied menu of guided tours at this preserve on a lovely 227-acre peninsula will keep nature lovers happy, night and day. Native plants, birds, arrowheads, and snakes are among the topics covered (though not at the same time) during daylight walks; come dark, moonlighting tours coinciding with the full moon and stargazing tours 3 or four days after the new moon are also offered. Call ahead or check the website for exact dates.

805 N. Capital of Texas Hwy. *©* **512/327-7622.** www.wildbasin.org. Preserve admission $2 adults, $1 seniors and ages 5–12; tours $3 adults, $1 ages 5–12, children under 5 free. Preserve open daily dawn–dusk; office daily 9am–4pm. Hiking tours every weekend, weather permitting, stargazing tours twice monthly, weather permitting, generally 8 or 8:30pm to 9:30 or 10pm.

SELF-GUIDED TOURS

In addition to the guided walking tours offered by the **Austin Convention and Visitors Bureau** (see below), the ACVB also publishes seven excellent, free self-guided tour booklets. Five tours (Bremond Block, Hyde Park, Congress Avenue and E. Sixth St., Texas State Cemetery, and Oakwood Cemetery) require foot power alone; the other two (West Austin and O. Henry Trail) combine walking and driving. They make for interesting reading even if you don't have time to follow the routes.

If you'd prefer to have a knowledgeable personal guide with you while you drive (along with, or as opposed to, a know-nothing friend, spouse or significant other), consider buying the **Hit the Road Austin** audio tour CD ($19), just out in November 2002. You'll be escorted from downtown Austin through Zilker Park, along Wild Basin Preserve, to Mt. Bonnell, through Clarksville, the University of Texas, the Capitol, and various other points of interest. The narrators have the requisite Texas twang, and their stories are accompanied by such audio effects as music, military drumbeats and birdcalls. Along with the CD, you'll also get a printed map of the tour route, so be nice; you might still have to rely on that person in the navigator seat. To order, call © 512/335-3300 or log on to www.hittheroadtours.com.

7 Staying Active

BALLOONING   For an uplifting experience, consider a hot-air balloon ride over Hill Country. **Austin Aeronauts Hot Air Balloons** (© 512/440-1492; www.austinaeronauts.com) and **Airwolf Adventures** (© 512/251-4024) are both reputable operators with FAA-licensed pilots. Their scenic excursions, including champagne breakfast, generally last about an hour.

BIKING   A city that has a "bicycle coordinator" on its payroll, Austin is a cyclist's dream. Contact **Austin Parks and Recreation,** 200 S. Lamar Blvd. (© 512/974-6700; www.ci.austin.tx.us/parks), for information on the city's more than 25 miles of scenic paths, the most popular of which are the Barton Creek Greenbelt (7¾ miles) and the Town Lake Greenbelt (10 miles). The **Veloway,** a 3.1-mile paved loop in Slaughter Creek Metropolitan Park, is devoted exclusively to bicyclists and in-line skaters. You can rent bikes and get maps and other information from **University Cyclery,** 2901 N. Lamar Blvd. (© 512/474-6696, www.ucycleaustin.com); a number of downtown hotels rent or provide free bicycles to their guests. For information on weekly road rides, contact the **Austin Cycling Association,** P.O. Box 5993, Austin, TX 78763 (© 512/282-7413; www.austincycling.org), which also publishes a monthly newsletter, *Southwest Cycling News;* only local calls or e-mails are returned. For rougher mountain-bike routes, try the **Austin Ridge Riders**—their website, www.austinridgeriders.com, will have the latest contact information.

BIRD WATCHING   Endangered golden-cheeked warblers and black-capped vireos are among the many species you might spot around Austin. The **Travis Audubon Society** (© 512/926-8751; www.travisaudubon.org) organizes regular birding trips and even has a rare-bird hot line. Texas Parks and Wildlife publishes "The Guide to Austin-Area Birding Sites," which points you to the best urban perches; you should be able to pick up a copy at the Austin Convention & Visitors Bureau or at the offices of any of Austin's parks and preserves (see "More Attractions," above). Avid birders should also enjoy *Adventures with a Texas Naturalist* by Roy Bedichek; the author is one of the three friends depicted on the Philosophers' Rock, also listed in the "More Attractions" section.

CANOEING   You can rent canoes at **Zilker Park,** 2000 Barton Springs Rd. (© 512/478-3852; www.fastair.com/zilker), for $8.50 an hour or $29 all day (Sat, Sun, and holidays only Oct–Mar). **Capital Cruises,** Hyatt Regency boat dock (© 512/480-9264; www.capitalcruises.com), also offers hourly rentals on Town Lake. If your paddling skills are a bit rusty, check out the instructional courses of UT's **Recreational Sports Outdoor Program** (© 512/471-3116).

FISHING   Go on the fly with downtown's **Austin Angler,** 312½ Congress Ave. (© 512/472-4553; www.austinangler.com), an excellent place to pick up a license, tackle, and information on where to find the big ones. **Git Bit** (© 512/280-2861; www.gitbitfishing.com) provides guide service for half- or full-day bass-fishing trips on Lake Travis.

GOLF   For information about Austin's **six municipal golf courses,** call ✆ **512/480-3020** or log on to www.ci.austin.tx.us/parks/golf.htm; all offer pro shops and equipment rental, and their greens fees are very reasonable. Among them are the 9-hole **Hancock,** which was built in 1899 and is the oldest course in Texas; and the 18-hole **Lions,** where Tom Kite and Ben Crenshaw played college golf for the University of Texas.

HIKING   Austin's parks and preserves abound in nature trails; see "More Attractions," above, for additional information. Contact the **Colorado River Walkers of Austin** (✆ **512/495-6294;** www.onr.com/user/dbarber/crw/home page.htm) or the **Sierra Club** (✆ **512/472-1767;** www.texas.sierraclub.org/austin), if you're interested in organized hikes. **Wild Basin Wilderness Preserve** (see "Organized Tours," above), is another source for guided treks, offering periodic "Haunted Trails" tours along with its more typical hikes.

ROCK CLIMBING   Those with the urge to hang out on cliffs can call **Mountain Madness** (✆ **512/329-0309;** www.mtmadness.com), which holds weekend rock-climbing courses at Enchanted Rock, a stunning granite outcropping in the Hill Country. **Austin Rock Gym,** 4401 Freidrich Lane, Suite 300 (✆ **512/474-4376;** www.austinrockgym.com), offers more than 10,000 square feet of indoor rock climbing in a climate-controlled environment.

SAILING   Lake Travis is the perfect place to let the wind drive your sails; among the operators offering boat rentals in the Austin area are **Commander's Point Yacht Basin** (✆ **512/266-2333;** www.cpyb.com), **Texas Sailing Academy** (✆ **512/261-6193;** www.texassailing.com), and **Dutchman's Landing** (✆ **512/267-4289;** www.dutchmanslanding.com); the first two companies also offer instruction.

SCUBA DIVING   The clarity of the limestone-filtered waters of Lake Travis makes it ideal for peeking around underwater. Boat wrecks and metal sculptures have been planted on the lake bottom of the private (paying) portion of **Windy Point Park** (✆ **512/266-3337**), and Mother Nature has provided the park's advanced divers with an unusual underwater grove of pecan trees. Equipment rentals and lessons are available nearby from **Pisces** (✆ **512/258-6646;** www. flash.net/~piscestx).

SPELUNKING   The limestone country in the Austin area is rife with dark places in which to poke around. In the city, two wild caves you can crawl into with the proper training are **Airman's Cave** on the Barton Creek Greenbelt and **Goat Cave Preserve** in southwest Austin. Check the Website of the Texas Speleological Association, www.cavetexas.org, and that of the University Speleological Society, www.utgrotto.org (you don't have to be a student to join), for links to statewide underground attractions. See also chapter 17 for other caves in nearby Hill Country.

SWIMMING   The best known of Austin's natural swimming holes is **Barton Springs Pool** (see "The Top Attractions," above), but it's by no means the only one. Other scenic outdoor spots to take the plunge include **Deep Eddy Pool,** 401 Deep Eddy Ave. at Lake Austin Boulevard (✆ **512/472-8546**), and **Hamilton Pool Preserve,** 27 miles west of Austin, off Texas 71 on FM 3238 (✆ **512/264-2740**). For lakeshore swimming, consider **Hippie Hollow** on Lake Travis, 2½ miles off FM 620, www.co.travis.tx.us/tnr/parks/hippie_hollow.asp, where you can let it all hang out in a series of clothing-optional coves, or **Emma Long Metropolitan Park** on Lake Austin (see "More Attractions," above). You can also get into the swim at a number of **free neighborhood pools;** contact the City Aquatics Department (© **512/476-4521;** www.ci.austin.tx.us/parks/aquatics.htm) for information.

TENNIS   The very reasonably priced **Austin High School Tennis Center,** 2001 W. Cesar Chavez St. (© **512/477-7802**), **Caswell Tennis Center,** 2312 Shoal Creek Blvd. (© **512/478-6268**), and **Pharr Tennis Center,** 4201 Brookview Dr. (© **512/477-7773**), all have enough courts to give you a good shot at getting one. To find out about additional public courts, contact the Tennis Administration office (© **512/480-3020,** www.ci.austin.tx.us/parks/tennis.htm).

8 Spectator Sports

There are no professional teams in Austin, but a new minor league baseball team has captured local attention. College sports are very big, particularly when the **University of Texas (UT) Longhorns** are playing. The most comprehensive source of information on the various teams is www.TexasSports.com, but you can phone the **UT Athletics Ticket Office** (© **512/471-3333**) to find out about schedules and **UTTM Charge-A-Ticket** (© **512/477-6060**) to order tickets.

BASEBALL   The **University of Texas** baseball team goes to bat February through May at Disch-Falk Field (just east of I-35, at the corner of Martin Luther King, Jr. Blvd. and Comal). Many players from this former NCAA championship squad have gone on to the big time, including two-time Cy Young award winner Roger Clemens. Nolan Ryan's **Round Rock Express,** a Houston Astros farm club, won the Texas League championship in 1999, their first year in existence. See them at the Dell Diamond, 3400 E. Palm Valley Road in Round Rock (© **512/255-BALL** or 512/244-4209; www.roundrock express.com), a 7,800-seat stadium where you can choose from box seats, stadium seating, or even a grassy berm in the outfield.

BASKETBALL   The **University of Texas** Longhorn and Lady Longhorn basketball teams, both former Southwest Conference champions, play in the Frank C. Erwin Jr. Special Events Center (just west of I-35 on Red River between Martin Luther King, Jr. Blvd. and 15th St.) November through March.

FOOTBALL   It's hard to tell which is more central to the success of an Austin Thanksgiving: the turkey or the UT–Texas A&M game. Part of the Big 12 Conference, the **University of Texas** football team often fills the huge Darrell K. Royal/Texas Memorial Stadium (just west of I-35 between 23rd and 21st sts., E. Campus Dr. and San Jacinto Blvd.) during home games, played August through November.

GOLF   Celebrities such as Joe Namath and Dennis Quaid tee off for a good cause at the **East Austin Youth Classic,** held at Barton Creek Resort (© **512/329-4000;** www.bartoncreek.com) in June. (It's been dubbed the "Ben-Willie-Darryl" because its benefactors are Ben Crenshaw, Willie Nelson, and Darryl Royal.)

HOCKEY   The **Austin Ice Bats** hockey team (© **512/927-PUCK;** www.icebats.com) has been getting anything but an icy reception. This typically rowdy team plays at the Travis County Exposition Center, 7311 Decker Lane (about 15 min. east of UT). Tickets, which run from $10 to $18, are available at any UTTM outlet or from Star Tickets (© **888/597-STAR** or 512/469-SHOW; www.startickets.com). The team generally plays on weekends mid-October through late March; a phone call will get you the exact dates and times.

HORSE RACING   Pick your ponies at **Manor Downs,** 8 miles east of I-35 on U.S. 290 East (© **512/272-5581;** www.manordowns.com). The track is open for quarterhorse and thoroughbred live racing on Saturday and Sunday in mid-February through May. The rest of the year, you can see simulcasts. Call or check the website for the current schedule.

SOCCER   August through December you can find the **University of Texas** women's soccer team working to defend their stellar record. In 2002 they garnered all the Big 12 soccer honors, including Player of the Year, Julie Gailey. Home games are played either Friday or Sunday at the Mike A. Myers Stadium and Soccer Field, just northeast of the UT football stadium at Robert Dedman Dr. and Mike Myers Dr.

15

Shopping in Austin

When it comes to things intellectual, musical, and gustatory, Austin is a match for many cities twice its size. Shopping here may not quite have evolved into the art it has in glitzier big cities like Houston or Dallas, but this town still offers a more-than-adequate range of choices.

1 The Shopping Scene

Austin is seeing a revitalization of its urban retail scene. Downtown, specialty shops and art galleries are filtering back to the renovated 19th-century buildings along **Sixth Street** and **Congress Avenue.** Below Town Lake, **South Congress Avenue,** from Riverside south to Annie Street, is especially trendy, with art galleries and boutiques joining its rows of secondhand clothing stores. Other rich shopping enclaves to mine include the **West End,** in the blocks around Sixth Street and Lamar, and, nearby, north of 12th Street and West Lynn. In the vicinity of **Central Market,** between West 35th and 40th streets and Lamar and Mo-Pac, such small shopping centers as Jefferson Square are similarly charming. Many stores on **the Drag**—the stretch of Guadalupe Street between Martin Luther King Jr. Boulevard and 26th Street, across from the University of Texas campus—are student-oriented, but a wide range of clothing, gifts, toys, and books can also be found here.

Still, much of Austin's shopping has moved out to the malls. The newest growth area is in the northwest, where three upscale shopping centers, **The Arboretum, The Arboretum Market,** and **The Gateway complex** (consisting of the Gateway Courtyard, the Gateway Market, and Gateway Sq.), have earned the area the nickname "South Dallas." Bargain hunters go farther afield to the huge collections of factory outlet stores in San Marcos and New Braunfels; see chapter 17 for details.

Specialty shops in Austin tend to open around 9 or 10am, Monday through Saturday, and close at about 5:30 or 6pm; many have Sunday hours from noon until 6pm. Malls tend to keep the same Sunday schedule, but Monday through Saturday they don't close their doors until 9pm. Sales tax in Austin is 8.25%.

2 Shopping A to Z

ANTIQUES

In addition to the one-stop antiques markets listed below, a number of smaller shops line Burnet Road north of 45th Street. See also the **Travis County Farmers' Market** under "Food," below.

Antique Marketplace   For people who like antiques but don't enjoy speaking in hushed tones, the Antique Marketplace offers bargains and treasures in a friendly, relaxed atmosphere. You'll find a little bit of everything under the roof of this large warehouse-type building in central Austin: Czech glass, funky collectibles, and expensive furnishings. 5350 Burnet Rd. ☎ 512/452-1000.

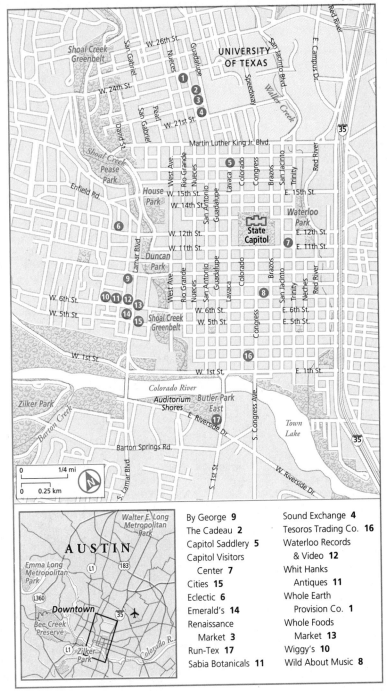

UNIVERSITY OF TEXAS

Shoal Creek Greenbelt

W. 26th St.

San Gabriel

Nueces

Guadalupe

San Jacinto Blvd.

Speedway

E. Campus Dr.

Walter Creek

Red River

W. 24th St.

Pearl

San Gabriel

David St.

W. 21st St.

35

Martin Luther King Jr. Blvd.

Shoal Creek

Pease Park

Enfield Rd.

House Park

W. 15th St.

W. 14th St.

West Ave

Rio Grande

Nueces

San Antonio

Guadalupe

Lavaca

Colorado

Congress

Brazos

San Jacinto

Trinity

Red River

E. 15th St.

Waterloo Park

Lamar Blvd.

Duncan Park

W. 12th St.

W. 11th St.

State Capitol

E. 12th St.

E. 11th St.

West Ave

Rio Grande

Nueces

San Antonio

Guadalupe

Lavaca

Colorado

Brazos

San Jacinto

Trinity

Neches

Red River

W. 6th St.

W. 5th St.

Shoal Creek Greenbelt

W. 6th St.

W. 5th St.

E. 6th St.

E. 5th St.

W. 1st St.

W. 1st St.

E. 1st St.

Congress

Colorado River

Zilker Park

Barton Creek

Auditorium Shores

Butler Park East

E. Riverside Dr.

S. Congress Ave.

Town Lake

35

Barton Springs Rd.

S. Lamar Blvd.

S. 1st St.

W. Riverside Dr.

0   1/4 mi

0   0.25 km

N

AUSTIN

Walter E. Long Metropolitan Park

Emma Long Metropolitan Park

183

L1

L360

Downtown

35

Bee Creek Preserve

L1

Zilker Park

Colorado R.

Greater Austin Shopping

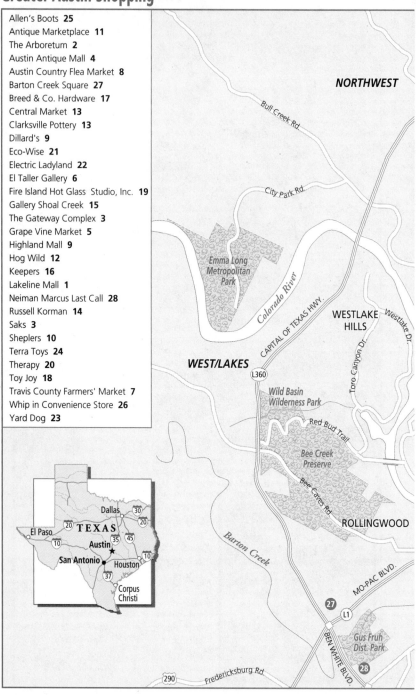

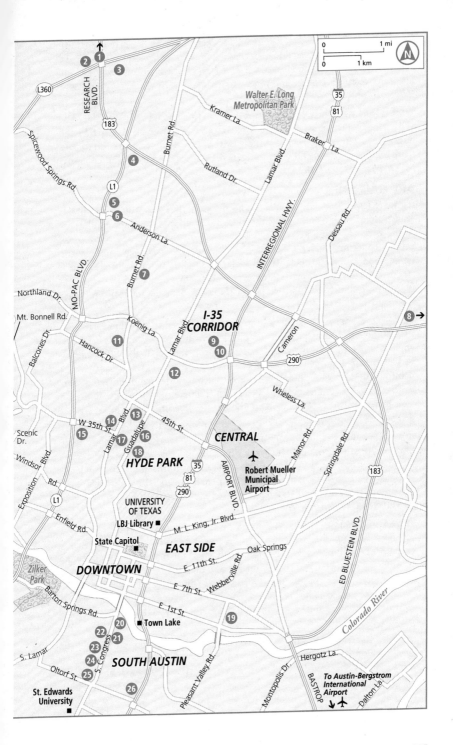

Austin Antique Mall You can spend anywhere from five bucks to thousands of dollars in this huge collection of antiques stores. More than 100 dealers inside a 30,000-square-foot indoor space sell Roseville pottery, Fiesta dishes, Victorian furniture, costume jewelry, and much, much more. 8822 McCann Dr. © 512/459-5900.

Whit Hanks Antiques More than a dozen independent dealers gather at tony Whit Hanks, just across the street from Treaty Oak. This is Austin's premier outlet for fine antiques. Even if you can't afford to buy anything, it's fun to ogle items from fine crystal and vases to Chinese cabinets and neoclassical columns. 1009 W. Sixth St. © 512/478-2101.

ART GALLERIES

It's not exactly SoHo, but the area just northwest of the Capitol and south of the University of Texas—specifically, the block bounded by Guadalupe and Lavaca to the west and east and 17th and 18th streets to the south and north—has a large concentration of galleries. They include the group clustered in the **Guadalupe Arts Building,** 1705 Guadalupe, as well as Women and their Work (see below). For additional information about other galleries and art events in Austin, call City Art Link at © 512/452-7773 or log on to www.cityart link.com.

El Taller Gallery Located just east of Mo-Pac, this appealing showcase for Southwestern art sells Santa Fe pieces at Austin prices. Amado Peña, Jr., who once owned the gallery, is represented here, and you'll also find work by R. C. Gorman and other Native American artists, as well as whimsical Western paintings by Darryl Willison. Handmade Pueblo pottery and vintage Southwestern jewelry are among the gallery's other interesting offerings. 8015 Shoal Creek Blvd., Suite 109. © 800/234-7362 or 512/302-0100. www.eltallergallery.com.

Gallery Shoal Creek Since it opened in 1965, Shoal Creek has moved away from an exclusive emphasis on Western art to encompass work from a wide range of American regions. The focus is on contemporary painting in representational or Impressionist styles—for example, Jerry Ruthven's Southwest landscapes or Nancy McGowan's naturalist watercolors. Like El Taller, this is an Austin outlet for many artists who also have galleries in Santa Fe. 1500 W. 34th St. © 512/454-6671. www.gshoalcreek.com.

Wild About Music Austin's commitment to music makes it a perfect location for this gallery and shop, strictly devoted to arts and crafts with a musical theme. Some of the pieces are expensive, but nearly all of them are fun. Come see the multimedia prints by Texas musician Joe Ely, the instrument-shaped furniture (a Moroccan prince picked up a guitar-shaped Jimi Hendrix chair), and the unique Texas music T-shirt collection. Gift items run the gamut from books and bola ties to watches and wind chimes. 721 Congress Ave. © 512/708-1700. www.wild aboutmusic.com.

Women & Their Work Gallery Founded in 1978, this nonprofit gallery is devoted to more than visual art—it also promotes and showcases women in dance, music, theater, film, and literature. Regularly changing exhibits have little in common except innovation. This art space got the nod for "Best Gallery" from the *Austin Chronicle* in 2001 and 2002. The gift shop has a great selection of unusual crafts and jewelry created by female artists. 1710 Lavaca St. © 512/477-1064. www.womenandtheirwork.org.

Yard Dog Folk Art "Outsider" art, created in the deep, rural South, usually by the poor and sometimes by the incarcerated, is not for everyone, but for those interested in contemporary American folk art, this gallery is not to be missed. Naturally, it's in the hip South Congress area, where no one would be so uncool as to admit they find some of this stuff incredibly ugly. 1510 South Congress Ave. ℂ 512/912-1613. www.yarddog.com.

CRAFTS

Eclectic A dazzling panoply of hand-painted furniture, pottery, and art—new and old—from around the world is beautifully presented in this large store (with a bonus parking lot in back). An outstanding jewelry section includes pieces from Mexico, Africa, Indonesia, Afghanistan and other exotic places. 700 N. Lamar. ℂ 512/477-1816.

Tesoros Trading Co. If you like exotic tchotchkes, be prepared to lose all sense of time when you enter this store. Colorful hand-woven cloth from Guatemala, intricate weavings from Peru, glassware and tinwork from Mexico—all these and more are available at Tesoros, which (in addition to its high-quality folk art) also offers a limited selection of furniture, dishes, and housewares from Latin America. Plenty of reasonably priced items mingle with expensive treasures. 209 Congress Ave. ℂ 512/479-8377. www.tesoros.com.

DEPARTMENT STORES

Dillard's This Little Rock–based chain, spread throughout the Southwest, carries a nice variety of mid- to high-range merchandise. In Highland Mall, there are two separate outlets, one focusing on home furnishings and women's clothing, the other devoted to men's and children's wear. All the stores have country shops with good selections of stylish Western fashions. Two other locations are at the Barton Creek Mall (ℂ 512/327-6100) and the Lakeline Mall (ℂ 512/257-8740). Highland Mall. ℂ 512/452-9393. www.dillards.com.

Saks Austin came of age in the late 1990s with the opening of a link in this golden chain. Although smaller than many of the other Saks stores, it offers the high-tone fashions and accouterments you'd expect, as well as a personal shopper service. 9722 Great Hills Trail. ℂ 512/231-3700. www.saksfifthavenue.com.

DISCOUNT SHOPPING

Neiman Marcus' Last Call ⭐ Fans of Texas-grown Neiman Marcus will want to take advantage of Last Call, which consolidates fashions from 27 of the chain's high-toned department stores and sells them here at prices 50% to 75% off retail. New merchandise shipments arrive every week. Not only can you find great bargains, but you needn't sacrifice the attention for which Neiman Marcus is famous; staff here is as helpful as at any other branch, and a personal shopper service is available. Brodie Oaks Shopping Center, 4115 S. Capital of Texas Hwy. at S. Lamar. ℂ 512/447-0701. www.neimanmarcus.com.

ECO-WARES

Eco-wise It's hard to typecast a shop that sells everything from greeting cards, natural insect repellent, and hand-woven purses to building materials and home decorating supplies. The common denominator? Everything you'll find here is created with an eye toward the environment—that is, it's either recycled, made from natural fabrics, and/or chemical-free. Staff is knowledgeable and helpful, and customers are passionately loyal. The store offers baby and wedding shower registries for earth-friendly brides and grooms or moms and dads. 110 W. Elizabeth. © 512/326-4474. www.ecowise.com.

ESSENTIAL OILS

Sabia Botanicals   All those soothing oils and lotions in their pretty bottles on the shelves seem to whisper, "Buy me, I'll make you feel better." This is aromatherapy central, but along with New Age products, the store also carries old-time herbal lines, such as Kiehl's. 500 N. Lamar, Suite 150. © 512/469-0447. www. sabia.com.

FASHIONS

MEN

See also **By George** under "Women," below.

Keepers   Austinites seeking to make the transition from geek to fashion chic turn to this locally owned men's specialty store for friendly but expert advice and the latest in well-made men's clothing. You'll find an "image consultant" and expert tailors on the premises. 1004 W. 38th St. © 512/302-3664. www.keepers clothing.com.

OUTDOOR

Run-Tex   If you've ever felt like saying "Feet, don't fail me now," you've come to the right place. Owned by the footwear editor for *Runner's World* magazine—and serving as the official wear-test center for that publication—this store not only has a huge inventory of shoes and other running gear, but also does everything it can to promote healthful jogging practices, even offering free running classes and a free injury-evaluation clinic. The staff will make sure any footwear you buy is a perfect fit for your feet and running style. There's a larger Run-Tex in Gateway Market, 9901 Capital of Texas Hwy. (© 512/343-1164); a location at 2201 Lake Austin Blvd., (© 512/477-9464); and a related WalkTex at 4001 N. Lamar (© 512/454-WALK). But this downtown store is best: It's near that runner's Mecca, Town Lake. 422 W. Riverside Dr. © 512/472-3254. www.runtex.com.

WOMEN

See also **The Cadeau,** listed under "Gifts/Souvenirs," below.

By George   In its various incarnations, By George has long been a prime pick for Austin fashion victims, and now the men's and women's outlets have been consolidated into a single huge clothing emporium. Both genders like the mix of well-established and up-and-coming designers with (somewhat) less pricey off-the-rack clothing here; the common denominator is hip, contemporary fashions in natural fabrics. There's also another, more casual women's store for the college crowd on the Drag at 2346 Guadalupe St. (© 512/472-2731). 524 N. Lamar Blvd. © 512/472-5951.

Emeralds   It's young, it's hip, it's got Carrie Bradshaw shoes by the boatload, plus racks of outrageous party dresses to wear them with. And—should your friends have the same tastes as Carrie's do—you can also buy cards, candles, aromatherapy bath salts, and funky jewelry here. 624 N Lamar Blvd. © 512/476-3660.

Therapy   Many of Austin's top singer/songwriters come to this hip SoCo boutique to seek out clothing as clever as the store's name (any shopper worth her credit card knows the value of retail therapy). You'll find a small but constantly changing inventory of inventive styles by local designers—everything from purses and casual halters to flowing skirts and evening gowns—sold at prices that fall well below what you'd find at the large national stores. Feeling better yet? 1113 S. Congress Ave. ✆ **877/326-2331** or 512/326-2331. www.therapyclothing.com.

VINTAGE

Electric Ladyland/Lucy in Disguise with Diamonds   Feather boas, tutus, flapper dresses, angel wings, and the occasional gorilla suit overflow the narrow aisles of Austin's best-known costume and vintage clothing outlet. The owner, who really *does* dress like that all the time, is a walking advertisement for her fascinating store. The story carries more-or-less subdued clothing like floral-print dresses and striped shirts, but you're likely to get sidetracked by rack after rack of outrageousness. At Halloween, this is costume-rental central. 1506 S. Congress Ave. ✆ **512/444-2002.**

FOOD

Central Market ★★   You'll think you've died and gone to foodie heaven. Not only can you buy every imaginable edible item here—fresh or frozen, local or imported—but these gourmet megamarkets also have a restaurant section, with a top-notch chef serving up cowboy, bistro, Italian, vegetarian, you name it. And it's all at very reasonable prices. A monthly newsletter announces what's fresh in the produce department, which jazz musicians are entertaining on the weekend, and which gourmet chef is holding forth at the market's cooking school; it has more classes for nonprofessional chefs than any other in the country. The newer Westgate Shopping Center branch, 4477 S. Lamar (✆ **512/899-4300**) in South Austin, is as impressive as its history-making sibling north of UT. 4001 N. Lamar. ✆ **512/206-1000.** www.centralmarket.com.

Travis County Farmers' Market   Not only does this market offer great fresh fruit and vegetables grown in the surrounding area, but it also hosts monthly festivals honoring particular crops and/or growing seasons. April, for example, honors the 1015 "Y" onion, lauded as sweet, mild, and tear-free, while June celebrates peaches with contests for the best peach cobbler, peach ice cream, and peach preserves. Want something less produce-oriented? The market also has a barbecue restaurant, a cowboy restaurant, a Mexican restaurant, and a bakery, as well as a store selling country-primitive antiques. 6701 Burnet Rd. ✆ **512/454-1002.**

Whole Foods Market   From chemical-free cosmetics to frozen tofu burgers, Whole Foods covers the entire (organic) enchilada. It's the place to find anything that comes in a low-fat or otherwise pure version. The northwest store in Gateway Market, 9607 Research Blvd. (✆ **512/345-5003**), is slightly smaller, but it's also less frenetic. 601 N. Lamar Blvd. ✆ **512/476-1206.** www.wholefoodsmarket.com.

GIFTS/SOUVENIRS

See also **Wild About Music,** listed under "Art Galleries" above, and **Emeralds,** listed under "Clothing/Women's," above.

The Cadeau   *Cadeau* means "gift" in French, and this is the perfect place to find one, whether it be beautiful contemporary kitchenware, pottery, jewelry, clothing, bibelots, tchotchkes, or knickknacks. Be forewarned: Just when you think you've narrowed down your choice, you may suddenly realize you've missed two whole rooms full of goodies to choose from. To add to the dilemma, there's a newer location, at 4001 N. Lamar Blvd. (✆ **512/453-6988**), near Central Market. 2316 Guadalupe St. (the Drag). ✆ **512/477-7276.**

Capitol Visitors Center   Over the years, visitors have admired—sometimes excessively—the intricately designed door hinges of the capitol. The gift shop at the visitors center sells brass bookends made from the original models used, during the capitol's renovation, to cast replacements for hinges that were cadged over the years. Other Texana includes paperweights made from reproductions of the capitol's Texas seal doorknobs and local food products. There's also a variety of educational toys and an excellent selection of historical books. 112 E. 11th St. (southeast corner of Capitol grounds). © 512/305-8400. www.texascapitolvisitorscenter.com.

GLASS & POTTERY

Clarksville Pottery & Galleries   This pottery emporium, filled with lovely pieces created by local artisans, has long been transplanted from its namesake location in the artsy section of downtown to a prime spot near Central Market (see "Food," above). You'll find everything ceramic, from candleholders to bird feeders, as well as hand-blown glass, woodcarvings, and contemporary jewelry in a variety of media; there's a unique selection of Judaica, too. Two additional outlets, in the Arboretum Market, 9722 Great Hills Trail, Suite 380 (© 512/ 794-8580), and on 3300 Bee Cave Rd. (© 512/732-2821), near Westlake Hills, carry equally impressive stock. 4001 N. Lamar, Suite 200. © 512/454-9079. www. clarksvillepottery.com.

Fire Island Hot Glass Studio, Inc.   This glassblowing studio, about 2 miles east of I-35, is a bit off the beaten track, but it's a treat to watch the owners/artists, Matthew LaBarbera and his wife, Teresa Ueltschey, at their delicate craft. Demonstrations are given every Saturday morning from 9am to noon (other times by appointment). Other galleries around Austin carry the couple's elegant perfume bottles, oil lamps, bowls, and paperweights, but this showroom naturally has the largest selection. If you have a certain design in mind, you can special-order a set of goblets. 3401 E. Fourth St. © 512/389-1100. www.fireislandglass.com.

HARDWARE & MORE

Breed & Co. Hardware   You don't have to be a power-drill freak to visit Breed & Co. How many hardware stores, after all, have bridal registries where you can sign up for Waterford crystal? This darling of Austin do-it-your-selfers has everything from nails to tropical plants, organic fertilizer, gardening and cookbooks, paté molds, and cherry pitters. There's a newer branch in the chic Westlake Hills area, 3663 Bee Cave Rd. (© 512/328-3960). 718 W. 29th St. © 512/474-6679. www.breedandco.com.

HOME FURNISHINGS

See also **Eclectic,** under "Crafts," above.

Cities   This sprawling store is urban hipster heaven, carrying everything from martini glass wall sconces and cocktail clocks to purses shaped like Chinese take-out containers (in both black and red). It's one of those places where you're likely to want everything you see—but need none of it. 524 N. Lamar. © 512/236-1200.

JEWELRY

See also **Eclectic** and **Tesoros,** under "Crafts," above.

Russell Korman   You'd never know it from his current elegant digs, but Russell Korman got his start in Austin's jewelry trade by selling beads on the Drag. Although he's moved on to fine 14-karat gold, platinum, and diamond pieces, along with fine pens and watches—there's an experienced watchmaker on the premises—his store still has a considerable collection of more casual sterling silver from Mexico. Prices are very competitive, even for the most formal baubles. 3806 N. Lamar Blvd. © 512/451-9292.

MALLS/SHOPPING CENTERS

The Arboretum   It's worth a trip to the far northwest part of town to a shopping center so chic that it calls itself a market, not a mall. This two-level collection of outdoor boutiques doesn't include any department stores, but it does have a Barnes & Noble Superstore and a huge Pottery Barn. You'll find your basic selection of yuppie shops—everything from upscale clothing stores to a cigar humidor. The Treetop Galleries section on the second floor features art galleries, a custom jeweler, and crafts shops. Dining options, including a sub shop, a T.G.I. Friday's, and an outlet for Amy's—Austin's local favorite ice cream—tend to be on the casual side, but there's also a good local steakhouse, Dan McKlusky's. 10000 Research Blvd. (Hwy. 183 and Loop 360). © 512/338-4437. www.shop simon.com.

Barton Creek Square   Set on a bluff with a view of downtown, Barton Creek tends to be frequented by upscale West-Siders; the wide-ranging collection of more than 150 shops is anchored by Dillard's, Foley's, Sears, and JCPenney. One of the newer malls in Austin, it's refined and low-key, but the presence of Frederick's of Hollywood and Victoria's Secret lingerie boutiques makes one wonder if the daytime soaps might not be onto something about the bored rich. 2901 S. Capital of Texas Hwy. © 512/327-7040. www.bartoncreeksquare.com.

The Gateway Complex   Comprising three not-so-distinct shopping areas, the Gateway Courtyard, the Gateway Market, and Gateway Square, this large, open complex includes everything from a handmade paper store and an audiobook store to national chains such as Blockbuster Music, REI, Old Navy, and CompUSA. There are also branches of Austin-based stores, including Run-Tex and Whole Foods Market, discussed individually in this chapter. Hwy. 183 and Capital of Texas Hwy. © 512/418-1600.

Highland Mall   Austin's first mall, built in the 1970s, is still one of the city's most popular places to shop. It's located at the south end of the hotel zone near the old airport, just minutes north of downtown on I-35. Reasonably priced casual-clothing stores like Gap and Express vie with high-end shops such as Ann Taylor. Dillard's (two of 'em!), Foley's, and JCPenney department stores coexist with specialty stores like Papyrus and the Warner Bros. Studio Store. The tonier Lincoln Plaza shops are just to the south, on I-35. The food court is impressive. 6001 Airport Blvd. © 512/454-9656. www.highlandmall.com.

Lakeline Mall   Austin's newest shopping Mecca, in an upscale far northwest location, is notable for its attention-grabbing design, featuring lots of colorful reliefs and murals of the city. The shops, including Foley's, Dillard's, Mervyn's, Sears, and JCPenney, are not nearly so unusual, but there are some interesting smaller shops, from Dollar Tree, where everything costs a buck, to The Stockpot, with state-of-the art cookware. 11200 Lakeline Mall Dr., Cedar Park. © 512/257-SHOP. www.lakelinemall.com.

MARKETS

Austin Country Flea Market   Every Saturday and Sunday year-round, more than 550 covered spaces are filled with merchants selling all the usual flea market goods and then some—new and used clothing, fresh herbs and produce, electronics, antiques. This is the largest flea market in central Texas, covering more than 130 paved acres. There's live music every weekend—generally a spirited Latino band—to step up the shopping pace. 9500 Hwy. 290 east (4 miles east of I-35). © 512/928-2795 or 512/928-4711.

Renaissance Market   Flash back or be introduced to tie-dye days at this hippie-ish crafts market, where vendors are licensed by the city of Austin (read: no commercial schlock). Billed as the only continuously operated, open-air crafts market in the United States, it's theoretically open daily 8am to 10pm, but most of the merchants turn up only on the weekends. You'll find everything from silver jewelry and hand-carved flutes to batik T-shirts. Many of the artisans come in from small towns in the nearby Hill Country. West 23rd St. and Guadalupe St. (the Drag). ✆ 512/397-1468.

MUSIC

Sound Exchange   Come to the Sound Exchange for hard-to-find older music, imports, and releases by local bands, especially in the rock-and-roll and punk-rock genres. You can get some pretty good bargains in vinyl, tapes, and CDs here, and browse obscure music magazines to your heart's content. The walls are plastered with posters announcing upcoming Austin shows. 2100A Guadalupe St. (the Drag). ✆ 512/476-8742. www.soundexchangeaustin.com.

Waterloo Records and Video   Carrying a huge selection of sounds, Waterloo is always the first in town to get the new releases. If they don't have something on hand, they'll order it for you promptly. The store offers preview listening, compilation tapes of Austin groups, and tickets to all major-label shows around town. It also hosts frequent in-store promotional performances by both local and mid-sized national bands. There's a video annex just west of the record store (✆ 512/474-2525) and, for purists, a vinyl section. 600A N. Lamar Blvd. ✆ 512/474-2500. www.waterloorecords.com.

OUTDOOR GEAR

See also **Run-Tex,** listed under "Fashions," above.

The Whole Earth Provisions Co.   Austin's large population of outdoor enthusiasts flocks to this store to be outfitted in the latest gear and earth-friendly fashions. If you wouldn't think of hiking without a two-way radio or a Magellan positioning navigator, you can find them here. The Austin-based chain also carries gifts, housewares, educational toys, and travel books. There are additional locations at 1014 N. Lamar Blvd. (✆ 512/476-1414) and Westgate Shopping Center, 4477 S. Lamar (✆ 512/899-0992). 2410 San Antonio St. ✆ 512/478-1577. www.wholeearthprovision.com.

TOYS

Hog Wild *(Kids*   Always regretted throwing out that Howdy Doody lunch box? You can get it back—for a few more bucks, of course—at this nostalgia-inducing little toy shop on the edge of Hyde Park. Photos of celebrity customers such as Quentin Tarantino and Mira Sorvino hang on the wall. 100A E. North Loop Blvd. ✆ 512/467-9453. www.gohogwild.com.

Terra Toys *(Kids*   Steiff teddy bears, the wooden Playmobil world, and other high-quality imported toys are among the kiddie delights at Terra, just south of the river. The store also carries a variety of miniatures, train sets, books, and kites. For unique children's apparel, try the owners' other place, **Dragonsnaps,** 1700 S. Congress (✆ 512/445-4497), just down the block. 1708 S. Congress Ave. ✆ 800/247-TOYS or 512/445-4489. www.terratoys.com.

Toy Joy *(Kids*   The name says it all; the only question is whether kids or grown-ups will have more Toy Joy here. Ambi and Sailor Moon are among the appealing children's lines sold in the large back room. Out front, things like lava lamps, yo-yos, and cartoon character watches keep both GenXers and boomers fasci-nated. Amazingly, it's open until midnight on Friday and Saturday. 2900 Guadalupe St. ℂ 512/320-0090.

WESTERN STORES

Allen's Boots   Name notwithstanding, Allen's sells a lot more than footwear. Come here too for hats, belts, jewelry, and other boot scootin' accouterments (bring the young 'uns too). This store, in now trendy SoCo, has been around since 1970. Its staying power through the area's sleazy years is a testament to its quality and fair prices. 1522 S. Congress St. ℂ 512/447-1413.

Capitol Saddlery   The custom-made boots of this classic three-level Western store near the capitol were immortalized in a song by Jerry Jeff Walker. Run by the same family for 7 decades, this place is a bit chaotic, but it's worth poking around to see the hand-tooled saddles, belts, tack, and altogether functional cowboy gear. 1614 Lavaca St. ℂ 512/478-9309.

Sheplers   Adjacent to Highland Mall, the huge Austin branch of this chain of Western-wear department stores has everything the well-dressed urban cowboy or cowgirl might require. If you're already back home and get a sudden urge for a concho belt or bolo tie, the mail-order and online business can see you through any cow-fashion crisis. 6001 Middle Fiskville Rd. ℂ 512/454-3000 or 800/835-4004 (mail order). www.sheplers.com.

WINE & BEER

See also **Central Market** in "Food," above.

Grape Vine Market   This warehouse-size wine store, with an expert staff, huge selection of bottles at good prices, and large menu of wine tastings and classes is yet another sign that Austin is coming of age. If you're seeking a unique wine gift, this is definitely the place to come. There's a good selection of brews and spirits here, too. 7938 Great Northern Blvd. ℂ 512/323-5900. www.grapevine market.com.

Whip In Convenience Store *(Finds*   Like the name says, it's a convenience store, and like the address says, it's just off the freeway. So don't expect atmos-phere. Do expect to find any obscure beer you're looking for, though, be it a lager or stout brewed anywhere from the Hill Country to New Delhi. At a con-servative estimate, the cooler is filled with almost 400 different types of brews at any given time—even more come Oktoberfest or other special beer-producing seasons. Wines also make a strong showing here (the staff is happy to track down obscure bottles for you), and there are two humidors for imported cigars. 1950 S. I-35, Woodland Avenue exit on southbound service road. ℂ 512/442-5337.

Wiggy's   If liquor and tobacco are among your vices, Wiggy's can help you indulge in high style. In addition to its extensive selection of wines (more than 1,500) and single-malt scotches, this friendly West End store also carries a huge array of imported smokes, including humidified cigars. Prices are reasonable and the staff is very knowledgeable. 1130 W. Sixth St. ℂ 512/474-WINE.

16

Austin After Dark

It's hard to imagine an itch for entertainment, high or low, that Austin couldn't scratch. The city's live music scene rivals those of Seattle and Nashville, and the performing arts run the gamut from classic lyric opera to high-tech modern dance. Ironically, the source of much of the city's high culture is literally crude: When an oil well on land belonging to the University of Texas system blew in a gusher in 1923, future money for the arts was all but assured.

The best sources for what's on around town are the *Austin Chronicle* and *XLent,* the entertainment supplement of the *Austin-American Statesman;* both are free and available in hundreds of outlets every Thursday.

For a quick take on the local club action, call the **KLBJ** hot line at C 512/832-4094.

The **Austin Circle of Theaters Hot Line** (C **512/416-5700,** ext. 1603; www.acotonline.org) can tell you what's on the boards each week. If you want to know who's kicking around, phone **Danceline** (C **512/416-5700,** ext. 3262).

The University of Texas is the locus for many of the city's performing arts

events. You can reach UTTM, its **Ticketmaster** outlet, at www.ticketmaster.com or C **512/477-6060;** there are also outlets in most HEB grocery stores. For other major venues, call C **512/494-1800.** Concerts at La Zona Rosa, the Backyard, and Austin Music Hall, and shows at the Paramount Theatre can be booked through **Star Tickets** (C **512/469-SHOW** or 888/597-STAR; www.startickets.com/Austin), with outlets in most Albertson's grocery stores.

The **Austix Box Office,** 3423 Guadalupe (C **512/454-8497** or 512/416-5700 ext. 1603; www.austix.com), handles phone charges for many of the smaller theaters in Austin, as well as half-price ticket sales (C **512/416-5700,** ext. 1602). Call for a recorded listing of what's currently being discounted, then pick up tickets at the Austix Box Office or at the **Austin Visitors Center,** 201 E. Second St., from Wednesday through Saturday from noon to 6pm. Half-price tickets are also on sale at Bookpeople, 603 N. Lamar Blvd. (C **512/472-5050**), on Thursday from 4 to 7pm.

FREE ENTERTAINMENT

Starting in late April or early May, the city sponsors 10 weeks of free **Wednesday night concerts** at Waterloo Park, which range from rock and reggae to Latin and country-and-western, as well as **Sunday concerts** at dusk at Wooldridge Park, 9th and Guadalupe, featuring the Austin Symphony Orchestra. Call C **512/442-2263** for current schedules of these two series and of the free **Zilker Park Jazz Festival** in September. Every other Wednesday night from June through August, **Blues on the Green** is held at Zilker Park Rock Island, 2100 Barton Springs Rd. Contact sponsor KGSR (C **512/390-KGSR;**

But There Are No Limits on the Entertainment

PBS's longest-running television program (it first aired in 1975), **Austin City Limits** has showcased such major talent as Lyle Lovett, Willie Nelson, Garth Brooks, Mary Chapin Carpenter, the Dixie Chicks, and Phish. Originally pure country, it has evolved to embrace blues, zydeco, Cajun, Tejano—you name it. The show is taped live from August through February at the KLRU-TV studio, 2504B Whitis St. (near Dean Keeton, 1 block in from Guadalupe), but the schedule is very fluid, so you have to be vigilant to nab the free tickets, which are distributed on a first-come, first-served basis on the day of the taping. Log on to **www.pbs.org/klru/austin** and click on "FAQ" for details of how to get tickets, or phone the show's hot line at ℂ **512/475-9077.**

You don't have to plan in advance to get a free tour of the recording studio, where you can watch an interesting video clip of the show's highlights, stroll through the control room, and get up on the studio stage and play air guitar. Tours are offered at the KLRU studio at 10:30am every Friday except holidays (call ℂ **512/471-4811** to verify the schedule around holidays).

You do, however, have to plan ahead if you want to attend the **Austin City Limits Music Festival,** which debuted in late September 2002; performers at this hugely successful premiere event included Emmylou Harris, Los Lobos, Shawn Colvin, Jimmie Vaughan, and Patty Griffin. For information on future festivals, log on to **www.aclfestival. com** or call **512/478-7211;** for tickets, call ℂ **888/597-7827.**

www.kgsr.com) for information. Some 75,000 people turn out to cheer the 1812 Overture and the fireworks at the Austin Symphony's **Fourth of July Concert** at the northeast triangle of Zilker Park (ℂ **512/476-6064;** www.austin symphony.org).

From mid-July through late August, the **Beverly F. Sheffield Zilker Hillside Theater,** across from Barton Springs Pool, hosts a summer musical (Zilker Theater Productions, ℂ **512/479-9491;** www.zilker.org). Started in the late 1950s, this is the longest-running series of its type in the United States. The summer **Austin Shakespeare Festival** is often held at the theater, too; for up-to-date information, call ℂ **512/454-BARD** or log on to www.austinshakespeare.org. More than 5,000 people can perch on the theater's grassy knoll to watch performances. Seating is first-come, first-served; bring your own blanket or lawn chairs.

1 The Performing Arts

Austin has its own symphony, theater, ballet, lyric opera, and modern dance companies, but it also draws major international talent to town. Much of the action, local and imported, goes on at the University of Texas's Performing Arts Center, but some terrific outdoor venues take advantage of the city's abundant greenery and mild weather.

OPERA & CLASSICAL MUSIC

In addition to putting on performances and sponsoring high caliber visiting artists, the **Austin Chamber Music Center,** 4930 Burnet Rd., Suite 203 (© 512/454-7562 or 512/454-0026; www.austinchambermusic.org), holds an annual summer festival. Its popular Intimate Concert series is held at elegant private homes. Austin's first professional opera company, founded in 1985, **Austin Lyric Opera,** 901 Barton Springs Rd. (© **800/31-OPERA** or 512/472-5992 [box office]; www.austinlyricopera.org), currently presents three productions a year at the Bass Concert Hall. Major national and international artists hit the high notes in such operas as *La Traviata* and *Dead Man Walking* in the 2002–03 season.

Austin Symphony   A resident in Austin since 1911, the symphony performs most of its classical works at Bass Concert Hall, although a new hall, which will also host Ballet Austin and the Austin Lyric Opera, is slated for completion in 2004. The informal Pops shows (such as the Kingston Trio in 2003) play to a picnic table–seated crowd at the Palmer Events Center. In addition, in June and July at Symphony Square, every Wednesday from 9:30am until about 11:30am, kids can try out various orchestral instruments in the symphony's version of a petting zoo. Symphony Square is a complex comprising an outdoor amphitheater and four historic structures dating from 1871 to 1877. Narrow Waller Creek runs between the seats and the stage of the amphitheater. 1101 Red River St. © 888/4-MAESTRO or 512/476-6064. www.austinsymphony.org. Tickets $19–$35 classical, $20 and $35 pops. Box office Mon–Fri 9am–5pm; concert days noon–5pm.

THEATER

You never know what you'll see at the intimate **Hyde Park Theatre,** 511 W. 43rd St. (© **512/479-PLAY** [box office] or 512/479-7530; www.frontera.org), but you can count on it to be intellectually engaging. and focused on Austin writers, actors, and designers. The annual 5-week-long FronteraFest, the largest fringe theater/performance art festival in the Southwest, showcases local and national talent of all kinds. There's a thriving theater department at St. Edward's University, where the **Mary Moody Northen Theatre,** 3001 S. Congress Ave. (© **512/448-8484** [box office] or 512/448-8483; www.stedwards.edu/hum/thtr/mmnt.html), gets support for its performances from a variety of professional directors and guest actors. The 2002–2003 season included Arthur Miller's drama *All My Sons* and the farcical *Nunsense*. It's tough to typecast **One World Theater,** 7701 Bee Cave Rd. (© **512/330-9500;** www.oneworld theatre.org), where performers might range from Cowboy Junkies to the American Ballet Theater, but you couldn't find a more appealing venue for them than this intimate (300-seat) Tuscan castle–style theater in countrified West Austin. The **State Theater Company,** 719 Congress Ave. (© **512/472-5143** [box office] or 512/472-7134; www.austintheatrealliance.org), which performs at the beautiful old theater for which it is named, is Austin's most professional troupe; their recent repertoire ran the gamut from *The Little Prince: The Musical,* to *Proof.* The Vortex theater, a converted warehouse with an outdoor courtyard and cafe, complements the avant-garde program of the **Vortex Repertory Company,** 2307 Manor Rd. (© **512/478-LAVA;** www.jollylox.com/vortex), just east of UT and I-35. You can tell by the titles alone—*Ratgirl's Holy Rockin' Christmas,* say, or *Conversations at a Bathhouse Can Be Tricky*—that you're way, way off-Broadway. Austin's oldest theater, incorporated in 1933, the **Zachary**

Kids **A Venerable Venue**

The Marx Brothers, Sarah Bernhardt, Helen Hayes, and Katharine Hepburn all entertained at the **Paramount Theatre**, 713 Congress Ave. (© **512/ 472-5470** [box office] or 512/472-5411; www.austintheateralliance.org), a former vaudeville house, which opened as the Majestic Theatre in 1915 and functioned as a movie palace for 50 years. Restored to its original opulence at the end of the 20th century, the Paramount now hosts Broadway shows, visiting celebrity performers, local theatrical productions, and, in the summer, old-time films.

Scott Theatre Center (© **512/476-0541** [box office] or 512/476-0594; www.zachscott.com), makes use of two adjacent venues at the edge of Zilker Park: the three-sided thrust John E. Whisenhut Arena at 1510 Toomey Rd., and the theater-in-the-round Kleberg at 1421 W. Riverside Dr. Its rich and varied offerings include a Mainstage series and an Off-Broadway series, supplemented by holiday productions.

DANCE

The two-dozen professional dancers of **Ballet Austin,** 3004 Guadalupe St. (© **512/476-2163** [box office] or 512/476-9051; www.balletaustin.org), leap and bound in such classics as *The Nutcracker* and *Giselle,* or more modern pieces like *Touch,* a non-narrative, multimedia work choreographed by the company's acclaimed long-time director Stephen Mills. When in town, the troupe performs at Bass Concert Hall or, for children's shows, the Paramount Theatre. An aptly high-tech ensemble for plugged-in Austin, **Sharir + Bustamante Dance Works,** 3724 Jefferson St., Suite 201 (© **512/458-8158** or 512/477-6060 [box office]), stretches the boundaries of dance toward virtual reality by including video projections and computer-generated images in its choreography. Most of the Austin performances are held at UT's Performing Arts Center, but there are also site-specific environmental pieces.

2 The Club & Music Scene

The appearance of country-and-western "outlaw" Willie Nelson at the Armadillo World Headquarters in 1972 united hippies and rednecks in a common musical cause, and is often credited with the birth of the live-music scene on Austin's Sixth Street. The city has since become an incubator for a wonderfully vital, crossbred alternative sound that mixes rock, country, folk, and blues. Although the Armadillo is defunct and Sixth Street is long past its creative prime—with some notable exceptions, it caters pretty much to a rowdy college crowd—live music in Austin is very much alive, just more geographically diffuse. There's always something happening downtown in the warehouse district and on the stretch of Red River between Sixth and Tenth streets. Some venues, like the Continental Club, have long been off the beaten path; others, like the Backyard, more recently expanded the boundaries of Austin's musical terrain. Poke around; you can never tell which dive might turn up the latest talent (Janis Joplin, Stevie Ray Vaughan, and Jimmie Dale Gilmore all played local gigs). If you're here during S×SW (see box, below), you'll see the town turn into one huge, music-mad party.

Note: Categories of clubs in a city known for crossover are often very rough approximations; those that completely defy typecasting are dubbed "eclectic." Cover charges range from $5 to $15 for well-liked local bands. Note, too, that in addition to the clubs detailed below, several of the restaurants discussed in chapter 13, including **Threadgill's** and **Manuel's,** offer live music regularly.

FOLK & COUNTRY

Broken Spoke   This is the genuine item, a Western honky-tonk dating from 1964 with a wood-plank floor and a cowboy-hatted, two-steppin' crowd. Still, it's in Austin, so don't be surprised if the band wears Hawaiian shirts, or if tongues are firmly in cheek for some of the songs. Photos of Hank Williams, Tex Ritter, and other country greats line the walls of the club's "museum." You can eat in a large, open room out front (the chicken-fried steak can't be beat), or bring your long necks back to a table overlooking the dance floor. 3201 S. Lamar Blvd. ✆ 512/442-6189. www.lone-star.net/bspoke. Cover $5–$15.

Continental Club ✫   Although it also showcases rock, rockabilly, and new-wave sounds, the Continental Club holds on to its traditional country roots by celebrating events such as Hank Williams's birthday. A small, smoky club with high stools and a pool table in the back room, this is a not-to-be-missed Austin classic. It's considered by many to have the best happy hour music in town, and the folksy Tuesday blues with Toni Price is a real crowd pleaser. 1315 S. Congress Ave. ✆ 512/441-2444. www.continentalclub.com. Cover $5–$20.

Jovita's   It's a winning recipe: Jovita's is part Mexican restaurant, part night-club, part Mexican-American cultural center—and all South Austin landmark.

⟲ Label It Successful—Austin's S×SW

Started in 1987 as a way to showcase unsigned Texas bands, S×SW soon became *the* place for fledgling musicians from around the world to come to schmooze music industry bigwigs. In the mid-1990s, film and interactive (high-tech and Internet) components were added to the event, and now they're almost as important as the original musical showcases. A list of festival participants could easily be mistaken for a *Rolling Stone* or *People* magazine table of contents.

Even if you're not looking to make it in the music, film, or Internet industries, this is still the hottest conference ticket around. Programs might include as many as 60 panels and workshops and 900 musical appearances at more than 40 venues around town. Prices for 2003 range from $150, if you register early for the film or interactive aspects alone, to $775 for the walkup Platinum rate, which affords access to all conference and music events.

The **South by Southwest (S×SW) Music and Media Conference & Festival** (its full name) is held during UT's spring break, usually the third week of March. For current schedules and speakers/performers, check the website at **www.sxsw.com** or call ✆ 512/467-7979.

How can you beat a place that's got terrific flautas and enchiladas, tasty margaritas, and some of the best sounds in town, ranging from salsa to country? 1617 S. First St. ℂ 512/447-7825. Cover $5–$10.

JAZZ & BLUES

Antone's ☆ Although Willie Nelson and crossover country-and-western bands like the Austin Lounge Lizards have been known to turn up at Clifford Antone's place, the club owner's name has always been synonymous with the blues. Stevie Ray Vaughan used to be a regular, and when major blues artists like Buddy Guy, Etta James, or Edgar Winter venture down this way, you can be sure they'll either be playing Antone's or stopping by for a surprise set. The owner's incarceration (for selling marijuana) and the club's relocation to the warehouse district hasn't changed anything—this is still where you come to hear the bad, sad songs. 213 W. Fifth St. ℂ 512/474-5314. www.antones.net. Cover $8–$35 (depending on performer).

Elephant Room Stars on location in Austin mingle with T-shirted students and well-dressed older aficionados at this intimate downtown venue, as dark and smoky as a jazz bar should be. The focus is on contemporary and traditional jazz, although the bill branches out to rock on occasion. 315 Congress Ave. ℂ 512/473-2279. www.arthiveonline.com/elephant. Cover $5–$15.

ROCK

Emo's Austin's last word in alternative music, Emo's draws acts of all sizes and flavors, from Johnny Cash to Green Day. It primarily attracts college kids, but you won't really feel out of place at any age. The front room holds the bar, pool tables, and pinball machines. You'll have to cross the outside patio to reach the back room where the bands play. 603 Red River St. ℂ 512/477-EMOS. www.emosaustin. com. Cover $8–$15.

Maggie Mae's Good rock cover bands, a great selection of beers, and plenty of space set Maggie Mae's apart from the collegiate-crowded clubs lining Sixth Street. Five separate bars make ordering easy, and the live music plays upstairs and down. The outside courtyard is generally reserved for blues. 512 Trinity St. ℂ 512/478-8541. Cover $3–$10.

SINGER/SONGWRITER

Cactus Cafe ☆ A small, dark cavern with great acoustics and a fully stocked bar, UT's Cactus Cafe is singer/songwriter heaven, a place where dramatic stage antics take a back seat to engaged showmanship. The crowd's attentive listening attracts talented solo artists like Alison Krauss, Jimmy LaFave, and Austin native Shawn Colvin, along with well-known acoustic combos. The adjacent **Texas Union Ballroom** (ℂ 512/475-6645) draws larger crowds with big names like Billy Bragg. Texas Union, University of Texas campus (24th and Guadalupe). ℂ 512/475-6515. www.utexas.edu/student/txunion/ae/cactus. Cover $10–$35.

Ego's Located in the parking garage of an apartment building, this '60s clubhouse is dark, smoky, seedy, and loads of fun. Locals throng here for the strong drinks and live nightly music, from piano to honky-tonk country. A couple of run-down pool tables and video games add to the funky charm. You can shoot pool for free after 10pm nightly. 510 S. Congress Ave. ℂ 512/474-7091. Cover $3–$8.

Saxon Pub You'll recognize the Saxon Pub by the giant knight in shining armor in the parking lot, an old friend among lots of new faces along South

---

Kids Girl Power

The Austin sound may have long been dominated by names like Willie, Stevie Ray, and Jerry Jeff (Janis was a too-brief blip on the all-male radar screen), but that's changing. Austin is now becoming known as the home of such prominent female performers as Sara Hickman, Shawn Colvin, and the Dixie Chicks.

Lamar Boulevard. This is a long-standing home to South Austin's large community of singer/songwriters. Don't be put off by the medieval kitsch outside; inside, the atmosphere is comfortable and no-nonsense. 1320 S. Lamar Blvd. © 512/448-2552. www.thesaxonpub.com. Cover $5–$15.

Speakeasy   The walk down a dark alley in the warehouse district to reach this multilevel club is all part of the 1920s Prohibition theme, which, mercifully, is not taken to an obnoxious extreme. Lots of dark wood and red velvet drapes help create a swanky atmosphere; walk up two flights of narrow stairs to enjoy a drink or dance on the romantic Evergreen terrace, which overlooks downtown. The booze is not bootleg, the music (mostly of the singer/songwriter type) is fine, and there's no prohibition on good times (in fact, in 2002, Austin Chronicle readers voted this "Best Place to Party Like It's 2000 . . . And You Still Have a Job"). 412 Congress Ave. © 512/476-8017. www.speakeasyaustin.com. Cover $3–$10.

ECLECTIC

The Backyard ⭐   A terrific sound system and a casual country atmosphere have helped make this one of Austin's hottest venues, although it rarely hosts local bands any more. Since it opened in the early 1990s, the Allman Brothers, Joan Baez, The Band, Elvis Costello, Chris Isaak, k.d. lang, Lyle Lovett, Bonnie Raitt, and Jethro Tull have all played the terraced outdoor amphitheater, which is shaded by ancient live oaks. Come early for dinner; the Waterloo Ice House serves a Texas menu, including barbecue from The Iron Works (see chapter 13). The food's all good and reasonably priced. Hwy. 71 West at R.R. 620, Bee Cave. © 512/263-4146 or 512/469-SHOW for tickets. www.thebackyard.net. Tickets $6–$8 local acts, $20–$45 national acts.

Carousel Lounge   In spite of (or maybe because of) its out-of-the-way location and bizarre circus theme—complete with elephant and lion-tamer murals and an actual carousel behind the bar—the Carousel Lounge is a highly popular local watering hole. You never know what will turn up on stage; this place has hosted everything from smaller musical acts to belly dancers. 1110 E. 52nd St. © 512/452-6790. Cover no more than $5.

Cedar Street Courtyard   Join the martini-and-cigar crowd—which has included the likes of Denzel Washington and Bob Dylan—in this sophisticated courtyard, where the nightly live sounds range from jazz to tango. Single gals take note: This place got the Austin Chronicle's nod as the "Best Place to Watch Too Many Men Compete for Too Few Women." 208 W. Fourth St. © 512/495-9669. www.cedarstreetcourtyard.com. Cover $5–$15.

La Zona Rosa ⭐⭐   Another Austin classic, LZR has departed from its funky roots a bit to go upmarket, featuring bigger names and bigger covers than in the past. But the venue has remained the same—a renovated garage brightly painted with monsters and filled with kitschy memorabilia—and this is still a fun place to listen to good bands, from Greg Allman and Friends to Los Lobos. 612 W. Fourth St. ✆ 512/263-4146. www.lazonarosa.com. Tickets $6–$8 local acts, $20–$45 national acts.

Stubb's Bar-B-Q   Within the rough limestone walls of a renovated historic building you'll find great barbecue and country Texas fare and three friendly bars—plus terrific music, ranging from singer/songwriter solos to hip-hop open mics to all-out country jams. Out back, the Waller Amphitheater hosts some of the bigger acts. See also chapter 13 for Stubb's Sunday gospel brunches. 801 Red River St. ✆ 512/480-8341. www.stubbsaustin.com. Cover $6–$25.

COMEDY CLUBS

Capitol City Comedy   Top ranked on the stand-up circuit, Cap City books nationally recognized comedians like Dave Chapell and Tommy Chong (late of Cheech and . . .). The cream of the crop turn up on Friday and Saturday, of course, but you'll find plenty to laugh at (including lower cover charges) the rest of the week. 8120 Research Blvd., Suite 100. ✆ 512/467-2333. www.hotcomedy.com/capcity. htm. Tickets $9 Sun, Wed–Thurs, $2 Mon, $4.50 Tues, $12 Fri–Sat. Performances Tues–Thurs and Sun 8pm; Fri–Sat 8 and 10:30pm.

Esther's Follies   You might miss a couple of the punch lines if you're not in on the latest twists and turns of local politics, but the no-holds-barred Esther's Follies doesn't spare Washington, either. It's very satirical, very irreverent, very Austin. 525 E. Sixth St. ✆ 512/320-0553. www.esthersfollies.com. Tickets $18 Thurs–Sat; $2 off for students. Performances Thurs 8pm; Fri–Sat 8 and 10pm.

Velveeta Room   For one-stop comedy consumption, go straight from Esther's to the Velveeta Room next door, a deliberately cheesy club serving more generic stand-up, local and national as well as, on Thursday night, an open mic. 525 E. Sixth St. ✆ 512/469-9116. www.thevelveetaroom.com. Tickets $5–$10. Thurs 9:30pm open mic night; performances Fri–Sat 9:30pm and 11pm.

3 The Bar Scene

BREWPUBS

Bitter End B-Side Lounge & Tap Room   Adjoining the Bitter End Bistro & Brewery, this intimate gathering spot serves up (canned) swing, jazz, and blues along with its excellent home brews. Additional yuppie draws are a cask-conditioned beer tap and a separate cigar room. 311 Colorado St. ✆ 512/478-5890.

Copper Tank Brewing Company   Within the confines of these thick limestone walls, sports fans catch games on one of the two large screens, couples dine from an eclectic menu, and singles hopefully scan the crowd, while beer aficionados of all stripes savor the light Whitetail Ale or the Big Dog Stout. A small courtyard provides a haven from the madding crowd. 504 Trinity St. ✆ 512/478-8444.

A BRITISH PUB

Dog & Duck Pub   I have it on the authority of British friends that this is the real deal, a comfy 'local' (British pub) with a relaxing atmosphere. You'll be touring all the British Isles with the mix of darts, Irish jams, bagpipes, and hearty brews. The bangers and mash taste authentic, too—not that that's necessarily a good thing. 406 W. 17th St. ✆ 512/479-0598.

GAY BARS

Oilcan Harry's Its name notwithstanding, this slick warehouse district bar attracts a clean-cut, upscale, mostly male crowd. Consistently voted Austin's Best Gay Club by readers of the *Austin Chronicle,* this is the place to go if you're looking for a buttoned-down, Brooks Brothers kind of guy. There's dancing, but not with the same frenzy as at many of the other clubs. 211 W. Fourth St. ℭ **512/320-8823.** www.oilcanharrys.com.

Rainbow Cattle Co. This is Austin's prime gay country-western dance hall. It's about 75% male, but also attracts a fair share of lesbian two-steppers, especially on Thursday—which is Ladies Night. 305 W. 5th St. ℭ **512/472-5288.** www. rainbowcattleco.com.

AN HISTORIC BAR

Scholz Garten ℱ Since 1866, when councilman August Scholz first opened his tavern near the state capitol, every Texas governor has visited it at least once (and many quite a few more times). In recent years, Texas's oldest operating biergarten was sold to the owners of the popular Green Mesquite BBQ, giving it new life. The extensive menu now combines barbecue favorites with traditional bratwurst and sauerkraut; a state-of-the-art sound system cranks out the polka tunes; and patio tables as well as a few strategically placed TV sets help Longhorn fans cheer on their team—a Scholz's tradition in and of itself. All in all, a great place to drink in some Austin history. 1607 San Jacinto Blvd. ℭ **512/474-1958.** www. scholzgarten.com.

> **Impressions**
>
> *There is a very remarkable number of drinking and gambling shops [in Austin], but not one book store.*
>
> —Frederick Law Olmsted, *A Journey Through Texas* (1853)

LOCAL FAVORITES

Cedar Door Think "Cheers" with a redwood deck in downtown Austin. In spite of the fact that it keeps changing location—it's moved four times in its 26-year history—the Cedar Door remains Austin's favorite neighborhood bar, drawing a group of potluck regulars ranging from hippies to journalists and politicos. The beer's cold, the drinks are strong, and to lots of folks (no doubt those whose families moved a lot when they were kids), it feels like home. 201 Brazos. ℭ **512/473-3712.** www.cedardooraustin.com.

Club de Ville This is one of the few bars in the area where you can actually have a conversation without shouting. Settle in on one of the couches inside—the low red light is both atmospheric and flattering—or lounge under the stars, where a natural limestone cliff creates a private walled patio. The cliff is also a great acoustical barrier for the bands that occasionally play here. 900 Red River. ℭ **512/457-0900.**

A PIANO BAR

The Driskill Sink into one of the plush chairs arrayed around a grand piano and enjoy everything from blues to show tunes in the upper-lobby bar of this newly opulent historic hotel. A pianist accompanies the happy-hour

Late-Night Bites

If it's 3am and you have a hankering for a huge stack of pancakes to soak up that last Shiner you probably shouldn't have downed, Austin has you covered. Part Texas roadhouse, part all-night diner, Austin's cafes offer extra-late hours, funky atmosphere, and large quantities of hippie food. To call them cafes is a bit misleading—there's nothing remotely resembling Gallic, or even Seattle, chic here—but it's as good a term as any for these Austin originals.

One of the earliest on the scene and still hugely popular is **Kerbey Lane,** 3704 Kerbey Lane (✆ **512/451-1436**). Sunday mornings, locals spill out on the porch of the comfortable old house, waiting for a table so they can order the signature "pancakes as big as your head." Musicians finishing up late-night gigs at the Continental Club usually head over to the **Magnolia Cafe South,** 1920 S. Congress Ave. (✆ **512/445-0000**); on nice nights, enjoy the Love Veggies sautéed in garlic butter or the Deep Eddy burrito on an outdoor deck. Both cafes are open 24 hours daily. Kerbey Lane has two other locations, and Magnolia Cafe has one clone, but the originals are far more interesting.

hors d'oeuvres (nightly 5–7pm), but the ivory thumping doesn't get going in earnest until 9pm on Tuesday through Saturday. 604 Brazos St. ✆ 512/474-5911. www.driskillgrill.com/bar.html.

A WINE AND TAPAS BAR

Málaga   Come to this sleek, sophisticated spot to sip fine wines at good prices—50 selections by the glass—and nibble Spanish appetizers (the swordfish bites are especially tasty). Only downside: This place is not for the smoke-sensitive. 208 W. 4th St. ✆ 512/236-8020.

4 Films

Not surprisingly, you can see more foreign films in Austin than anywhere else in the state. Nearly every cinema in town devotes at least one screen to something off Hollywood's beaten track. In the university area, the largest concentration of art films can be found at the **Dobie Theatre,** 2021 Guadalupe St., on the Drag (✆ **512/472-FILM**), and at the two venues of the **Texas Union Film Series,** UT campus, Texas Union Building and Hogg Auditorium (✆ **512/475-6656**). If you'd like something a little more substantial than popcorn with your flicks, check out the **Alamo Drafthouse,** 409 Colorado St. (✆ **512/476-1320;** www.drafthouse.com), offering all-you-can-eat pizza nights, two-for-one pasta date nights, and theme events like "Hong Kong Sundays" with kung-fu films, Chinese food, and Chinese beer—all at terrifically low prices. If you're around on Friday, don't miss the live film spoofs of Mr. Sinus Theater, The newer northern location, 2700 W. Anderson Lane (✆ **512/785-75150**), does variations on the downtown themes but adds first-run hits to the menu.

Celluloid Clout

Austin has long had an undercover Hollywood presence. During the past two and a half decades, more than 80 films were shot in the city and its vicinity. But you'd be hard pressed to identify Texas's capital in any of them: Because it has such a wide range of landscapes, Austin has filled in for locations as far-flung as Canada and Vietnam.

The city has less of an identity crisis behind the camera. It first earned its credentials as an indie director–friendly place in 1982, when the Coen brothers shot *Blood Simple* here. And when University of Texas graduate Richard Linklater captured some of the loopier members of his alma mater in *Slackers*—adding a word to the national vocabulary in the process—Austin arrived on the *cineaste* scene. Linklater is often spotted around town with Robert Rodriguez, who shot all or part of several of his films (*Alienated, The Faculty,* and the *Spy Kids* series), in Austin, and with Quentin Tarantino, who owns property in town. Mike Judge, of "Beavis and Butthead" and "King of the Hill" fame, lives in Austin, too.

Of the many cinematic events held in town, October's **Austin Film Festival** is among the most interesting. Held in tandem with the Heart of Films Screenwriters Conference, it focuses on movies with great scripts. For current information, contact the Austin Film Festival, 1604 Nueces, Austin, TX 78701 (© **800/310-FEST** or 512/478-4795; fax 512/478-6205; www.austinfilmfest.com). And the come-lately film component of SxSW (see sidebar above) gets larger every year. Panelists have included Linklater and John Sayles, whose film *Lone Star* had its world premiere here.

But the most recent development may be the most exciting yet: In 2000, the old Robert Mueller airport was transformed into Austin Studios, a film/video/multimedia production facility. During its first year of operation, the studio helped generate $41.5 million and 700 jobs for the local economy. Scenes from *Miss Congeniality* and *The Rookie* were among its early projects.

17

Touring the Texas Hill Country

A rising and falling dreamscape of lakes, rivers, springs, and caverns, the Hill Country is one of Texas's prettiest regions—especially in early spring, when wildflowers daub it with every pigment in nature's palette. Dotted with old dance halls, country stores, and quaint Teutonic towns—more than 30,000 Germans emigrated to Texas during the great land-grant years of the Republic—and birthplace to one of the U.S.'s more colorful recent presidents, the region also lays out an appealing tableau of the state's history.

San Antonio lies at the southern edge of the Hill Country, while Austin is the northeastern gateway to the region. The following tour traces a roughly circular route from San Antonio, but it's only 80 miles between the two cities; distances in this area are sufficiently short that you can design excursions based on your point of origin and your particular interests. The highlights are covered here, but those with extra time will find far more to explore. To find out what's blooming and where, phone the **Texas Travel Information Center** (© 800/452-9292) in March, April, or May.

Note: Driving in the Hill Country can be a delight, but the speed limit on some roads is 70 mph. If you want to enjoy the scenery, be prepared to pull over.

1 Boerne ⚊

From downtown San Antonio, it's a straight shot north on I-10 to Boerne (rhymes with "journey"). It's a good base for travelers, as it's near both a big city (just 30 miles from San Antonio) and some very rural areas. A popular health resort in the 1880s, the little (2¼ miles long) town was first settled 30 years earlier by freedom-seeking German intellectuals, including firebrand journalist Ludwig Börne, for whom it was named. A gazebo with a Victorian cupola in the center of the main plaza often hosts concerts by the Boerne Village Band, the oldest continuously operating German band in the world outside Germany (it first tuned up in 1860). A number of the town's 19th-century limestone buildings house small historical museums, boutiques, and restaurants, and old-fashioned lampposts and German street signs add atmosphere. But Boerne's biggest draw is its antiques shops—more than 20 line the "Hauptstrasse," or main street. For a self-guided tour, stop in at the **Greater Boerne Chamber of Commerce**, 1 Main Plaza, Boerne, TX 78006 (© 888/842-8080 or 830/249-8000; www.boerne.org).

SEEING THE SIGHTS

Those who want to spend their time outdoors can explore four distinct ecosystems—grassland, marshland, woodland, and river bottom—via short treks on the **Cibolo Wilderness Trail,** City Park Road, off Hwy. 46 East next

The Texas Hill Country

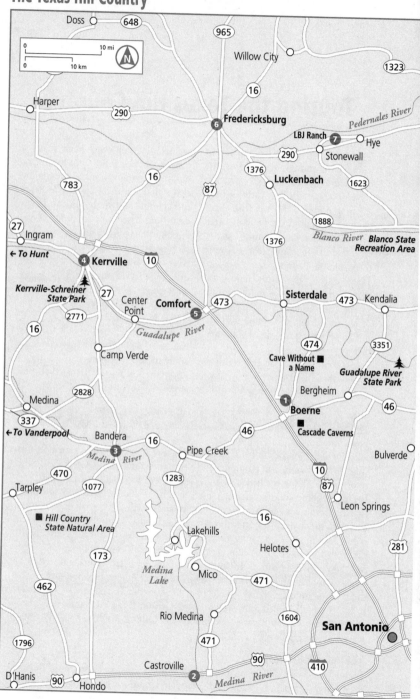

Doss · 648
965
Willow City · 1323
16
Harper · 290
Fredericksburg 6
Pedernales River
LBJ Ranch 7 · Hye
290 · Stonewall
783 · 16 · 1376 · Luckenbach · 1623
87
1888
27 Ingram
← To Hunt
Blanco River · Blanco State Recreation Area
1376
4 Kerrville · 10
Kerrville-Schreiner State Park
27 · Center Point · Comfort 5 · 473 · Sisterdale · 473 · Kendalia
16 · 2771
Guadalupe River
474 · 3351
Camp Verde
Cave Without a Name ■
Guadalupe River State Park
2828
Bergheim
1 · Boerne · 46
Medina · 337
← To Vanderpool
Bandera 3 · 16 · Pipe Creek · Cascade Caverns ■
Medina River
46 · 10
Bulverde
470 · 1077 · 1283 · 87
Tarpley
Hill Country State Natural Area ■ · 16 · Leon Springs
173 · Lakehills · Helotes · 281
Medina Lake · Mico · 471
462
Rio Medina · 1604
San Antonio
1796 · 471
D'Hanis · 90 · Castroville 2 · 90 · 410
Hondo · Medina River

236

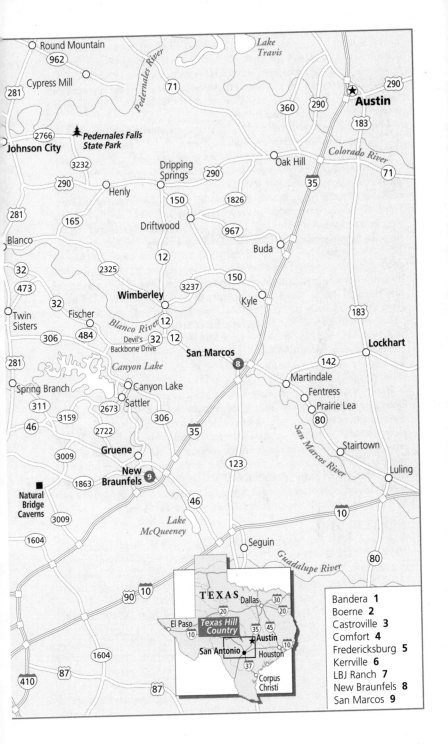

Bandera **1**
Boerne **2**
Castroville **3**
Comfort **4**
Fredericksburg **5**
Kerrville **6**
LBJ Ranch **7**
New Braunfels **8**
San Marcos **9**

to the Kendall County Fair grounds (© **830/249-4616;** www.cibolo.org). A dinosaur trackway traces the route of *Acrocanthosaurus atokensis* and friends, whose fossilized footprints were uncovered when the area was flooded in 1997. If you like your strolls to include sand traps, the top-rated **Tapatio Springs Golf Course,** Johns Road exit off I-10 West (© **800/999-3299** or 830/537-4611; www.tapatio.com), is the place for you.

One of the most popular nearby attractions is **Cascade Caverns** (© **830/ 755-8080**); drive about 3 miles south of Boerne on I-10, take exit 543, and drive 2.7 miles east. This active cave boasts huge chambers, a 90-foot underground waterfall, and comfortable walking trails; guides provide 1-hour interpretive tours every 30 minutes. It's open March 1 until Memorial Day Monday to Friday 10am to 4pm, Saturday and Sunday 9am to 5pm; Memorial Day to Labor Day daily 9am to 6pm; the rest of the year Saturday, Sunday, and holidays 9am to 5pm. Admission is $11 adults, $6.95 children. It's also easy to tour the stalactite- and stalagmite-filled **Cave Without a Name,** 325 Kreutzberg Rd., 12 miles northeast of Boerne (© **830/537-4212;** www.cavewithoutaname. com). A naming contest held when the cavern was discovered in 1939 was won by a little boy who wrote that it was too pretty to name; the $500 he earned put him through college. Open Memorial Day through Labor Day daily 9am to 6pm; off season, daily 10am to 5pm. Admission $9 adults, $5 children.

Rafters and canoeists like **Guadalupe River State Park,** some 13 miles east of Boerne, off Hwy. 46 on P.R. 31 (© **830/438-2656;** www.tpwd.state.tx.us), comprising more than 1,900 acres surrounding a lovely, cypress-edged river. Keep an eye out: You might spot white-tailed deer, coyotes, armadillos, or even a rare golden-cheeked warbler.

If your tastes run to the above-ground and Epicurean, drive 12 miles north of Boerne on FM 1376 to the **Sister Creek Vineyards** (© **830/324-6704;** www. sistercreekvineyards.com), located in a converted century-old cotton gin on the main—actually the only—street in Sisterdale (pop. 50). Traditional French wines are made using traditional French techniques, but the attitude is Texas friendly. Open daily noon to 5pm. Weave down the road afterward to the **Sisterdale General Store** (© **830/324-6767**), opened in 1954 and not changed very much since then. You can still buy a pickled egg to accompany your Coke or Bud at the beautiful old handcrafted bar, made of East Texas pine.

WHERE TO STAY

Now a lovely Victorian-style B&B, **Ye Kendall Inn,** 128 W. Blanco, Boerne, TX 78006 (© **800/364-2138** or 830/249-2138; www.yekendallinn.com), opened as a stagecoach lodge in 1859. The rooms (costing $99–$139 each) and suites ($140–$190 each) are beautifully appointed, but the former have their bathtubs in the middle of the room, and commodes are located behind a screen. If you're traveling with a companion with whom you're not willing to be that intimate, book a suite.

The **Guadalupe River Ranch Resort and Spa,** P.O. Box 877, Boerne, TX 78006 (© **800/460-2005;** www.guadaluperiverranch.com), was owned by actress Olivia de Havilland in the 1930s, and served as an art colony for a time. This gorgeous spread offers abundant activities ranging from river rafting and porch sitting to getting wrapped and polished at the spa. Basic rates run about $299 per night for two, including a room, three meals, and snacks, but specials and spa packages are frequently offered.

WHERE TO DINE

The Limestone Grill, in Ye Kendall Inn (see above), 128 W. Blanco (© **830/ 249-9954**), sets an elegant tone for the steaks, seafood, poultry, pasta, and sandwiches it serves. It's open for lunch and dinner Tuesday to Saturday, brunch only Sunday, and lunch only Monday; entrees are moderate to expensive. The more casual **Bear Moon Bakery,** 401 S. Main St. (© **830/816-BEAR**), is ideal for a hearty breakfast or light lunch. Organic ingredients and locally grown produce enhance the flavor of the inventive soups, salads, sandwiches, and wonderful desserts. It's open Tuesday to Saturday 6am to 5pm, Sunday 8am to 4pm, and is inexpensively prices.

2 Castroville ★★

Castroville, located on a scenic bend of the Medina River, is closer to San Antonio than Boerne—it's just 20 miles from the big city via U.S. 90 West—it has maintained a pristine rural atmosphere. In 1842, Henri Castro, a Portuguese-born Jewish Frenchman (yes, really), received a 1.25-million-acre grant from the Republic of Texas in exchange for his commitment to colonize the land. Second only to Stephen F. Austin in the number of settlers he brought over, Castro recruited most of his 2,134 immigrants from the Rhine Valley, especially from the French province of Alsace. You can still hear Alsatian, an unwritten dialect of German, spoken by some of the older members of town though the language is likely to die out in the area when they do.

SEEING THE SIGHTS

Make your first stop the **Castroville Chamber of Commerce,** 802 London St., P.O. Box 572, Castroville, TX 78009 (© **800/778-6775** or 830/538-3142; www.castroville.com), where you can pick up a walking tour booklet of the town's historical buildings, as well as a map that details the local boutiques and antiques shops (they're not concentrated in a single area).

Almost 100 of the original settlers' unevenly slope-roofed houses remain in Castroville, some still occupied by the builders' descendants. The oldest standing structure, the **First St. Louis Catholic Church,** went up in 1846 on the corner of Angelo and Madrid. Many of the European-style headstones in the **cemetery** at the western edge of town, where Henri Castro's wife, Amelia, is buried, date back to the 1840s.

Get some insight into the town's history at the **Landmark Inn State Historical Park,** 402 E. Florence St., Castroville, TX 78009 (© **830/931-2133**; www.tpwd.state.tx.us/park/landmark/landmark.htm), which also counts a nature trail, an old gristmill, and a stone dam among its attractions.

Tip: Castroville closes down on Monday and Tuesday, and some places are shuttered on Wednesdays and Sundays as well. If you want to find everything open, come on Thursday, Friday, or Saturday.

AN HISTORIC INN

The centerpiece of the State Historical Park, the **Landmark Inn** offers eight simple rooms decorated with early Texas pieces dating up until the 1940s. Prices for a double with a private bathroom are $61; with a shared bathroom, $55. None of the rooms have phones or TVs, but all do have air-conditioning. A continental breakfast is included in the rate. Don't come here for luxurious appointments, but for a uniquely peaceful setting in the woods near the Medina

River. Note that the inn is closed Tuesdays and Wednesdays, so no reservations are accepted for Monday or Tuesday nights.

WHERE TO DINE

Get a delicious taste of the past at **Haby's Alsatian Bakery,** 207 U.S. 90 East (© **830/931-2118**), owned by the Tschirhart family since 1974 and featuring apple fritters, strudels, stollens, breads, and coffeecakes. Open Monday to Saturday 5am to 7pm.

A gourmet surprise in this rural area, **La Normandie Restaurant,** 1302 Fiorella St. (© **830/538-3070** or 800/261-1731), features a classic French menu, including escargot and coq au vin and the delicious house special veal *à la normande.* Strains of songs from Normandy, homeland of one of the proprietor/chefs, float through the pretty, lace-curtained cottage. Open Tuesday buffet lunch, dinner Thursday through Saturday, champagne brunch Sunday.

3 Bandera ★★★

North of Castroville and west of Boerne, Bandera is a slice of life out of the Old West, a town that could easily serve as a John Ford film set. Established as a lumber camp in 1853, this popular guest-ranch center still has the feel of the frontier: Not only are many of its historic buildings intact, but people are as genuinely friendly as any you might imagine from America's small-town past.

WHAT TO SEE & DO

Interested in delving into the town's roots? Pick up a self-guided tour brochure of historic sites—including **St. Stanislaus** (1855), the country's second-oldest Polish church—at the **Bandera County Convention and Visitors Bureau,** 1134 A Main St., Bandera, TX 78003 (© **800/364-3833** or 830/796-3045; www.banderacowboycapital.com), open weekdays 9am to 5:30pm, Saturday 10am to 4pm. Or explore the town's living traditions by strolling along Main Street, where a variety of crafters work in the careful, hand-hewn style of yesteryear. Be sure to stop in at the **Cowboy Palace** (© **830/796-3450**), a working blacksmith shop (as well as casual restaurant and live country music venue); the **Stampede** (© **830/796-7650**), a good spot for Western collectibles; and the huge **Love's Antique Mall** (© **830/796-3838**), a one-stop shopping center for current local crafts as well as things retro. **Country Accent Antiques,** Hwy. 16, 6 miles south of Bandera (© **830/535-4979**), includes among its array of furnishings beds, benches, and gates crafted from wrought iron by Warren Lee. Naturally, plenty of places in town such as **The Cowboy Store,** 302 Main St. (© **830/796-8176**), can outfit you in Western duds.

If you want to break those clothes in, the Convention and Visitors Bureau can direct you to the outfitter who can match you with the perfect mount. The CVB is also the place to check whether any rodeos or roping exhibitions are in the area. (They occur often in summer and less regularly in fall.)

THE GREAT OUTDOORS

You don't have to go farther than **Bandera Park** (© **830/796-3765**), a 77-acre green space within city limits, to enjoy nature, whether you want to stroll along the River Bend Native Plant Trail or picnic by the Medina River. Or you can canter through the **Hill Country State Natural Area,** 10 miles southwest of Bandera (© **830/796-4413**), the largest state park in Texas allowing horseback riding. The nearest outfitter is the reliable **Running R Ranch,** Route 1

(© **830/796-3984**); cost is $23 an hour for adults, $20 for those 12 and under. A visit to the nonprofit **Brighter Days Horse Refuge,** 682 Krause Rd., Pipe Creek, about 9 miles northeast of Bandera (© **830/510-6607**), will warm any animal lover's heart. The price of admission to this rehabilitation center for abandoned and neglected horses is a bag of carrots or apples; donations are also welcome.

About 20 miles southeast of town (take Hwy. 16 to RR 1283), **Medina Lake** is the place to hook crappie, white or black bass, and especially huge yellow catfish; the public boat ramp is on the north side of the lake, at the end of P.R. 37. The Bandera Convention and Visitors Bureau can provide the names of various outfitters for those who want to kayak, canoe, or tube the Medina River.

Most people visit the **Lost Maples State Natural Area,** about 40 miles west of Bandera in Vanderpool (© **830/966-3413;** www.tpwd.state.tx.us/park/lostmap), in autumn, when the leaves put on a brilliant show. But birders come in winter to look at bald eagles, hikers like the wildflower array in spring, and anglers try to reduce the Guadalupe bass population of the Sabinal River in summer. Those seeking accommodations more upscale than the campground should try **Fox Fire Log Cabins,** 1 mile south of Lost Maples State Natural Area, HC 01, Box 142, Vanderpool, TX 78885 (© **830/966-2200;** www.foxfirecabins. com), where two-bedroom cabins offer full kitchens, wood-burning fireplaces, and comfy antique-country furnishings (but new beds). Barbecue pits, volleyball and basketball courts, myriad outdoor activities, and low rates ($85 for two adults, $98 for four; children under 12 free) make this place ideal for families. Even higher on the lodgings food chain, the **Texas Stagecoach Inn,** HC 02, Box 166, Vanderpool, TX 78885 (© **888/965-6272** or 830/966-6272), is a beautiful 6,000-square-foot ranch-style house that dates back to 1885. The location, on the banks of the Sabinal River, couldn't be more idyllic, and the hot breakfast buffets are elaborate. Rates range from $115 to $145 for a double room.

STAYING AT A GUEST RANCH

For the full flavor of this region, plan to stay at one of Bandera's many guest ranches; you'll find a full listing on the Bandera website. Note that most of them have a 2-night (or more) minimum stay. You wouldn't want to spend less time at a dude ranch, anyway; it'll take at least half a day to start to unwind and get attuned to the slower ranch rhythms. Expect to encounter lots of European visitors (you'd be amazed at how popular country-and-western dancing is in England); these places are great for cultural exchange, and you'll learn about all the best beers in Texas—and Germany.

At the **Dixie Dude Ranch,** P.O. Box 548, Bandera, TX 78003 (© **800/375-YALL** or 830/796-4481; www.dixieduderanch.com), a long-time favorite retreat, you're likely to see white-tailed deer or wild turkeys as you trot on horseback through a 725-acre spread; overnight trail rides can be booked in fall and winter. The down-home, friendly atmosphere keeps folks coming back year after year. Rates are $95 to $105 per adult per night. The neighboring Dixie Dude Ranch West (formerly Bald Eagle Ranch), offers more upscale accommodations for $15 more per person per night.

Tubing on the Medina River and swimming in an Olympic-size pool are among the many activities at the **Mayan Ranch,** P.O. Box 577, Bandera, TX 78003 (© **830/796-3312** or 830/460-3036; www.mayanranch.com), another well-established family-run place ($130 per adult); corporate groups often come for a bit of loosening up. Both ranches provide lots of additional Western fun for their guests during high season—things like two-step lessons, cookouts, hayrides, singing cowboys, or trick-roping exhibitions. Rates are based on double occupancy and include three meals, two trail rides, and most other activities.

WHERE TO DINE

When you're ready to put on the feed bag, try Main Street's **O.S.T.** (© 830/796-3836), named for the Old Spanish Trail that used to run through Bandera. Serving up down-home Texas and Tex-Mex victuals since 1921, this cafe has a room dedicated to The Duke and other cowboy film stars. It's open daily for breakfast, lunch, and dinner; entrees are inexpensive to moderate.

Billy Gene's, 1105 Main St. (© 830/460-3200), lays on huge platters of down-home country standards like calf's liver and onions or meatloaf for seriously retro prices. Less health-defying food is available here, too. An open deck and huge windows afford excellent Medina River vistas. It's open daily for breakfast, lunch, and dinner; meals are inexpensive to moderate.

If you're just up for an old-fashioned milkshake or some fresh-squeezed lemonade, grab a stool at the soda fountain of the **Bandera General Store,** 306 Main St. (© 830/796-4925), open 10am to 6pm Monday to Saturday, 10am to 4pm on Sunday.

One of the best country-and-western clubs in South Texas, the **Cabaret Dance Hall** (see below) has a cafe known for its good prime rib and Gulf Coast seafood.

A COUPLE OF HONKY-TONKS

Don't miss **Arkey Blue & The Silver Dollar Bar** ★★ (© 830/796-8826), a genuine spit-and-sawdust cowboy honky-tonk on Main Street usually called Arkey's. When there's no live music, plug a quarter in the old jukebox and play a country ballad by the owner. And look for the table where Hank Williams, Sr. carved his name.

Just down the road a piece, the old **Cabaret Dance Hall** (© 830/796-8166), established in 1936, was resuscitated in the late 1990s. Larger than Arkey's, it can accommodate bigger-draw names like Don Walser (the "Pavarotti of the Plains"), local resident Robert Earl Keen, and Chris Ledoux.

EN ROUTE TO KERRVILLE

Each of the roads from Bandera to Kerrville has its distinct allure. The longer Hwy. 16 route—37 miles compared to 26—is one of the most gorgeous in the region, its scenic switchbacks introducing a new forest, river, or rolling ranchland vista at every turn (don't worry, the road is curvy but not precipitous; you're at river level most of the time). Go this way and you'll also pass through Medina. You won't doubt the little town's self-proclaimed status as Apple Capital of Texas when you come to **Love Creek Orchards Cider Mill and Country Store** (© 800/449-0882 or 830/589-2588) on the main street. Along with apple pies and other fresh-baked goods, you can buy apple cider, apple syrup, apple butter, apple jam, apple ice cream—you can even have an apple sapling shipped back home. Not feeling fruity? The restaurant out back serves some of the best burgers in the area.

Military buffs and souvenir-seekers might want to take the more direct but also scenic Hwy. 173, which passes through **Camp Verde,** the former headquarters (1856–69) of the short-lived U.S. Army camel cavalry. Widespread ignorance of the animals' habits and the onset of the Civil War led to the abandonment of the attempt to introduce "ships of the desert" into dry Southwest terrain, but the commander of the post had great respect for his humpbacked recruits. There's little left of the fortress itself, but you can tour the **1877 General Store and Post Office** (© **830-634-7722**), chock-full of camel memorabilia and artifacts, as well as country-cute contemporary crafts. The store also sells fixings for picnics at the pleasant roadside park nearby.

4 Kerrville

With a population of about 20,000, Kerrville is larger than the other Hill Country towns described here. Now a popular retirement and tourist area, it was founded in the 1840s by Joshua Brown, a shingle-maker attracted by the area's many cypress trees. A rough-and-tumble camp surrounded by more civilized German towns, Kerrville soon became a ranching center for longhorn cattle and, more unusually, for Angora goats, eventually turning out the most mohair in the United States. After it was lauded in the 1920s for its healthful climate, Kerrville began to draw youth camps, sanitariums, and artists.

SEEING THE SIGHTS

It's a good idea to make your first stop the **Kerrville Convention and Visitors Bureau,** 2108 Sidney Baker, Kerrville, TX 78028 (© **800/221-7958** or 830/792-3535; www.ktc.net/kerrcvb), where you can get a map of the area as well as of the historic downtown district. Open weekdays 8:30am to 5pm, Saturday 9am to 3pm, Sunday 10am to 3pm.

Tip: If you're planning to come to Kerrville around Memorial Day weekend, when the huge, 18-day **Kerrville Folk Festival** kicks off and the **Official Texas State Arts and Crafts Fair** is held, book far in advance.

 A Bit of Old England in the Old West

Several attractions, some endearingly offbeat, plus beautiful vistas along the Guadalupe River, warrant a detour west of Kerrville. Drive 5 miles from the center of town on Hwy. 27 West to reach tiny **Ingram.** Take Hwy. 39 West to the second traffic light downtown. After about ⅛ mile, you'll see a sign for the Historic Old Ingram Loop, essentially 2 blocks of **antiques and crafts shops.** Back on Hwy. 39, continue another few blocks to the **Hill Country Arts Foundation** (© 830/ 367-5120; www.hcaf.com), a complex comprising two theaters, an art gallery, and studios where arts-and-crafts classes are held. Every summer since 1948, a series of musicals has been offered on the outdoor stage. Continue 7 miles west on Hwy. 39 to the junction of FM 1340, where you'll find **Hunt,** which pretty much consists of a combination general store, bar, and restaurant that would look right at home in any Western. Now head west on FM 1340 for about ¼ mile. Surprise: There's a replica of **Stonehenge** sitting out in the middle of a field. It's not as large as the original, but this being Texas, it's not exactly diminutive, either. There are a couple of reproduction Easter Island heads here, too. Where will it end? Well, Al Shepherd, the wealthy eccentric who commissioned the pieces, passed away in the mid-1990s. So there are unlikely to be any more local forays into ancient mysteries.

The restored downtown, flanked by the Guadalupe River and a pleasant park, is the most interesting part of town. For a glimpse of affluent Hill Country life in the early days, visit the **Hill Country Museum,** 226 Earl Garrett St. (© **830/ 896-8633**), a mansion built of native stone by Alfred Giles for pioneer rancher and banker Capt. Charles Schreiner. Open Monday to Saturday 10am to 3pm; admission $5 adults, $2 students. A collection of ball gowns is among the antique treasures. Old Republic Square (off Lemos, between Main and Water sts.) hosts a collection of quaint gift shops and boutiques, among them **Hill Country Western Wear** (© **830/257-7333**), selling chic cowpoke duds. The **Sunrise Antique Co.,** 820 Water St. (© **830/257-5044**), offers remembrances of things past in another restored turn-of-the-century building. More interested in the present than the past? **Artisans Group, Inc.,** 826 Water St. (© **830/896-4220**), sells beautiful contemporary crafts on weekdays.

At the headquarters of **James Avery Craftsman,** about 3½ miles north of town on Harper Road (© **830/895-1122**), you can watch artisans work on silver and gold jewelry designs, many of which incorporate Christian symbols, then head for the retail shop.

Whether or not you think you like Western art, the **Cowboy Artists of America Museum,** 1550 Bandera Hwy. (© **830/896-2553;** www.caamuseum. com), is not to be missed. Lying just outside the main part of town, the high-quality collection is housed in a striking Southwestern structure. Open Tuesday to Saturday 9am to 5pm, Sunday 1 to 5pm; $5 adults, $3.50 seniors, $1 ages 6 to 18. Outdoor enthusiasts will enjoy the nearby **Kerrville-Schreiner State Park,** 2385 Bandera Hwy. (© **830/257-5392;** www.tpwd.state.tx.us/park/ kerrvill/kerrvill.htm), a 500-acre green space boasting 7 miles of hiking trails, as well as swimming and boating on the Guadalupe River.

A NEARBY RANCH

You'll need a reservation to visit the **Y. O. Ranch,** 32 miles from Kerrville, off Hwy. 41, Mt. Home, TX 78058 (© **800/YO-RANCH** or 830/640-3222; www.yoranch.com). Originally comprising 550,000 acres purchased by Charles Schreiner in 1880, the Y. O. Ranch is now a 40,000-acre working ranch known for its exotic wildlife and Texas longhorn cattle. Daily activities include everything from organized hunts and cattle drives to horseback rides and hayrides.

WHERE TO STAY

The **Y. O. Ranch Resort Hotel and Conference Center,** 2033 Sidney Baker, Kerrville, TX 78028 (© **877/YO-RESORT** or 830/257-4440; www.yoresort. com)—not near the Y. O. Ranch (see above), but in Kerrville itself—offers large and attractive Western-style quarters. Its Branding Iron dining room features big steaks as well as continental fare, and the gift shop has a terrific selection of creative Western-theme goods. Double rooms range from $79 to $119, depending on the season.

Inn of the Hills River Resort, 1001 Junction Hwy., Kerrville, TX 78028 (© **800/292-5690** or 830/895-5000; www.innofthehills.com), looks like a motel from the outside, but it has the best facilities in town, including tennis courts, three swimming pools, a putting green, two restaurants, a popular pub, and free access to the excellent health club next door. Rates for double rooms range seasonally from $79 to $90.

The **River Run Bed & Breakfast Inn,** 120 Francisco Lemos St., Kerrville, TX 78028 (© **800/460-7170** or 830/896-8533; www.riverrunbb.com), was built in the late 20th century, but its native limestone and sloping tin roof hearken back to 19th-century German Hill Country architecture. A welcoming front porch, proximity to the Guadalupe River, rooms done in Texas country style, and big, down-home breakfasts make you feel way out in the country. But whirlpool tubs and TVs with (in the suites) VCRs remind you you're actually near the civilized center of town. Rooms rates are $100 to $105; suites cost $139.

WHERE TO DINE
Because of its focus on salads and its somewhat froufrou look, more women than men tend to lunch at the **Old Republic Inn** (© 830/896-7616) in Old Republic Square, 225 Junction Hwy. But the guys are missing out on some incredible desserts. You can minimize the damage by getting a half order, but most people just end up trying two. It's open Monday through Saturday, 11am to 4pm; entrees are moderately priced.

Although the menu at **Patrick's Lodge,** 2190 Junction Hwy. (© 830/895-4111), is primarily French, and the tables are covered with white cloths, you can't accuse a restaurant with wood-paneled walls, mounted deer heads, and a view of Goat Creek of not being macho. Gallic classics such as escargot and filet mignon *au poivre* turn up alongside venison and chicken-fried steak. Prices are reasonable, and the excellent wine list includes lots of local bottles. The lodge is open for dinner Monday and for lunch and dinner Tuesday through Saturday.

5 Comfort ★★
The most direct route from Kerrville to Fredericksburg is via Hwy. 16 North, but it's well worth detouring 18 miles southeast along Hwy. 27 to seek Comfort. True to its name, it's one of the most pleasant of the Hill Country towns. It has been said that the freethinking German immigrants who founded Comfort in 1852 were originally going to call it Gemütlichkeit—a more difficult-to-pronounce native version of its current name—when they arrived at this welcoming spot after an arduous journey from New Braunfels. The story is probably apocryphal, but it's an appealing explanation of the name, especially as no one is quite sure what the truth is.

The rough-hewn limestone buildings in the center of Comfort may compose the most complete 19th-century business district in Texas. Some of the offices were designed by architect Alfred Giles, who also left his distinctive mark on San Antonio's streets. The earliest church in town was built some 40 years after the first settlers arrived because during the initial period, the founders' antireligious beliefs, for which they had been persecuted in the old country, prevailed. Most of the settlers were also opposed to the Confederacy during the Civil War. The Treue der Union (True to the Union) Monument, on High Street between Third and Fourth streets, was erected in 1866 to commemorate 36 antislavery settlers killed by Confederate soldiers when they tried to defect to Mexico.

SHOPPING FOR ANTIQUES
A majority of the town's high-quality and high-priced antiques shops are in the limestone buildings along High Street; more than 30 dealers gather at the **Comfort Antique Mall,** 734 High St. (© 830/995-4678). But make your first stop the **Ingenhuett Store,** 830–834 High St. (© 830/995-2149), set in an 1880 Alfred Giles building. The business has been owned and operated by the same German-American family since 1867. Along with groceries, outdoor gear, and

---

Kids   Bats & Ostriches Along a Back Road to Fredericksburg

If you missed the bats in Austin, you've got a chance to see even more in an abandoned railroad tunnel supervised by the Texas Parks and Wildlife Department. From Comfort, take Hwy. 473 North 4 or 5 miles. When the road winds to the right toward Sisterdale, keep going straight on Old Hwy. 9. After another 8 or 9 miles, you'll spot a parking lot and a mound of large rocks on top of a hill. During migration season (May–Nov), you can watch as many as 2½ million Mexican free-tailed bats set off on a food foray around dusk. The viewing on the Upper Observation Area is free, and in past years, state-sponsored naturalist tours ($5 adults, $3 seniors, $2 children 6–16) have been given on Thursday and Saturday evenings, June through October. There are 60 seats, filled on a first-come, first-served basis. Try the Old Tunnel Wildlife Management Area (© 830/995-4154; www.tpwd.state.tx.us/hillcountry/wma/otwma/public_access.htm) for current information.

Even if you don't stop for the bats, this is a wonderfully scenic route to Fredericksburg. You won't see any road signs, but have faith—this really will take you to town, eventually. You're likely to spot grazing goats and cows and even some strutting ostriches.

---

sundries, the store carries maps and other sources of tourist information; you'll find everyone there extremely helpful. It's open far more frequently than the **Comfort Chamber of Commerce,** P.O. Box 777, Comfort, TX 78013 (© 830/995-3131), on Seventh and High streets, which has very limited hours.

WHERE TO STAY

One of the largest and most interesting antiques shops in town, **Comfort Common,** 818 High St., Comfort, TX 78013 (© 830/995-3030; www.comfort common.com), doubles as a bed-and-breakfast. Two reasonably priced ($80) rooms, in what was once the 19th-century Faust-Ingenhuett Hotel, are imaginatively decorated and look out onto a peaceful garden. Nearby, two separate cottages and a log cabin go for $110 to $175.

WHERE TO DINE

The chef/owner of **Arlene's,** 426 Seventh St., just off High Street (© 830/995-3330), used to be a food columnist for the *San Antonio Express-News,* and her freshly made soups, quiches, sandwiches, and desserts prove she knew whereof she wrote. The converted old house is charming, and Arlene has the ability to pinpoint your place of origin as soon as you open your mouth. Hours are limited to Thursday through Sunday, from 11am to 4pm. Prices are moderate.

Mimi's Cafe, 814 High St. (© 830/995-3470), also specializes in light repasts prepared daily on the premises. The chocolate French silk pie and apple cherry crisp are particularly popular. Mimi's is open Tuesday to Friday 11am to 2pm, Saturday 11am to 3pm, and Fridays 6 to 8:30pm for steak dinners. It is moderately priced.

6 Fredericksburg ★★★

San Antonians and Austinites flock to Fredericksburg in droves on the weekends—and with good reason. It's got outstanding shopping, lots of historic sites (so you can pretend you're not just there to shop), and some of the most unusual accommodations around, all in a pretty rural setting.

Fredericksburg may be getting a bit trendy—"chick flick" producer Linda Obst lives here, and film-star sightings are becoming increasingly common—but the town also remains devoted to its European past. Baron Ottfried Hans von Meusebach was one of ten nobles who formed a society designed to help Germans resettle in Texas, where they would be safe from political persecution and economic hardship. In 1846, he took 120 settlers in ox-drawn carts from New Braunfels to this site, which he named for Prince Frederick of Prussia. The town's mile-long main street is still wide enough for a team of oxen to turn around in (although that hasn't been tested lately). The permanent peace treaty Meusebach negotiated with the Comanches in 1847, claimed to be the only one in the United States that was ever honored, and the gold rush of 1849—Fredericksburg was the last place California-bound prospectors could get supplies—both helped the town thrive. Fredericksburg became and remains the seat of Gillespie County, the largest peach-producing county in the state—which explains the many roadside stands selling the fruit from late May through mid-August, and the profusion of peachy products found around this area.

SEEING THE SIGHTS
IN TOWN

For a virtual preview, go to **www.fredericksburg-texas.com**. Once you're in town, the new **Visitor Information Center,** 302 E. Austin St., Fredericksburg, TX 78624 (© **888/997-3600** or 830/997-6523), can direct you to the many points of interest in the town's historic district. Open weekdays 8:30am to 5pm, Saturday 9am to noon and 1 to 5pm, Sunday noon to 4pm. Points of interest include a number of little **Sunday Houses,** built by German settlers in distant rural areas because they needed a place to stay overnight when they came to town to trade or attend church. You'll also notice many homes built in the Hill Country version of the German *fachwerk* design, made out of limestone with diagonal wood supports.

The unusual octagonal **Vereins Kirche (Society Church)** in Market Square once functioned as a town hall, school, and storehouse. A 1935 replica of the original 1847 building now holds the archives of the Gillespie County Historical Society. The Historical Society also maintains the **Pioneer Museum Complex,** 309 W. Main St., anchored by the 1849 Kammlah House, which was a family residence and general store until the 1920s. Open Monday to Saturday 10am to 5pm, Sunday 1 to 5pm; $3 for ages 12 and up. Among the other historical structures here are a one-room schoolhouse and a blacksmith's forge. For information on both places and on the other historical structures in town, phone © **830/997-2835.**

The 1852 Steamboat Hotel, originally owned by the grandfather of World War II naval hero Chester A. Nimitz, is now part of the **National Museum of the Pacific War** ★★, 340 E. Main St. (© **830/997-4379;** www.nimitz-museum.org), a 9-acre Texas State Historical Park and the world's only museum focusing solely on the Pacific theater. It just keeps expanding and getting better. In addition to the exhibits in the steamboat-shaped hotel devoted to Nimitz and his comrades, there are also the Japanese Garden of Peace, a lovely gift from the people of Japan; the Memorial Wall, the equivalent to the Vietnam wall for Pacific War veterans; the life-size Pacific Combat Zone (2½ blocks east of the museum), which replicates a World War II battle scene; and the George Bush Gallery, where you can see a captured Japanese midget submarine and a multimedia simulation of a bombing raid on Guadalcanal. The Center for Pacific War Studies, a major research facility, is slated to open in 2005 as part of an expansion that will double the exhibition area of the George Bush Gallery. Until then, limited access to the library archives can be arranged by special request. Indoor exhibits open daily from 10am to 5pm, outdoor exhibits daily from 8am to 5pm; it is closed at Christmas. Adult admission costs $5, students pay $3, and children under 6 enter for free.

If you're interested in saddles, chaps, spurs, sheriffs' badges, and other cowboy-o-bilia, visit **Gish's Old West Museum,** 502 N. Milam St. (© 830/997-2794). A successful illustrator for Sears & Roebuck, Joe Gish started buying Western props to help him with his art. After more than 40 years of trading and buying with the best, he has gathered a very impressive collection. Joe opens the museum when he's around (he generally is); if you don't want to take a chance, phone ahead to make an appointment.

NEARBY

One of the many attractions in the Fredericksburg vicinity is **Lady Bird Johnson Municipal Park,** 2 miles southwest of town off Hwy. 16 (© 830/997-4202). It features an 18-hole golf course (which has a spiffy new clubhouse), six tennis courts, a volleyball court, a swimming pool (open summer only), a 17-acre lake for fishing, and a new Live Oak Wilderness Trail.

In the heart of town, the family-run **Fredericksburg Winery,** 237 W. Main St. (© 830/990-8747), sells its own hand-bottled, hand-corked, and hand-labeled vintages, and specializes in dessert wines. But more respected are the three wineries nearby, all of which offer tastings and tours: the newest, **Chisholm Trail Winery,** 2367 Usener Rd. (© 830/990-2675), 9 miles west off Hwy. 290; **Bell Mountain/Oberhellmann Vineyards,** 14 miles north on Hwy. 16 (© 830/685-3297); **Grape Creek Vineyard,** 9 miles east on Hwy. 290 (© 830/644-2710); and **Becker Vineyards,** 1 mile farther east on Hwy. 290 (© 830/644-2681), which many contend is the best of the bunch. Check **www.texaswinetrail.com** for details on these and other wineries in the Hill Country.

A visit to the **Wildseed Farms** ✵, 7 miles east on Hwy. 290 (© 830/990-1393; www.wildseedfarms.com), will disabuse you of any naive notions you may have had that wildflowers grew wild. At this working wildflower farm, beautiful fields of blossoms are harvested for seeds that are sold throughout the world (26 states buy wildflowers from this company). For $5 you can grab a bucket and pick bluebonnets, poppies, or whatever's blooming when you visit. There's a gift shop and the Brew-Bonnet beer garden, which sells light snacks.

For a scenic loop drive, head northwest to **Willow City.** The 13-mile route, which leads back to Hwy. 16, is especially spectacular in wildflower season.

Take FM 965 some 18 miles north to reach **Enchanted Rock State Natural Area** ✵✵ (© 915/247-3903; www.tpwd.state.tx.us/park/enchantd), a 640-acre, pink-granite dome that draws hordes of hikers. The creaking noises that emanate from it at night—likely caused by the cooling of the rock's outer surface—led the area's Native American tribes to believe that evil spirits inhabited the rock.

Fredericksburg

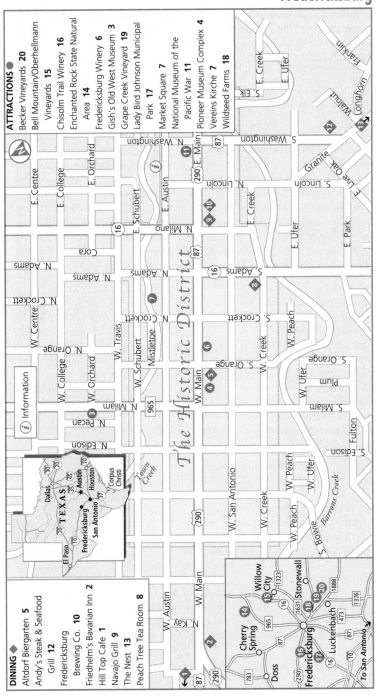

The Historic District

249

Note: Because of the rock's popularity, a limit is placed on visitors. If the park is considered full, you will be asked to return around 4pm. It's best to call in advance to check.

SHOPPING

Ladies and gentleman, start your acquisition engines. If you're pressed for time, concentrate on Main Street between Elk and Milam, although other sections are worth exploring, too. You may overdose on the cuteness, however. More than 100 specialty shops, many of them in mid-19th-century houses, feature work by Hill Country artisans. You'll find candles, lace coverlets, cuckoo clocks, hand-woven rugs, even dulcimers. Yuppies come from all over Texas to grab up the ultra-fashionable home furnishings sold at the three-story **Homestead,** 230 E. Main (© **830/997-5551**), where European rural retro (chain-distressed wrought-iron beds from France, for example) meets contemporary natural fabrics. One room is devoted entirely to the color white. You can also get an idea of just how chic the town has become by visiting **Parts Unknown,** 146 E. Main St. (© **830/997-2055**), a travel clothing store so exclusive that its only other branches are located in Santa Fe, Scottsdale, and Carmel. For something less effete, check out **Texas Jack,** 117 N. Adams St. (© **830/997-3213**), which has outfitted actors for Western films and TV shows, including *Lonesome Dove, Tombstone,* and *Gunsmoke.* This is the place to stock up on red long johns.

Becoming increasingly well known via its mail-order business is the **Fredericksburg Herb Farm,** 405 Whitney St. (© **800/259-HERB** or 830/997-8615; www.fredericksburgherbfarm.com), just a bit south of town. You can visit the flower beds that produce salad dressings, teas, fragrances, and air fresheners (the chocolate mint smells good enough to eat), and then sample some of them in the on-site restaurant (lunch only; moderate), B&B, and day spa.

One of several such places to crop up in town recently, the **European Day Spa,** 901 N. Llano St. (© **877/997-5267** or 830/997-5267; www.european dayspa.citysearch.com), has a list of treatments—everything from ear candling to heel massages—covering every stress imaginable.

WHERE TO STAY

Perhaps even more than for its shopping, Fredericksburg is well known for its appealing accommodations. In addition to the usual rural motels, the town boasts more than 300 bed-and-breakfasts and *gastehauses* (guest cottages). If you choose one of the latter, you can spend the night in anything from an 1865 homestead with its own wishing well to a bedroom above an old bakery or a limestone Sunday House. Most *gastehauses* are romantic havens complete with robes, fireplaces, and even spas. And, unlike the typical B&B, these places ensure privacy because breakfast is provided the night before (the perishables are left in a refrigerator). *Gastehauses* are comparatively reasonable; for about $100 to $150, you can get loads of history and charm. The main reservation services are: **Bed & Breakfast of Fredericksburg,** 619 W. Main St. (© 877/396-9240 or 830/997-4712; www. bandbfbg.com); **Be My Guest,** 110 N. Milam (© 866/997-7227 or 830/997-7227; www.bemyguestfredericksburgtexas.com); **Gastehaus Schmidt,** 231 W. Main St. (© 866/427-8374 or 830/997-5612; www.fbglodging.com); and **Hill Country Lodging & Reservation Service,** 215 W. Main St. (© 800/745-3591 or 830/990-8455; www.fredericksburgbedbreakfast.com); and **First Class Bed & Breakfast Reservation Service,** 909 E. Main (© **888/991-6749** or 830/997-0443; www.fredericksburg-lodging.com). Specializing in the more familiar type

Going Back (in Time) to Luckenbach

About 11 miles southeast of Fredericksburg on R.R. 1376, but light years away in spirit, the town of **Luckenbach** (pop. 25) was immortalized in song by Waylon Jennings and Willie Nelson. The town pretty much consists of a dance hall and a post office/general store/bar. But it's a great place to hang out on weekend afternoons, when someone's almost always strumming a guitar, or Friday or Saturday evening, when Jerry Jeff Walker or Robert Earl Keen might be among the names who turn up at the dance hall. Tying the knot? You can rent the dance hall—or even the entire town. Call *©* **830/997-3224** for details. And to get a feel for Luckenbach, log on to www.luckenbachtexas. com, a hoot of a website.

Whenever you visit, lots of beer is likely to be involved, so consider staying at the **Luckenbach Inn,** 3234 Luckenbach Rd., Fredericksburg, TX 78624 (*©* **800/997-1124** or 830/997-2205; www.luckenbachtx.com), just ½ mile from the action on a rise overlooking the wildflower-dotted countryside. The best of the accommodations, which range in price from $125 to $200, is the 1800s log cabin, large enough to sleep four. Rooter, the resident pot-bellied pig, is usually around to greet guests.

of B&B is **Fredericksburg Traditional Bed & Breakfasts** (*©* 800/494-4678; www.fredericksburgtrad.com).

WHERE TO DINE

Fredericksburg's dining scene is very diverse, catering to the traditional and the trendy alike. The former tend to frequent the **Altdorf Biergarten,** 301 W. Main St. (*©* **830/997-7865**), open Wednesday to Monday for lunch and dinner, and **Friedhelm's Bavarian Inn,** 905 W. Main St. (*©* **830/997-6300**), open Tuesday to Sunday for lunch and dinner, both featuring moderately priced, hearty German schnitzels, dumplings, and sauerbraten, and large selections of beer. The **Fredericksburg Brewing Co.,** 245 E. Main St. (*©* **830/997-1646**), offers its home brews in a friendly atmosphere, but the menu includes lots of lighter selections. Book one of the rooms upstairs and you can relax in your own bed after a pizza and a pint of Pedernales Pilsner. It's open daily for lunch and dinner; prices are moderate. For blue-plate specials and huge breakfasts of eggs, biscuits, and gravy, locals converge on **Andy's Steak & Seafood Grill,** 413 S. Washington St. (*©* **830/997-3744**), open since 1957. Be sure to look up at the miniature train circling the restaurant. Andy's is open daily for breakfast, lunch, and dinner; meals are inexpensive.

The more health-conscious turn up at the **Peach Tree Tea Room,** 210 S. Adams St. (*©* **830/997-9527**), although they often order a slice of heavenly ice cream pie after their salads. The tearoom is open Monday to Saturday for lunch; meals are moderately priced. Local foodies like to roost in **The Nest,** 607 S. Washington St. (*©* **830/990-8383**), which serves updated American cuisine in a lovely old house. It's open for dinner Thursday through Monday; meals are expensive. Equally popular and a bit more cutting-edge, the contemporary-chic **Navajo Grill,** 209 E. Main St. (*©* **830/990-8289**), offers food inspired by New

Orleans (chef/owner Steve Howard has cooked at Emeril's, K-Paul's, and Nola), the Southwest, and occasionally the Caribbean. Open Tuesday to Sunday for lunch and dinner; expensive.

About 11 miles north of Fredericksburg on I-87, the **Hill Top Cafe** (© **830/ 997-8922**) serves excellent Cajun and Greek food. You might find the owner, a former member of the band Asleep at the Wheel, very much awake at the piano. It's open for lunch and dinner Wednesday to Sunday; prices are moderate to expensive.

7 Lyndon B. Johnson Country 🅰

Welcome to Johnson territory, where the forebears of the 36th president settled almost 150 years ago. Even before he attained the country's highest office, Lyndon Baines Johnson was a local hero whose successful fight for funding a series of dams provided the region with inexpensive water and power. Try to make a day out of a visit to LBJ's boyhood home and the sprawling ranch that became known as the Texas White House. Even if you're not usually drawn to the past, you're likely to find yourself fascinated by Johnson's frontier lineage.

LBJ HISTORICAL PARKS

From Fredericksburg, take U.S. 290 East for 16 miles to the entrance of the **Lyndon B. Johnson State and National Historical Parks at LBJ Ranch** 🅰, near Stonewall (© **830/868-7128** or 830/644-2252), jointly operated by the Texas Parks and Wildlife Department (www.tpwd.state.tx.us/park/lbj) and the National Park Service (www.nps.gov/lyjo). Tour buses depart regularly from the state park visitors center, which displays interesting memorabilia from Johnson's boyhood, to the still-operating Johnson Ranch. You probably won't spot Lady Bird Johnson, who spends about a third of her time here, but don't be surprised to see grazing longhorn cattle.

Crossing over the swiftly flowing Pedernales River and through fields of phlox, Indian blanket, and other wildflowers, you can easily see why Johnson used the ranch as a second, more comfortable White House, and why, discouraged from running for a second presidential term, he came back here to find solace and, eventually, to die. A reconstruction of the former president's modest birthplace lies close to his (also modest) final resting place, shared with five generations of Johnsons.

On the side of the river from which you started out, period-costumed "occupants" of the **Sauer-Beckmann Living History Farm** give visitors a look at typical Texas-German farm life at the turn of the century. Chickens, pigs, turkeys, and other farm animals roam freely or in large pens, while the farmers go about their chores, which might include churning butter, baking, or feeding the animals. The midwife who attended LBJ's birth grew up here. As interesting as Colonial Williamsburg, but much less known (and thus not as well funded), this is a terrific place to come with kids. Nearby are nature trails, a swimming pool (open only in summer), and lots of picnic spots. Bring your pole (or rent one in Austin) if you want to fish in the Pedernales River.

Admission is $3 per person for bus tours; all other areas are free. All state park buildings, including the visitors center, are open daily 8am to 5pm; the Sauer-Beckmann Living History Farm is open daily 8am to 4:30pm. The Nature Trail, grounds, and picnic areas are open until dark every day. National Park Service tours of the LBJ Ranch, lasting from 1 to 1½ hours, depart from the state park visitors center daily 10am to 4pm (tours may be shortened or canceled due to excessive heat and humidity). All facilities in both sections of the park are closed Thanksgiving, Christmas, and New Year's Day.

It's 14 miles farther east along U.S. 290 to **Johnson City,** a pleasant agricultural town named for founder James Polk Johnson, LBJ's first cousin once removed. The **Boyhood Home** 𝆑—the house on Elm Street where Lyndon was raised after age 5—is the centerpiece of this unit of the **Lyndon B. Johnson National Historical Park.** The modest white clapboard structure the family occupied from 1913 on was a hub of intellectual and political activity: LBJ's father, Sam Ealy Johnson, Jr., was a state legislator, and his mother, Rebekah, was one of the few college-educated women in the country at the beginning of the 20th century. From here, be sure to walk over to the **Johnson Settlement,** where LBJ's grandfather, Sam Ealy Johnson, Sr., and his great-uncle, Jessie, engaged in successful cattle speculation in the 1860s. The rustic dogtrot cabin out of which they ran their business is still intact. Before exploring the two sites, stop at the **visitor center** (© **830/868-7128**); from U.S. 290, which turns into Main Street, take F Street to Lady Bird Lane, and you'll see the signs—where a number of excellent displays and a touching film about Johnson's presidency provide background for the buildings you'll see.

The Boyhood Home, visitors center, and Johnson Settlement are all open 8:45am to 5pm daily except Christmas, Thanksgiving, and New Year's Day. Admission is free.

The **Johnson City Visitor and Tourism Bureau,** P.O. Box 485, Johnson City, TX 78636 (© **830/868-7684;** www.johnsoncity-texas.com), can provide information about local dining, lodging, and shopping options; they're not this area's strong suit, however. Those interested in staying at a local B&B should call © **830/868-4548.**

If you're heading on to Austin, take a short detour from U.S. 290 to **Pedernales Falls State Park,** 8 miles east of Johnson City on F.R. 2766 (© **830/868-7304;** www.tpwd.state.tx.us/park/pedernal). When the flow of the Pedernales River is normal to high, the stepped waterfalls that give the 4,860-acre park its name are quite dramatic.

WINE, LAKES, AND EAGLES: A DETOUR NORTH

Oenophiles and nature lovers might want to make a far longer detour to Austin via the westernmost of the Highland Lakes (see chapter 14). From Johnson City, drive 23 miles north on Hwy. 281 to Marble Falls, then go west on R.R. 1431; after 20 miles, it meets Hwy. 261. Turn left (north) on Hwy. 261 and drive 6 miles along Lake Buchanan to Bluffton, then take a right on R.R. 2241, which will trail off after about 8 miles (2¼ miles beyond the town of Tow) into **Fall Creek Vineyards** (© **915/379-5361;** www.fcv.com). The bottles produced by these 65 acres of lakeside vineyards have garnered national praise—especially the Chardonnays, and Rieslings. The vineyards are open Monday to Friday from 11am to 4pm; Saturday from noon to 5pm; and Sunday from noon to 4pm.

Perhaps you'd like to cruise to the vineyards on Lake Buchanan and see some wildflowers and migratory birds along the way? From March through May, that's one of the options offered by **Vanishing Texas River Cruise** 𝆑𝆑 (© **800/4-RIVER-4** or 512/756-6986; www.vtrc.com). Other times of the year you might see bald eagles (Nov–Mar) or wild deer and turkey (spring through fall). Various naturalist tours depart from the north shore of Lake Buchanan, about 45 minutes from Fall Creek Vineyards; call for directions and details, or check the website, which also lists the latest tour schedules and prices (they range from about $15 for 2 ½-hr. naturalist tours to $27 for dinner cruises).

If you've enjoyed this beautiful region so much that you'd like to stay awhile, no problem: The river cruises depart from the 940-acre grounds of the **Canyon of the Eagles Lodge and Nature Park,** 16942 R.R. 2341, Burnet TX 78611 (© **800/977-0081** or 512/756-8787; www.canyonoftheeagles.com), opened in 1999 on land owned by the Lower Colorado River Authority and most of it still wilderness preserve. You can go canoeing on Lake Buchanan, stargaze at the lodge's observatory, or just kick back on your porch and watch birds flitting by. The lodge's restaurant offers everything from baby back ribs to Asian-style red snapper. Rates for the rooms, which are country-style rustic—but with all the usual conveniences you'd expect—range from $99 to $159.

8 San Marcos 🖈

Some 26 miles south of Austin via I-35, San Marcos was first settled by a tribe of nomadic Native Americans around 12,000 years ago. Some scholars claim it is the oldest continuously inhabited site in the Western Hemisphere. Temporary home to two Spanish missions in the late 1700s, as well as to Comanches and Apaches (which explains the "temporary" part), this site at the headwaters of the San Marcos River was permanently settled by Anglos in the middle of the 19th century. Now host to Southwest Texas State University, the alma mater of LBJ— and the only university in the state to graduate a future president—San Marcos has the laid-back feel of a college town. It's also fast becoming a bedroom community of Austin, only half an hour away.

WHAT TO SEE & DO

In the center of town—and, clearly, the reason for its existence—more than 1,000 springs well up from the Balcones Fault to form Spring Lake; its astonishingly clear waters maintain a constant temperature of 72°F (22°C). On the lake's shore sits the **Center** 🖈🖈, 1 Aquarena Springs Dr. (© **512/245-7575;** www.continuing-ed.swt.edu/aquarena), an exemplar of tourism trends. The first theme park to be opened in Texas, and once home to Ralph the Swimming Pig, it was purchased in the mid-1990s by Southwest Texas State University, which then spent $16 million to convert it into an environmental research center. Glass-bottom boat tours, which allow you to view the lake's rare flora and fauna, cost $6 for adults, $5 for seniors 55 and older, and $4 for children 4 to 14. In addition, there are environmental tours (2 weeks advance arrangement required), an endangered species exhibit, a natural aquarium, hikes, and a boardwalk over the wetlands, where more than 100 species of birds have been spotted. You can also visit the log home of General Edward Burleson, who built the dam that created Spring Lake to power his gristmill.

The **San Marcos River,** which begins at Spring Lake, is also getting (somewhat) eco-conscious. Log on to www.sanmarcosriver.org to find out about conservation measures taken by the San Marcos River Foundation. Not-so-rare species on the river include canoeists and rafters: Between May and September, the local Lions Club (© **512/396-LION**) rents inner tubes and operates a river shuttle at City Park.

When the Balcones Fault was active some 30 million years ago, an earthquake created the cave at the center of **Wonder World,** 1000 Prospect St., off Bishop (© **800/782-7653,** ext. 2283, or 512/392-3760; www.wonderworldpark.com). If you're short on time, don't go out of your way to visit this much-hyped attraction. (Skip the petting farm, for example, which is essentially a tram ride through an enclosure of depressed-looking deer.) A tour of the cave eventually takes you to the so-called Anti-Gravity House, where you can see water flowing upward. The cave ($11 adults, $9 children 4–11) is okay, but the Anti-Gravity House ($3 all ages) is just tacky. This attraction is open daily in winter from 9am to 5pm, (varying) longer hours during summer, spring, and fall; it is closed Christmas Eve and Christmas.

San Marcos's entire downtown area is listed in the National Register of Historic Places. Its hub is **Courthouse Square,** where several turn-of-the-century buildings are being restored. The **Old State Bank Building** was robbed by the Newton Gang in 1924 and (most likely) by Machine Gun Kelly in 1933.

To get an inside look at one of the town's two tree-lined residential districts, make an appointment to view the **Millie Seaton Collection of Dolls and Toys,** 1104 W. Hopkins (✆ **512/396-1944**), housed in the opulent 1908 Augusta Hofheinz mansion. Thousands of tiny eyes peer at you from the three stories crammed with figurines that Mrs. Seaton has been collecting since 1965, including some rare historical specimens; you're likely to recognize a few of them from your childhood.

Southwest Texas State University's Albert B. Alkek Library isn't old, but it's home to some of the state's most important literary artifacts as well as to a gem of a gallery, not to be missed if you're in town. The **Southwestern Writers Collection** 𝒜, on the seventh floor of the library at 601 University Dr. (✆ **512/245-3861;** www.library.swt.edu/swwc/index.html), showcases materials donated by the region's leading filmmakers, musicians, and wordsmiths. You might see anything from a 1555 printing of the journey of Spanish adventurer Cabeza de Vaca to a songbook created by an 11-year-old Willie Nelson to the costumes worn by Tommy Lee Jones and Robert Duvall in *Lonesome Dove.* (The collection was founded by screenwriter Bill Wittliff, who wrote the script for that TV miniseries as well as for *Legends of the Fall* and *A Perfect Storm.*) The collection is open to the public Monday to Friday 8am to 5pm (Tues until 9pm), Saturday 1 to 5pm, Sunday 2 to 6pm; weekdays only when the university is not in session. The **Wittliff Gallery of Southwestern & Mexican Photography** 𝒜 (✆ **512/245-2313**) exhibits not only works from an excellent permanent collection, but also temporary shows by other renowned photographers. Call ahead for directions to the building and parking garage; hours are the same as for the Southwestern Writers Collection.

OUTLET SHOPPING

If truth be told, lots of people bypass San Marcos altogether and head straight for the two factory outlet malls a few miles south of downtown—the biggest discount shopfest in Texas. Take exit 200 from I-35 for both the **Tanger Factory Outlet Center** (✆ **800/408-8424** or 800-4TANGER; www.tangeroutlet.com) and the larger and tonier **Prime Outlets** (✆ **800/628-9465** or 512/396-7183; www.primeoutlets.com) right next door. Among the almost 150 stores, you'll find everything from Donna Karan, Anne Klein, Calvin Klein, and Brooks Brothers to Samsonite and Waterford/Wedgwood. There's also a Saks Fifth Avenue outlet.

The **San Marcos Convention and Visitors Bureau,** 202 N. C. M. Allen Pkwy., San Marcos, TX 78666 (✆ **888/200-5620** or 512/393-5900; www.sanmarcostexas.com/tourism), can provide you with information on mall bus transportation, as well as a complete list of places to eat and stay in town.

> *Tips*   **A Spectacular Drive**
>
> San Marcos is a convenient jumping-off point for one of Texas's most breathtaking drives. Take R.R. 12 West to R.R. 32 to reach the Devil's Backbone, a 15-mile, switchback-filled route affording spectacular Hill Country views.

WHERE TO STAY & DINE

The **Crystal River Inn,** 326 W. Hopkins, San Marcos, TX 78666 (© **888/396-3739** or 512/396-3739; www.crystalriverinn.com), offers something for everyone. Nine rooms and three suites, beautifully decorated with antiques, occupy a large 1883 Victorian main house and two smaller historic structures behind it. There's also a fully furnished executive apartment across the street. Rates, which range from a low of $90 for a room during the week to a high of $160 for a two-bedroom suite on the weekend, include a full breakfast. The elaborately scripted (and enthusiastically acted) murder-mystery weekends are extremely popular.

The prettiest place to have a meal in town is the fountained courtyard at **Palmers,** 216 W. Moore (© **512/353-3500**), where you can sit among lovely native plants and trees and enjoy dishes ranging from fusilli pasta with herbed pesto or charbroiled ahi tuna to a hefty New York strip steak. "Conservative" portions of many dishes are available; they're a smart option if you want to save room for the delicious Key lime or chocolate satin pies. The restaurant is open for lunch and dinner daily, and meals are moderately priced.

NEARBY WIMBERLEY

A river resort town some 15 miles northwest of San Marcos, Wimberley attracts Austinites with a slew of bed-and-breakfasts—it's a favorite setting for family reunions—and a concentration of resident artists. From April through December, the first Saturday of each month is **Market Day,** a huge crafts gathering on Lion's Field.

I don't think most of the shops and boutiques in Wimberly are anything special, but **Sable V Fine Art Gallery** (© 512/847-8975), on the town square, is a quality exception. And **Wimberley Glass Works,** Spoke Hill Road, 1½ miles south of the town square (© **512/847-9348;** www.wgw.com), stands out for its rainbow-like array of blown glassware; you can watch artist Tim de Jong at work much of the time.

Right next door is perhaps the best reason to come to Wimberley. The **Blair House,** 100 Spoke Hill Rd., Wimberley, TX 78676 (© **877-549-5450** or 512/847-8828; www.blairhouseinn.com), is a luxurious inn on 85 Hill Country acres, offering beautifully decorated rooms in a Texas limestone ranch complex. Talk about relaxing: Six of the eight rooms have Jacuzzis, and there's a massage room and sauna on the property. Innkeeper Jonnie Stansbury is a gourmet chef, and rates ($125–$175 for a double) include her elaborate breakfasts, evening desserts, and wine served in your room. Most Saturday nights, she also offers outstanding, multi-course dinners ($55 per person) that draw people all the way from Austin. Weekend cooking classes are also very popular, so book ahead if you are interested.

For information about other places to stay, eat, or shop in Wimberley, contact the **Chamber of Commerce,** 14100 R.R. 12, just north of the town square

(© 512/847-2201; www.wimberley.org). Another resource for accommodations is **All Wimberley Lodging,** 400 River Road (© **800/460-3909** or 512/847-3909; www.texashillcountrylodging.com).

A MEATY DETOUR TO LOCKHART

The scenic loop from San Marcos to Lockhart and back (or up to Austin) is a must for those who love barbecue. Take Hwy. 80 some 27 miles east to Luling and the junction of Hwy. 183; it's 15 miles north to Lockhart, Texas's smoked-meat Mecca. Many people swear by the barbecue at **Kreuz Market** ⟨, 619 N. Colorado (© **512/398-2361**), where the brisket, prime rib, and sausage come with little other than some white bread; your food is slapped down on butcher paper, and the seating is family style. It's open for lunch and dinner Monday to Saturday. Those who enjoy side dishes such as homemade coleslaw and pinto beans—or prefer eating off plates on tables that aren't shared with other diners—will be happier at **Black's Barbecue,** 215 N. Main St. (© **512/398-2712**), open daily for lunch and dinner. Although these two are the main contenders, **Chisholm Trail Barbecue,** 1323 S. Colorado (© **512/398-6027**), also has its die-hard defenders; its niceties extend to a salad bar. It is open Monday to Saturday for lunch and dinner. Kreuz's was established in 1900, Black's in 1932, and Chisholm Trail in 1978—enough time for all of them to have perfected their recipes. All three are inexpensively priced.

But there's more to Lockhart than just barbecue. At the center of town, the 1893 **Caldwell County Courthouse** ⟨ is said to be the most photographed town hall in Texas. Though it's impossible to verify or refute the claim, there's no question that the ornate French Second Empire–style structure is photogenic: Its film credits include *The Great Waldo Pepper, What's Eating Gilbert Grape,* and *Waiting for Guffman.* You can pick up a guide to downtown Lockhart's historic structures, many of which house antiques shops, at the **Lockhart Chamber of Commerce,** 205 S. Main Street at Prairie Lea (© **512/398-2818;** www.lockhart-tx.org), open Monday to Friday from 9am to 5pm.

PICKING OUT A HAT IN BUDA

There's not a whole lot happening in the town of Buda (pronounced *byou*-duh), but if you get off I-35 at the Buda exit (exit 220, about halfway between Austin and San Marcos), you'll see **Texas Hatters** (© **800/421-HATS** or 512/312-0036; www.texashatters.com) on the access road on the east side of the highway. In business for more than 50 years, this Western hatter has had an unlikely mix of famous customers, from Tip O'Neill, George Bush, and the king of Sweden to Al Hirt, Willie Nelson, and Arnold Schwarzenegger—to name just a few.

A LITERARY ASIDE

Pulitzer Prize–winning author Katherine Anne Porter, best known for her novel *Ship of Fools,* spent most of her childhood just a few miles south of Buda, in the town of Kyle. In 2001, the 1880 **Katherine Anne Porter House,** 508 W. Center St. (© **512/268-6637;** www.english.swt.edu/kap), was dedicated and opened to the public, as well as to a visiting writer chosen by the Southwest Texas State University (SWTU) in San Marcos. The house, which was restored and furnished with period antiques, hosts Porter's works and a collection of her photographs; you can also see her papers at SWTU. There's no admission charge, but you need to call ahead for an appointment.

9 New Braunfels (★)

Some 16 miles south of San Marcos on I-35, New Braunfels sits at the junction
of the Comal and Guadalupe rivers. German settlers were brought here in 1845
by Prince Carl of Solms-Braunfels, the commissioner general of the Society for
the Protection of German Immigrants in Texas, the same group that later
founded Fredericksburg. Although Prince Carl returned to Germany within a
year to marry his fiancée, who refused to join him in the wilderness, his colony
prospered. By the 1850s, New Braunfels was the fourth-largest city in Texas after
Houston, San Antonio, and Galveston. Today it's not one of the Hill Country's
quieter or quainter towns, but still might be worth a short stop if you like Germanic history.

WHAT TO SEE & DO

At the **New Braunfels Chamber of Commerce,** 390 S. Seguin, New Braunfels,
TX 78130 (© **800/572-2626** or 830/625-2385; www.nbchamb.org), open
weekdays 8am to 5pm, you can pick up the *Prosit Visitor's Guide,* which can help
you take an antiques-lovers' crawl. Those who prefer the modern retail world
should head for the **New Braunfels Marketplace,** 651 Business Loop I-35
North (© **830/620-7475;** www.nbmarketplace.com), where factory outlet
stores such as American Tourister, Bass, and Easy Spirit vie with several specialty
shops for visitors' dollars. Some of the stores in midtown straddle two eras:
Henne Hardware, 246 W. San Antonio (© **830/606-6707**), established in
1857, sells modern bits and bobs, but maintains its original tin roof ceiling,
rings for hanging buggy whips, and an old pulley system for transporting cash
and paperwork through the back business office. It's said to be the oldest hardware store in Texas. **Naeglin's,** 129 S. Seguin Ave. (© **830/625-5722**), opened
in 1868, stakes its claim as the state's longest-running bakery. It's the place to try
some *kolaches*—Czech pastries filled with cheese, fruit, poppy seeds, sausage or
ham, among other delicious fillings.

Henne's Hardware and Naeglin's are on a 40-point **historic walking tour** of
midtown, also available at the Chamber of Commerce. Other buildings of note
include the Romanesque-Gothic Comal County Courthouse (1898) on Main
Plaza; the nearby Jacob Schmidt Building (193 W. San Antonio), built on the
site where William Gebhardt, of canned chili fame, perfected his formula for
chili powder in 1896; and the 1928 Faust Hotel (240 S. Seguin), believed by
some to be haunted by its owner. These days, draughts pulled from the micro-
brewery on the Faust's premises help allay even the most haunting anxieties.

Several small museums are worth a visit. Prince Carl never did build a
planned castle for his sweetheart, Sophia, on the elevated spot where the
Sophienburg Museum (★), 401 W. Coll St. (© **830/629-1572;** www.nbtx.com/
sophienburg), now stands, but it's nevertheless an excellent place to learn about
the history of New Braunfels and other Hill Country settlements. Open Monday to Saturday 10am to 5pm, Sunday 1 to 5pm; $5 adults, students under 19
free. The **Museum of Texas Handmade Furniture** (★), 1370 Church Hill Dr.
(© **830/629-6504;** www.nbheritagevillage.com), also sheds light on local
domestic life of the 19th century with its beautiful examples of Texas Bieder-
meier by master craftsman Johan Michael Jahn. They're displayed at the gracious
1858 Breustedt-Dillon Haus. The 11-acre Heritage Village complex also
includes an 1848 log cabin and a barn that houses a reproduction cabinetmaker's
workshop. The museum is open daily February through November from 1 to

4pm, with the last tour beginning at 3:30pm. Admission costs $5 for adults, $1 for children ages 6 to 12.

You can tour other historic structures, including the original 1870 schoolhouse and such transported shops as a tiny music studio, at the nearby **Conservation Plaza,** 1300 Church Hill Dr. (© **830/629-2943**), centered around a gazebo and garden with more than 50 varieties of antique roses. Guided tours (included in admission) are offered every day except Monday. It's open Tuesday to Friday, 10am to 3pm, and Saturday and Sunday, 2 to 5pm; adult admission costs $2.50, while children 6 to 17 pay 50¢. Also owned by the New Braunfels Conservation Society, the 1852 **Lindheimer Home** ⚘, 491 Comal Ave. (© **830/608-1512**), is probably the best example of an early *fachwerk* house still standing in New Braunfels. Ferdinand J. Lindheimer, one of the town's first settlers—he scouted out the site for Prince Solms—was an internationally recognized botanist and editor of the town's German-language newspaper. Museum hours are limited—in summers, it's open Thursday to Tuesday from 2 to 5pm; the rest of the year, it's only open weekends, from 2 to 5pm—but you can wander the lovely grounds planted with Texas natives (38 species of plant were named for Lindheimer) even if you can't get in to see the house.

HISTORIC GRUENE ⚘⚘

You can get a more concentrated glimpse of the past at Gruene (pronounced "Green"), 4 miles northwest of downtown New Braunfels. First settled by German farmers in the 1840s, Gruene was virtually abandoned during the Depression in the 1930s. It remained a ghost town until the mid-1970s, when two investors realized the value of its intact historic buildings and sold them to businesses rather than raze them. These days, tiny Gruene is crowded with day-trippers browsing the specialty shops in the wonderfully restored structures, which include a smoked-meat shop, lots of cutesy gift boutiques, and several antiques shops.

The **New Braunfels Museum of Art & Music** 1259 Gruene Rd, on the river behind Gruene Mansion (© **800/456-4866** or 830/625-5636), was moved to Gruene in 2001 from its home in downtown New Braunfels. Subjects of recent exhibits, which change quarterly and combine music and art components, have included Texas accordion music, central Texas dance halls, and cowboy art and poetry. Local singers and songwriters perform the first Thursday of each month. It's open Monday to Saturday from 10am to 5pm, Sunday noon to 5pm, with more extended summer hours; admission costs $5 for adults, $4.50 for seniors, $3 for students ages 6 to 18.

A brochure detailing the town's retailers, restaurants, and accommodations is available from the New Braunfels Chamber of Commerce (see above) or at most of Gruene's shops. You can also get information on the town's website, www.gruene.net.

WATERSPORTS

Gruene also figures among the area's impressive array of places to get wet, most of them open only in summer. Outfitters who can help you ride the Guadalupe River rapids on raft, tube, canoe, or inflatable kayak include **Rockin "R" River Rides** (© **800/553-5628** or 830/629-9999) and **Gruene River Raft Company** (© **830/625-2800** or 625-2873), both on Gruene Road just south of the Gruene Bridge.

You can go tubing, too, at **Schlitterbahn,** Texas's largest water park and one of the best in the country, 305 W. Austin St. in New Braunfels (© **830/**

625-2351; www.schlitterbahn.com). If there's a way to get wet 'n' wild, this place has got it. Six separate areas feature gigantic slides, pools, and rides, including Master Blaster, the tallest, steepest uphill water coaster in the world. The combination of a natural river-and-woods setting and high-tech attractions make this splashy 65-acre playland a standout. Schedule varies, so call or check the website. All-day passes cost $27 for adults, $22 for children 3 to 11; children under 3 enter free.

Those who like their waterplay a bit more low-key might try downtown New Braunfels' **Landa Park** (© **830/608-2160**), where you can either swim in the largest spring-fed pool in Texas or calmly float in an inner tube down the Comal River—at 2½ miles the "largest shortest" river in the world, according to *Ripley's Believe It or Not.* There's an Olympic-size swimming pool, and you can rent paddleboats. Even if you're not prepared to immerse yourself, you might take the lovely 22-mile drive along the Guadalupe River from downtown's Cypress Bend Park to **Canyon Lake,** whose clarity makes it perfect for scuba diving.

NEARBY CAVERNS AND ANIMALS

Natural Bridge Caverns, 26495 Natural Bridge Caverns Rd. (© **210/651-6101;** www.naturalbridgecaverns.com), 12 miles west of New Braunfels, is named for the 60-foot limestone arch spanning its entryway. More than a mile of huge rooms and passages are filled with stunning, multihued formations—still being formed, as the dripping water attests. The daring—and physically fit—can opt to join one of the recently established Adventure Tours, which involve crawling and, in some cases, rappelling, in an unlighted cave not open to the general public. The caverns are open 9am to 6pm June through Labor Day, 9am to 4pm rest of the year; closed Thanksgiving Day, Christmas Day, and New Year's Day; admission costs $14 adults, $13 seniors 65 and older, $8.50 ages 4 to 12.

Just down the road, the **Natural Bridge Wildlife Ranch,** 26515 Natural Bridge Caverns Rd. (© **830/438-7400;** www.nbwildliferanchtx.com), lets you get up close and personal—from the safety of your car—with some 50 threatened and endangered species from around the world. Packets of food sold at the entryway inspire even some generally shy types to amble over to your vehicle. It is open daily 9am to 5pm, with extended summer hours until 6:30pm; admission costs $11 adults, $10 seniors 65 and older, $6 ages 3 to 11.

WHERE TO STAY IN NEW BRAUNFELS & GRUENE

The **Prince Solmes Inn,** 295 E. San Antonio St., New Braunfels, TX 78130 (© **800/625-9169** or 830/625-9169), has been in continuous operation since it opened its doors to travelers in 1898. A prime downtown location, tree-shaded courtyard, downstairs wine bar, and gorgeously florid, high Victorian–style sleeping quarters have put accommodations at this charming bed-and-breakfast in great demand. Three Western-themed rooms in a converted 1860 feed store next door are ideal for families, and there's an ultraromantic separate cabin in the back of the main house. Rates range from $125 to $150.

For a river view, consider the **Gruene Mansion Inn,** 1275 Gruene Rd., New Braunfels, TX 78130 (© **830/629-2641;** www.gruenemansioninn.com). The barns that once belonged to the opulent 1875 plantation house were converted to rustic elegant cottages with decks; some also offer cozy lofts (if you don't like stairs, request a single-level room). Accommodations for two go from $115 to $210 per night, including breakfast served in the plantation house.

About 5 miles north of Gruene, the **Hunter Road Stagecoach Stop B & B,** 5441 FM 1102, New Braunfels, TX 78132 (© **800/201-2912** or 830/ 620-9453; www.stagecoachbedandbreakfast.com), offers accommodations in an 1848 log cabin and an 1850 German *fachwerk* house. As its name suggests, this was the stop for stagecoaches traveling between San Antonio and New Braunfels on the Butterfield line. Cedar-beamed rooms are furnished in primitive antiques, in keeping with the era, but all offer modern amenities such as private bathrooms, TVs, and telephones. A lovely 1850s garden highlights antique roses and native Texas plants; the herbs that grow here turn up in the breakfast dishes. Prices range from $105 to $145 for a double, with discounts available for stays of 2 days or more.

The **Bed & Breakfast & Getaways Reservation Service,** 295 E. San Antonio St., New Braunfels, TX 78130 (© **800/239-8282** or 830/625-8194; www.bedbreakfastgetaways.com), lists many other similarly cozy places in the area. If you're planning to come to town during *wurstfest* (late Oct to early Nov), be sure to book well in advance, no matter where you stay—that is high season here.

WHERE TO DINE IN NEW BRAUNFELS & GRUENE

The oldest restaurant in New Braunfels, **Krause's Cafe,** 148 S. Castell Ave. (© **830/625-7581**), serves substantial German dishes like sauerbraten, schnitzel, and homemade sausage in a homey diner-type setting. The **New Braunfels Smokehouse,** 140 Hwy. 46 South, at I-35 (© **830/625-2416**), has been around only since 1951; it opened as a tasting room for the meats it started hickory smoking in 1945. Savor it in platters or on sandwiches, or have some shipped home as a savory souvenir (www.nbsmokehouse.com). It's open for breakfast, lunch, and dinner; prices are moderate. The far newer **Huisache Grille,** 303 W. San Antonio St. (© **830/620-9001**), has an updated American menu that draws foodies from as far as San Antonio. The pecan-grilled catfish and Yucatán chicken are excellent. Lunch and dinner are served daily; prices are moderate to expensive. Another recent arrival on downtown's fine dining scene, pretty **Giovani's,** 367 Main Plaza (© **830/626-2235**), serves sophisticated Italian specialties, such as chicken with artichokes and veal saltimbocca at reasonable prices. Save room for the tiramisu. It is open for dinner, Tuesday to Saturday; prices are moderate to expensive.

In Gruene, the **Gristmill River Restaurant & Bar,** 1287 Gruene Rd. (© **830/625-0684**), a converted 100-year-old cotton gin, includes burgers and chicken-fried steak as well as healthful salads on its Texas-casual menu. Kick back on one of its multiple decks and gaze out at the Guadalupe River. Lunch and dinner daily; moderate. The somewhat more upscale **Restaurant at River's Edge,** 1275 Gruene Rd. (© **830/620-0760**), serving German and continental cuisine, looks like an old European hall though it was built in the late 20th century. It also has an outside deck with a river view. It is open for lunch and dinner daily; prices are moderate to expensive.

GRUENE AFTER DARK

Lyle Lovett and Garth Brooks are just a few of the big names who have played **Gruene Hall** 🎵🎵, Gruene Road, corner of Hunter Road (© **830/629-7077;** www.gruenehall.com), the oldest country-and-western dance hall in Texas and still one of the state's most mellow and wonderful places to listen to live music. Some of the scenes in *Michael,* starring John Travolta, were shot here. By itself, the hall is worth a detour; when in town, if there's live music playing, it is an absolute must—just remember to wear your cowboy boots and hat.

Appendix A:
San Antonio & Austin in Depth

Texans, who consider their state the center of the universe, are surprised when not everyone knows exactly what went on at the Alamo, or what the latest tech developments are in Austin. You won't learn everything there is to know about these two cities from this necessarily brief overview, but at least you'll be armed with some background information.

1 San Antonio Past & Present

San Antonio's past is the stuff of legend, the Alamo being but the most famous episode. If it were a movie, the story of the city would be an epic with an improbably packed plot, encompassing the end of a great empire, the rise of a republic, and the rescue of the river with which the story began.

ON A MISSION

Having already established an empire by the late 17th century—the huge Viceroyalty of New Spain, which included, at its high point, Mexico, Guatemala, and large parts of the southwestern United States—Spain was engaged in the far less glamorous task of maintaining it. The remote regions of east Texas had been coming under attack by the native Apache and Comanche; now with rumors flying of French forays into the Spanish territory, search parties were dispatched to investigate.

On one of these search parties in 1691, regional governor Domingo Teran de los Ríos and Father Damian Massenet came upon a wooded plain fed by a fast-flowing river. They named the river—called Yanaguana by the native Coahuiltecan Indians—San Antonio de Padua, after the saint's day on which they arrived. When, some decades later, the Spanish Franciscans proposed building a new mission halfway between the ones on the

Dateline

- 1691 On June 13, feast day of St. Anthony of Padua, San Antonio River discovered and named by the Spanish; governor of Spanish colonial province of Texas makes contact with Coahuiltecan Indians.
- 1718 Mission San Antonio de Valero (later nicknamed the Alamo) founded; presidio San Antonio de Béxar established to protect it and other missions to be built nearby.
- 1720 Mission San José founded.
- 1731 Missions Concepción, San Juan Capistrano, and Espada relocated from East Texas to San Antonio area; 15 Canary Island families sent by Spain to help populate Texas establish the first civil settlement in San Antonio.
- 1793–94 The missions are secularized by order of the Spanish crown.
- 1820 Moses Austin petitions Spanish governor in San Antonio for permission to settle Americans in Texas.
- 1821 Mexico wins independence from Spain.
- 1835 Siege of Béxar: first battle in San Antonio for Texas independence from Mexico.
- 1836 The Alamo falls after 13-day siege by Mexican general Santa Anna; using "Remember the Alamo" as a rallying cry, Sam Houston defeats Santa Anna at San Jacinto.
- 1836 Republic of Texas is established.
- 1845 Texas annexed to the United States.

Rio Grande and those more recently established in east Texas, the abundant water and friendliness of the local population made the plain near the San Antonio River seem like a good choice.

And so it was that in 1718, Mission San Antonio de Valero—later known as the Alamo—was founded. To protect the religious complex from Apache attack, the presidio (fortress) of San Antonio de Béxar went up a few days later. In 1719, a second mission was built nearby, and in 1731, three ill-fated east Texas missions, nearly destroyed by French and Indian attacks, were moved hundreds of miles to the safer banks of the San Antonio River. Also, in March 1731, 15 weary families arrived from the Spanish Canary Islands with a royal dispensation from Philip V to help settle his far-flung New World kingdom. Near the protection of the presidio, they established the village of San Fernando de Béxar.

Thus, within little more than a decade, what is now downtown San Antonio became home to three distinct, though related, settlements: a mission complex, the military garrison designed to protect it, and the civilian town known as Béxar (pronounced "bear"), which was officially renamed San Antonio in 1837. To irrigate their crops, the early settlers were given narrow strips of land stretching back from the river and from the nearby San Pedro Creek; centuries later, the paths connecting these strips, which followed the winding waterways, were paved as the city's streets.

- 1861 Texas secedes from the Union.
- 1876 Fort Sam Houston established as new quartermaster depot.
- 1877 The railroad arrives in San Antonio, precipitating new waves of immigration.
- 1880s King William, first residential suburb, begins to be developed by German immigrants.
- 1939–40 Works Project Administration builds River Walk, based on plans drawn up in 1929 by architect Robert H. H. Hugman.
- 1968 HemisFair exposition—River Walk extension, Convention Center, Mansión del Río, and Hilton Palacio del Río completed for the occasion, along with Tower of the Americas and other fair structures.
- 1988 Rivercenter Mall opens.
- 1989 Premier of the newly refurbished Majestic Theatre.
- 1993 Alamodome, huge new sports complex, completed.
- 1995 Southbank and Presidio complexes open on the river.
- 1998 Opening of the Nelson A. Rockefeller Center for Latin American Art, a three-story, $11 million addition to the San Antonio Museum of Art; reopening of the Empire Theatre.
- 1999 San Antonio Spurs outgrow the Alamodome; funding approved for the new SBC Center.
- 2001 Completion of Convention Center expansion.
- 2002 Opening of SBC Center, new home to the Spurs, the rodeo, and more.

REMEMBER THE ALAMO

As the 18th century wore on, the missions came continuously under siege by hostile Indians, and the mission Indians fell victim to a host of European diseases against which they had no natural resistance; by the end of the 1700s, the Spanish mission system itself was nearly dead. In 1794, Mission San Antonio de Valero was secularized, its rich farmlands redistributed. In 1810, recognizing the military potential of the thick walls of the complex, the Spanish authorities turned the former mission into a garrison. The men recruited to serve here all hailed from the Mexican town of San José y Santiago del Alamo de Parras; the name of their station was soon shortened to the Alamo (Spanish for "cottonwood tree").

Impressions

From all manner of people, business men, consumptive men, curious men, and wealthy men, there came an exhibition of profound affection for San Antonio. It seemed to symbolize for them the poetry of life in Texas.

—Stephen Crane, *Patriot Shrine of Texas* (1895)

By 1824, all five missions had been secularized and Spain was, once again, worried about Texas. Apache and Comanche roamed the territory freely, and with the incentive of converting the native populations eliminated, it was next to impossible to persuade Spaniards to live there. Although the Spanish were rightly suspicious of Anglo-American designs on their land, when land agent Moses Austin arrived in San Antonio in 1820, the government reluctantly gave him permission to settle some 300 Anglo-American families in the region. Austin died before he could see his plan carried out, however. And Spain lost its hold on Mexico in 1821, when the country gained its independence after a decade of struggle. But Moses's son Stephen convinced the new government to honor the terms of the original agreement.

By 1830, however, the Mexicans were growing nervous about the large numbers of Anglos descending on their country from the north. They had already repealed many of the tax breaks they had initially granted the settlers; now they prohibited all further U.S. immigration to the territory. When, in 1835, General Antonio López de Santa Anna abolished Mexico's democratic 1824 constitution, Tejanos (Mexican Texans) and Anglos alike balked at his dictatorship, and a cry rose up for a separate republic.

The first battle for Texas independence fought on San Antonio soil fell to the rebels; Mexican general Martín Perfecto de Cós surrendered after a short, successful siege of the town in December 1835. But it was the return engagement, that glorious, doomed fight against all odds, that forever captured the American imagination. From February 23 through March 6, 1836, some 180 volunteers—among them Davy Crockett and Jim Bowie—serving under the command of William Travis, died trying to defend the Alamo fortress against a vastly greater number of Santa Anna's men. One month later, Sam Houston spurred his troops on to victory at the Battle of San Jacinto with the cry "Remember the Alamo," thus securing Texas's freedom.

AFTER THE FALL

Ironically, few Americans came to live in San Antonio during Texas's stint as a republic (1836–45), but settlers came from overseas in droves: By 1850, 5 years after Texas joined the United States, Tejanos (Mexican Texans) and Americans were outnumbered by European, mostly German, immigrants. The Civil War put a temporary halt to the city's growth—in part because Texas joined the Confederacy and most of the new settlers were Union sympathizers—but expansion picked up again soon afterward; the coming of the railroad in 1877 set off a new wave of immigration. Riding hard on its crest, the King William district of the city, a residential suburb named for Kaiser Wilhelm, was developed by prosperous German merchants.

Some of the immigrants set up Southern-style plantations, others opened factories and shops, and more and more who arrived after the Civil War earned their keep by driving cattle. The Spanish had brought Longhorn cattle and *vaqueros* (cowboys) from Mexico into the area; now Texas cowboys drove herds north on the Chisholm Trail from San Antonio to Kansas City, where they were shipped east. Others moved cattle west, for use as seed stock in the fledgling ranching industry.

Over the years, San Antonio had never abandoned its role as a military stronghold. In 1849, the Alamo was designated a quartermaster depot for the U.S. Army; in 1876, the much larger Fort Sam Houston was built to take over those duties. Apache chief Geronimo was held at the clock tower in the fort's Quadrangle for 40 days in 1886, en route to exile in Florida, and Teddy Roosevelt outfitted his Rough Riders—some of whom he recruited in San Antonio bars—at Fort Sam 12 years later.

As the city marched into the 20th century, Fort Sam Houston continued to expand. In 1910, it witnessed the first military flight by an American; early aviation stars like Charles Lindbergh honed their flying skills here. From 1917 to 1941, four Army air bases—Kelly Field, Brooks Field, Randolph Field, and Lackland Army Air Base—shot up, making San Antonio the largest military complex in the United States outside the Washington, D.C., area. Although Kelly was downsized and privatized, the military remains the city's major employer today.

A RIVER RUNS THROUGH IT

As the city moved farther and farther from its agrarian roots, the San Antonio River became much less central to the economy; by the turn of the century, its constant flooding made it a downright nuisance. When a particularly severe storm caused it to overflow its banks in 1921, killing 50 people and destroying many downtown businesses, there was serious talk of cementing over the river.

In 1925, the newly formed San Antonio Conservation Society warned the city council against killing the goose that was laying the golden eggs of downtown economic growth. And in 1927, Robert H.H. Hugman, an architect who had lived in New Orleans and studied that city's Vieux Carré district, came up with a detailed plan for saving the waterway. His proposed River Walk, with shops, restaurants, and entertainment areas buttressed by a series of floodgates, would render the river profitable as well as safe, and also preserve its natural beauty. The Depression intervened, but in 1941, with the help of a federal Works Project Administration (WPA) grant, Hugman's vision became a reality.

Still, for some decades more, the River Walk remained just another pretty space; not until the 1968 HemisFair exposition drew record crowds to the rescued waterway did the city really begin banking on its banks.

Fun Fact The Lay of the Land

Three geographical zones meet in San Antonio: The Balcones Fault divides the farms and forests of east Texas from the scrubby brushland and ranches of west Texas, and the Edwards Plateau drops off to the southern coastal plains. Frederick Law Olmsted's description in his 1853 *A Journey Through Texas* is more poetic. San Antonio, he writes, "lies basking on the edge of a vast plain, through which the river winds slowly off beyond where the eye can reach. To the east are gentle slopes toward it; to the north a long gradual sweep upward to the mountain country, which comes down within five or six miles; to the south and west, the open prairies, extending almost level to the coast, a hundred and fifty miles away."

SAN ANTONIO TODAY

The ninth largest city in the United States (its population is approximately 1.15 million), and one of the oldest, is undergoing a metamorphosis. For a good part of last century, San Antonio was a military town that happened to have a nice river promenade running through its decaying downtown area. Now, with the continuing growth in tourism (which brings in some $3.51 billion each year), the city is increasingly perceived by outsiders as a place with a terrific river walk.

Although the city's outlying theme parks and central area attractions are also benefiting from increased visitation, downtown is by far the most affected section. The city's Henry B. Gonzales Convention Center doubled in size at the end of the 1990s, and its $187 million expansion was completed in 2001. And, as though the Alamodome, the state-of-the-arts sports arena built in the last decade of the 20th century, wasn't high-tech enough for the Spurs, the huge new SBC Center opened nearby in 2002. But the biggest trend is recycling: Suddenly historic is hot. The Majestic Theatre was restored and reopened in the late 1980s, the Empire Theater followed in the late 1990s, and the Alameda and Aztec theaters should be ready to welcome audiences again in the first decade of the new millennium. And every time you turn around it seems as though another old building has been converted into a hotel. Between restorations and new construction, nearly 3,000 guest rooms were added to downtown in the 1990s.

Middle-class residential growth still lags behind commercial development in this area. San Antonians who moved downtown in the past decade initially patted themselves on the back for their prescience, but many are now beginning to second-guess the changes they helped bring about. Not only are there few residential services (the area still has no major supermarket, for example), but the huge success of the riverside Southbank and Presidio complexes, opened in the mid-1990s, destroyed what little quiet there was at night. Ordinances to cut down on late-night noise and the opening up of a dialogue between residents and businesses have begun to resolve that friction.

This is not to suggest there's no growth in any business sectors besides tourism. Boeing and Lockheed-Martin are among the aviation companies that have been attracted to Kelly Air Force Base, while other businesses like SBC (formerly Southwestern Bell) and oil giant Diamond Shamrock both moved their headquarters to San Antonio in the mid 1990s.

The North American Free Trade Agreement, signed in 1994, was also a boon for the city, which hosts the North American Development Bank—the financial arm of NAFTA—in its downtown International Center. Representatives from the various states of Mexico are housed in the same building as part of the "Casas" program. With its large Hispanic population, regular flights to Mexico City, cultural attractions such as the Latin American wing of the San Antonio Museum of Art and the Centro Alameda project—the cornerstone of which, the Alameda National Center for Latino Arts and Culture, is slated to open in 2004—and a history of strong business relations with Mexico, San Antonio is ideally positioned to take advantage of the economic reciprocity between the two nations.

Even with its rosy outlook, the city is facing some major problems, ones it shares with other rapidly growing Southwest urban centers. San Antonio and Austin are 80 miles and political light-years apart, but the two cities are growing ever closer. Although they haven't yet melded to form the single, huge metropolis that futurists predict, the increasing suburban sprawl and the growth of New Braunfels and San Marcos, two small cities that lie between San Antonio and Austin, are causing a great deal of congestion on I-35, which connects all four cities.

> ## ⌒Fun Fact Did You Know?
>
> - More jars of salsa than ketchup are consumed in the United States today.
> - The first military flight by an American took place at Fort Sam Houston in 1910; in 1915, the entire U.S. Air Force—six reconnaissance planes—resided at the fort.
> - The Fairmount Hotel in San Antonio is the heaviest building ever moved.
> - Barbed wire was first demonstrated in San Antonio's Military Plaza.

An even more serious concern is the city's water supply. Currently, the Edwards Aquifer is the city's only source of water; no one knows exactly how many years' worth of water it contains. And that supply is being threatened by development: Plans to build a vast new golf complex, PGA Village, are being contested by members of Save Our Aquifer, who contend the project, slated to be built on the aquifer's recharge zone, would have a negative impact on the city's water supply. In addition, several citizens' groups contend they didn't have a say in the issue, which was not put to a public vote. At the time of this writing, PGA Village was on hold due to ongoing litigation.

2 Austin Past & Present

A vast territory that threw off foreign rule to become an independent nation—remember the Alamo?—Texas has always played a starring role in the romance of the American West. So it's only fitting that Texas's capital should spring, full-blown, from the imagination of a man on a buffalo hunt.

A CAPITAL DILEMMA

The man was Mirabeau Buonaparte Lamar, who had earned a reputation for bravery in Texas's struggle for independence from Mexico. In 1838, when our story begins, Lamar was vice president of the 2-year-old Republic of Texas; Sam Houston, the even more renowned hero of the Battle of San Jacinto, was president. Although they shared a strong will, the two men had very different ideas about the future of the republic: Houston tended to look eastward, toward union with the United States, while Lamar saw

Dateline

- 1730 Franciscans build a mission at Barton Springs, but abandon it within a year.
- 1836 Texas wins independence from Mexico; Republic of Texas established.
- 1838 Jacob Harrell sets up camp on the Colorado River, calling the settlement Waterloo; Mirabeau B. Lamar succeeds Sam Houston as president of Texas.
- 1839 Congressional commission recommends Waterloo as site for new capital of the republic. Waterloo's name changes to Austin.
- 1842 Sam Houston succeeds Lamar as president, reestablishes Houston as Texas's capital, and orders nation's archives moved there. Austinites resist.
- 1844 Anson Jones succeeds Houston as president and returns capital to Austin.
- 1845 Constitutional convention in Austin approves annexation of Texas by the United States.

continues

independence as the first step to establishing an empire that would stretch to the Pacific.

That year, an adventurer named Jacob Harrell set up a camp called Waterloo at the western edge of the frontier. Lying on the northern banks of Texas's Colorado River (not to be confused with the larger waterway up north), it was nestled against a series of gentle hills. Some 100 years earlier, the Franciscans had established a temporary mission here; in the 1820s, Stephen F. Austin, Texas's earliest and greatest land developer, had the area surveyed for the smaller of the two colonies he was to establish on Mexican territory.

But the place had otherwise seen few Anglos before Harrell arrived; for thousands of years, it had been visited mainly by nomadic Indian tribes, including the Comanches, Lipan Apaches, and Tonkawas. Thus, it was to a rather pristine spot that, in the autumn of 1838, Harrell invited his friend Mirabeau Lamar to take part in a shooting expedition. The buffalo hunt proved extremely successful, and when Lamar gazed at the rolling, wooded land surrounding Waterloo, he saw that it was good.

In December of the same year, Lamar became president of the Republic. He ordered the congressional commission that had been charged with the task of selecting a site for a permanent capital, to be named after Stephen F. Austin, to check out Waterloo. Much to the dismay of residents of Houston—home to the temporary capital—who considered Waterloo a dangerous wilderness outpost, the commission recommended Lamar's pet site.

In early 1839, Lamar's friend Edwin Waller was dispatched to plan a city— the only one in the United States besides Washington, D.C. designed to be an independent nation's capital.

- 1850s Austin undergoes a building boom; construction of the capitol (1853), Governor's Mansion (1856), and General Land Office (1857).
- 1861 Texas votes to secede from the Union (Travis County, which includes Austin, votes against secession).
- 1865 General Custer is among those who come to restore order in Austin during Reconstruction.
- 1871 First rail line to Austin completed.
- 1883 University of Texas opens.
- 1923 Santa Rita No. 1, an oil well on University of Texas land, strikes a gusher.
- 1937 Lyndon Johnson elected U.S. representative from Tenth Congressional District, which includes Austin.
- Late 1930s to early 1950s Six dams built on the Colorado River by the Lower Colorado River Authority, resulting in formation of the Highland Lakes chain.
- 1960s High-tech firms, including IBM, move to Austin.
- 1972 Willie Nelson moves back to Texas from Nashville; helps spur live-music scene on Sixth Street.
- 1976 PBS's *Austin City Limits* airs for the first time.
- 1980s Booming real-estate market goes bust, but South By Southwest (S×SW) Music Festival debuts (1987).
- 1993 S×SW adds interactive (tech) and film components to its festival.
- 1995 Capitol, including new annex, reopens after massive refurbishing.
- 1997 Completion of the refurbishing of the capitol's grounds and of the Texas State Cemetery.
- 1999 Opening of Austin-Bergstrom International Airport.
- 2000 The Driskill revamp completed, the Stephen F. Austin Hotel reopens, and plans to turn Robert Mueller Airport into film production studio approved.
- 2001 The Bob Bullock Texas State History Museum opens.
- 2002 The tech recession hits, but Austin's still partying like it's 2000, as the Austin City Limits Music Festival debuts.

The first public lots went on sale on August 1, 1839; by November of that year, Austin was ready to host its first session of Congress.

Austin's position as capital was far from entrenched, however. Attacks on the republic by Mexico in 1842 gave Sam Houston, now president again, sufficient excuse to order the national archives to be relocated out of remote Austin. Resistant Austinites greeted the 26 armed men who came to repossess the historic papers with a cannon. After a struggle, the men returned empty-handed, and Houston abandoned his plan, thus ceding to Austin the victory in what came to be called the Archive War.

Although Austin won this skirmish, it was losing a larger battle for existence. Houston refused to convene Congress in Austin. By 1843 Austin's population had dropped down to 200 and its buildings lay in disrepair. Help came in the person of Anson Jones, who succeeded to the presidency in 1844. The constitutional convention he called in 1845 not only approved Texas's annexation to the United States, but also named Austin capital until 1850, when voters of what was now the state of Texas would choose their governmental seat for the next 20 years. In 1850, Austin campaigned hard for the position and won by a landslide.

A CAPITAL SOLUTION

Austin thrived under the protection of the U.S. Army. The first permanent buildings to go up during the 1850s construction boom following statehood included an impressive limestone capitol; two of the buildings in its complex, the General Land Office and the Governor's Mansion, are still in use today.

The boom was short-lived, however: Although Austin's Travis County voted against secession, Texas decided to join the Confederacy in 1861. By 1865, Union army units—including one led by General George Armstrong Custer—were sent to restore order in a defeated and looted Austin.

But once again Austin rebounded. With the arrival of the railroad in 1871, the city's recovery was sealed. The following year, when Austin won election as state capital, it was delivered.

Still, there were more battles for status to be fought. Back in 1839, the Republic of Texas had declared its intention to build a "university of the first class"; in 1876, a new state constitution mandated its establishment. Through yet another bout of heavy electioneering, Austin won the right to establish the flagship of Texas's higher educational system on its soil. In 1883, the classrooms not yet completed, the first 221 members of what is now a student body of more than 50,000 met the eight instructors of the University of Texas.

The university wasn't the only Austin institution without permanent quarters that year: The old limestone capitol had burned in 1881, and a new, much larger home for the legislature was being built. In 1888, after a series of mishaps—the need to construct a railroad branch to transport the donated building materials, among them—the current capitol was completed. The grand red-granite edifice looking down upon the city symbolized Austin's arrival.

DAMS, OIL & MICROCHIPS

The new capitol notwithstanding, the city was once again in a slump. Although some believed that quality of life would be sacrificed to growth—a view still strongly argued today—most townspeople embraced the idea of harnessing the fast-flowing waters of the Colorado River as the solution to Austin's economic woes. A dam, they thought, would not only provide a cheap source of electricity for residents, but also supply power for irrigation and new factories. Dedicated in 1893, the Austin Dam did indeed fulfill these goals—but only temporarily. The energy source proved to be limited, and when torrential rains pelted the city in April 1900, Austin's dreams came crashing down with its dam.

Impressions

Like the ancient city of Rome, Austin is built upon seven hills, and it is impossible to conceive of a more beautiful and lovely situation.
—George W. Bonnell, Commissioner of Indian Affairs of the Republic of Texas (1840)

Another dam, attempted in 1915, was never finished. It wasn't until the late 1930s that a permanent solution to the water-power problem was found. The successful plea to President Roosevelt for federal funds on the part of young Lyndon Johnson, the newly elected representative from Austin's Tenth Congressional District, was crucial to the construction of six dams along the lower Colorado River. These dams not only afforded Austin and central Texas all the hydroelectric power and drinking water they needed, but also created the seven Highland Lakes—aesthetically appealing and a great source of recreational revenue.

Still, Austin might have remained a backwater capital seat abutting a beautiful lake had it not been for the discovery of oil on University of Texas (UT) land in 1923. The huge amounts of money that subsequently flowed into the Permanent University Fund—worth some $4 billion today—enabled Austin's campus to become truly first-class. While most of the country was cutting back during the Depression, UT went on a building binge and began hiring a faculty as impressive as the new halls in which they were to hold forth.

The indirect effects of the oil bonus reached far beyond College Hill. Tracor, the first of Austin's more than 250 high-tech companies, was founded by UT scientists and engineers in 1955. Lured by the city's natural attractions and its access to a growing bank of young brainpower, many outside companies soon arrived: IBM (1967), Texas Instruments (1968), and Motorola's Semiconductor Products Section (1974). In the 1980s, two huge computer consortiums, MCC and SEMATECH, opted to make Austin their home. And wunderkind Michael Dell, who started out selling computers from his dorm room at UT in 1984 and is now the CEO of the hugely successful Austin-based Dell Computer Corporation, spawned a new breed of local "Dellionaires" by rewarding his employees with company stock.

Willie Nelson's return to Austin from Nashville in 1972 didn't have quite as profound an effect on the economy, but it certainly had one on the city's live-music scene. Hippies and country-and-western fans could now find common ground at the many clubs that began to sprout up along downtown's Sixth Street, which had largely been abandoned. These music venues, combined with the construction that followed in the wake of the city's high-tech success, helped spur a general downtown resurgence.

AUSTIN TODAY

During the 1990s, Austin's population increased by 41% (from 465,600 to 656,600), as high-paying tech jobs drew out-of-staters—quite a few of them Californians with lots of disposable cash. Many of the new residents moved to the suburban west and northwest, but the economic expansion also fueled a resurgence in the older central city.

Downtown projects included the restoration of the capitol and its grounds; the refurbishing of the State Theatre; and the reopening of the Stephen F. Austin Hotel, a 1924 property that's giving The Driskill—also newly refurbished and once the only grand historic lodging in town—a run for its money. The convention center doubled in size and the Bob Bullock Texas History Center, a major new tourist attraction, opened in 2001. The transformation of the historic Brown building into an apartment complex and the ongoing conversion of former warehouses and commercial lofts into residential housing are even more crucial signs that downtown is returning to the land of the living. Both the Jack Blanton Museum of Art (on the University of Texas campus) and the downtown branch of the Austin Museum of Art are slated to open in the near future.

In addition, the debut of the Austin-Bergstrom International Airport south of downtown in 1999 enhanced the development of an area that had already started to make a comeback. South Congress Street (dubbed SoCo) is drawing an increasing number of hip galleries and boutiques, and the airport is attracting more restaurants and hotels to this older area. And, in an ultimate Austin act of recycling, the abandoned hangers of the old Robert Mueller airport were transformed into a film production studio in 2000, which has meant more jobs and more activity in a once-decaying north-central neighborhood.

But there are many signs that Austin is becoming a victim of its own success. Locals complain that the people moving in from California drive like they're still in L.A.; formerly bicycle-friendly streets are no longer as hospitable to two-wheelers. The low-key, libertarian atmosphere of the city may be changing too; there's now a gated residential complex right down the street from the famed Continental Club. In the mid-1990s, with thefts of microchips and circuit boards on the rise, the Austin Police Department introduced a high-tech crime unit.

With the rise in rents, many of the struggling musicians who gave Austin's music scene its vitality can no longer afford to live here. Gentrification is similarly resulting in the displacement of the poor and older people on fixed incomes. While newer arts venues move into downtown, older ones like the Capitol Theater in the warehouse district were pushed out by high rents. Many of the restaurants in that burgeoning district are owned by groups of outside investors rather than locals, and some funky midtown restaurants like Kerbey Lane are spinning off characterless counterparts in the city's soulless northwest. And although the new airport prides itself on its use of local concessionaires, the restaurants and hotels that are springing up alongside the facility are chains.

One of the most pressing problems is out-of-control traffic. Although the freeways are perpetually being expanded, they can't keep pace with the ever-burgeoning population; in downtown, construction is forcing detours on already choked narrow streets. And there's no solution in sight. A proposed light-rail

---

(Fun Fact **And the Beat Goes On . . .**

Both Janis Joplin, who attended the University of Texas for a while, and Stevie Ray Vaughan, enshrined in a statue overlooking Town Lake, got their starts in Austin clubs in the 1960s. During the 1970s the area was a hotbed for "outlaw" country singers Willie Nelson, Waylon Jennings, and Jerry Jeff Walker. During the 1980s there was a national surge of interest in local country-folk artists Lyle Lovett, Eric Taylor, Townes Van Zandt, Darden Smith, Robert Earl Keen, and Nanci Griffith. And the tradition continues: Austin's current musical residents include Grammy Award winners Shawn Colvin and the Dixie Chicks, among others.

system was voted down in 2000—in part, its opponents said, because it was too little too late; in part because they worried that Capitol Metro, the city transport system, wasn't up to the task of building it; and in part because . . . well, no one can ever agree on anything in Austin.

The current tech-recession has halted some of the new construction, but quite a bit is still ongoing. Perhaps the full impact of the economic turndown just hasn't hit yet. But Austin is resilient. Although the oil and savings-and-loan crashes of the mid-1980s left many of the office towers built downtown in the 1970s partially empty, within a decade, Austin had already made a complete recovery. There's no reason to think that this comeback-kid of cities, which became capital because of its hubris and feistiness, will stay down for long this time.

Appendix B:
For International Visitors

Whether it's your first visit or your tenth, a trip to the United States may require an additional degree of planning. This chapter will provide you with essential information, helpful tips, and advice for the more common problems that some visitors encounter.

1 Preparing for Your Trip

ENTRY REQUIREMENTS

Immigration laws are a hot political issue in the United States these days, and the following requirements might have changed somewhat by the time you plan your trip. Check at any U.S. embassy or consulate for current information and requirements. You can also obtain a visa application and other information online at the **U.S. State Department**'s website, at **www.travel.state.gov**.

VISAS The U.S. State Department has a **Visa Waiver Program** allowing citizens of certain countries to enter the United States without a visa for stays of up to 90 days. At press time these included Andorra, Australia, Austria, Belgium, Brunei, Denmark, Finland, France, Germany, Iceland, Ireland, Italy, Japan, Liechtenstein, Luxembourg, Monaco, the Netherlands, New Zealand, Norway, Portugal, San Marino, Singapore, Slovenia, Spain, Sweden, Switzerland, the United Kingdom, and Uruguay. Citizens of these countries need only a valid passport and a round-trip air or cruise ticket in their possession upon arrival. If they first enter the United States, they may also visit Mexico, Canada, Bermuda, and/or the Caribbean islands and return to the United States without a visa. Further information is available from any U.S. embassy or consulate. Canadian citizens may enter the United States without visas; they need only proof of residence.

Citizens of all other countries must have (1) a valid passport that expires at least 6 months later than the scheduled end of their visit to the United States, and (2) a tourist visa, which may be obtained without charge from any U.S. consulate.

To obtain a visa, the traveler must submit a completed application form (either in person or by mail) with a 1½-inch-square photo, and must demonstrate binding ties to a residence abroad. Usually you can obtain a visa at once or within 24 hours, but it may take longer during the summer rush from June through August. If you cannot go in person, contact the nearest U.S. embassy or consulate for directions on applying by mail. Your travel agent or airline office may also be able to provide you with visa applications and instructions. The U.S. consulate or embassy that issues your visa will determine whether you will be issued a multiple- or single-entry visa and any restrictions regarding the length of your stay.

British subjects can obtain up-to-date passport and visa information by calling the **U.S. Embassy Visa Information Line** (© 0891/200-290) or the **London Passport Office** (© 0990/210-410 for recorded information) or they can find the visa information on the U.S. Embassy Great Britain website at www.passport.gov.uk.

Irish citizens can obtain up-to-date passport and visa information through the **Embassy of USA Dublin,** 42 Elgin Rd., Dublin 4, Ireland (© **353/1-668-8777;** or checking the visa page on the website at www.usembassy.ie.

Australian citizens can obtain up-to-date passport and visa information by calling the **U.S. Embassy Canberra,** Moonah Place, Yarralumla, ACT 2600 (© **02/6214-5600**) or check the website's visa page at www.usis-australia.gov/consular/niv.html.

Citizens of **New Zealand** can obtain up-to-date passport and visa information by calling the **U.S. Embassy New Zealand,** 29 Fitzherbert Terr., Thorndon, Wellington, New Zealand (© **644/472-2068**), or get the information directly from the website at http://usembassy.org.nz.

MEDICAL REQUIREMENTS   Unless you're arriving from an area known to be suffering from an epidemic (particularly cholera or yellow fever), inoculations or vaccinations are not required for entry into the United States. If you have a medical condition that requires **syringe-administered medications,** carry a valid signed prescription from your physician—the Transportation Security Administration (TSA) no longer allows airline passengers to pack syringes in their carry-on baggage without documented proof of medical need. If you have a disease that requires treatment with **narcotics,** you should also carry documented proof with you—smuggling narcotics aboard a plane is a serious offense that carries severe penalties in the U.S.

For **HIV-positive visitors,** requirements for entering the United States are somewhat vague and change frequently. According to the latest publication of *HIV and Immigrants: A Manual for AIDS Service Providers,* the Immigration and Naturalization Service (INS) doesn't require a medical exam for entry into the United States, but INS officials may stop individuals because they look sick or because they are carrying AIDS/HIV medicine.

If an HIV-positive noncitizen applies for a non-immigrant visa, the question on the application regarding communicable diseases is tricky no matter which way it's answered. If the applicant checks "no," INS may deny the visa on the grounds that the applicant committed fraud. If the applicant checks "yes" or if INS suspects the person is HIV-positive, it will deny the visa unless the applicant asks for a special waiver for visitors. This waiver is for people visiting the United States for a short time, to attend a conference, for instance, to visit close relatives, or to receive medical treatment. It can be a confusing situation. For further up-to-the-minute information, contact the Centers for Disease Control's **National Center for HIV** (© **404/332-4559;** www.hivatis.org) or the **Gay Men's Health Crisis** (© **212/367-1000;** www.gmhc.org).

DRIVER'S LICENSES   Foreign driver's licenses are mostly recognized in the U.S., although you may want to get an international driver's license if your home license is not written in English.

PASSPORT INFORMATION

Safeguard your passport in an inconspicuous, inaccessible place like a money belt. Make a copy of the critical pages, including the passport number, and store it in a safe place, separate from the passport itself. If you lose your passport, visit the nearest consulate of your native country as soon as possible for a replacement. Passport applications are downloadable from the Internet sites listed below.

Note that the International Civil Aviation Organization (ICAO) has recommended a policy requiring that *every* individual who travels by air have his or her own passport. In response, many countries are now requiring that children must be issued their own passport to travel internationally, where before those under 16 or so may have been allowed to travel on a parent or guardian's passport.

FOR RESIDENTS OF CANADA

You can pick up a passport application at one of 28 regional passport offices or most travel agencies. As of December 11, 2001, Canadian children who travel must have their own passport. However, if you hold a valid Canadian passport issued before December 11, 2001, that bears the name of your child, the passport remains valid for you and your child until it expires. Passports cost C$85 for those 16 years and older (valid 5 years), C$35 children 3 to 15 (valid 5 years), and C$20, children under 3 (valid 3 years). Applications, which must be accompanied by two identical passport-sized photographs and proof of Canadian citizenship, are available at travel agencies throughout Canada or from the central **Passport Office,** Department of Foreign Affairs and International Trade, Ottawa, ON K1A 0G3 (✆ **800/567-6868;** www.dfait-maeci.gc.ca/passport). Processing takes 5 to 10 days if you apply in person, or about 3 weeks by mail.

FOR RESIDENTS OF THE UNITED KINGDOM

To pick up an application for a standard 10-year passport (5-year passport for children under 16), visit your nearest passport office, major post office, or travel agency. You can also contact the **United Kingdom Passport Service** at ✆ **0870/ 521-0410** or search its website at www.ukpa.gov.uk. Passports are £30 for adults and £16 for children under 16. Processing takes about 2 weeks.

FOR RESIDENTS OF IRELAND

You can apply for a 10-year passport, costing €57, at the **Passport Office,** Setanta Centre, Molesworth Street, Dublin 2 (✆ **01/671-1633;** www.irlgov. ie/iveagh). Those under age 18 and over 65 must apply for a €12 3-year passport. You can also apply at 1A South Mall, Cork (✆ **021/272-525**) or over the counter at most main post offices.

FOR RESIDENTS OF AUSTRALIA

You can pick up an application from your local post office or any branch of Passports Australia, but you must schedule an interview at the passport office to present your application materials. Call the **Australian Passport Information Service** at ✆ **131-232,** or visit the government website at www.passports.gov.au. Passports for adults are A$144 and for those under 18 are A$72.

FOR RESIDENTS OF NEW ZEALAND

You can pick up a passport application at any New Zealand Passports Office or download it from their website. Contact the **Passports Office** at ✆ **0800/ 225-050** in New Zealand or 04/474-8100, or log on to www.passports.govt.nz. Passports for adults are NZ$80 and for children under 16 NZ$40.

CUSTOMS
WHAT YOU CAN BRING IN

Every visitor more than 21 years of age may bring in, free of duty, the following: (1) 1 liter of wine or hard liquor; (2) 200 cigarettes, 100 cigars (but not from Cuba), or 3 pounds of smoking tobacco; and (3) $100 worth of gifts. These exemptions are offered to travelers who spend at least 72 hours in the United States and who have not claimed them within the preceding 6 months.

It is altogether forbidden to bring into the country foodstuffs (particularly fruit, cooked meats, and canned goods) and plants (vegetables, seeds, tropical plants, and the like). Foreign tourists may bring in or take out up to $10,000 in U.S. or foreign currency with no formalities; larger sums must be declared to U.S. Customs on entering or leaving, which includes filing form CM 4790. For more specific information regarding U.S. Customs, contact your nearest U.S. embassy or consulate, or the **U.S. Customs** office (℡ **202/927-1770** or www.customs. ustreas.gov).

WHAT YOU CAN TAKE HOME

U.K. citizens returning from a non-EU country have a customs allowance of: 200 cigarettes; 50 cigars; 250g of smoking tobacco; 2 liters of still table wine; 1 liter of spirits or strong liqueurs (over 22% volume); 2 liters of fortified wine, sparkling wine or other liqueurs; 60cc (ml) perfume; 250cc (ml) of toilet water; and £145 worth of all other goods, including gifts and souvenirs. People under 17 cannot have the tobacco or alcohol allowance. For more information, contact HM Customs & Excise at ℡ **0845/010-9000** (from outside the U.K., 020/8929-0152), or consult their website at www.hmce.gov.uk.

For a clear summary of **Canadian** rules, request the booklet *I Declare,* issued by the **Canada Customs and Revenue Agency** (℡ **800/461-9999** in Canada, or 204/983-3500; www.ccra-adrc.gc.ca). Canada allows its citizens a C$750 exemption, and you're allowed to bring back duty-free one carton of cigarettes, 1 can of tobacco, 40 imperial ounces of liquor, and 50 cigars. In addition, you're allowed to mail gifts to Canada valued at less than C$60 a day, provided they're unsolicited and don't contain alcohol or tobacco (write on the package "Unsolicited gift, under $60 value"). All valuables should be declared on the Y-38 form before departure from Canada, including serial numbers of valuables you already own, such as expensive foreign cameras. Note: The $750 exemption can only be used once a year and only after an absence of 7 days.

The duty-free allowance in **Australia** is A$400 or, for those under 18, A$200. Citizens age 18 and over can bring in 250 cigarettes or 250 grams of loose tobacco, and 1,125 milliliters of alcohol. If you're returning with valuables you already own, such as foreign-made cameras, you should file form B263. A helpful brochure available from Australian consulates or Customs offices is *Know Before You Go.* For more information, call the **Australian Customs Service** at ℡ **1300/363-263,** or log on to www.customs.gov.au.

The duty-free allowance for **New Zealand** is NZ$700. Citizens over 17 can bring in 200 cigarettes, 50 cigars, or 250 grams of tobacco (or a mixture of all three if their combined weight doesn't exceed 250g); plus 4.5 liters of wine and beer, or 1.125 liters of liquor. New Zealand currency does not carry import or export restrictions. Fill out a certificate of export, listing the valuables you are taking out of the country; that way, you can bring them back without paying duty. Most questions are answered in a free pamphlet available at New Zealand consulates and Customs offices: *New Zealand Customs Guide for Travellers, Notice no. 4.* For more information, contact **New Zealand Customs,** The Customhouse, 17–21 Whitmore St., Box 2218, Wellington (℡ **0800/428-786** or 04/473-6099; www.customs.govt.nz).

HEALTH INSURANCE

Although it's not required of travelers, health insurance is highly recommended. Unlike many European countries, the United States does not usually offer free or low-cost medical care to its citizens or visitors. Doctors and hospitals are expensive, and in most cases will require advance payment or proof of coverage before they render their services. Policies can cover everything from the loss or theft of your baggage and trip cancellation to the guarantee of bail in case you're arrested. Good policies will also cover the costs of an accident, repatriation, or death. See "Insurance" in chapter 2 for more information. Packages such as **Europ Assistance's "Worldwide Healthcare Plan"** are sold by European automobile clubs and travel agencies at attractive rates. **Worldwide Assistance Services,** Inc. (© **800/821-2828;** www.worldwideassistance.com) is the agent for Europ Assistance in the United States.

Though lack of health insurance may prevent you from being admitted to a hospital in nonemergencies, don't worry about being left on a street corner to die: the American way is to fix you now and bill the living daylights out of you later.

INSURANCE FOR BRITISH TRAVELERS   Most big travel agents offer their own insurance and will probably try to sell you their package when you book a holiday. Think before you sign. **Britain's Consumers' Association** recommends that you insist on seeing the policy and reading the fine print before buying travel insurance. **The Association of British Insurers** (© **020/7600-3333;** www.abi.org.uk) gives advice by phone and publishes *Holiday Insurance,* a free guide to policy provisions and prices. You might also shop around for better deals: Try **Columbus Direct** (© **020/7375-0011;** www.columbusdirect.net).

INSURANCE FOR CANADIAN TRAVELERS   Canadians should check with their provincial health plan offices or call **Health Canada** (© **613/957-2991;** www.hc-sc.gc.ca) to find out the extent of their coverage and what documentation and receipts they must take home in case they are treated in the United States.

MONEY

CURRENCY   The U.S. monetary system is very simple: The most common **bills** are the $1 (colloquially, a "buck"), $5, $10, and $20 denominations. There are also $2 bills (seldom encountered), $50 bills, and $100 bills (the last two are usually not welcome as payment for small purchases). All the paper money was recently redesigned, making the famous faces adorning them disproportionately large. The old-style bills are still legal tender.

There are seven denominations of coins: 1¢ (1 cent, or a penny); 5¢ (5 cents, or a nickel); 10¢ (10 cents, or a dime); 25¢ (25 cents, or a quarter); 50¢ (50 cents, or a half dollar); the new gold "Sacagawea" coin worth $1; and, prized by collectors, the rare, older silver dollar.

Note: The "foreign-exchange bureaus" so common in Europe are rare even at airports in the United States, and nonexistent outside major cities. It's best not to change foreign money (or traveler's checks denominated in a currency other than U.S. dollars) at a small-town bank, or even a branch in a big city; in fact, leave any currency other than U.S. dollars at home—it may prove a greater nuisance to you than it's worth.

CREDIT CARDS & ATMS   Credit cards are the most widely used form of payment in the United States: **Visa** (BarclayCard in Britain), **MasterCard** (Eurocard in Europe, Access in Britain, Chargex in Canada), **American Express, Diners Club, Discover,** and **Carte Blanche.** You must have a credit or charge card to rent a car. There are, however, a handful of stores and restaurants that do not take credit cards, so be sure to ask in advance. Most businesses

Travel Tip

Be sure to keep a copy of all your travel papers separate from your wallet or purse, and leave a copy with someone at home should you need it faxed in an emergency.

display a sticker near their entrance to let you know which cards they accept. *Note:* Often, businesses require a minimum purchase price, usually around $10, to use a credit card.

It is strongly recommended that you bring at least one major credit card. Hotels, car-rental companies, and airlines usually require a credit-card imprint as a deposit against expenses, and in an emergency, a credit card can be priceless.

You'll find automated teller machines (ATMs) on just about every block—at least in almost every town—across the country. Some ATMs will allow you to draw U.S. currency against your bank and credit cards. Check with your bank before leaving home, and remember that you will need your personal identification number (PIN) to do so. Most accept Visa, MasterCard, and American Express, as well as ATM cards from other U.S. banks. Expect to be charged up to $3 per transaction, however, if you're not using your own bank's ATM.

TRAVELER'S CHECKS   Although traveler's checks are widely accepted, make sure that they're denominated in U.S. dollars, as foreign-currency checks are often difficult to exchange. The three traveler's checks that are most widely recognized—and least likely to be denied—are **Visa, American Express,** and **Thomas Cook.** Be sure to record the numbers of the checks, and keep that information separately in case they get lost or stolen. Most businesses are pretty good about taking traveler's checks, but you're better off cashing them at a bank (in small amounts, of course) and paying in cash. You'll need identification, such as a driver's license or passport, to change a traveler's check.

SAFETY

GENERAL SUGGESTIONS   While tourist areas are generally safe, U.S. urban areas tend to be less safe than those in Europe or Japan. You should always stay alert. It is wise to ask your hotel front desk staff or the city or area's tourist office if you're in doubt about which neighborhoods are safe. Avoid deserted areas, especially at night. Don't go into any city parks at night unless there's an event that attracts crowds, such as a concert or similar occasion.

Avoid carrying valuables with you on the street, and don't display expensive cameras or electronic equipment. If you are using a map, consult it inconspicuously—or better yet, try to study it before you leave your room. Hold onto your pocketbook, and place your billfold in an inside pocket. In theaters, restaurants, and other public places, keep your possessions in sight.

Remember also that hotels are open to the public, and in a large hotel, security may not be able to screen everyone entering. Always lock your room door—don't assume that, once inside your hotel, you are automatically safe and no longer need to be aware of your surroundings.

You may want to contact the **San Antonio Convention and Visitors Bureau,** P.O. Box 2277, San Antonio, TX 78298 (© **800/447-3372;** www.sanantoniovisit.com), or the **Austin Convention and Visitors Bureau,** 201 E. Second St., Austin, TX 78701 (© **800/926-2282;** www.austintexas.org), ahead of time for additional advice on safety precautions.

DRIVING   Driving safety is important too, and carjacking is not unprecedented. Question your rental agency about personal safety and ask for a traveler-safety brochure when you pick up your car. Obtain written directions—or a map with the route clearly marked—from the agency showing how to get to your destination. (Many agencies now offer the option of renting a cellphone for the duration of your car rental; check with the rental agent when you pick up the car.) And, if possible, arrive and depart during daylight hours.

If you drive off a highway and end up in a dodgy-looking neighborhood, leave the area as quickly as possible. If you have an accident, even on the highway, stay in your car with the doors locked until you assess the situation or until the police arrive. If you're bumped from behind on the street or are involved in a minor accident with no injuries, and the situation appears to be suspicious, motion to the other driver to follow you. Never get out of your car in such situations. Go directly to the nearest police precinct, well-lit service station, or 24-hour store. You may want to look into renting a cellphone on a short-term basis. One recommended wireless rental company is **InTouch USA** (© **800/872-7626;** www.intouchusa.com).

Park in well-lit and well-traveled areas whenever possible. Always keep your car doors locked, whether the vehicle is attended or unattended. Never leave any packages or valuables in sight. If someone attempts to rob you or steal your car, don't try to resist the thief/carjacker. Report the incident to the police department immediately by calling © **911.**

2 Getting to the United States

Houston is the hub for international flights into Texas. **Air Canada** (© 888/ 247-2262; www.aircanada.ca) offers daily nonstop flights from Toronto and Calgary to Houston. **Continental** (© 0800/776-464; www.continental.com) and **British Airways** (© 0845/773-3377; www.britishairways.com) both have nonstop service from London. **Aerolitoral** (© 01800/021-26622; www.aero litoral.com), **Continental** (© 01800/900-5000; www.continental.com), and **Mexicana** (© 800/531-7921 in the U.S.; www.mexicana.com) offer service from Mexico to San Antonio.

For further information about travel to San Antonio and Austin, see the "Getting There" sections of chapters 2 and 10, respectively.

AIRLINE DISCOUNTS   You can find numerable ways to reduce the price of a plane ticket simply by taking time to shop around. For example, overseas visitors can take advantage of the APEX (Advance Purchase Excursion) reductions offered by all major U.S. and European carriers. For the best rates, compare fares and be flexible with the dates and times of travel.

IMMIGRATION AND CUSTOMS CLEARANCE   Visitors arriving by air, no matter what the port of entry, should cultivate patience and resignation before setting foot on U.S. soil. Getting through immigration control can take as long as 2 hours on some days, especially on summer weekends, so be sure to carry this guidebook or something else to read. This is especially true since the September 11, 2001, terrorist attacks; security clearances have been considerably beefed up at U.S. airports.

People traveling by air from Canada, Bermuda, and certain countries in the Caribbean can sometimes clear Customs and Immigration at the point of departure, which is much quicker.

3 Getting Around the United States

BY PLANE   Some large airlines (for example, Northwest and Delta) offer travelers on their transatlantic or transpacific flights special discount tickets under the name **Visit USA,** allowing mostly one-way travel from one U.S. destination to another at very low prices. These discount tickets are not on sale in the United States and must be purchased abroad along with your international ticket. This system is the best, easiest, and fastest way to see the United States at low cost. You should get information well in advance from your travel agent or the office of the airline concerned since the conditions attached to these discount tickets can be changed without advance notice.

BY TRAIN   International visitors (excluding Canada) can also buy a **USA Rail Pass,** good for 15 or 30 days of unlimited travel on Amtrak (© **800/USA-RAIL;** www.amtrak.com). The pass is available through many foreign travel agents. With a foreign passport, you can also buy passes at some Amtrak offices in the United States, including locations in San Francisco, Los Angeles, Chicago, New York, Miami, Boston, and Washington, D.C. Reservations are generally required and should be made for each part of your trip as early as possible. Regional rail passes are also available.

BY BUS   Although bus travel is often the most economical form of public transit for short hops between U.S. cities, it can also be slow and uncomfortable—certainly not an option for everyone (particularly when Amtrak, which is far more luxurious, offers similar rates). **Greyhound/Trailways** (© **800/231-2222;** www.greyhound.com), the sole nationwide bus line, offers an **International Ameripass** that must be purchased before coming to the United States, or by phone through the Greyhound International Office at the Port Authority Bus Terminal in New York City (© **212/971-0492**). The pass can be obtained from foreign travel agents or through Greyhound's website (order at least 21 days before your departure to the U.S.) and costs less than the domestic version. You can get more info on the pass at the website, or by calling © **402/330-8552.** In addition, special rates are available for seniors and students.

BY CAR   The most cost-effective, convenient, and comfortable way to travel around the United States is by car. The interstate highway system connects cities and towns all over the country; in addition to these high-speed, limited-access roadways, there's an extensive network of federal, state, and local highways and roads. Some of the national car-rental companies include **Alamo** (© 800/462-5266; www.alamo.com), **Avis** (© 800/230-4898; www.avis.com), **Budget** (© 800/527-0700; www.budget.com), **Dollar** (© 800/800-3665; www.dollar.com), **Hertz** (© 800/654-3131; www.hertz.com), **National** (© 800/227-7368; www.nationalcar.com), and **Thrifty** (© 800/847-4389; www.thrifty.com).

If you plan to rent a car in the United States, you probably won't need the services of an additional automobile organization. If you're planning to buy or borrow a car, automobile-association membership is recommended. The **American Automobile Association** (**AAA;** © **800/222-4357**), is the country's largest auto club and supplies its members with maps, insurance, and, most important, emergency road service. The cost of joining runs from $63 for singles to $87 for two members, but if you're a member of a foreign auto club with reciprocal arrangements, you can enjoy free AAA service in America.

For details about San Antonio and Austin, see the "Getting Around" sections of chapters 3 and 10, respectively.

FAST FACTS: For the International Traveler

Automobile Organizations Auto clubs will supply maps, suggested routes, guidebooks, accident and bail-bond insurance, and emergency road service. The **American Automobile Association (AAA)** is the major auto club in the United States. If you belong to an auto club in your home country, inquire about AAA reciprocity before you leave. You may be able to join AAA even if you're not a member of a reciprocal club; to inquire, call AAA (© **800/222-4357**). AAA is actually an organization of regional auto clubs, so look under "AAA Automobile Club" in the white pages of the telephone directory. AAA has a nationwide emergency road service telephone number (© **800/AAA-HELP**).

Business Hours Offices are usually open weekdays 9am to 5pm. Banks are open weekdays 9am to 3pm or later and sometimes Saturday mornings. Stores, especially those in shopping complexes, tend to stay open late: until about 9pm on weekdays and 6pm on weekends.

Climate See "When to Go," in chapters 2 and 10.

Currency & Currency Exchange See "Entry Requirements" and "Money" under "Preparing for Your Trip," above.

Drinking Laws See liquor laws in "Fast Facts: San Antonio," in chapter 3, and "Fast Facts: Austin," in chapter 11.

Electricity Like Canada, the United States uses 110 to 120 volts AC (60 cycles), compared to 220 to 240 volts AC (50 cycles) in most of Europe, Australia, and New Zealand. If your small appliances use 220 to 240 volts, you'll need a 110-volt transformer and a plug adapter with two flat parallel pins to operate them here. Downward converters that change 220–240 volts to 110–120 volts are difficult to find in the United States, so bring one with you.

Embassies & Consulates All embassies are located in the nation's capital, Washington, D.C. Some consulates are located in major U.S. cities, and most nations have a mission to the United Nations in New York City. Foreign visitors can find telephone numbers for their embassies and consulates by calling directory information in Washington, D.C. (© **202/555-1212**).

There's a Canadian Consulate in Dallas at 750 N. St. Paul St., Suite 1700, Dallas, TX 75201 (© **214/922-9806**). Houston is home to a consulate for the United Kingdom at 1000 Louisiana St., Suite 1900, Houston, TX 77002 (© **713/659-6270**).

Emergencies Call © **911** to report a fire, call the police, or get an ambulance anywhere in the United States. This is a toll-free call (no coins are required at public telephones).

If you encounter traveler's problems, check the local telephone directory to find an office of the **Traveler's Aid Society,** a nationwide, nonprofit, social-service organization geared to helping travelers in difficult straits. Their services might include reuniting families separated while traveling, providing food and/or shelter to people stranded without cash, or even emotional counseling. If you're in trouble, seek them out.

Gasoline (Petrol) One U.S. gallon equals 3.75 liters, and 1.2 U.S. gallons equals 1 imperial gallon. You'll notice there are several grades (and price levels) of gasoline available at most gas stations, and you'll also notice their names change from company to company. Most cars use unleaded gasoline; higher-octane gasoline is more expensive and usually unnecessary, thus most rental cars take the least expensive "regular" unleaded gas.

Holidays Banks, government offices, post offices, and many stores, restaurants, and museums are closed on the following legal national holidays: January 1 (New Year's Day), the third Monday in January (Martin Luther King, Jr., Day), the third Monday in February (Presidents' Day, Washington's Birthday), the last Monday in May (Memorial Day), July 4 (Independence Day), the first Monday in September (Labor Day), the second Monday in October (Columbus Day), November 11 (Veterans' Day/Armistice Day), the fourth Thursday in November (Thanksgiving Day), and December 25 (Christmas). Also, the Tuesday following the first Monday in November is Election Day and is a federal government holiday in presidential-election years—which occur every 4 years, and next in 2004.

Languages Major hotels may have multilingual employees. Unless your language is obscure, they can usually supply a translator. Many people in San Antonio are fluent in Spanish.

Legal Aid The foreign tourist will probably never become involved with the American legal system. If you are "pulled over" for a minor infraction (for example, of the highway code, such as speeding), never attempt to pay the fine directly to a police officer; this could be construed as attempted bribery, a much more serious crime. Pay fines by mail or directly into the hands of the clerk of the court. If accused of a more serious offense, say and do nothing before consulting a lawyer. Here, the burden is on the state to prove a person's guilt beyond a reasonable doubt, and everyone has the right to remain silent, whether he or she is suspected of a crime or actually arrested. Once arrested, a person can make one telephone call to a party of his or her choice. Call your embassy or consulate.

Mail If you aren't sure what your address will be in the United States, mail can be sent to you, in your name, c/o General Delivery at the main post office of the city or region where you expect to be (call ✆ **800/275-8777** for information on the nearest post office). The addressee must pick mail up in person and must produce proof of identity (driver's license, passport, and so on). Most post offices will hold your mail for up to 1 month, and are open Monday to Friday 8am to 6pm, and Saturday 9am to 3pm.

Generally found at intersections, mailboxes are blue with a red-and-white stripe and carry the inscription U.S. MAIL. If your mail is addressed to a U.S. destination, don't forget to add the five-digit postal code (or ZIP code) after the two-letter abbreviation of the state to which the mail is addressed.

At press time, domestic postage rates were 23¢ for a postcard and 37¢ for a letter. For international mail, a first-class letter of up to one-half ounce costs 80¢ (60¢ to Canada and Mexico); a first-class postcard costs 70¢ (50¢ to Canada and Mexico); and a preprinted postal aerogramme costs 70¢.

Newspapers/Magazines National newspapers include the *New York Times, USA Today,* and the *Wall Street Journal.* National newsweeklies include *Newsweek, Time,* and *U.S. News & World Report.* San Antonio and Austin each have one major newspaper: the *San Antonio Express-News* and the *Austin-American Statesman.*

Radio/Television Nationally there are six commercial over-the-air television networks—ABC, CBS, NBC, FOX, UPN, and WB—along with the Public Broadcast System (PBS) and the cable news network CNN. In big cities, viewers have a choice of dozens of channels (including basic cable), most of which transmit 24 hours a day. Most hotels have at least basic cable, and many offer access to "premium" movie channels that show uncut theatrical releases. You'll find a wide choice of local radio stations, each broadcasting particular kinds of talk shows and/or music punctuated with news broadcasts and frequent commercials.

Safety See "Safety" in "Preparing for Your Trip," above.

Taxes In the United States, there is no value-added tax (VAT) or other indirect tax at the national level. Every state, county, and city has the right to levy its own local tax on all purchases, including hotel and restaurant checks, airline tickets, and so on.

Telephone, Telegraph, Telex & Fax The telephone system in the United States is run by private corporations, so rates, especially for long-distance service and operator-assisted calls, can vary widely. Generally, hotel surcharges on long-distance and local calls are astronomical, so you're usually better off using a **public pay telephone,** which you'll find clearly marked in most public buildings and private establishments, as well as on the street. Convenience grocery stores and gas stations always have them. Many convenience groceries and packaging services sell **prepaid calling cards** in denominations up to $50; they can be the least expensive way to call home. Many public phones at airports now accept American Express, MasterCard, and Visa credit cards. **Local calls** made from public pay phones in most locales cost either 25¢ or 35¢. Pay phones do not accept pennies, and few will take anything larger than a quarter.

Most long-distance and international calls can be dialed directly from any phone. **For calls within the United States and to Canada,** dial 1 followed by the area code and the seven-digit number. **For other international calls,** dial 011 followed by the country code, city code, and the telephone number of the person you are calling.

Calls to area codes **800, 888,** and **877** are toll-free. However, calls to numbers in area codes **700** and **900** (chat lines, bulletin boards, "dating" services, and so on) can be very expensive—usually a charge of 95¢ to $3 or more per minute, and they sometimes have minimum charges that can run as high as $15 or more.

For **reversed-charge or collect calls,** and for person-to-person calls, dial 0 (zero, not the letter *O*) followed by the area code and number you want; an operator will then come on the line, and you should specify that you are calling collect, or person-to-person, or both. If your operator-assisted call is international, ask for the overseas operator.

For **local directory assistance** ("information"), dial ℂ **411;** for long-distance information, dial 1, then the appropriate area code, then 555-1212.

Telegraph and telex services are provided primarily by Western Union. You can bring your telegram into the nearest Western Union office (there are hundreds across the country) or dictate it over the phone (© **800/ 325-6000**). You can also telegraph money or have it telegraphed to you very quickly over the Western Union system, but this service can cost as much as 15% to 20% of the amount sent.

Most hotels have **fax machines** available for guest use (be sure to ask about the charge to use it), and many hotel rooms are even wired for guests' fax machines. A less expensive way to send and receive faxes may be at stores such as Kinko's, a national chain of copy shops, and Mail Boxes Etc., a national chain of packing service shops (look in the Yellow Pages directory under "Packing Services").

Telephone Directories There are two kinds of telephone directories in the United States. The so-called **White Pages** list private households and business subscribers in alphabetical order. The inside front cover lists emergency numbers for police, fire, ambulance, the Coast Guard, poison-control center, crime-victims hot line, and so on. The first few pages will tell you how to make long-distance and international calls, complete with country codes and area codes. Government numbers are usually printed on blue paper within the White Pages. Printed on yellow paper, the so-called **Yellow Pages** list all local services, businesses, industries, and houses of worship according to activity with an index at the front or back. (Drugstores/pharmacies and restaurants are also listed by geographic location.) The Yellow Pages also include city plans or detailed area maps, postal ZIP codes, and public transportation routes.

Time The continental United States is divided into **four time zones:** Eastern Standard Time (EST), Central Standard Time (CST), Mountain Standard Time (MST), and Pacific Standard Time (PST). Alaska and Hawaii have their own zones. For example, noon in New York City (EST) is 11am in Chicago (CST), 10am in Denver (MST), 9am in Los Angeles (PST), 8am in Anchorage (AST), and 7am in Honolulu (HST).

Most of Texas, including San Antonio and Austin, is on Central Standard Time. The far western part of the state, around El Paso, observes Mountain Standard Time (clocks are set 1 hr. earlier). Daylight saving time, which moves the clock 1 hour ahead of standard time, is in effect from the first Sunday in April through the last Sunday in October (starting at 2am), except in Arizona, Hawaii, most of Indiana, and Puerto Rico.

Tipping Tips are a very important part of certain workers' salaries, so it's necessary to leave appropriate gratuities. In hotels, tip **bellhops** at least $1 per bag ($2–$3 if you have a lot of luggage) and tip the **chamber staff** $1 to $2 per day (more if you've left a disaster area for him or her to clean up). Tip the **doorman** or **concierge** only if he or she has provided you with some specific service (for example, calling a cab for you or obtaining difficult-to-get theater tickets). Tip the **valet-parking attendant** $1 every time you get your car.

In restaurants, bars, and nightclubs, tip **service staff** 15% to 20% of the check, tip **bartenders** 10% to 15%, tip **checkroom attendants** $1 per garment, and tip **valet-parking attendants** $1 per vehicle. Tip the **doorman** only if he has provided you with some specific service (such as calling a cab for you).

As for other service personnel, tip **cab drivers** 15% of the fare; tip **sky-caps** at airports at least $1 per bag ($2–$3 if you have a lot of luggage); and tip **hairdressers** and **barbers** 15% to 20%.

Toilets You won't find public toilets or "restrooms" on the streets in most U.S. cities, but they can be found in hotel lobbies, bars, restaurants, museums, department stores, railway and bus stations, or service stations. Note, however, that restaurants and bars in resorts or heavily visited areas may reserve their restrooms for the use of their patrons. Some establishments display a notice that toilets are for the use of patrons only. You can ignore this sign or, better yet, avoid arguments by paying for a cup of coffee or a soft drink, which will qualify you as a patron. Museums, cafés, department stores, and large hotels are probably the best place to find good, clean facilities; fast-food restaurants always have restrooms, but quality is variable. If possible, avoid the toilets at parks and beaches, as they tend to be dirty.

Appendix C: Useful Toll-Free Numbers & Websites

AIRLINES

Aeromar Airlines
☎ 888/627-0207 in the U.S.
www.aeromarairlines.com

Air Canada
☎ 888/247-2262
www.aircanada.ca

Air New Zealand
☎ 800/262-1234 in the U.S.
☎ 0800/737-767 in New Zealand
www.airnewzealand.com

Alaska Airlines
☎ 800/252-7522
www.alaskaair.com

American Airlines
☎ 800/433-7300
www.aa.com

American Trans Air
☎ 800/I-FLY-ATA
www.ata.com

America West Airlines
☎ 800/235-9292
www.americawest.com

British Airways
☎ 800/247-9297
☎ 0845/773-3377 in the U.K.
www.ba.com

Continental Airlines
☎ 800/525-0280
www.continental.com

Delta Air Lines
☎ 800/221-1212
www.delta.com

Frontier Airlines
☎ 800/432-1359
www.frontierairlines.com

Mexicana Airlines
☎ 800/531-7921 in the U.S.
www.mexicana.com

Midwest Express
☎ 800/452-2022
www.midwestexpress.com

Northwest Airlines
☎ 800/225-2525
www.nwa.com

Qantas
☎ 800/227-4500 in the U.S.
☎ 13-13-13 in Australia
www.qantas.com

Southwest Airlines
☎ 800/435-9792
www.iflyswa.com

United Airlines
☎ 800/241-6522
www.united.com

US Airways
☎ 800/428-4322
www.usairways.com

Virgin Atlantic Airways
☎ 800/862-8621 in continental U.S.
☎ 0293/747-747 in the U.K.
www.virgin-atlantic.com

CAR-RENTAL AGENCIES

Advantage
© 800/777-5500
www.advantagerentacar.com

Alamo
© 800/327-9633
www.goalamo.com

Avis
© 800/331-1212
www.avis.com

Budget
© 800/527-0700
www.budget.com

Dollar
© 800/800-4000
www.dollarcar.com

Enterprise
© 800/325-8007
www.enterprise.com

Hertz
© 800/654-3131
www.hertz.com

National
© 800/CAR-RENT
www.nationalcar.com

Payless
© 800/PAYLESS
www.paylesscar.com

Rent-A-Wreck
© 800/944-7501
www.rentawreck.com

Thrifty
© 800/367-2277
www.thrifty.com

MAJOR HOTEL & MOTEL CHAINS

Best Western International
© 800/780-7234
www.bestwestern.com

Clarion Hotels
© 800/CLARION
www.hotelchoice.com

Comfort Inns
© 800/228-5150
www.hotelchoice.com

Courtyard by Marriott
© 800/321-2211
www.courtyard.com

Days Inn
© 800/325-2525
www.daysinn.com

Doubletree Hotels
© 800/222-TREE
www.doubletree.com

Econo Lodges
© 800/55-ECONO
www.hotelchoice.com

Embassy Suites
© 800/EMBASSY
www.embassy-suites.com

Fairfield Inn by Marriott
© 800/228-2800
www.fairfieldinn.com

Hampton Inns
© 800/HAMPTON
www.hampton-inn.com

Hilton Hotels
© 800/HILTONS
www.hilton.com

Holiday Inn
© 800/HOLIDAY
www.holiday-inn.com

Howard Johnson
© 800/I-GO-HOJO
www.hojo.com

Hyatt Hotels & Resorts
© 888/591-1234
www.hyatt.com

InterContinental Hotels & Resorts
© 888/567-8725
www.intercontinental.com

La Quinta Motor Inns
© 800/531-5900
www.laquinta.com

Marriott Hotels
© 888/236-2427
www.marriott.com

Motel 6
© 800/4-MOTEL6
www.motel6.com

Omni Hotels
© 800/THE-OMNI
www.omnihotels.com

Quality Inns
© 800/228-5151
www.hotelchoice.com

Radisson Hotels
© 888/201-1717
www.radisson.com

Ramada Inns
© 888/298-2054
www.ramada.com

Red Roof Inns
© 800/RED-ROOF
www.redroof.com

Residence Inn by Marriott
© 800/331-3131
www.residenceinn.com

Rodeway Inns
© 800/228-2000
www.hotelchoice.com

Sheraton Hotels & Resorts
© 888/625-5144
www.sheraton.com

Super 8 Motels
© 800/800-8000
www.super8.com

Travelodge
© 800/578-7878
www.travelodge.com

Vagabond Inns
© 800/522-1555
www.vagabondinn.com

Westin Hotels & Resorts
© 800/937-8461
www.westin.com

Wyndham Hotels and Resorts
© 800/WYNDHAM
www.wyndham.com

Index

See also Accommodations and Restaurant indexes, below.

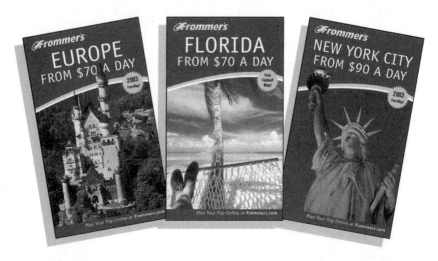

FROMMER'S® COMPLETE TRAVEL GUIDES

Alaska
Alaska Cruises & Ports of Call
Amsterdam
Argentina & Chile
Arizona
Atlanta
Australia
Austria
Bahamas
Barcelona, Madrid & Seville
Beijing
Belgium, Holland & Luxembourg
Bermuda
Boston
Brazil
British Columbia & the Canadian Rockies
Budapest & the Best of Hungary
California
Canada
Cancún, Cozumel & the Yucatán
Cape Cod, Nantucket & Martha's Vineyard
Caribbean
Caribbean Cruises & Ports of Call
Caribbean Ports of Call
Carolinas & Georgia
Chicago
China
Colorado
Costa Rica
Denmark
Denver, Boulder & Colorado Springs
England
Europe
European Cruises & Ports of Call
Florida
France
Germany
Great Britain
Greece
Greek Islands
Hawaii
Hong Kong
Honolulu, Waikiki & Oahu
Ireland
Israel
Italy
Jamaica
Japan
Las Vegas
London
Los Angeles
Maryland & Delaware
Maui
Mexico
Montana & Wyoming
Montréal & Québec City
Munich & the Bavarian Alps
Nashville & Memphis
Nepal
New England
New Mexico
New Orleans
New York City
New Zealand
Northern Italy
Nova Scotia, New Brunswick & Prince Edward Island
Oregon
Paris
Philadelphia & the Amish Country
Portugal
Prague & the Best of the Czech Republic
Provence & the Riviera
Puerto Rico
Rome
San Antonio & Austin
San Diego
San Francisco
Santa Fe, Taos & Albuquerque
Scandinavia
Scotland
Seattle & Portland
Shanghai
Singapore & Malaysia
South Africa
South America
South Florida
South Pacific
Southeast Asia
Spain
Sweden
Switzerland
Texas
Thailand
Tokyo
Toronto
Tuscany & Umbria
USA
Utah
Vancouver & Victoria
Vermont, New Hampshire & Maine
Vienna & the Danube Valley
Virgin Islands
Virginia
Walt Disney World® & Orlando
Washington, D.C.
Washington State

FROMMER'S® DOLLAR-A-DAY GUIDES

Australia from $50 a Day
California from $70 a Day
Caribbean from $70 a Day
England from $75 a Day
Europe from $70 a Day
Florida from $70 a Day
Hawaii from $80 a Day
Ireland from $60 a Day
Italy from $70 a Day
London from $85 a Day
New York from $90 a Day
Paris from $80 a Day
San Francisco from $70 a Day
Washington, D.C. from $80 a Day

FROMMER'S® PORTABLE GUIDES

Acapulco, Ixtapa & Zihuatanejo
Amsterdam
Aruba
Australia's Great Barrier Reef
Bahamas
Berlin
Big Island of Hawaii
Boston
California Wine Country
Cancún
Charleston & Savannah
Chicago
Disneyland®
Dublin
Florence
Frankfurt
Hong Kong
Houston
Las Vegas
London
Los Angeles
Los Cabos & Baja
Maine Coast
Maui
Miami
New Orleans
New York City
Paris
Phoenix & Scottsdale
Portland
Puerto Rico
Puerto Vallarta, Manzanillo & Guadalajara
Rio de Janeiro
San Diego
San Francisco
Seattle
Sydney
Tampa & St. Petersburg
Vancouver
Venice
Virgin Islands
Washington, D.C.

FROMMER'S® NATIONAL PARK GUIDES

Banff & Jasper
Family Vacations in the National Parks
Grand Canyon
National Parks of the American West
Rocky Mountain
Yellowstone & Grand Teton
Yosemite & Sequoia/ Kings Canyon
Zion & Bryce Canyon

FROMMER'S® MEMORABLE WALKS

Chicago
London

New York
Paris

San Francisco
Washington, D.C.

FROMMER'S® GREAT OUTDOOR GUIDES

Arizona & New Mexico
New England

Northern California
Southern New England

Vermont & New Hampshire

SUZY GERSHMAN'S BORN TO SHOP GUIDES

Born to Shop: France
Born to Shop: Hong Kong,
   Shanghai & Beijing

Born to Shop: Italy
Born to Shop: London

Born to Shop: New York
Born to Shop: Paris

FROMMER'S® IRREVERENT GUIDES

Amsterdam
Boston
Chicago
Las Vegas
London

Los Angeles
Manhattan
New Orleans
Paris
Rome

San Francisco
Seattle & Portland
Vancouver
Walt Disney World®
Washington, D.C.

FROMMER'S® BEST-LOVED DRIVING TOURS

Britain
California
Florida
France

Germany
Ireland
Italy
New England

Northern Italy
Scotland
Spain
Tuscany & Umbria

HANGING OUT™ GUIDES

Hanging Out in England
Hanging Out in Europe

Hanging Out in France
Hanging Out in Ireland

Hanging Out in Italy
Hanging Out in Spain

THE UNOFFICIAL GUIDES®

Bed & Breakfasts and Country
   Inns in:
   California
   Great Lakes States
   Mid-Atlantic
   New England
   Northwest
   Rockies
   Southeast
   Southwest
Best RV & Tent Campgrounds in:
   California & the West
   Florida & the Southeast
   Great Lakes States
   Mid-Atlantic
   Northeast
   Northwest & Central Plains

Southwest & South Central
   Plains
   U.S.A.
Beyond Disney
Branson, Missouri
California with Kids
Chicago
Cruises
Disneyland®
Florida with Kids
Golf Vacations in the Eastern U.S.
Great Smoky & Blue Ridge Region
Inside Disney
Hawaii
Las Vegas
London

Mid-Atlantic with Kids
Mini Las Vegas
Mini-Mickey
New England and New York with
   Kids
New Orleans
New York City
Paris
San Francisco
Skiing in the West
Southeast with Kids
Walt Disney World®
Walt Disney World® for Grown-ups
Walt Disney World® with Kids
Washington, D.C.
World's Best Diving Vacations

SPECIAL-INTEREST TITLES

Frommer's Adventure Guide to Australia &
   New Zealand
Frommer's Adventure Guide to Central America
Frommer's Adventure Guide to India & Pakistan
Frommer's Adventure Guide to South America
Frommer's Adventure Guide to Southeast Asia
Frommer's Adventure Guide to Southern Africa
Frommer's Britain's Best Bed & Breakfasts and
   Country Inns
Frommer's Caribbean Hideaways
Frommer's Exploring America by RV
Frommer's Fly Safe, Fly Smart
Frommer's France's Best Bed & Breakfasts and
   Country Inns
Frommer's Gay & Lesbian Europe

Frommer's Italy's Best Bed & Breakfasts and
   Country Inns
Frommer's New York City with Kids
Frommer's Ottawa with Kids
Frommer's Road Atlas Britain
Frommer's Road Atlas Europe
Frommer's Road Atlas France
Frommer's Toronto with Kids
Frommer's Vancouver with Kids
Frommer's Washington, D.C., with Kids
Israel Past & Present
The New York Times' Guide to Unforgettable
   Weekends
Places Rated Almanac
Retirement Places Rated